3D Game Development with Blender 5 and Unity 6

Create immersive 3D games in Blender and Unity using a real-time, elegant workflow

Paolo Acampora

<packt>

3D Game Development with Blender 5 and Unity 6

Portfolio Director: Rohit Rajkumar
Relationship Lead: Tanisha Mehrotra
Project Manager: Sandip Tadge
Content Engineer: Anuradha Joglekar
Technical Editor: Tejas Vijay Mhasvekar
Copy Editor: Safis Editing
Indexer: Manju Aarsan
Proofreader: Anuradha Joglekar
Production Designer: Vijay Kamble
Growth Lead: Namita Velgekar
Marketing Owner: Nivedita Pandey

First published: March 2026

Production reference: 2300426

Published by Packt Publishing Ltd.
Grosvenor House
11 St Paul's Square
Birmingham
B3 1RB, UK

ISBN 978-1-83664-321-0
www.packtpub.com

Do You Think This Is a Game?

– Some cat on the internet

Foreword

The story of modern game development is inseparable from the tools that empower creativity.

Over the years, *Blender* has grown from a quirky underdog with an unconventional interface into one of the most respected tools in the open-source world. Driven by its community, the project redefined what free 3D creation software can achieve. That evolution stands as a testament to how collective passion and open collaboration can rival even the largest commercial offerings.

Unity 6, as a game engine, strikes a balance between approachability and professional capability. It invites newcomers with an intuitive interface and a vibrant ecosystem, while offering experts the advanced features needed to push the boundaries of interactive design.

Together, Blender and Unity form a creative duo that allows developers and artists alike to bring their visions to life.

Paolo and I last met at the Blender Conference in Amsterdam after his talk about modern widgets for character animation. During our conversation, Paolo shared his strong belief in the importance of open and approachable software, speaking with genuine enthusiasm. It's the same principle I sense throughout all his publications.

In his second book, Paolo combines his deep technical background with his enduring commitment to education. Paolo has the rare ability to demystify complex topics without resorting to oversimplification. His didactic clarity, paired with years of hands-on development experience, makes this book not just a tutorial collection but a guided journey through the art and science of modern game creation.

May your games come true!

Nils Zweiling

Contributors

About the author

Paolo Acampora is a programmer and technical director for animation, visual effects, and real-time computer graphics. He is a long-time Blender user and contributor and helps studios streamline their pipelines. He teaches Interactive Systems at Accademia di Belle Arti di Napoli and is the author of the book "Python Scripting in Blender".

I would like to thank Rosa and Ferdinando, who let me keep their CDs and have excellent music taste, my family for tolerating all those hours spent on writing this book, the amazing people at Royal Render for delivering new bits of knowledge every day, and my colleagues and students at the Academy for nurturing the joy that I find in teaching.

I would like to extend my thanks to the people at the Blender Institute for working selflessly and with dedication on some of the most remarkable projects in the last decades, and to my friends for demonstrating so much more fondness than I could ever have possibly earned.

I would like to thank Anuradha and Vania for their valuable input, Tanisha and Sandip for wanting this project, and the entire Packt team for making it come true.

About the reviewer

Vania De Rosa is an Italian 3D rigger working across animation and video games. She studied digital filmmaking at SAE Institute and specialized in 3D digital production at the Rainbow Academy. She worked at MAD Entertainment as a 3D generalist, rigger, and technical artist, contributing to the animated films *Gatta Cenerentola* (2017), winner of two David di Donatello awards, and *Yaya and Lennie – The Walking Liberty* (2021), supporting modeling and rigging. Later, she joined Tiny Bull Studios as a 3D rigger, contributing to the recently released video game *The Lonesome Guild* (2025), consolidating her expertise in both animated film and video game development.

Table of Contents

Preface

It might be news to those who think of videogames as a mere form of entertainment, but building a game is an articulated activity. One has to account for artistic choices, technical constraints, input logic, and deployment. Luckily, there are tools like Unity, a cross-platform game engine for interactive graphics, and Blender, a production software for modeling, rendering, and animation, that help handle the complexity of those tasks.

They are widely used applications, with different histories and the common goal of making computer graphics available to everyone.

As established software in their fields, they have gained a lot of strong points:

- Blender is free and open source, and Unity is free for small independent teams.
- Both applications are fast and powerful, with immediate feedback and attention to creative demands.
- Both systems can be customized easily, with user-defined and native elements integrating seamlessly.

In this book dedicated to combining Unity and Blender, we will first discuss how to exchange assets and smooth the differences between the two.

Then we will work on a game level in Unity and create models using Blender's procedural operations.

We will create textures and materials for the finished product and set up the level exploration with a simple, yet explanatory, first-person character.

The two applications can share the same project for asset creation and game building, which makes the workflow much smoother.

The chapters will guide you through the process, as all the described actions can be performed by following the instructions.

In writing this book, I wanted to share how smooth game development can become if the goals are clear and the nature of the software is understood.

Who this book is for

This book is ideal for solo developers, technical artists, and small studios who want to unify their creative and technical workflows using Blender and Unity. Whether you're a Unity user looking to move away from costly 3D tools or a Blender artist eager to bring your creations to life through gameplay, this book will walk you through every step of the production pipeline. Production managers and visual artists interested in migrating their pipeline to Blender/Unity would also benefit.

What this book covers

Chapter 1, Mixing Unity and Blender, explains how to set up the two applications and bring a Blender scene into Unity.

Chapter 2, Creating with Blender, explores the differences in coordinate systems, offsets for asset orientation, and the exchange of vertex color information.

Chapter 3, Prototyping in Unity, shows how to draft a level using ProBuilder and export the result to Blender.

Chapter 4, Customizing Blender, explains how to use the Asset Browser in Blender and how to automate common procedures by extending the software via Python.

Chapter 5, Modeling with Geometry Nodes, introduces Geometry Nodes for procedural modeling in Blender.

Chapter 6, Assembling the Level, explains how to automate the scene clean-up in Blender during importation, re-purpose Geometry Nodes to finish the level, and replace placeholders with finished models in the game.

Chapter 7, Shading the Models, covers the creation, exportation, and usage of textures in a physically based rendering workflow.

Chapter 8, Baking Detail Maps, guides through the generation, exportation, and usage of texture maps from high-resolution geometry.

Chapter 9, Creating Gameplay and Animation, illustrates the creation of a playable first person character with articulated animation and input controls.

To get the most out of this book

Readers are assumed to be familiar with how objects are moved, rotated, and scaled in Blender and Unity, and to have a basic understanding of 3D in general, in terms of how mesh models are structured in vertices, edges, faces, and objects. The book does its best to offer a brief explanation of new concepts as they are introduced, but fundamental information like navigating a folder structure is taken for granted. Elements of the user interface are addressed with terms like Viewport, Panel, and Area, which are intuitive enough but better understood with a basic knowledge of the software. Knowledge of common modeling operations like bevel or extrusion definitely helps undestand the chapters on model generation.

Mac users are supposed to be aware that the *Ctrl* and *Alt* keys are equivalent, respectively, to the *Cmd* and *Option* keys on their keyboards, and to figure out the minor differences between the screenshots in the book and what they see on their monitors.

The software used in this book is limited to Unity 6.3, Blender 5.1, and occasionally a programmer text editor, like Notepad++ for Windows or CotEditor for Mac. Blender 5.2 LTS, which will be released a few months after the publication of this book, might be a good replacement for Blender 5.1, which is the latest available at the time of writing.

Download the example code files

This book includes a complete downloadable code bundle containing all the example projects and files used throughout the chapters. We recommend downloading the bundle so you can follow along smoothly and experiment with the examples.

Use the bundle as a practical starting point. Modify it, extend it, and apply what you learn by creating your own variations as you progress through the chapters.

Get the code bundle

If you bought the book directly from Packt:

1. Go to `packtpub.com`
2. Click your **profile picture** and select **Your Orders**
3. Find this book and click **Download Code**

If you bought this book from Amazon or any other channel partner:

1. Go to `packtpub.com/unlock` or scan the following QR code

1. Search for this book
2. Sign up or log in to your free Packt account
3. Upload your proof of purchase and download the code bundle locally

> Note
>
> **Usage note:** You're free to use and modify this code for personal learning and non-commercial projects.

Download the color images

Your purchase includes a color, DRM-free PDF copy of this book, ideal for viewing color images, screenshots, and diagrams. Refer to the *Free benefits with your book section* at the end of the *Preface* to unlock your PDF copy.

This book contains long screenshots captured to provide you with an overview of the entire Blender or Unity interface. As a result, the text on these images may appear small at 100% zoom. We recommend referring to the DRM-free PDF copy for ease of understanding.

Conventions used

There are a number of text conventions used throughout this book.

`CodeInText`: Indicates code words in text, database table names, folder names, filenames, file extensions, pathnames, dummy URLs, user input, and Twitter handles. For example: "The folder `_to_blender_` will be displayed among the Asset Libraries."

A block of code is set as follows:

```
When I say "main":
    for each object of the scene:
        display its name in the text console
```

When we wish to draw your attention to a particular part of a code block, the relevant lines or items are set in bold:

```
class ZeroLockOperator(bpy.types.Operator):
    """Clear objects' location and lock transforms"""
    bl_idname = "object.b2u_zerolock_operator"
    bl_label = "Lock at Origin"
    @classmethod
    def poll(cls, context):
        return context.active_object is not None
    def execute(self, context):
        main(context)
        return {'FINISHED'}
```

Any command-line input or output is written as follows:

```
blender -b scene.blend -P Unity-BlenderToFBX.py -- temp.fbx
```

Bold: Indicates a new term, an important word, or words that you see on the screen. For instance, words in menus or dialog boxes appear in the text like this. For example: "From the top bar menu, click Edit | Preferences...."

> **Note**
>
> Warnings or important notes appear like this

> **Tip**
>
> Tips and tricks appear like this

Get in touch

Feedback from our readers is always welcome.

General feedback: If you have questions about any aspect of this book or have any general feedback, please email us at `customercare@packt.com` and mention the book's title in the subject of your message.

Errata: Although we have taken every care to ensure the accuracy of our content, mistakes do happen. If you have found a mistake in this book, we would be grateful if you reported this to us. Please visit `http://www.packt.com/submit-errata`, click **Submit Errata**, and fill in the form.

Piracy: If you come across any illegal copies of our works in any form on the internet, we would be grateful if you would provide us with the location address or website name. Please contact us at `copyright@packt.com` with a link to the material.

If you are interested in becoming an author: If there is a topic that you have expertise in and you are interested in either writing or contributing to a book, please visit `http://authors.packt.com/`.

Subscribe to Game Dev Assembly!

We are excited to introduce **Game Dev Assembly**, our brand-new newsletter dedicated to everything game development. Whether you're coding, designing, animating, or managing a studio, we've got insights, trends, and expert advice to help you create, innovate, and thrive. Sign up now and get exciting benefits.

`https://packt.link/gamedev-newsletter`

Free benefits with your book

This book includes free benefits designed to support your learning and help you apply what you learn effectively. Activate them now for instant access (see the *How to unlock* section for instructions).

Here's a quick overview of what you can instantly unlock with your purchase:

How to unlock

Scan the QR code (or go to `packtpub.com/unlock`) Search for this book by name, confirm the edition, and then follow the steps on the page.

UNLOCK NOW

Note: Have your invoice handy. Purchases made directly from the Packt website do not require an invoice.

Share your thoughts

Once you've read *3D Game Development with Blender 5 and Unity 6*, we'd love to hear your thoughts! Scan the QR code below to go straight to the Amazon review page for this book and share your feedback.

https://packt.link/r/1836643217

Your review is important to us and the tech community and will help us make sure we're delivering excellent quality content.

Part 1

Jumping in Game Development

In this first part of the book, you'll take your first steps in populating a Unity project with objects created in Blender. We'll explore workflows for handling geometry and address the differences in coordinates, and we will exchange assets in both directions as we export Unity prototypes to Blender for refinements.

Most importantly, we lay the foundation for the joint use of the two applications, where model creation and game assets coexist.

This part of the book includes the following chapters:

- *Chapter 1, Mixing Unity and Blender*
- *Chapter 2, Creating with Blender*
- *Chapter 3, Prototyping in Unity*

Part 1

1

Mixing Unity and Blender

Video games are an impressive mix of art and technology, and an acknowledged medium in modern storytelling. As technology marches on, entry barriers have progressively broken down: only a few decades ago, even producing low-budget video games took specialized hardware, engineering teams, and expensive software licenses. That is still the case for blockbuster games, but independent projects can be created on consumer hardware or laptop computers.

Things have improved on the software side too, thanks to the availability of tools for computer graphics and publicly available game engines, that is, editors for interactive applications.

Unity is an advanced game engine that combines 3D models and other assets with interactive scripts. It's fast, and it is the go-to solution for independent and professional game developers. Unity games run on PCs, telephones, tablets, and the web. Small developers can use Unity for free, with payments starting after a $100,000 annual revenue is reached.

As for game assets such as models, pictures, and animations, Blender, the free software for computer graphics, can be used to create impressive three-dimensional scenes, textures, characters, and animations.

Unity and Blender work surprisingly well together, so it is possible to create original 3D artwork for our projects without worrying about compatibility.

At the same time, those two applications have evolved independently and have adopted different approaches to implementing similar technologies.

The good news is that both are flexible enough that, with some technical savviness, a workflow for seamless sharing can be put in place.

In this first chapter, we will start our journey by setting up Unity and Blender and exchanging a simple scene created in Blender.

By the end of this chapter, you will understand how to explore your Blender files inside Unity.

In this chapter, we're going to cover the following main topics:

- Setting up Unity
- Creating your project and scene
- Getting started with Blender

Note

Your purchase includes a free PDF copy + code bundle

Your purchase includes a DRM-free PDF copy of this book, the code bundle, and additional exclusive extras. See the *Free benefits with your book* section in the *Preface* to unlock them instantly and maximize your learning.

Technical requirements

In this chapter, we will use the game engine to load and navigate a 3D scene, so we are going to need:

- **Unity**: Use version 6.3 LTS of Unity, which can be installed from the Unity Hub. The Unity Hub can be downloaded from the Unity Technologies website at `https://unity.com/`.
- **Blender**: Use version 5.1 of Blender, which can be found at the website `www.blender.org`.
- **Programmer text editor**: Any text editor will do, but here are a few suggestions:
    - *Notepad++* for Windows, downloadable from `https://notepad-plus-plus.org/downloads/`.
    - *CotEditor* for Mac, available at `https://coteditor.com`.
    - *xed*, or the default text editor for most Linux distributions.

You can download the example project and code for this book by following the instructions in the *Download the example code files* section in the *Preface* of this book.

This chapter's code files are included in the downloadable code bundle.

Setting up Unity

The Unity editor is available for the main operating systems: Windows, Mac, and Linux. Although some features, such as **resolution scale**, are only available on Windows, the overall experience is similar across all platforms.

Some of the screenshots presented in this book might differ slightly, but not significantly, from what is displayed on a specific system.

Unity installations and projects are managed through the **Unity Hub**. The Hub is the only application that must be installed manually, following the standard procedure for the computer's operating system. Once the Hub is installed, we can log in with our Unity credentials and select a version of the game engine to install on disk.

Installing the Unity Hub

The **Unity Hub** covers the following functions:

- Creating and opening game projects
- Installing and removing versions and modules of the engine
- Accessing documentation and pre-made content

The Unity Hub installer must be downloaded from the Unity website at `unity.com/download`. The **Download** button detects the operating system automatically, and there are hyperlinks to download installers for the other platforms.

The installation procedure is typical for each system:

- Execute `UnityHubSetup.exe` on Microsoft Windows
- Launch `UnityHubSetup.dmg` on Mac and drag Unity Hub to **Applications**
- Add the Unity repository to the software manager on Linux, then install the `unityhub` package

Once installed, Unity Hub can be launched from the **Applications** menu or from the **tray** icon near the system clock.

Registering a Unity account

While the Unity Hub can be downloaded and installed without authentication, a Unity account is required to use the game engine.

The account contains our user information and is also useful for using assets that we might buy on the Unity Asset Store.

If no account has been created yet, we can open the registration page by clicking **Create account** the first time that we launch the hub. Once we have our credentials, we click **Sign In** to enter the hub.

Installing Unity

The left vertical bar of the Unity Hub window has four options: **Projects**, **Installs**, **Learn**, and **Resources**.

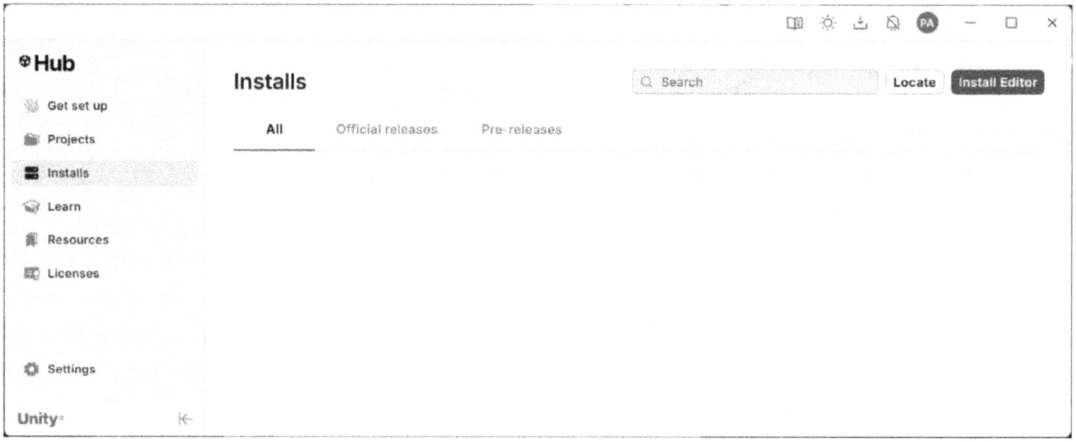

Figure 1.1: The Unity Hub on Windows

Clicking **Installs** displays the versions of Unity that are already on disk. Different versions might be recommended for different projects or for compatibility reasons.

The version used in this book, 6.3, might differ from other versions already present on the system. It's not a problem, since multiple versions of Unity can coexist on one system.

Understanding release numbers

Like most applications, Unity marks every release with progressive numbers separated by dots (e.g., **6.0**).

The first number marks the **major release**, and the second number marks the **minor release**. A minor release provides improvements and new features over the previous one without breaking compatibility, so a project developed using Unity 6.0 is supposed to work without issues with Unity 6.3.

While the `major.minor` format is useful on most occasions, the full version format employs 4 digits for the major number (e.g., `6000` rather than `6`), and a third element: the **build number**, which marks a bug-fix release where errors were fixed but no features were added. For instance, at the time of writing, the full version number of *Unity 6.3* is `6000.3.10f1`.

The first version of the engine, `Unity 1.0`, was released in 2005, with new versions being published every two to three years until *Unity 5.0*, released in 2015. The numbering switched to an annual format with *Unity 2017* until *Unity 2023*, only to go back to progressive release numbers in 2024 with the release of *Unity 6.0*.

Although all of that might seem complicated, it is very important that all the people working on the same project use the exact same version of the engine, or unexpected incompatibilities may arise.

Sticking with long-term support

Important major releases of Unity are marked as **long-term support** (**LTS**), with maintenance assured for about two years. Developers who enter production of a game are recommended to stick with the LTS release of Unity.

Since the team only maintains the latest non-LTS release of the engine, if features introduced with a minor version are required, it is recommended to update each release until an LTS release is reached.

With that in mind, we can proceed with the installation of *Unity 6.3 LTS*.

Installing the engine and modules

Once we have entered our credentials in the Unity Hub, select **Install** from the navigation bar on the left, click the **Install Editor** button at the top right, and then click the **Install** button displayed alongside the *Unity 6.3 LTS* release. This will open the installation dialog.

It is possible to install optional modules alongside the engine; these are required to package our games on specific platforms, such as mobile phones, web pages, or computers. We can install these later, so for now, just click **Install** at the bottom right of the window and proceed.

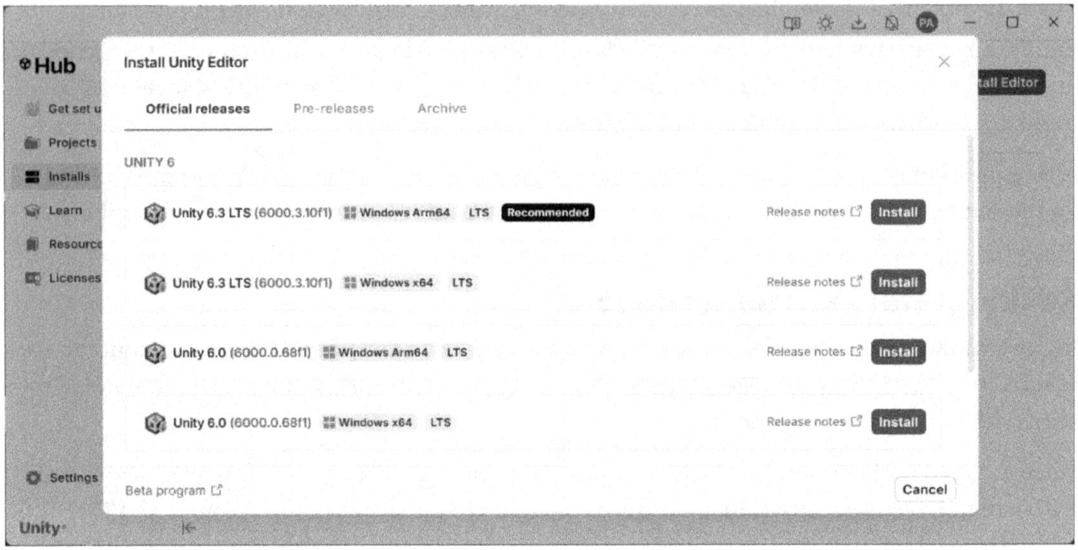

Figure 1.2: Installing the Unity Editor

Now that Unity is installed on the system, we can start working on our game. To do that, we proceed with creating a Unity project along with our first scene.

Creating your project and scene

We will work on a game throughout the book: a first-person, explorative, 3D adventure. This project will be very simple, as our focus is to set up a workflow rather than publishing this title, but it will become more articulated as we progress through the chapters.

All resources required for one game are contained in one folder on disk, which is referred to as the **project** directory. Projects can be created from the Unity Hub. Here's the standard procedure for creating a new project:

1. Select the **Projects** tab from the navigation bar on the left.
2. Click the **New Project** button at the top right.
3. We must select a **template**, that is, a starter collection of assets and settings for a typology of games. Since our focus is on 3D assets, we pick **Universal 3D** from the list at the center of the window. This template is for games that don't aim for extreme photorealism and are displayed through the **Universal Render Pipeline** (**URP**).
4. Click on the **Project Name** field on the right and choose a name for our project – for instance, `BlendToUni_URP`.

5. We can change, if we wish, the location on disk where the project is stored by clicking the **Location** field. It's a good idea to create a folder in `Documents` and name it `UnityProjects`.
6. Finally, click the **Create project** button at the bottom right.

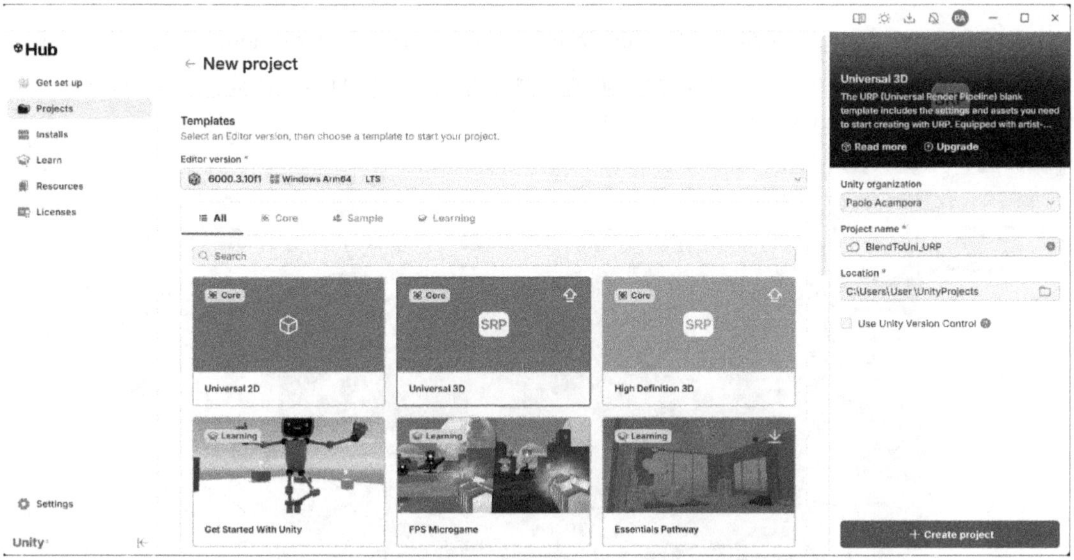

Figure 1.3: Creating a Universal Render Pipeline project

That will create the project and open Unity. By default, Unity displays an empty scene called `SampleScene`. This scene is stored at `Assets` | `Scenes` and contains only one camera that acts as the point of view, one directional light to simulate sunlight, and the Global Volume, which contains post-processing effects such as tone mapping, bloom, and vignette.

The project folder can be navigated using the editor's browser.

Navigating the project

The default layout displays the **Project** browser on the lower part of the screen. The browser's vertical navigation bar on the left displays the folders. By default, the hierarchy contains three top folders: `Favorites`, `Assets`, and `Packages`:

- `Favorites` contains presets for quick searches, such as the following:
    - `All Materials`: Display all assets that define a model's colors and look
    - `All Models`: Display all 3D models
    - `All Prefabs`: Display all the prefabs, that is, constructs created by assembling models and simple elements

- `Assets` contains the elements of the game, such as the following:
    - `Scenes`: Default directory for Unity levels
    - `Settings`: Values for project or level settings
    - `TutorialInfo`: Icons and scripts used by the template help files
- `Packages` contains utilities for development. There are many of them, and additional ones can be installed with the **Package Manager**. We will explore the functions of some of them in other chapters of this book.

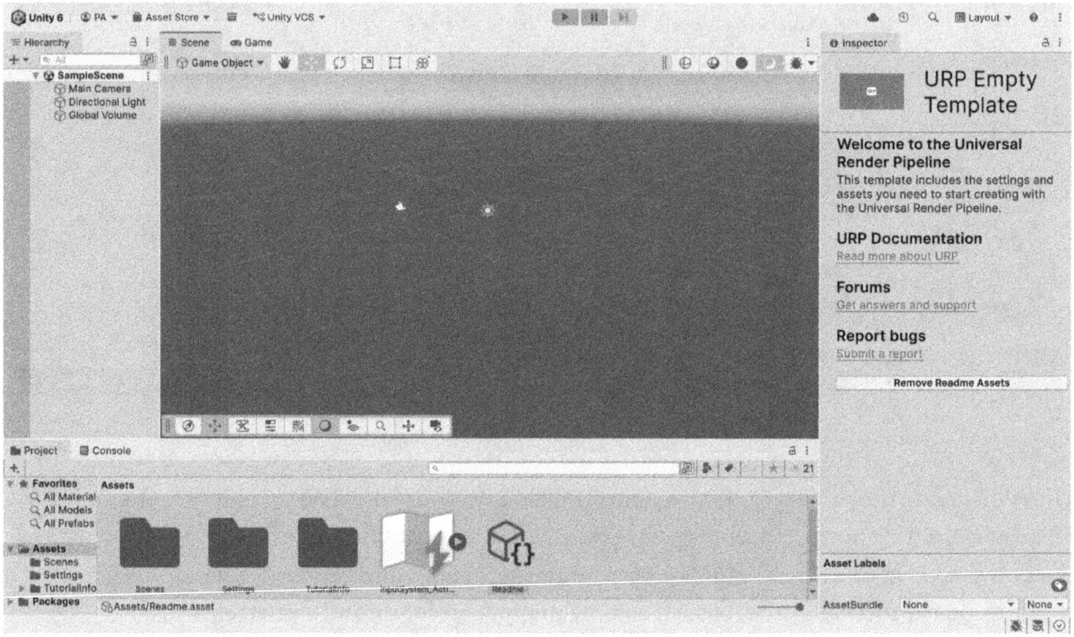

Figure 1.4: A brand-new Unity project

Favorite searches are saved directly from the search bar. Assets are either created in Unity or imported from tools such as Blender, and packages are either optional functionalities of the engine or third-party plugins. A scene is a level displayed during the actual game. We can use the **Scene** editor to add elements to a scene and move the objects around. Let's see how.

Editing the scene

By default, **Scene** is a tab of the central widget, beside the **Game** tab. It is easy to get confused between the two as both display the current level, but there are major differences:

- **Scene** has navigation toolbars and a floor grid
- **Game** is a preview of the final runtime and is only responsive in Play mode

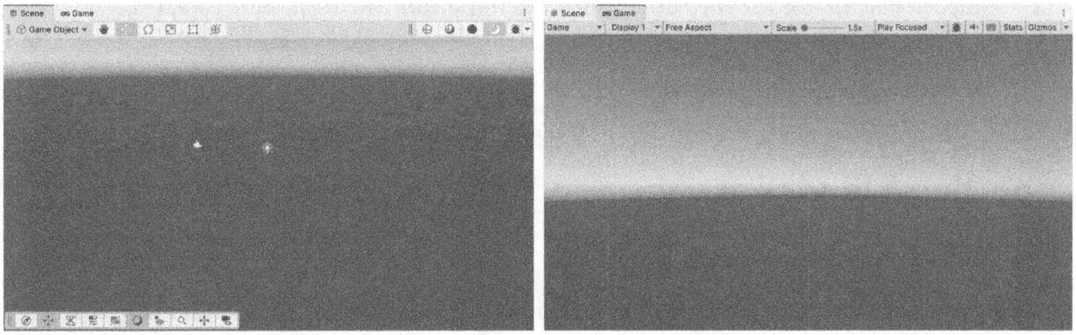

Figure 1.5: Scene and Game tabs side by side

Although we can add simple objects to our level without leaving Unity, actual models require editing at the geometry level, which can be done in Blender. Scenes created in Blender can be easily imported into Unity.

Getting started with Blender

Blender is a powerful application for creating, animating, and rendering three-dimensional scenes. It's open source, so it is not just free, but also without restrictions on usage, modification, study, and distribution.

Blender has gained popularity and a wide user base in the last decade, along with a stable team of highly skilled developers and impressive functionalities such as geometry nodes and high-quality rendering.

With Blender, we can create three-dimensional scenes for our games. Blender follows a 3-releases-per-year timeline, with one of them offering LTS. At the time of writing, the latest LTS release is *Blender 4.5*, which dates to the previous major cycle, since the current version is *Blender 5.1*.

To be up to date with the latest changes, version *5.1* will be used in this book; as *Blender 5.2 LTS* will be out in mid-2026, readers are encouraged to prefer that LTS release as soon as it becomes available.

Installing Blender

Follow these steps to install Blender on your system:

1. From `www.blender.org`, select **Download**.
2. Download either *Blender 5.1* or follow the **LTS** link and select **Blender 5.2 LTS**, which will take you to its subpage.

3. Select a distributor for your operating system (*Steam*, *Microsoft Store*, *Snapcraft*), an installer, or a portable release.
4. Once downloaded and installed, launch Blender.

Now that Blender is running, we can export a scene for Unity.

Importing Blender scenes into Unity

When we open Blender for the first time, we are presented with a new scene that contains a cube, a light, and a camera. As a quick test, we can explore this scene in Unity by saving it into the game project. Moreover, we can bookmark the Unity project folder in Blender to access it quickly. Here's how:

1. Open the **Save** dialog by selecting **File** | **Save As** from the menu bar.
2. In the **Blender File View**, navigate to the folder of the Unity project. If the project path is difficult to find, right-clicking **Show in File Browser** in the Unity Hub or in the Unity **Project** browser opens the project directory in the system file manager. From there, we can copy the path and paste it in the top field of the **Blender File View**.

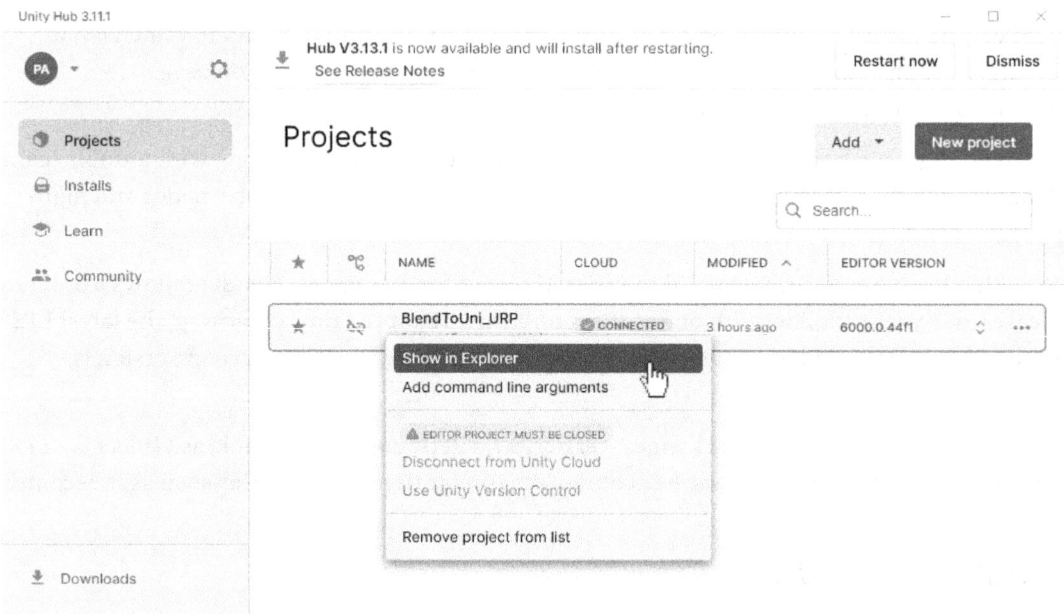

Figure 1.6: Opening the project directory from the Unity Hub

3. Once we reach the `BlendToUni_URP` directory, we can click **Add Bookmark** in the top-left corner of the **Blender File View**. Note that if a bookmarks list is already present, the **Add** button is displayed as a **+** beside the list.

Figure 1.7: The Unity project bookmarked in Blender

Whenever we want to access our project folder, we will be able to select it from the bookmarks; now we will create a folder for our artwork and save this scene:

1. Go to the `Assets/Scenes` subfolder.
2. Type `BlenderDefault` as the filename at the bottom. Blender will add the `.blend` extension automatically if we don't.
3. Click the **Save As** button, close Blender, and switch back to Unity.

Once we are back to the game engine, the **Project** browser will display our new asset in `Assets | Scenes`.

> Note
>
> **Check the system association**
>
> When a file is added to a project, Unity tries to open it with the application associated with that file format in the operating system. If, for some reason, Unity doesn't import the Blender file, make sure that clicking on it in the file manager launches Blender.

By dragging the **BlenderDefault** asset over the Unity **Scene** viewport, we can place the Blender objects in the current level. Unity considers the Blender scene a **prefab**, a container of objects.

The **Inspector** panel on the right displays the **Transform** properties of **BlenderDefault**, so we can reset its position.

1. In the **Inspector** panel, right-click **Position**.
2. Click **Revert** in the context menu.

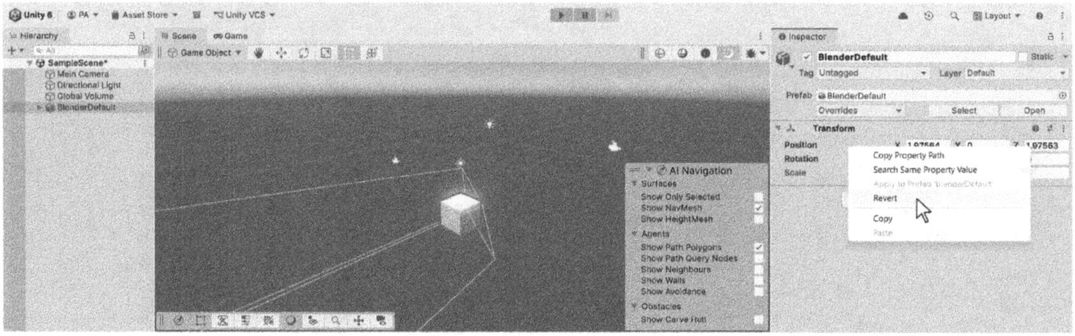

Figure 1.8: Revert position with the Inspector panel

Once the transformation is reset, the imported objects have the same positions they had in Blender; for instance, the cube is at the center of the scene.

When our prefab is added to the level, we find **Camera**, **Cube**, and **Light** by expanding **BlenderDefault** in the **Hierarchy**. Clicking the **Play** button starts the game from the point of view of **Camera**.

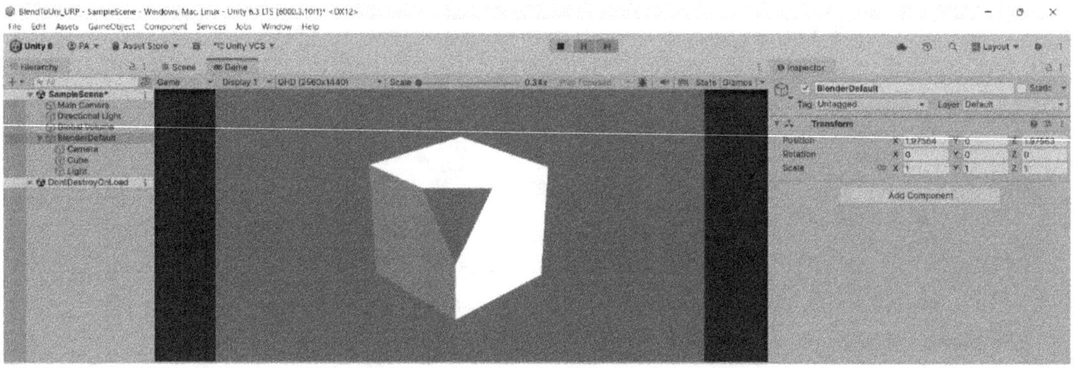

Figure 1.9: Playing Blender's default scene in Unity

While the point of view of the game matches the one from the Blender render, we can see through the cube in Unity. We can fix this mismatch by editing the `.blend` file.

Adjusting the clipping plane

The unwanted look-through geometry is due to a conversion factor of the **clipping plane**, that is, the nearest and farthest look distance, between the two applications. We can adjust the clipping start in Blender:

1. In the **Project** browser, navigate to the `Assets` | `Scenes` folder and double-click **BlenderDefault**.
2. That will open the scene in Blender. Select **Camera**.
3. In the properties on the right, click the **Camera** tab marked with a green camera icon.
4. Set **Clip Start** to `0.01`.
5. Save the scene with *Ctrl* + *S* or **File** | **Save** from the top bar menu, and close Blender.

After the scene is saved, Unity reloads the asset with the new settings:

1. If Unity is still in **Game** mode, click the **Stop** button, or Unity will not update the camera attributes in the scene.
2. In the **Game** tab, we will see that the cube is no longer clipped.
3. We can save the changes to **SampleScene** with *Ctrl* + *S* or **File** | **Save** from the menu bar.

In the **Project** browser, a blank document appears alongside the **BlenderDefault** asset.

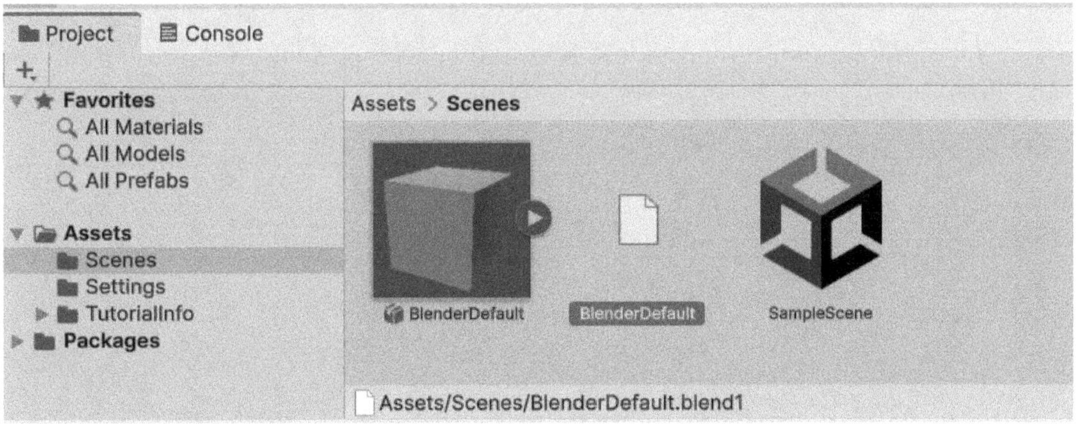

Figure 1.10: BlenderDefault.blend1 polluting our project

Blender creates backup copies with the extensions `.blend1`, `.blend2`, and so on, every time a scene is saved. Although those extra files do no harm, they add unnecessary weight to the project and would get in the way if we were using a versioning system, which is very common in games. For that reason, we will delete the `.blend1` file and disable that feature:

1. In the **Project** browser, right-click the **BlenderDefault** asset with the blank document icon. The status bar will display the address `Assets` | `Scenes` | `BlenderDefault.blend1`.
2. Click **Delete** from the context menu, then click the **Delete** button in the confirmation dialog.

It's advisable to move and delete assets using the **Project** browser exclusively, rather than the operating system's file manager, to allow Unity to keep track of the project files. Now for the Blender setting:

1. Open Blender and click **Edit** | **Preferences** in the top menu bar.
2. Click the **Save & Load** button in the navigation column on the left, then set **Save Versions** to `0`.

This way, Blender will not create extra files in the game project: it won't create backup files at all, so we'd better be careful!

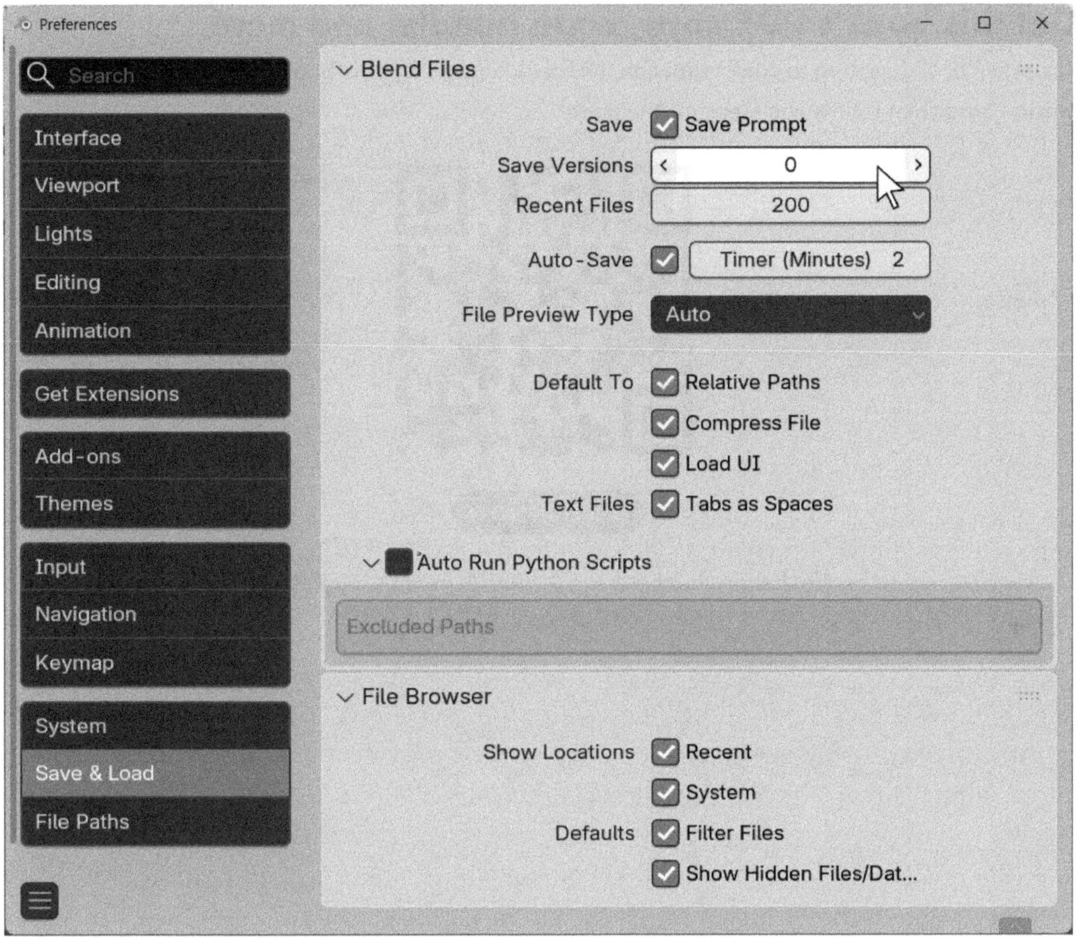

Figure 1.11: Disabling versioned backup in the Blender preferences

We cannot explore our level yet, as we have not set up any input handling. We will do that in *Chapter 9*. Until then, we will focus on populating our game assets.

Summary

In this chapter, we took our first steps toward integrating Blender and Unity. We imported a `.blend` file into Unity and applied our corrections by just saving the scene. It's just the beginning, as there is much more to do: we can create more complex scenes and character movement.

In the next chapter, we will explore materials and transformations.

Get this book's PDF copy, code bundle, and more

Scan the QR code (or go to `packtpub.com/unlock`). Search for this book by name, confirm the edition, and then follow the steps on the page.

UNLOCK NOW

Note: Have your invoice handy. Purchases made directly from the Packt website don't require an invoice.

2

Creating with Blender

Blender covers all aspects of 3D: modeling, lighting, texturing, animation, and rendering. In theory, it is possible to deliver visuals without ever leaving the application.

It is possible to use a specific application for each step, resorting to exchange file formats to pass data between them.

Starting with version 2.8, Blender doesn't feature a game engine anymore, making exporting to game engines an urgent requirement. This has also led to better support for FBX, a proprietary format and de facto standard in game pipelines.

That allows Unity to import and display Blender scenes, although some information, such as most modifiers and material properties, is inevitably lost.

Combining Unity's ability to read `.blend` files and update imported assets on the fly with a few conversion expedients, we can transfer our scenes with as much consistency as possible.

In this chapter, we are going to cover the following topics:

- Coordinate systems
- Rotation offsets
- Materials and geometry input

Technical requirements

In this chapter, we will use Unity 6.3 and Blender 5.1, which can be installed by following the instructions from *Chapter 1* or from their respective websites.

Addressing exchange and coordinates

Blender files are loaded in Unity via drag and drop from the file manager or, as we saw in *Chapter 1*, by saving them in the game project folder.

Unity does not read `.blend` files directly; it launches a hidden instance of Blender to export a `.fbx` file. **FBX** stands for **Filmbox**, a motion capture application from the 1990s, later acquired by Autodesk and renamed **Motion Builder**. The popularity of Autodesk products made `.fbx` the standard format for exchanging game assets.

It is possible to export `.fbx` files manually from Blender. We can test the `.fbx` workflow on a simple model.

Exporting monkey.fbx

Blender provides primitive solids of type **mesh** (polygonal model), such as **Cube**, **Cone**, and **Sphere**, as starting points for modeling. As an easter egg, the model of a monkey head was added to that list. The monkey, named *Suzanne*, is useful for evaluating materials and light sets, or for quick experiments such as the one we are about to do: exporting a model to Unity with a `.fbx` file. First, let's create the model:

1. Launch Blender.
2. Delete all objects by pressing *A* (*Select All*) and then pressing the *Delete* key.
3. Create a Suzanne mesh by selecting **Add** | **Mesh** | **Monkey** from the **Viewport** menu.

Now we can save the mesh as `monkey.fbx`:

1. Select **File** | **Export** | **FBX (.fbx)** from the top-bar menu.
2. In the **Export** dialog, navigate to the `BlendToUni_URP` project. We bookmarked that folder in *Chapter 1*, so it should be listed at the top left of the export window.
3. Go to the **Assets** subfolder and click the *New Directory* button at the top, which is the folder icon with a plus sign.
4. Type `Art` as the name of the new folder, enter the **Art** folder, and create a new folder named `Models`.
5. Enter the **Models** subfolder, and type `monkey.fbx` as the filename in the field at the bottom.
6. Click the **Export FBX** button or press *Enter*.

Exporting Suzanne.blend

When saving our scene to the game project as a `.blend` file, we will use a different filename to avoid confusion:

1. Go back to the Blender scene containing the monkey, or recreate it by repeating the first steps in the *Exporting monkey.fbx* section.
2. From the top-bar menu, select **File** | **Save As...** to bring up the save dialog.
3. Navigate to **BlendToUni_URP** | **Assets** | **Art** | **Models** again.
4. Type `suzanne.blend` as the filename at the bottom.
5. Click **Save As** or press *Enter*.

The **Project** browser will display two identical assets, **monkey** and **suzanne**.

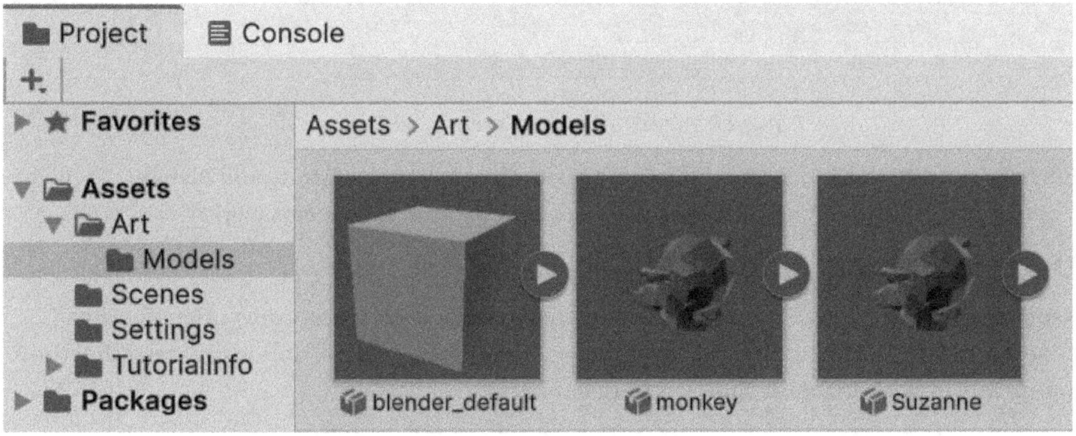

Figure 2.1: Blender's monkey imported as an .fbx file and a .blend file

We can close Blender and focus on the assets. The gray thumbnails are not very helpful, but we can see that something is wrong: the models appear rotated.

Dragging the **monkey** or **suzanne** asset into a Unity level displays the correct orientation, but in the Inspector, we can see that the object is rotated by approximately 90 degrees on the *X* axis.

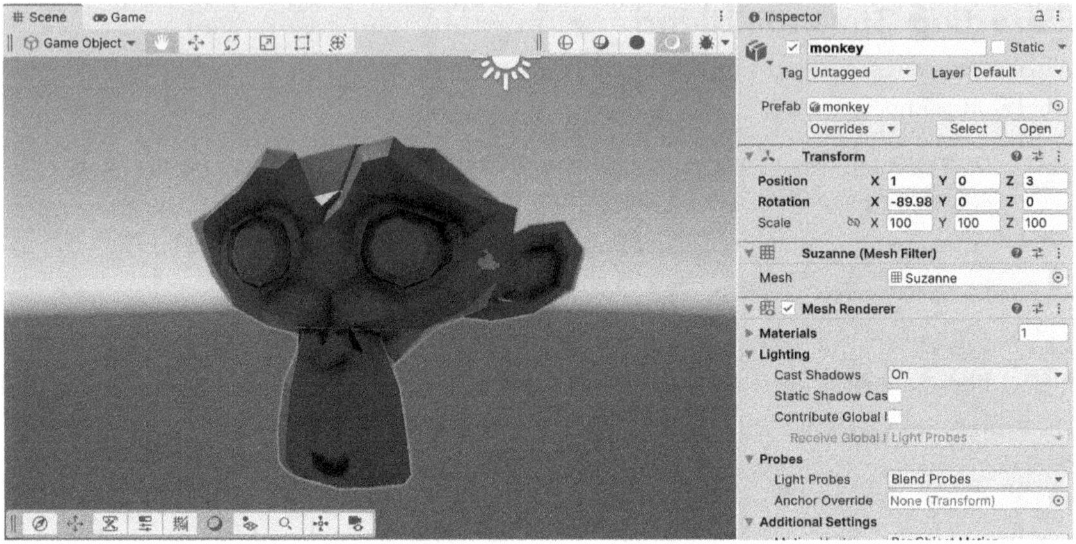

Figure 2.2: monkey's Rotation X value is -89.98 degrees

It's not our fault; this is due to a difference in coordinates between Unity and Blender. To have a better grasp of that, let's take a deep dive into how coordinate systems work.

Understanding coordinate systems

Representing 3D objects obviously requires three spatial dimensions. Conventionally, most people agree on representing three Cartesian axes named *X*, *Y*, and *Z*. It is also agreed that the *X* axis points in the horizontal direction from left to right.

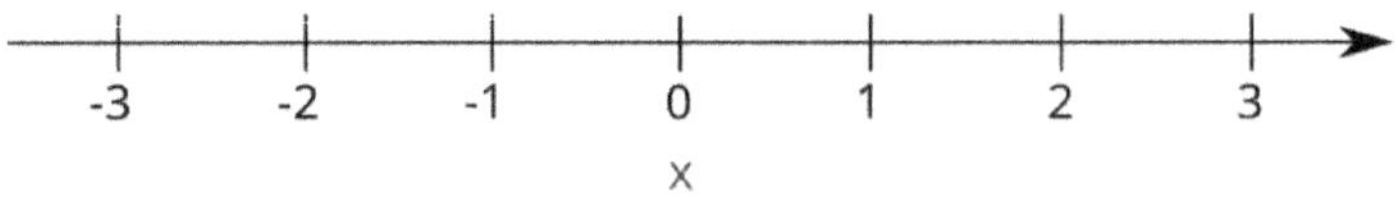

Figure 2.3: The X axis, easy-peasy

This is where the general agreement stops; in a 2D plane, the vertical axis is usually named *Y*, but the same doesn't hold in a 3D space. At best, 3D people have agreed to disagree on which letter represents height and which one depth.

3D software is split between **Y-up** tools, such as Unity and Autodesk Maya, and **Z-up** tools, such as Blender. One solution is not more valid than the other; it can be argued that on a vertical surface, such as a chalkboard, *Y* is the natural choice for the vertical axis, and the remaining letter, *Z*, would be assigned to depth, making it a Y-up space, like Unity.

Conversely, on a horizontal workspace, such as a table, depth is easily considered the second coordinate and marked with a *Y*, leaving the letter *Z* for the height of a Z-up system, like Blender.

Unity compensates for this difference and rotates the imported models. Although it's no big deal with simple objects, rotated assets might cause problems with animations, simulations, and movement. Luckily, there are workarounds to this issue.

Editing Blender assets

In Unity, we can open `.blend` assets in Blender directly from the **Project** browser. The only requirement is to associate Blender with `.blend` files in the operating system.

We can then double-click the **Suzanne** asset in Unity to open the scene in Blender.

If multiple versions of Blender are installed, we must make sure that our intended version is called. That can be set up using **Open with** from the right-click context menu in the file manager or, in Blender, with **Edit | Preferences** from the menu bar, selecting **System** in the left pane and, under **Operating System Settings**, clicking the **Register** button.

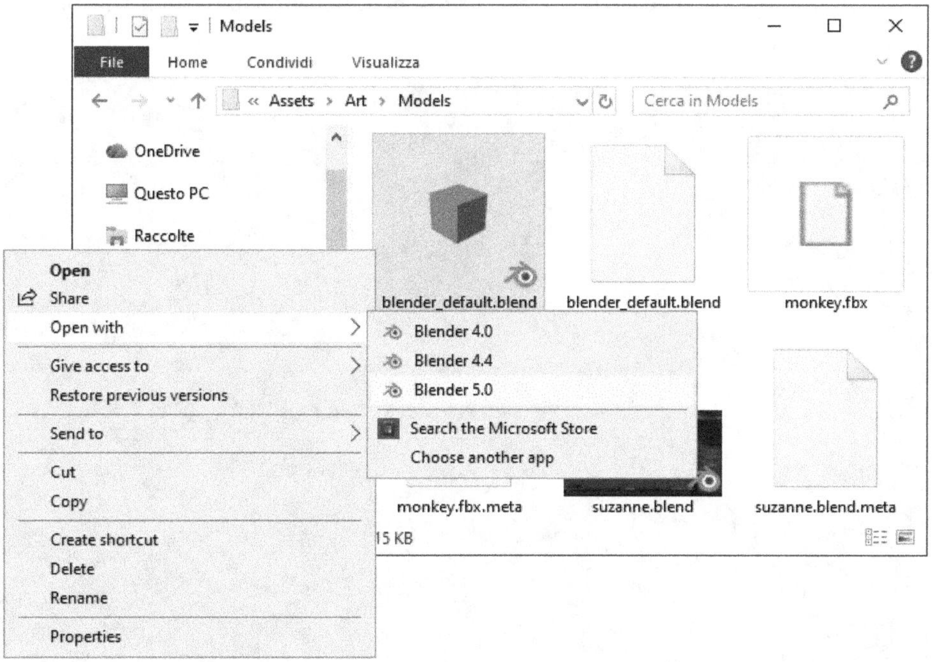

Figure 2.4: Associating .blend files with Blender 5.0 in Windows

Once the scene is open in Blender, we can fix the asset's rest rotation.

Working in Y-up in Blender

It is not possible to change Blender coordinates from a Z-up to a Y-up system, as that is defined in the software architecture, but we can mimic a Y-up space by grouping our geometries under a rotated object.

To counter the rotation, we only need something that can be transformed, not a geometry. A class of objects called Empty can be moved, rotated, and scaled, but doesn't contain any data. There are various types of Empty; they differ only in how they are displayed, but are equivalent in every other aspect. They are found under the **Add** menu:

1. From the top bar, select **Add** | **Empty** | **Arrows** to add a new Empty to the scene.
2. New objects are placed where the 3D cursor is. The 3D cursor is a pointer that can be moved in space, much like how a traditional cursor in a text application determines the position of new letters. If the cursor was moved and the Empty is not created at the origin, click **Object** | **Clear** | **Location** from the top bar, or press *Alt* + *G* to reset the position.
3. Press *R* to rotate the object, then *X* to lock on the horizontal axis, then type `90` for a 90-degree rotation.

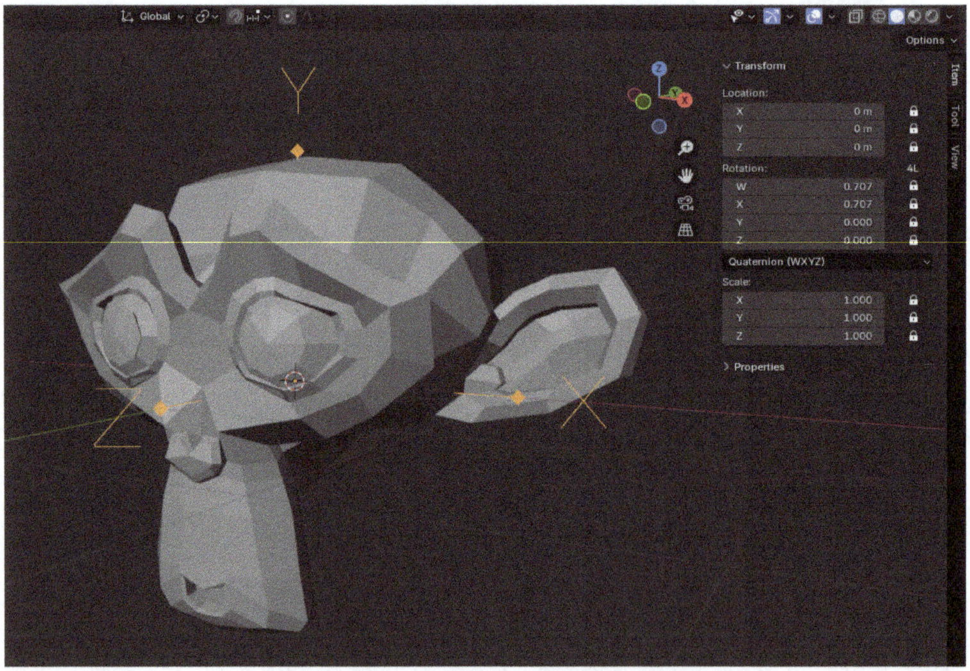

Figure 2.5: An Empty as a Y-up object

Now the Empty displays a Y-up orientation in Blender. We don't want to transform this object accidentally, so we lock its location, rotation, and scale by clicking the locker icons in the properties:

1. If translation, rotation, and scale are not displayed on the **Properties** panel on the right, press the *N* key.
2. Left-click on every locker icon and lock all transforms. We can keep the mouse button pressed while hovering through the properties.
3. Rotation modes such as quaternions have a fourth rotational value, so we switch from **Euler** to **Quaternion** rotation and lock the **W** channel.

Now that the Empty cannot be moved by mistake, let's parent our model to it:

1. Select **Suzanne**; then, while keeping *Shift* pressed, select **Empty** so that both are selected.
2. Press *Ctrl* + *P* (*Cmd* + *P* on Mac) to bring up the **Object** | **Parent** menu and select **Object (Keep Transform Without Inverse)**. That will bring the monkey under the Y-up space and rotate it to compensate for the different orientation.
3. Select **Suzanne**, and we can see a `-90` degree rotation in the **Properties**.
4. Press *Ctrl* + *A* (*Cmd* + *A* on Mac) to bring up the **Apply** menu, and select either **Rotation** or **All Transforms**; we only performed rotation, so the two are equivalent here.

We can save this scene to the game project, as we did for `BlenderDefault`:

1. Open the save dialog with *Ctrl* + *Shift* + *S* or **File** | **Save As** from the menu bar.
2. In the Blender file view, navigate to **BlendToUni_URP** | **Assets** | **Art** | **Models**.
3. Click the filename field at the bottom, type `Suzanne`, and press *Enter* or the **Save As** button.

Now, the objects placed under **Empty** behave as they would in a Y-up space. We can switch to Unity and see how it looks in the project.

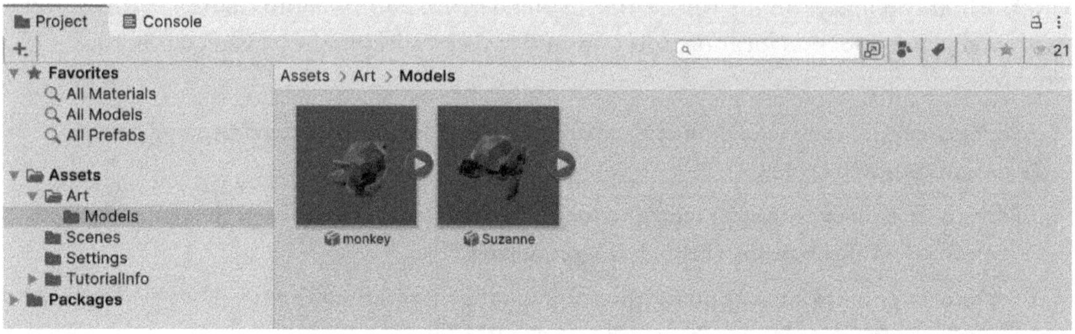

Figure 2.6: Suzanne's rotation is displayed correctly in Unity

Clicking on the expansion triangle beside a Unity thumbnail displays the content of an asset; we can observe a subtle difference in our two monkeys.

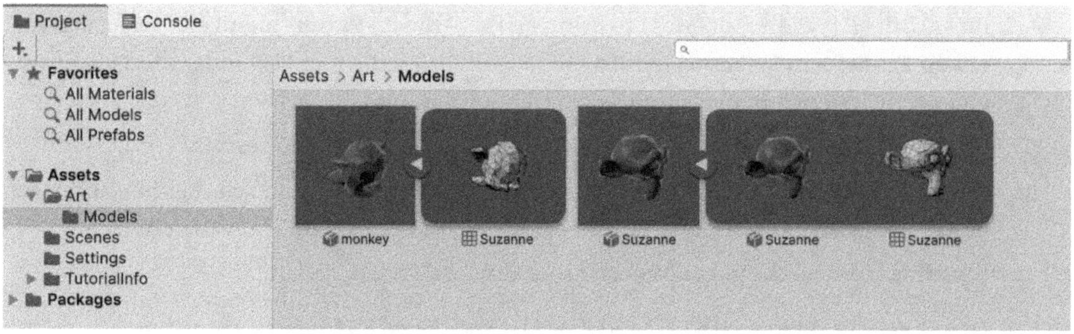

Figure 2.7: monkey and Suzanne are slightly different in content

While **monkey** contains only a mesh named **Suzanne**, the other asset presents a container before the mesh. That reflects the object/data structure that is displayed in the outliner and in *Figure 2.8*. **Empty** is omitted by the `.fbx` exporter as long as we don't change its name.

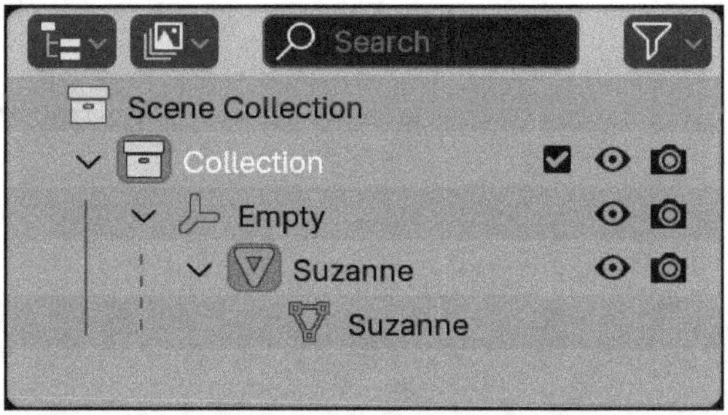

Figure 2.8: Blender data structure

The default material is a flat gray, but we can create new materials for our models.

Setting materials and creating a look

It is common for game assets to start as initial drafts and get refined during production, which is why saving `.blend` files in the game project helps us edit our assets quickly. In this section, we will add some color to Suzanne.

Smoothing polygons

A low-poly model like Suzanne has a sharp, angular appearance, but that is mostly due to its surface normals.

A face normal is the direction of a polygon. Polygons have a lighter shade if they face a light source and become darker as they point in a different direction, so we can notice differences in shade between two adjacent polygons. We can endow our models with a smoother look by just averaging their normals:

1. Open the **Suzanne** asset in Blender and select the model.
2. From the top-bar menu, click **Object** | **Shade Smooth**.
3. Save the scene with *Ctrl* + *S* or **File** | **Save**.

Shade Smooth mediates through neighboring normals across the model's surface. We can see that the asset is updated in Unity and displayed accordingly.

Creating a material

We haven't specified any material for **Suzanne**, so it is just gray. We need to assign a material to set a different color:

1. Open the **Suzanne** asset in Blender and select the model.

2. Go to the **Material** tab in the properties; the icon is a checkered sphere.
3. Click the **+** button to create and assign a material.
4. Click on the material name (the default is **Material** or **Material.001**) and rename it `Monkey`.
5. In the material properties, click the base color (white by default) and select an orange shade on the picker's color wheel.

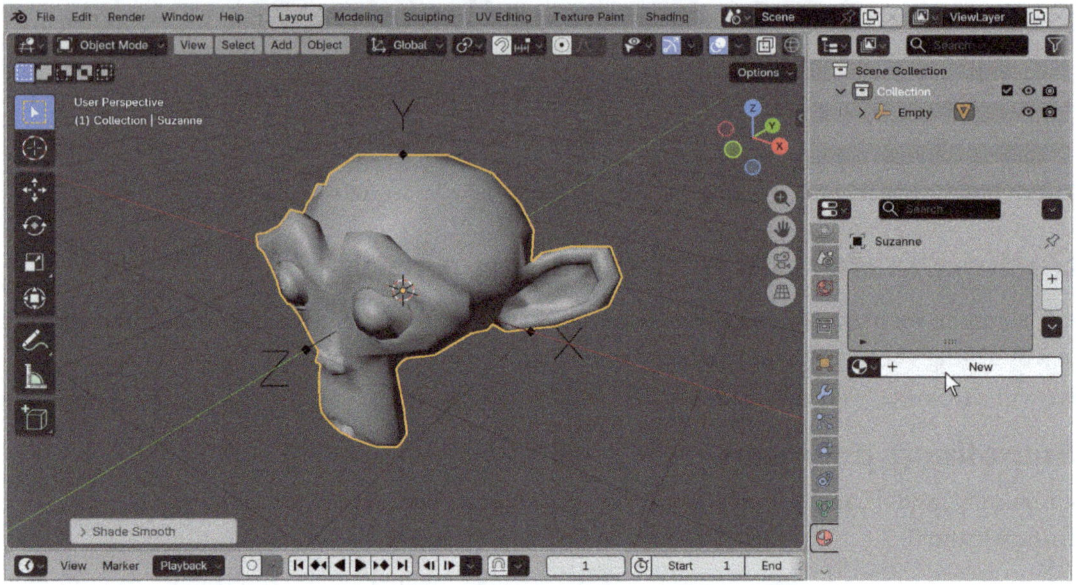

Figure 2.9: Creating a new material in Blender

The default **Viewport** mode still displays a gray model; to look at our materials, we can switch to **Preview** mode in the Viewport settings, using the buttons in the top right.

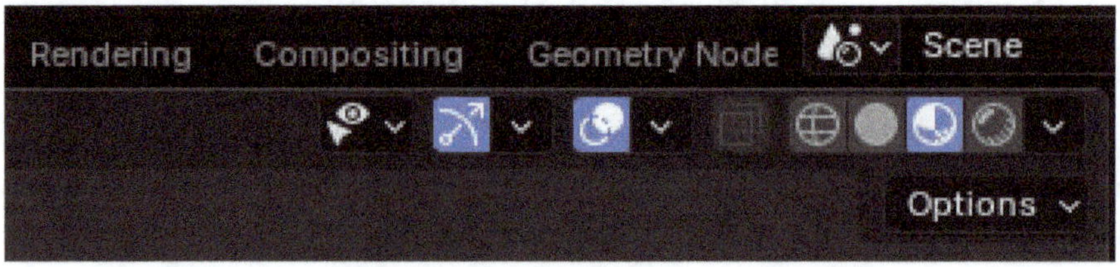

Figure 2.10: Enabling the material preview in Blender

Saving the scene will make Unity import and display the new material.

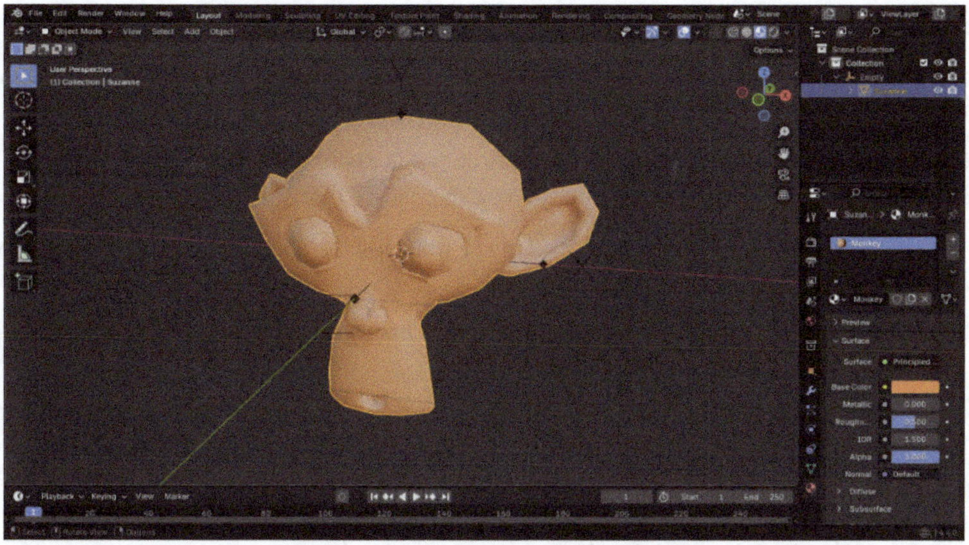

Figure 2.11: An orange monkey in Blender

We have set one color for the whole model, but we can add a different material for the eyes.

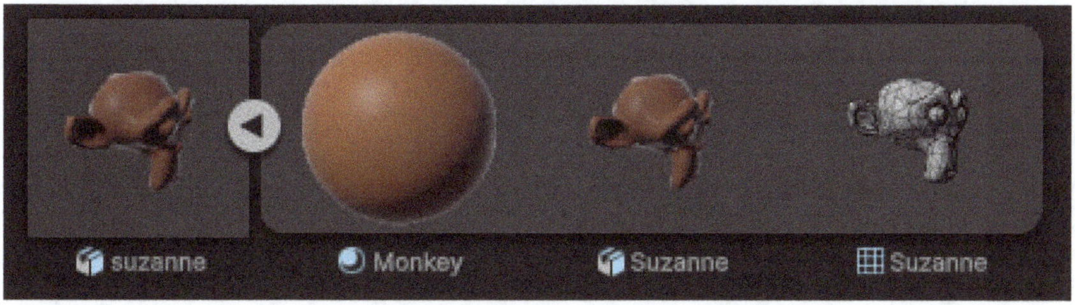

Figure 2.12: Monkey material in Unity

To do that, we will create a new slot for our material and assign it only to a part of the model.

Creating multiple materials

Materials are assigned to models through **material slots**, which affect all or part of the geometry.

Objects can have multiple slots, and while the first one is assumed to cover the entire model, additional slots must be assigned manually. We can create a material for the eyes:

1. Select **Suzanne** in the Viewport, and in the material properties, click the **+** button to create a new entry.
2. The new slot is empty, and clicking the **New** button creates a material; rename it `Eyes`. It's already white, so we don't need to set the color.

To assign a slot to specific faces, we must change mode to access and select the geometry:

1. Enter **Edit** mode either by pressing *Tab* or by selecting it from the drop-down box on the top left.
2. By default, all of the mesh is selected. Press *A* to deselect it, or click a region outside the model.
3. Move the mouse pointer over one eye and press *L*. The **Select Linked** shortcut will select the entire eye.
4. Move the mouse pointer over the other eye and press *L* to select both.
5. In the **Material** tab, click the **Assign** button.
6. Save the scene.

We will see a white-eyed Suzanne, so we need to mark the pupils. We don't need another material, as we can set a color for the vertices.

Painting vertex colors

Assigning different materials to adjacent polygons is usually discouraged; every vertex at the junction is evaluated twice, and that might affect performance. Besides, too many materials are redundant, so we would rather paint the details.

There are two ways to paint a model: image textures and vertex colors. Images are stored as files on disk, while vertex colors are part of the geometry and are exported with the mesh. We can paint black pupils on Suzanne's eyes:

1. In the Viewport, select **Suzanne**.
2. Expand the mode drop-down box on the top left and select **Vertex Paint**.

3. Vertex paint starts in **Draw** mode, with black and white as the default foreground and background colors. Press *X* to invert them so that white is the first color, as shown in *Figure 2.13*.
4. Press *Ctrl* + *X* to assign white as the vertex color for the entire model.

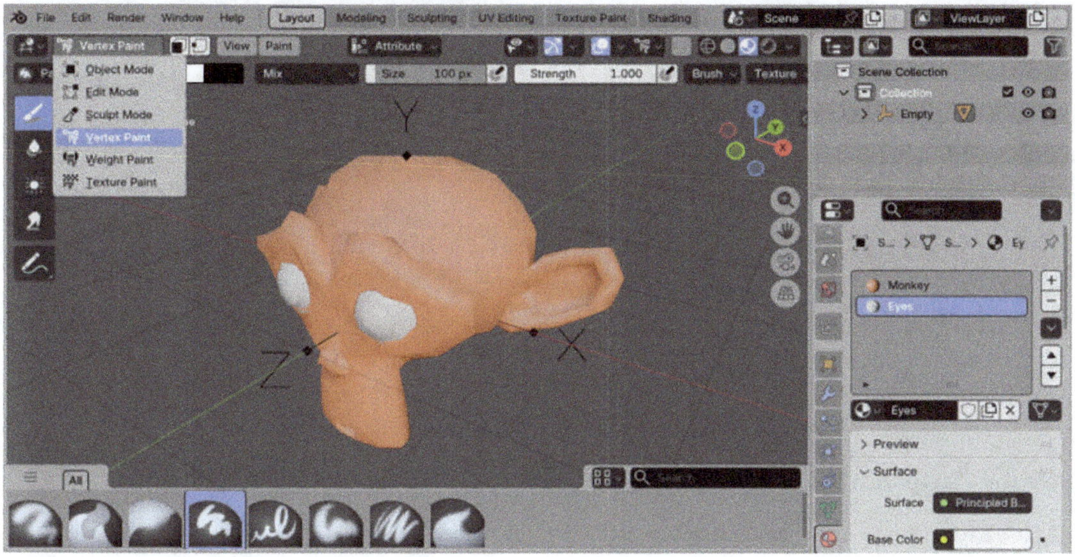

Figure 2.13: Vertex Paint mode in Blender. Pressing X switches the primary and secondary colors

We can see from the **Operation** properties at the bottom left that something was done, but we cannot see any changes, as vertex colors are not part of the shader yet. We are going to add vertex color to our shaders in the next section, *Editing materials*; in the meantime, we can switch **Viewport Shading** back to **Solid** and select **Attribute**, as in *Figure 2.14*.

Figure 2.14: Displaying the vertex color attribute with Solid shading

Now the Viewport will display the vertex colors as we paint the pupils:

1. Press *Tab* to enter **Edit** mode.
2. Make sure that **Vertex Selection** is enabled in the top-left buttons. The eyes are likely selected, as we assigned a material slot earlier.
3. Click the central vertex of one eye so that it is the only selected element, then keep *Shift* pressed and click the central vertex of the other eye to select both.
4. Expand the selection using *Ctrl* and *+* or **Select** | **More/Less** | **More** from the Viewport top menus.

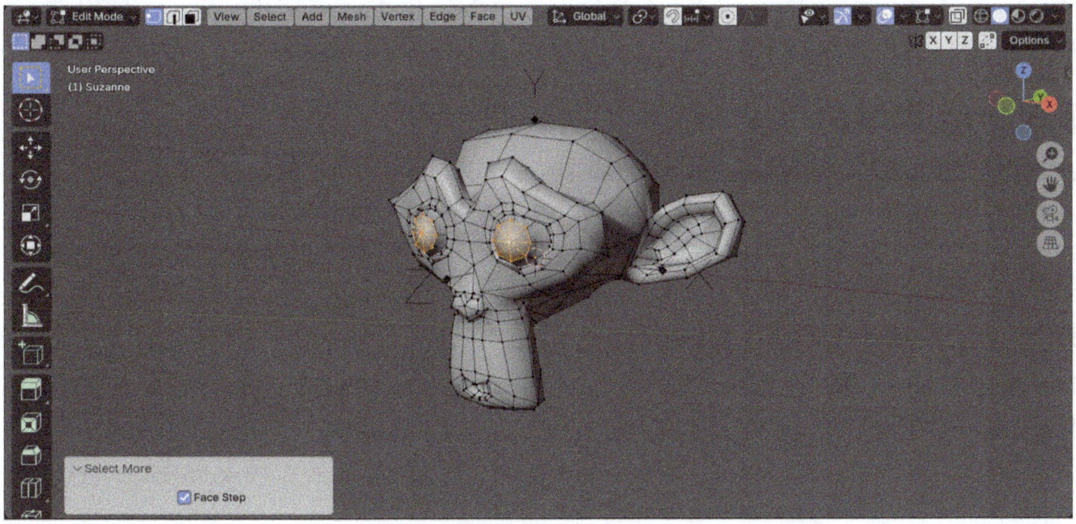

Figure 2.15: Selecting the pupils

We have selected the areas of both pupils. Now let's paint them black:

1. Press *Tab* to go back to **Paint** mode.
2. Enable **Vertex Selection**, the right button just above the paint colors.
3. Press *X* to invert the background and foreground colors. Now we are painting it black.
4. Press *Ctrl* + *X* to paint the pupils black.

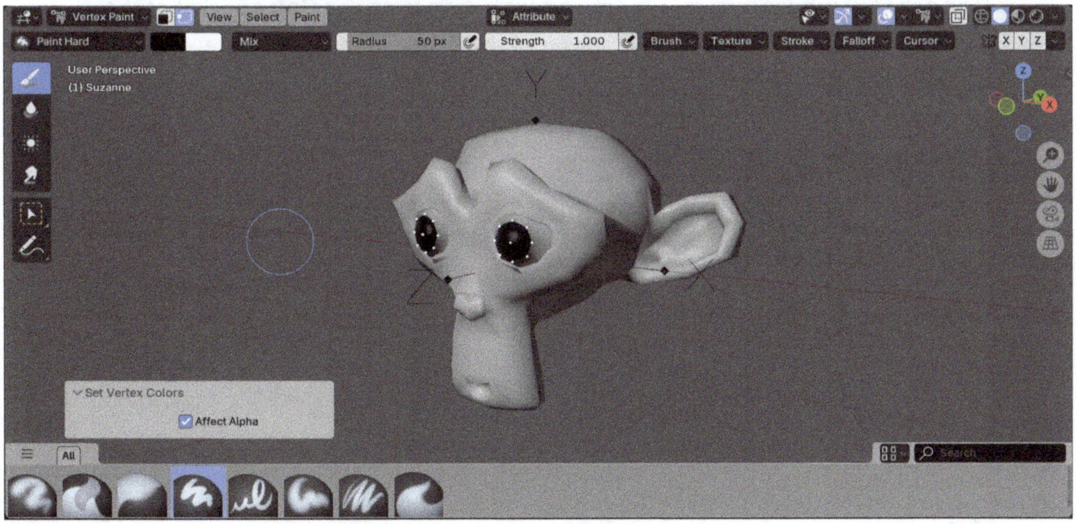

Figure 2.16: Painting selected vertices

We can see our vertex colors in solid view, but to see them in the material preview as well, we need to edit the **Eyes** material.

Editing materials

Materials are linked to **shaders**, a set of properties and rules for how an object looks. Each application implements materials in a different way; the most popular solutions are shader programming languages and graph networks with visual interfaces. Both Blender and Unity feature network-based shaders.

Editing materials in Blender

Blender provides a **Shader Editor** for its materials; clicking the **Shading** tab to switch workspace displays the Shader Editor at the bottom.

The connections between the nodes determine how a material looks. We need to connect the vertex colors to the material nodes.

Displaying vertex colors

Vertex colors are a geometric attribute, so they require an **Attribute** node:

1. From the **Shader Editor** menu bar, select **Add** | **Input** | **Attribute**.
2. The attribute node is already set to **Geometry**, but we need to type `Attribute` in its **Name** field. That's the default name for vertex colors and can be found in the color attributes of the **Mesh** properties (green triangle icon).
3. Using the left mouse button, we drag a connection from the **Color** socket of the **Attribute** node to the **Base Color** socket of the **Principled BSDF** node.
4. Save the file with *Ctrl* + *S* or **File** | **Save**.

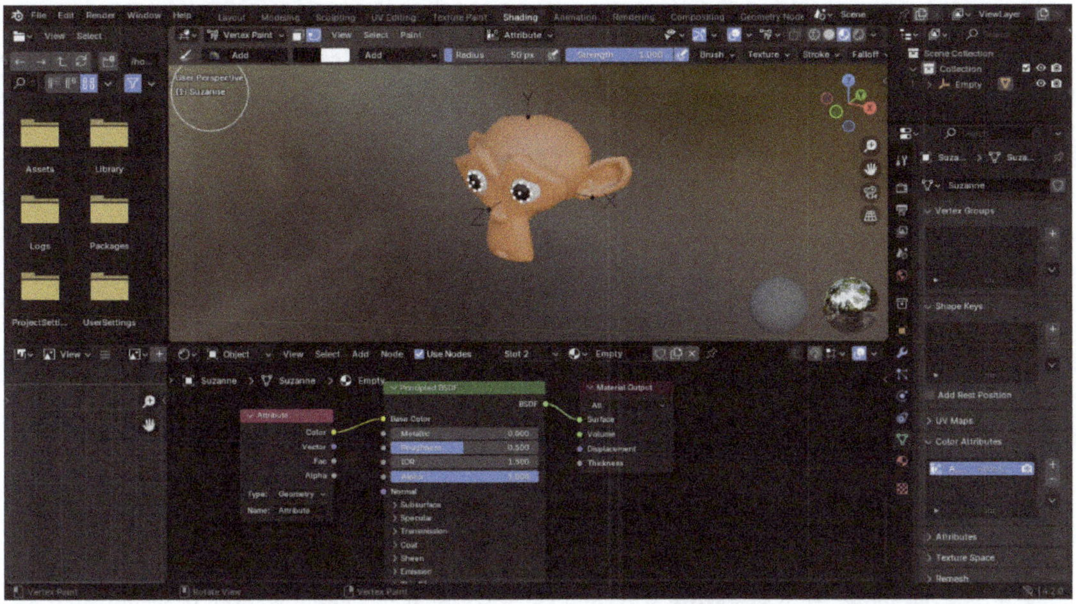

Figure 2.17: Using vertex colors in Blender materials

Once the nodes are connected, the material preview will display black pupils. Shaders are not exported, but we can switch to Unity and look for the vertex color information.

Editing materials in Unity

Once the assets are updated, we can see that Suzanne has two materials and colors.

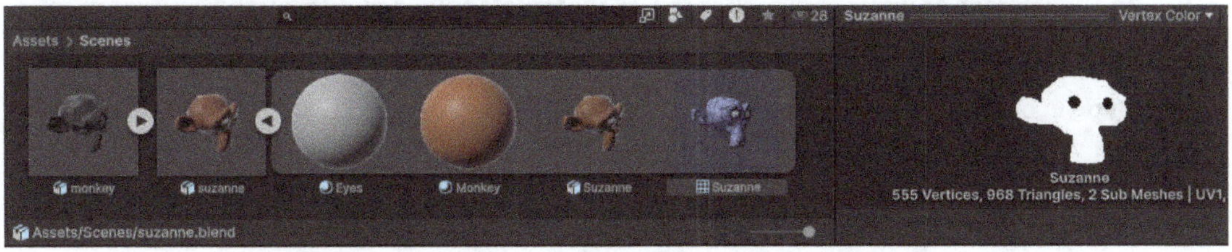

Figure 2.18: Materials and vertex colors in Unity

The eyes are still white, but in the Inspector, we can check that vertex colors were passed:

1. Click the **Suzanne** mesh, the wireframed one with a grid icon beneath it.
2. In the Inspector's preview, select **Vertex Color** in the display drop-down menu.

We can see that the pupils are black, and the rest of the model is white in the preview. To display that in-game, we need to create a Unity shader.

Extracting materials from prefabs

Unity cannot edit the materials from a `.blend` file, so we need to extract **Eyes** from the asset:

1. Expand the **Suzanne** asset in the **Project** browser.
2. Right-click on the **Eyes** material and select **Extract Material SubAsset**.
3. In the file dialog, navigate to the **Assets** | **Art** directory and create a new folder named `Materials`.
4. Select the new folder and click the confirmation button (**Select Folder** or **Save**, depending on the operating system).

Eyes will be detached from **Suzanne** and saved as its own asset. The next step is assigning it a Unity shader.

Using Shader Graph in Unity

Traditionally, game shaders were coded with a shader programming language; modern frameworks, such as the **Universal Render Pipeline**, provide a **Shader Graph**, similar to Blender's Shader Editor. To use it, we must create a Shader Graph asset:

1. In the **Project** browser, right-click in the **Materials** folder to display the context menu.
2. Select **Create** | **Shader Graph** | **URP** | **Lit Shader Graph**.
3. Type `vCol_LitShader` as the name of the new asset.
4. Double-click **vCol_LitShader** to open the editor.

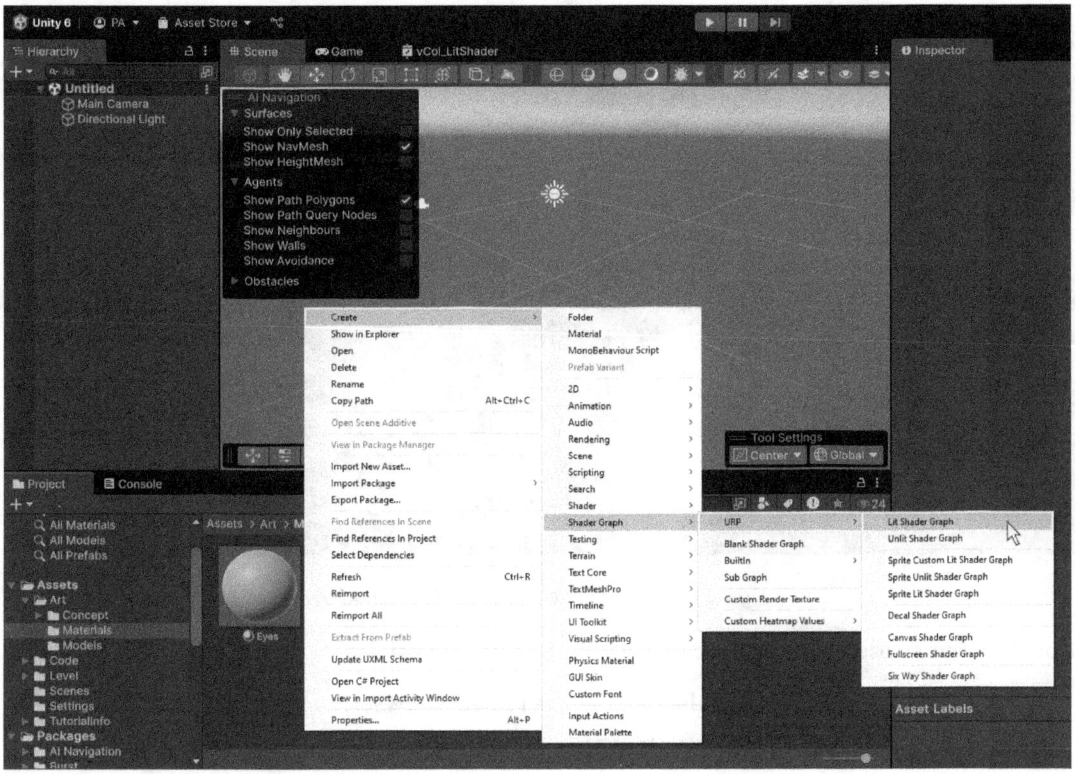

Figure 2.19: Creating a Lit Shader Graph in Unity

Unlike Blender shaders, URP graphs have two output groups: **Vertex** and **Fragment**. The first performs geometrical operations such as vertex displacement; color is generally an input of **Fragment**.

To display vertex colors in this shader, do the following:

1. Right-click an empty zone in the graph and select **Create Node**.
2. Select **Input** | **Geometry** | **Vertex Color** from the menu.
3. Drag **Vertex Color**'s output socket onto **Fragment**'s **Base Color** input.
4. Save this work using *Ctrl* + *S* or **File** | **Save** from the menu bar.

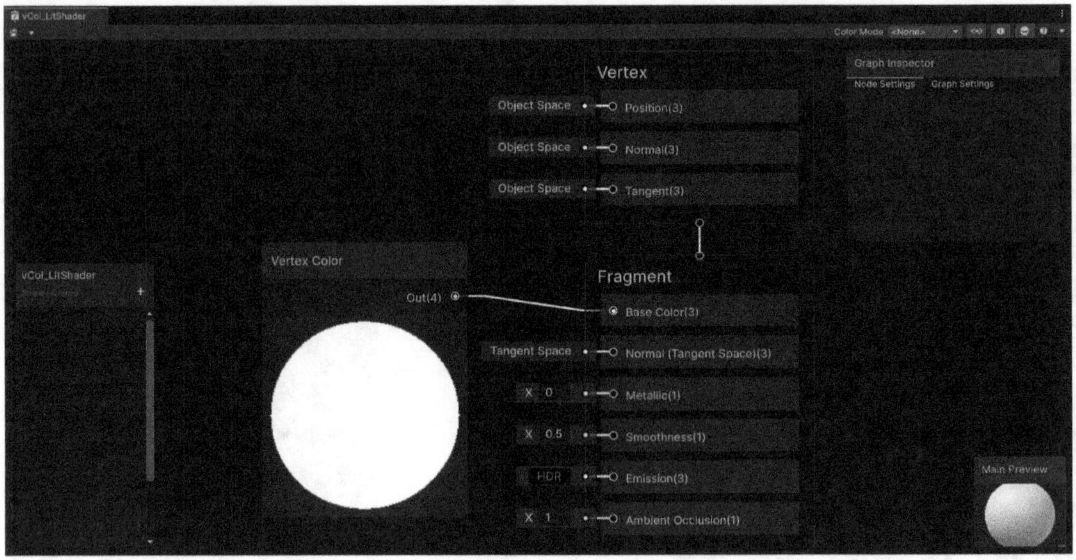

Figure 2.20: Using vertex color in a Unity shader

Now that our shader is ready, we can use it in the **Eyes** materials:

1. Select **Eyes** in the **Materials** folder of the Project Browser.
2. In the Inspector, expand the **Shader** combo box at the top and select **Shader Graphs** | **vCol_LitShader**; we can also type vco in the search filter and select the option, as shown in *Figure 2.21*.

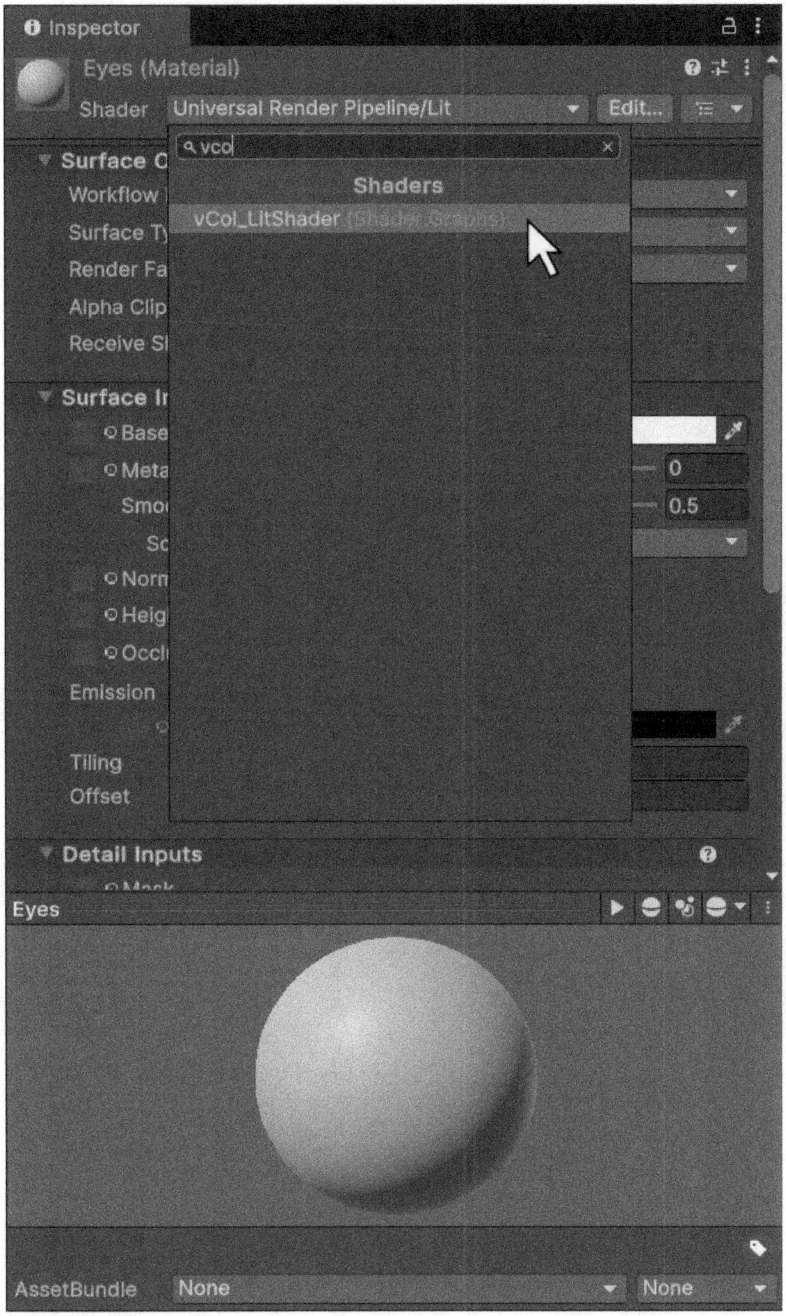

Figure 2.21: Selecting vCol_LitShader for the Eyes material

If we select the **Suzanne** asset in the **Models** folder, we can see the color painted in Blender.

Clicking the **Materials** tab in the Inspector displays the remap between the Blender and Unity materials that will be applied every time the model is reimported.

With this setup, we can paint different colors in Blender, save our edits, and see them in Unity. For instance, we can go back to the Blender scene and, in **Vertex Paint** mode, select a blue color for painting the iris:

1. In **Vertex Paint** mode, which should still be active, select the primary color on top and pick a blue tint from the wheel. The **Hue**, **Saturation**, and **Value** parameters in *Figure 2.22* are `0.6`, `0.7`, and `0.9`, respectively.
2. With **Vertex Selection** still active, press *Ctrl* + *X* to paint the pupils blue.
3. Press *Ctrl* + *S* or **File** | **Save** to write the changes to disk.

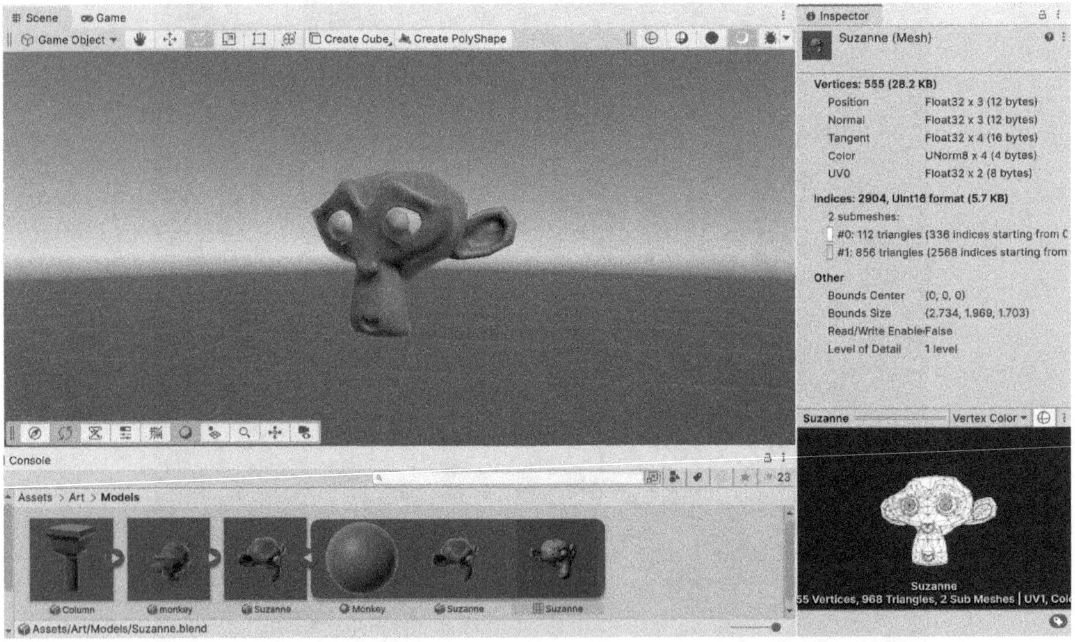

Figure 2.22: Painting blue-eyed Suzanne

Once we switch back to Unity, the **Suzanne** asset will be updated, as shown in *Figure 2.23*.

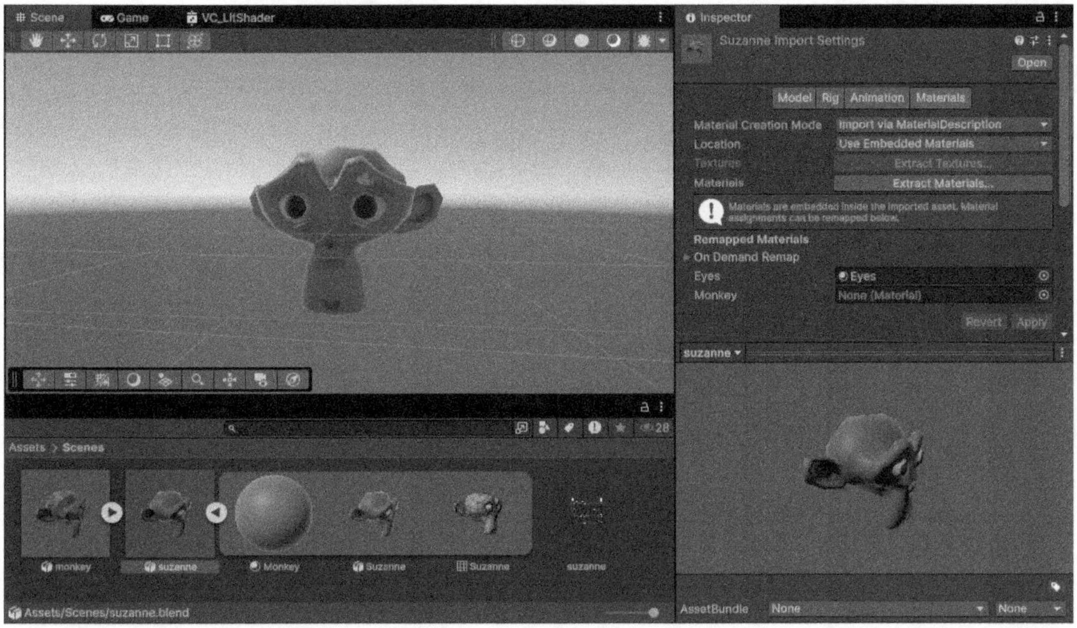

Figure 2.23: Suzanne has blue eyes in Unity

Summary

This chapter dived into the Blender-to-Unity mesh pipeline, comparing manual and automatic techniques and testing the auto-update workflow. Starting with a simple model, we experimented with how information is shared and how we can paint vertices, working incrementally on our assets.

Now that we have established a modeling pipeline, we can proceed with a more complex scene in *Chapter 3*.

3

Prototyping in Unity

Blender is our modeling tool, but we can prototype in Unity. It's a convenient solution for blocking, that is, defining the bulk volumes of a level and leaving the refinement for later. Drafting a location without leaving the game engine also allows for quick checks and corrections at the design stage.

Levels are part of the narrative, and we should plan our maps before we start modeling. In this chapter, we will design a simple level and bring the concept to life.

After a brief introduction to the **Package Manager**, we will install the **ProBuilder** package and create a quick location. Finally, we will import our creation into Blender and ensure visual uniformity with Unity.

By the end of this chapter, you will be able to design levels in Unity and bring them into Blender, maintaining consistency between the concept, the game engine prototype, and the 3D application.

In this chapter, we'll cover the following topics:

- Designing a level
- Modeling with **ProBuilder**
- Passing prototypes to Blender

Technical requirements

In this chapter, we will use Unity 6.3 and Blender 5.2, which can be installed by following the instructions from *Chapter 1* or from their respective websites.

You can download the example project and code for this book by following the instructions in the *Download the example code files* section in the *Preface* of this book.

This chapter's code files are included in the downloadable code bundle.

Designing a level

A **level**, or **map**, is the space that is explored in the game. In terms of location, an indoor level consists of architectural blocks like rooms, walls, doors, and everything that makes up a building, while outdoor levels use urban or natural elements depending on the setting.

Besides being walkable, a game level must feel purposeful, so rather than rushing to the modeling stage, we should think of our map and consider entrance and exit, resources, and obstacles.

Planning the map

Our level is very simple: a wide, ancient rectangular map of an underground crypt, with columns and vaults and an entry and exit corridor. Scribbling it down in a drawing app, we come up with something like *Figure 3.1*.

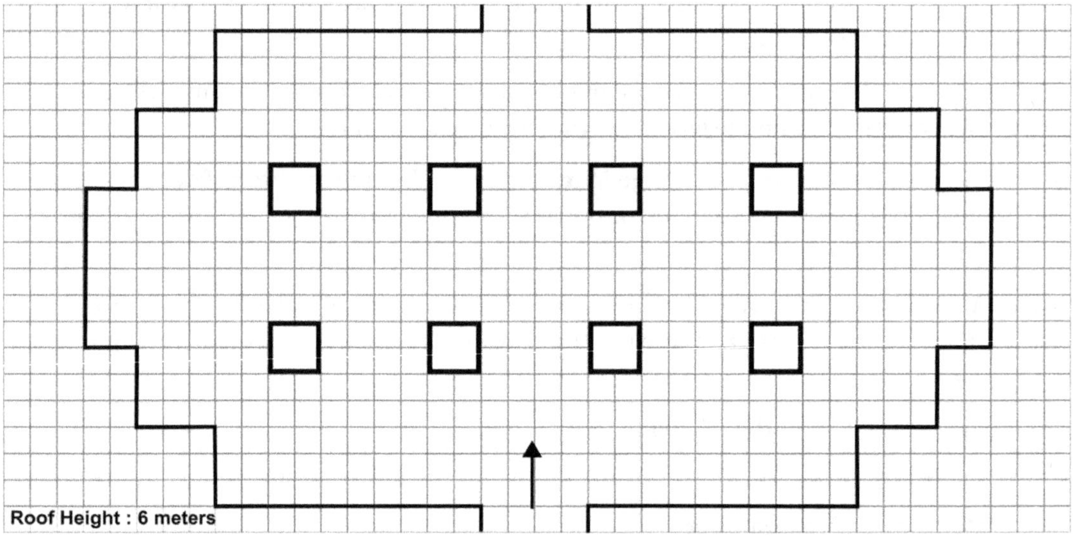

Figure 3.1: Concept map of our level

The arrow at the bottom is the entrance, and each of the six squares is a pillar. With this information, we can model the location, and we can start by importing the map in Unity.

Importing concept art in Unity

We want to test our concepts before modeling, so we create a few assets for that purpose. First, we need a directory for the concept art of this location:

1. Open the project **BlendToUni_URP** from the Unity Hub.
2. In the **Project** browser, *right-click* on the folder **Assets** | **Art**, select **Create** | **Folder**, and name it `Concept`.

Now we can import our map in this folder:

1. Download the map from `https://github.com/PacktPublishing/3D-Game-Development-with-Blender-5-and-Unity-6/blob/main/Assets/Art/Concept/CryptMap.png`
2. From the file manager, drag the file **CryptMap.png** to **Assets** | **Art** | **Concept** in the **Project Browser**.

Figure 3.2: CryptMap.png as an asset

Now our map is a Unity asset, a 2D texture that we can attach to a plane.

> **Note**
>
> **In the event of a crash**
>
> If Unity seems to crash for no apparent reason when importing images, it might be due to conflicts between Unity's file tracking system and other remote drive services. In case of repeated failures, check if the project directory was added to any synced folder.

We will create a new scene to work on our level:

1. In the **Project** browser, *right-click* on the folder **Assets**, select **Create** | **Folder**, and name it `Level`.
2. Drag the folder **Assets** | **Scenes** with the left mouse button and release it in **Assets** | **Level** to move it there.
3. *Right-click* on the folder **Assets** | **Level** | **Scenes**, select **Create** | **Scene** | **Scene**, and name it `CryptBlocking`.

Now, we can finally bring our drawing to the three-dimensional scene:

1. *Double-click* **Assets** | **Level** | **Scenes** | **CryptBlocking** to open it in the scene editor.
2. From the top bar menu, select **Game Object** | **3D Object** | **Plane**; a plane will be added to the scene.
3. In the **Inspector**, *right-click* on the **Transform** header and select **Reset**.
4. Drag the texture **CryptMap** from the folder **Assets** | **Art** | **Concept** in the **Project** browser and release it onto the **Plane** displayed in the scene view.

You will see that a new **Material** is created from our texture, along with the folder **Assets** | **Art** | **Concept** | **Materials**.

We can scale the map plane to fix the proportions: by default, a new plane is 10 units long on each side, but our map has respectively 20 and 40 squares on its shorter and longer side. We can resize the plane and match the two metrics:

1. Select **Plane** in the **Scene** or **Hierarchy**.
2. In the **Inspector** on the right, under the **Transform** panel, in the **Scale** row, set the **X** value to 4 and the **Z** value to 2.

> Note
>
> **The power of ten**
>
> Our map is a 20x40 square grid, so we match the Unity grid by just scaling the original 10x10 plane by 4 and 2 on its X and Z axes. It is possible to match any number of squares by varying that ratio, but grid dimensions that are multiples of ten make that easier.

Our texture's grid now matches the floor grid in Unity, so we can already have a grasp of the level's extent.

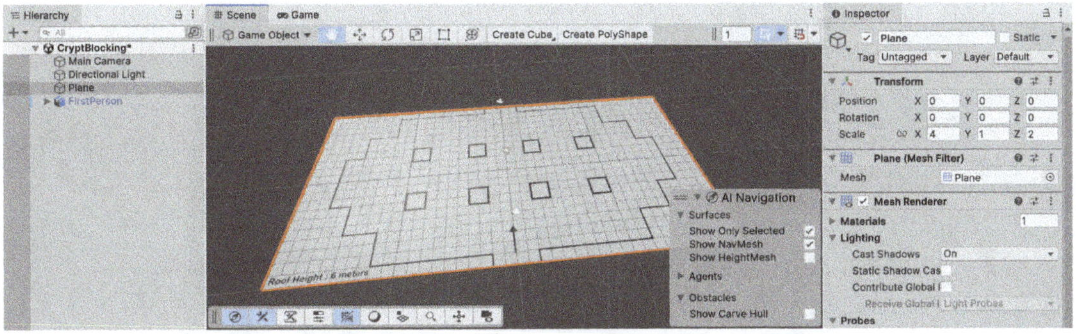

Figure 3.3: Our concept map as a floor in Unity

We want to visualize the volumes of the room, though, so we will create a quick prototype.

Modeling with ProBuilder

We can create models in Blender and bring them to Unity, as discussed in *Chapter 2*, but we can also create solids in our level. This way, we can test the volumes and spaces before working on the details.

ProBuilder, an optional package from **Unity Technologies**, is a tool for sketching walkable levels quickly by creating and merging geometries and architectural elements. **ProBuilder** models can be exported and then refined with another application. Since it is not included in the standard installation, we need to fetch it manually.

Installing ProBuilder

Some functionalities that cover specific needs are not part of the core editor but are released as optional packages and installed on a per-project basis. We can install the **ProBuilder** package using the **Package Manager** through the following steps:

1. Click **Window | Package Manager** from the menu bar. By default, it displays all the packages already installed in the project.
2. Select **Unity Registry** in the navigation list on the left. It will display all the packages authored by **Unity Technology**. ProBuilder is among them, but it is a very long list!
3. Start typing `probuilder`, even in lowercase, in the search bar at the top of the packages list. It takes only a few letters before the package we are looking for is displayed, as shown in *Figure 3.4*.

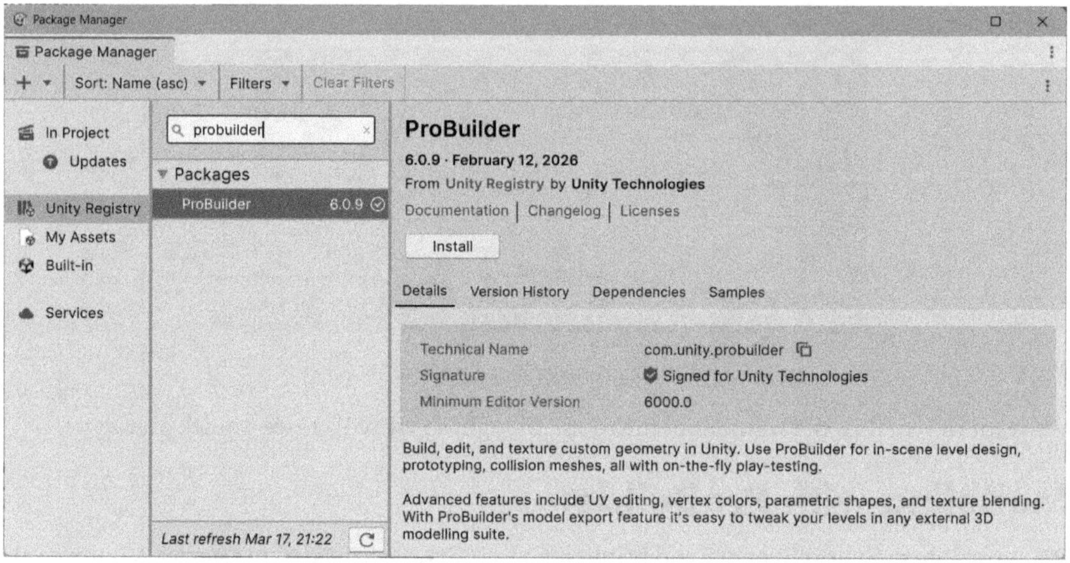

Figure 3.4: Filtering ProBuilder in the Package Manager

4. Click **Install** under the package description to add ProBuilder to the current project.

Once the installation is finished, we can start modeling in Unity.

Using ProBuilder

All ProBuilder actions can be accessed from the **Tools** menu in the top bar. Those actions perform mesh operations, but they don't work on common geometries; we need to create ProBuilder objects. The main advantage over ordinary objects is the support for interactive modeling. For instance, here are the steps for creating an editable plane:

1. From the top bar, select **Tools** | **ProBuilder** | **Editors** | **Create Shape** | **Plane**. That activates the **Shape** tool in the **Scene** editor; now, a small yellow square is displayed at the tip of the mouse pointer.

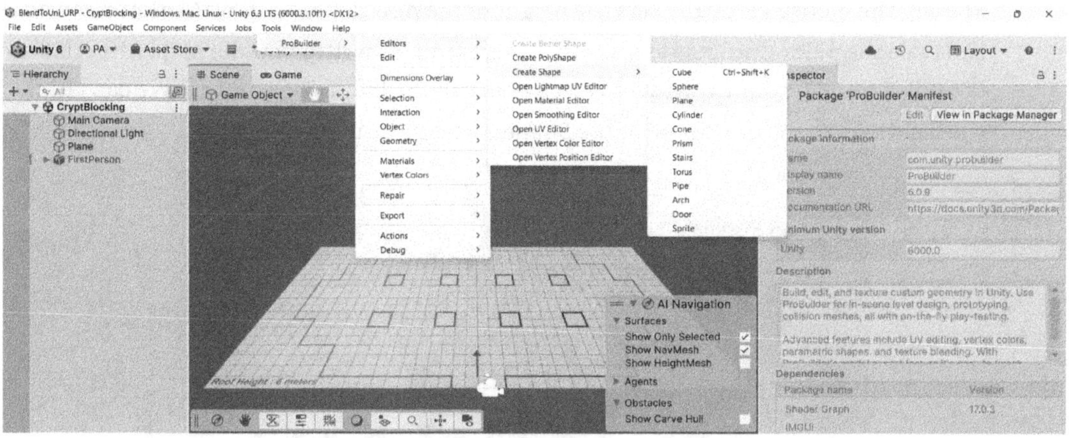

Figure 3.5: ProBuilder Editors menu

2. Click anywhere in the viewport and drag the mouse; that will create a plane and adjust its size in real time.

We do not need this plane, so we undo its creation using the combination *Ctrl* + *Z*, or *Cmd* + *Z* on Mac, and proceed with modeling our map's elements.

Creating the pillars

Since our columns have a square section, we can create them from a cube primitive. Also, since our map's squares match Unity's grid, we use grid snap for modeling:

1. Enable the *Tool Settings* visibility, using the fourth button in the overlay menu at the lower border of the viewport, as shown in *Figure 3.6*.
2. In the *Tool Settings*, set the *Handle Rotation*, the menu button on the right, to **Global**.

Global orientation allows Probuilder to snap to the grid while drawing. Now we can create Probuilder constructs:

1. From the top bar, select **Tools** | **ProBuilder** | **Editors** | **Create Shape** | **Cube**. We can see in the viewport that we have entered **Shape** mode.
2. Enable grid snap by pressing the `Ctrl` key (`Cmd` key on Mac) and keeping it pressed while moving the mouse. The yellow pointer sticks to the nearest grid vertex.
3. Without leaving the snap mode, click on one corner of one of the pillars on the map and drag the mouse to the other corner. That creates the base of a new cube and matches the square on the map exactly. You can now release the mouse click.

4. Moving the mouse vertically sets the height of the new cube. Keeping `Ctrl` pressed, we can raise the pillar until it is exactly six squares tall, as written on the map. After raising the pillar, we can confirm with `Enter` or a click of the left mouse button. We can check the height on the `Y` coordinate of the Shape Settings, as in *Figure 3.6*.

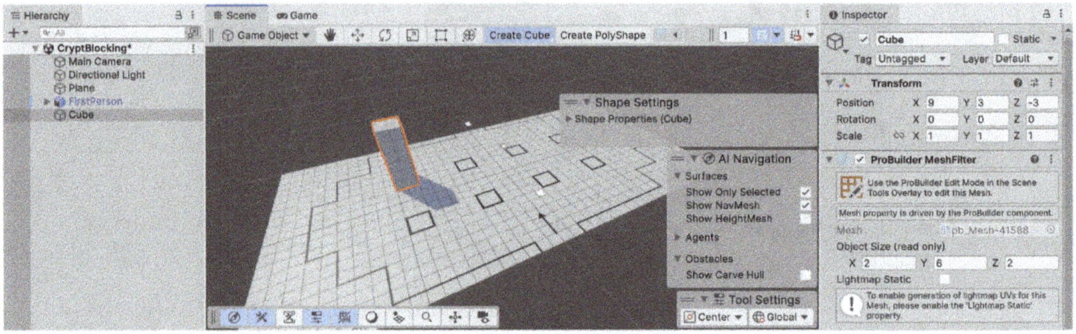

Figure 3.6: A pillar created with ProBuilder

We can create the other columns easily using the **Repeat Last** feature:

1. With the **Create Cube** tool still active, keep `Ctrl` pressed and move the yellow pointer to the center of the next square.
2. Release `Ctrl` and keep `Shift` pressed. ProBuilder will display a blue "ghost" of a new column.
3. Confirm with a click of the left mouse button

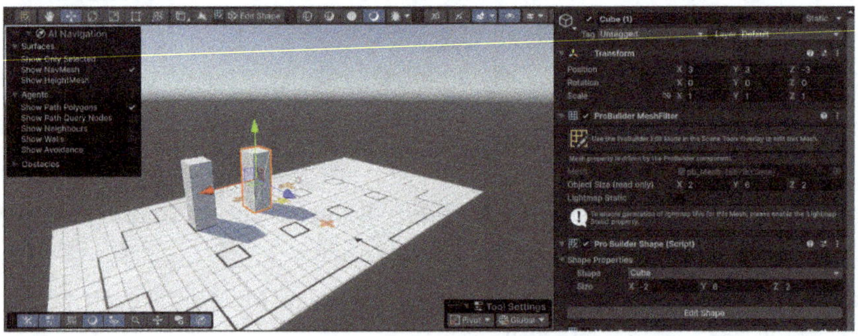

Figure 3.7: Placing copies of the pillar

We can repeat those steps and create the remaining six columns by combining `Ctrl` for snapping to the next center, `Shift` to create a copy of the previous column, and left click to confirm.

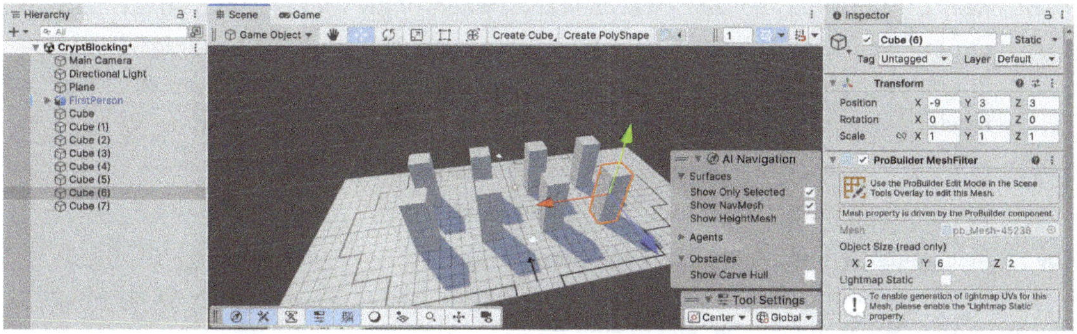

Figure 3.8: The finished colonnade

Now that we have populated the inside of the location, we can proceed to model the room.

Creating the walls

The wall of this room is not a regular geometry, but it is still polygonal, so we can use a **PolyShape**:

1. From the top bar, select **Tools** | **ProBuilder** | **Editors** | **Create Shape** | **PolyShape**. The vertex indicator on the mouse pointer is a tiny gray square.
2. In the viewport, keep the `Ctrl` key pressed to snap to the grid. Click one of the room corners in the drawing to begin tracing the PolyShape.

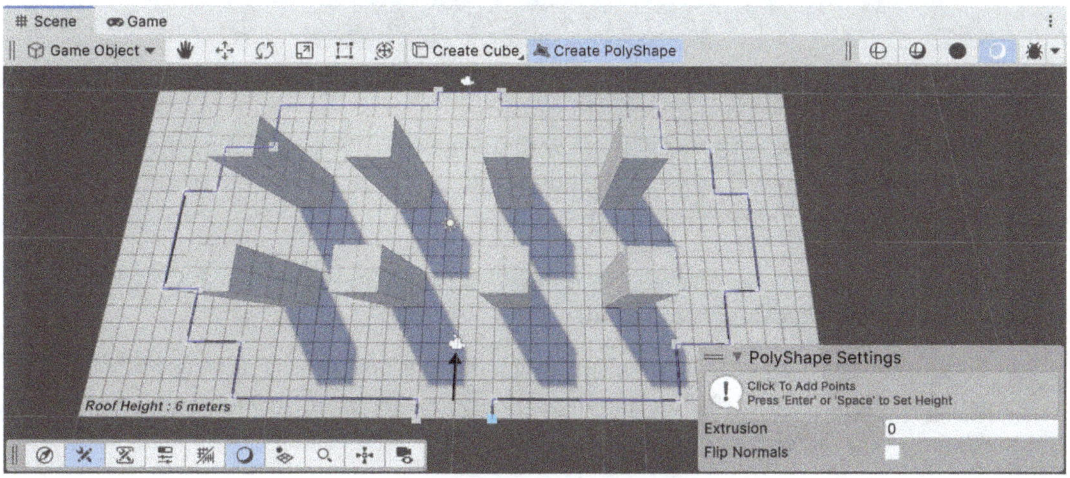

Figure 3.9: Drawing a PolyShape

3. Keep `Ctrl` pressed and click on each of the corners of the wall as drawn on the map until the other end is reached. We don't bother with the openings and draw a closed line. We can pan and zoom in the scene regularly as we add more vertices. Once we reach the first vertex and click it to close the loop, a planar base is created.
4. Moving the mouse sets the height of the room. By keeping the `Ctrl` key pressed, we can easily raise it until it's six squares tall, then press `Enter`.

The room is modeled, but it looks like a solid box. Since the player will see it from the inside, we reverse the direction of the faces by enabling **Flip Normals** in the **Inspector**'s **Poly Shape (Script)** panel. The result can be seen in *Figure 3.10*.

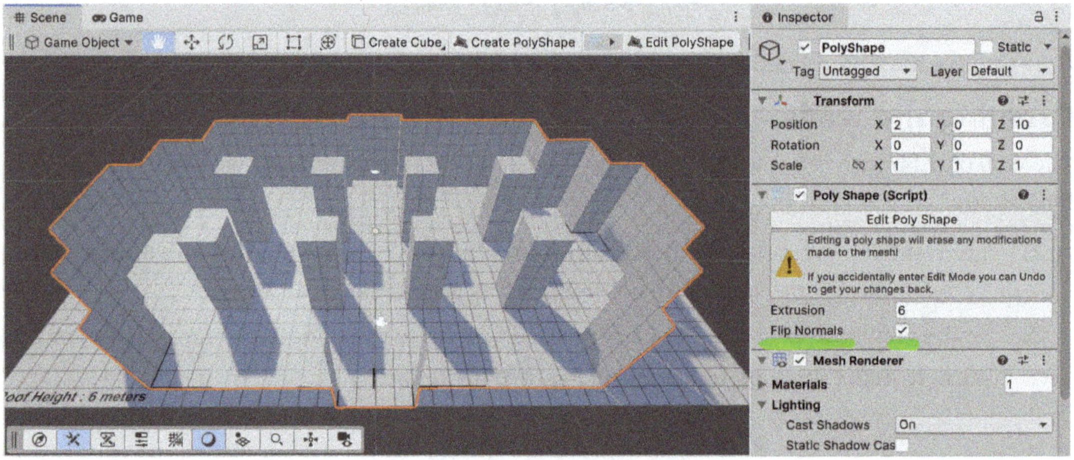

Figure 3.10: Checking Flip Normals on the right renders the wall from the inside

As of now, a raw version of our concept is ready for navigation. We could refine those shapes using more complex primitives and editing, but our focus is integration with Blender, so we will carry on with the rest of the modeling there.

> **Note**
>
> **Your face turned invisible? It's normal!**
>
> In 3D, polygons have a direction, called a normal, which is positive on one side and negative on the other. By default, game engines only render the positive side of a face, making the other side invisible.
>
> Most objects are viewed from the outside, so their normals should point outward. Interiors are explored from the inside, so their normals should point inward.

Exporting from Unity

ProBuilder can export to disk and use exchange formats. One of the available options, **Wavefront Obj**, is easily imported in Blender. To save our level to disk:

1. Select the eight columns and the **PolyShape**, either from the **Hierarchy** or the **Scene** viewport.
2. From the top bar menu, click **Tools** | **ProBuilder** | **Export** | **Export Obj**. A file dialog will open, which points to `BlendToUni_URP` | `Assets`.
3. This is not a game asset, so we will move up to the parent folder, `BlendToUni_URP`, where we will create a new directory with the name `_to_blender_`.
4. Now, create a new folder inside `BlendToUni_URP` | `_to_blender_` and name it `CryptBlocking`.
5. Enter the folder `BlendToUni_URP` | `_to_blender_` | `CryptBlocking` and save the file as `proBuilder_crypt.obj`.

> Note
>
> **Everybody speaks .obj**
>
> The now-defunct *Wavefront Technologies Inc.* developed the `.obj` format as part of their 3D software *Advanced Visualizer*. Since the specifics are open, it is now implemented in virtually every 3D application and, although very basic, is still useful when no animation or effects are involved.

The practice of prototyping with simple blocks is called **White Boxing**. It lets us check the gameplay in advance and reveal possible flaws.

Now that our prototype is exported, we can conclude our experience with **ProBuilder** and continue modeling in Blender.

Passing models to Blender

An `.obj` file contains the position of vertices, a list of which vertices are connected by edges, and which edges are connected by polygons. It doesn't retain any of the information that makes parametric editing possible, so the models are going to be imported as static meshes.

Importing ProBuilder_crypt.obj

All the import operators in Blender can be accessed from the File menu. Here are the steps for importing our geometries:

1. Launch Blender and delete the default content: press *A* to select everything, then press *Delete* or *X* and confirm to remove all the objects.
2. From the top bar, click **File** | **Import** | **Wavefront (.obj)** to open the import file dialog.
3. Navigate to the `BlendToUni_URP` folder; we have added it to the bookmarks in *Chapter 1*.
4. Walk to the folder `BlendToUni_URP` | `_to_blender_` | `CryptBlocking`; you will see two files: `proBuilder_crypt.obj` and `proBuilder_crypt.mtl`. The latter contains information about the material.
5. Select `proBuilder_crypt.obj` and enable **Split By Group** in the options on the right. That will import the ProBuilder models as separate objects.
6. Click the Import **Wavefront OBJ** button.

Blender will import the `.obj` scene, and the result might be disappointing at first, as all we can see is a closed box. The reason is that, unlike Unity, Blender doesn't skip back-facing polygons by default.

This is conventional among non-game apps and the cause of many avoidable issues, as artists might not realize that their models are flipped until they are exported to the engine. We must change this Blender setting immediately:

1. Click the expansion triangle beside the shading spherical icons on the top-right corner of the viewport to expand the display options.
2. From the **Viewport Shading** options, check the **Backface Culling** box.

Once enabled, you will be able to see only the inside of the walls, and the model will display correctly.

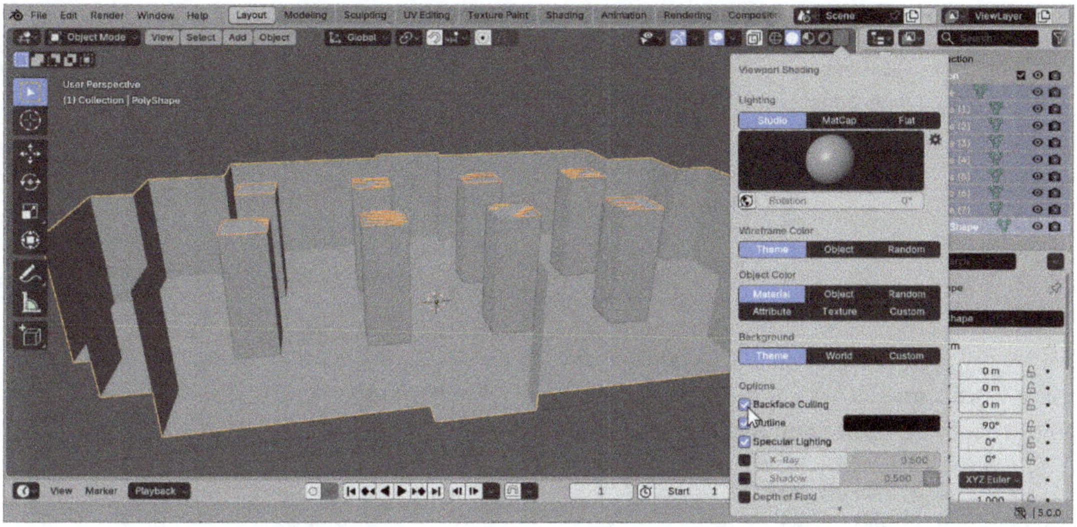

Figure 3.11: Our crypt normals displayed correctly in Blender

What about the material? **ProBuilder**'s metric texture is useful at this stage, and we could see the `.mtl` file in the directory, so we should be able to display that too.

Displaying material preview

The spherical icons at the top right corner of the 3D view select one of the four **Viewport Shading** modes. They are, from left to right:

- **Wireframe**: Displays only the edges of the model. Useful for a quick check of the topology or for saving resources while navigating heavy scenes. The icon is a wireframe sphere.
- **Solid**: Displays the polygons using quick shading, so lighting is not considered. The icon is a flat circle.
- **Material Preview**: Displays lit materials using Blender's almost real-time engine Eevee. The icon is a lit sphere with a solid quarter.
- **Rendered**: Displays the render engine set in the scene render properties, even if it is slow. The icon is a lit sphere.

Each shading mode has its own render options, which can be set using the expansion button at the right end of the toolbar. The shading modes toolbar is displayed in *Figure 3.12*.

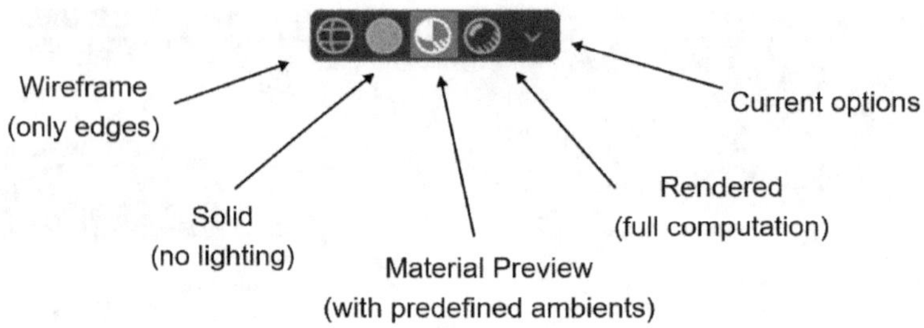

Figure 3.12: Viewport display modes

We are not using **Rendered** in this book, as we are not rendering with Blender, and we are not using **Wireframe** either, as there is no reason to display our models without faces. We are going to focus on **Solid** and **Material Preview**.

Adjusting solid view

Solid is the default method in Blender and is probably the fastest (wireframe display can be more expensive on highly subdivided models). It is usually associated with an ugly gray view, but that's inaccurate, as there are many ways to improve how it looks.

For instance, we can display the texture rather than the solid color:

1. Click the expansion triangle beside the **Viewport Shading** icons to display the **Viewport Shading** options again.
2. In the **Color** section, click **Texture**. This will display the **ProBuilder** grid rather than solid gray. We can also change the Lighting mode:
3. In the **Viewport Shading** options, there are three buttons under the **Lighting** section:
    - **Studio**: Uses four directional lights set in **Preferences** | **Lights** | **Studio Lights** for direct shading. Useful for a first assessment of a model.
    - **MatCap**: Wraps the drawing of a sphere around a model based on its face normals to give the illusion of fixed direct shading. Useful for sculpting and checking the uniformity of a model.
    - **Flat**: No shading at all, only color
4. There are plenty of combinations to check. We click the **Matcap** button to explore a few.
5. Click the preview image with a lit sphere under the **Lighting** buttons to browse the **Matcap Options**. Click the fourth entry from the left for a sideways illumination reminiscent of what we had in Unity. The result is displayed in *Figure 3.13*.

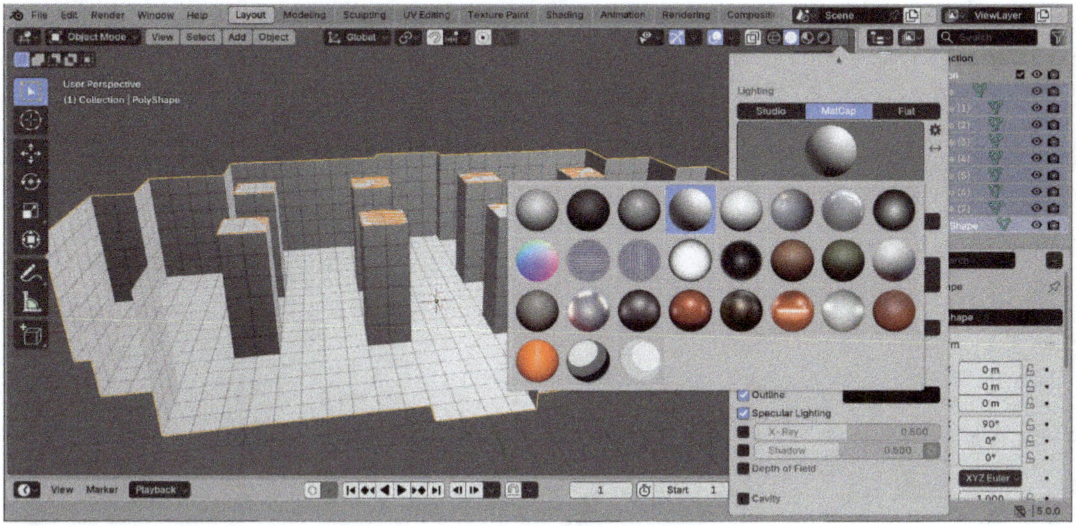

Figure 3.13: Matcap shading in Blender

With this setup, we can work on our scene without consuming render power and display textures at little to no cost.

Although very useful at this stage, solid display is restricted by its limited settings and absence of actual lighting. For that reason, we will set up **Material Preview** as well.

Using Material Preview

We have already approached materials in *Chapter 2*. In this case, the objects are already assigned the material exported by **ProBuilder**.

We can check that by activating **Material Preview**, the central icon in the **Viewport Shading** toolbar, as shown in *Figure 3.14*.

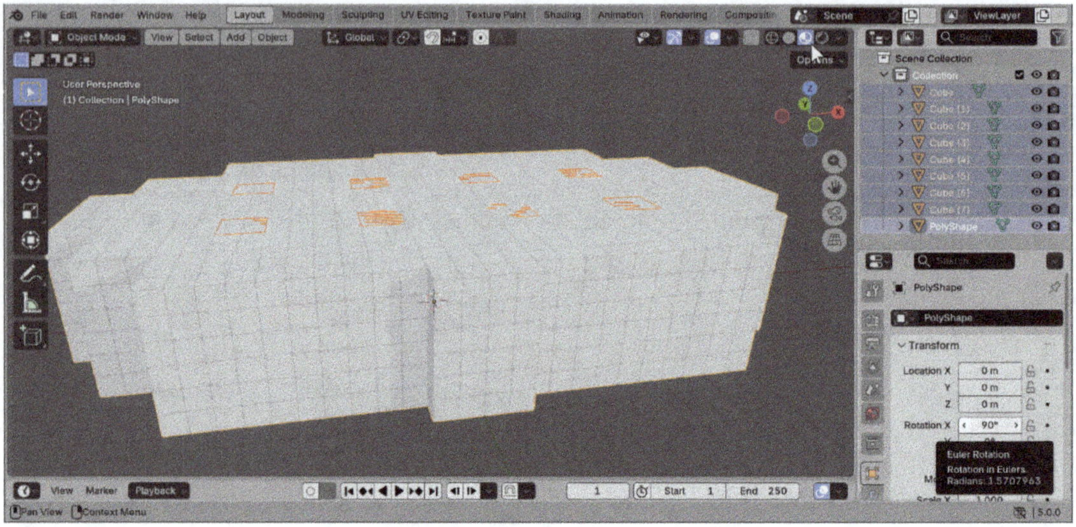

Figure 3.14: The crypt seen from the outside

Again, we will not be able to see the inside of the crypt, as the **Backface Culling** option from earlier is for solid shading and does not affect materials.

Blender shading system is much more flexible, and we can set different culling options on each material. To enable backface culling on the crypt's material:

1. Select the crypt geometry and, in the **Properties** view to the right, select the **Material** tab. It's the bottommost icon, a sphere with stylized highlights, as shown in *Figure 3.15*.
2. We can see the properties of the material **ProBuilderDefault**. Scroll down to the **Settings** panel. If it is collapsed, click on the expansion triangle.
3. Under the **Surface** | **Backface Culling** section, check the boxes for **Camera** and **Shadow**: the former makes flipped faces invisible to the camera, and the latter prevents them from casting shadows.

The **Properties** tabs display the attributes of the scene and objects and consist of two main blocks: tabs like **Render**, **Output**, and **View Layer** are valid for the entire scene, while the second group is related to the active object. The **Materials** tab is part of the latter group.

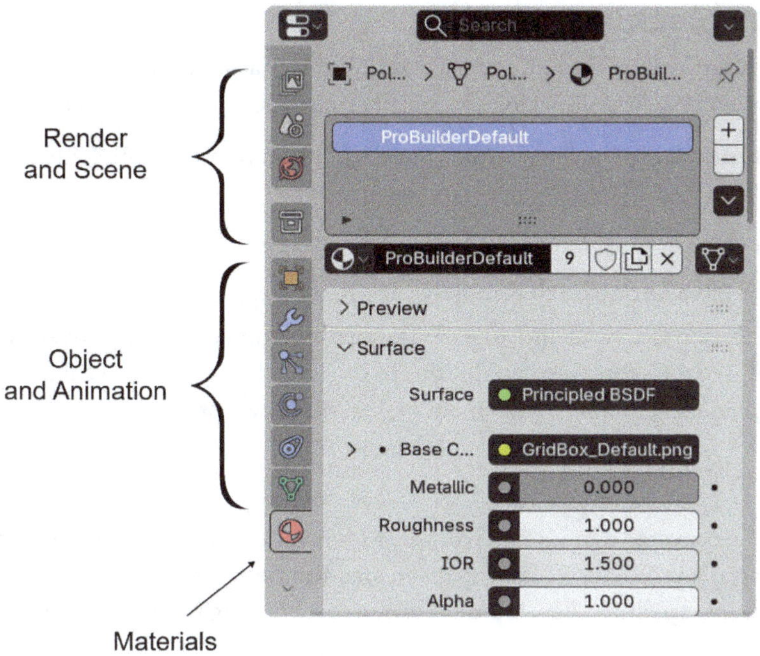

Figure 3.15: Blender Properties

Once we enable the culling options for the material, the preview is displayed correctly.

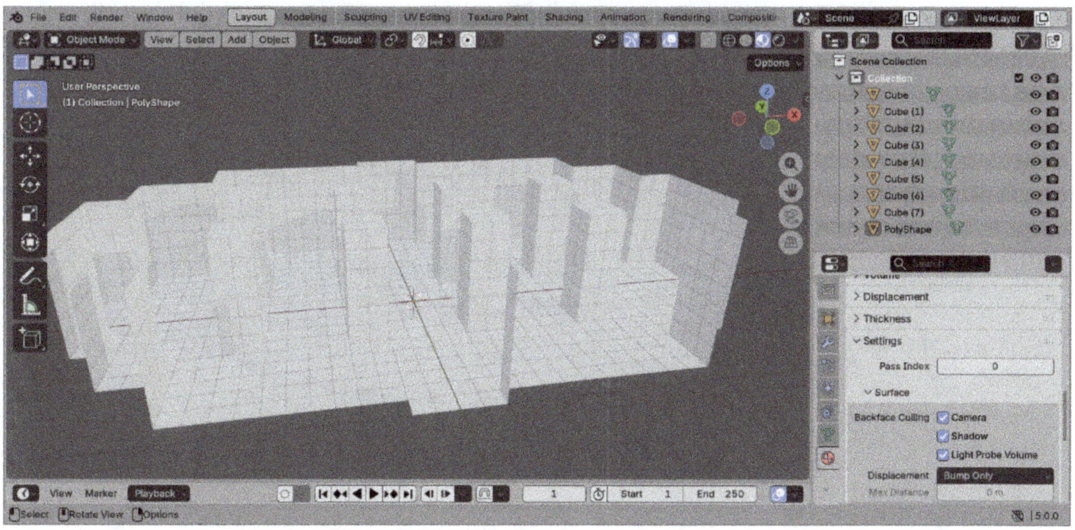

Figure 3.16: ProBuilder's material in Blender

Before we start working on the final model, we might want to save our file first.

Saving our blocking

This is only an intermediate file and not a game object, so rather than saving it along with the game assets, we will place it alongside the .obj file from which it was sourced:

1. From Blender's top bar, select **File** | **Save As**, then navigate to the folder `BlendToUni_URP` | `_to_blender_` | `CryptBlocking`.
2. Type `CryptBlocking.blend` as the filename.
3. Click the **Save As** button to complete the procedure.

Using two applications for modeling one environment might seem like an over-complication at first, but merging the sketching capabilities of Unity with the generative features of Blender pays off and will make it easier to match our assets' size as we progress through the chapters.

Summary

In this chapter, we covered a modeling workflow for levels. Rather than going deep into the technical aspects of modeling, we have focused on a simple, consistent, and streamlined workflow that allows planned development without sacrificing immediacy and control.

The prototype built in this chapter marks the end of the first part of this book and is going to be the starting point for more sophisticated techniques that will be presented in *Part 2, Building Assets*.

In *Chapter 4*, we will integrate this scene into the Blender asset system and build the utilities for turning this model into a proper game environment.

Get this book's PDF copy, code bundle, and more

Scan the QR code (or go to `packtpub.com/unlock`). Search for this book by name, confirm the edition, and then follow the steps on the page.

UNLOCK NOW

Note: Have your invoice handy. Purchases made directly from the Packt website don't require an invoice.

Part 2

Building Assets

In creating elements for the game, the software integration unravels along two main themes: how can we better adapt Blender to Unity, and how can we get the most from such a combination.

Blender is malleable enough to accommodate new workflows; on the other hand, it can bring innovative solutions to established practices, like procedural modeling and programmable routines.

In this part of the book, you will learn how to customize Blender and use its Asset Browser and plugin system to ease the development of assets. You will then bring your creations to Unity, replacing the placeholders created in the previous part with finished models.

This part of the book includes the following chapters:

- *Chapter 4, Customizing Blender*
- *Chapter 5, Modeling with Geometry Nodes*
- *Chapter 6, Assembling the Level*

4

Customizing Blender

Even a simple project can become hard to follow as the assets increase in number, while repetitive tasks can introduce potential mistakes. Customization and automation of tasks mitigate the effort required to keep a production together.

Blender is a generic, adaptable platform, so there is room for improvements that make a Unity workflow easier.

A well-designed process involves splitting our tasks into separate files and sharing them across different scenes. That has become easier to do in Blender since the introduction of the **Asset Browser** with version 3.0.

Once properly configured, the content of Blender files is displayed as thumbnails and can be dragged to the current scene, much like with Unity's Project Browser.

A second degree of customization—the addition of new commands—can be implemented with Python, the programming language that powers Blender's user interface.

Coding is not as hard as most people think, and video games can hardly be developed without programming.

This introduction to tool development for Blender will help set up an environment for working with Unity and present an overview of tool design for production.

This chapter covers the following topics:

- Working with collections and assets
- Creating custom commands
- Automating object creation

Technical requirements

In this chapter, we will use Blender 5.1, which can be installed by following the instructions from *Chapter 1* or from the website `blender.org`.

You can download the example project and code for this book by following the instructions in the *Download the example code files* section in the *Preface* of this book.

This chapter's code files are included in the downloadable code bundle.

Working with collections and assets

Collections are a flexible way to organize objects in Blender: objects grouped in collections can be hidden and displayed collectively, duplicated together at once, and shared through different files. A `.blend` file format is like a database from which Blender can pick any data, including objects, geometries, or materials.

Blender also provides the **Asset Browser**, a thumbnail viewer for resources contained in `.blend` files, much like the Unity Project Browser.

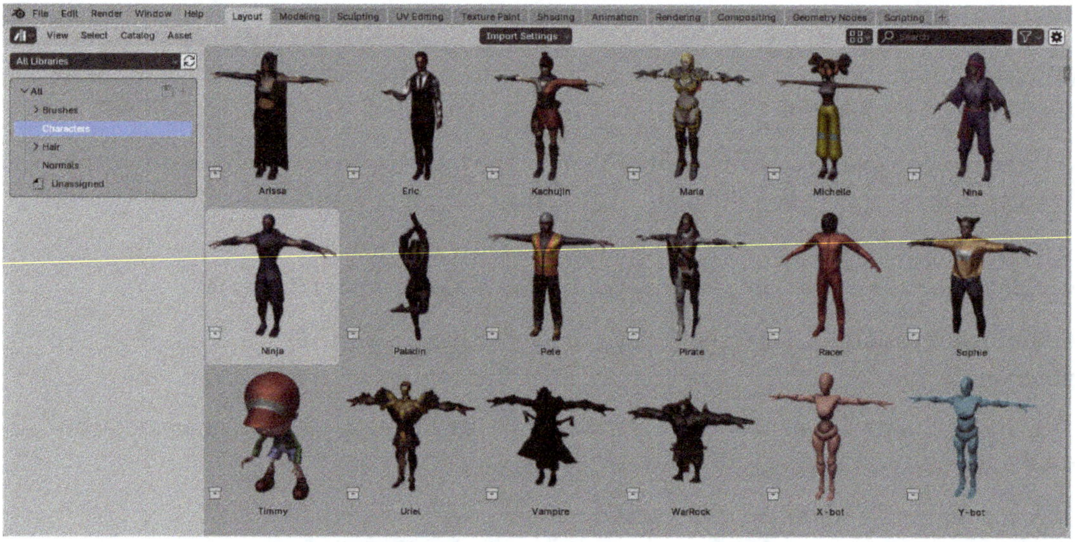

Figure 4.1: Characters on disk displayed in the Asset Browser

In our case, we want to display the blocking of our level as a read-only reference so that we can model over it. We also want the blocking to stay in its own file while we use it as a reference, because our assets should contain only their final model.

We will create a Blender asset from the **ProBuilder** level exported in *Chapter 3*, so that it can be dragged and dropped into our 3D scenes.

Preparing library scenes

We will start with the file `CryptBlocking.blend` created in *Chapter 3*. At this point, there should be two ways to open that scene:

- From the **Recent Files**, either from Blender's splash screen or from the **File** | **Open Recent** menu
- By reaching the `BlendToUni_URP` file folder from the bookmarks and navigating to `_to_blender_` | `CryptBlocking` | `CryptBlocking.blend`

Once it is open, we should see the level in Blender, already set up for display. We can see that the model has a 90-degree rotation on its X axis because it comes from a different coordinate system, as explained in *Chapter 2*.

Rather than sharing our geometries directly, we create a collection that will be passed to other Blender files. This way, if we make changes to the objects, external files will still read the content of the collection without raising any errors.

Creating collections

Collections are displayed in the **Outliner** as folders and can be enabled or hidden in their **View Layer**. In *Chapter 3*, we imported `proBuilder_crypt.obj` inside the default **Collection**, as we can see in the **Outliner**:

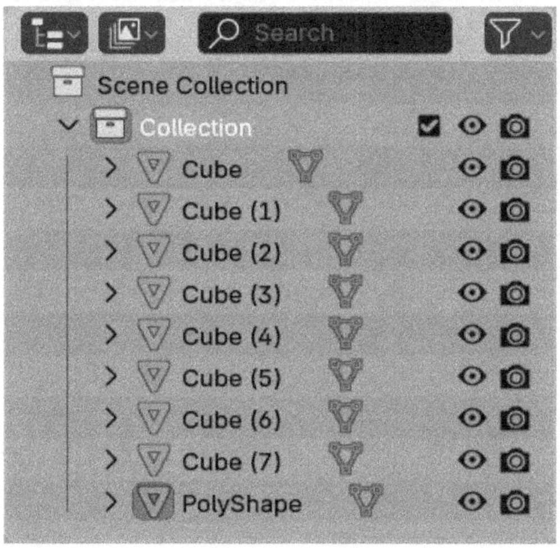

Figure 4.2: proBuilder_crypt in the scene's View Layers

Once a collection is marked as an asset, its name will be displayed under the thumbnail, so we need a more descriptive name for ours. Rather than renaming the existing collection, we can create another one: that will leave the default collection available in case it's needed for other tools and objects:

1. Press *A* to select all the objects.
2. Press *M* and select **Move to Collection** | **+ New Collection...**
3. Type `Crypt Blocking` when asked for a name.

The collection is ready for linking, but if we want it to appear in the **Asset Browser**, we need to make it an asset.

Marking collections as assets

There are no limitations on how many assets a scene can contain, although in this case, `Crypt Blocking` is going to be the only asset of this `.blend` file. The process of marking an asset is straightforward:

1. In the **Outliner**, *right-click* on the `Crypt Blocking` collection.
2. Select **Mark as Asset** from the menu.

The outliner will display the icon of a bookshelf alongside the collection. Now, we can check the **Asset Browser**.

Using the Asset Browser

Like many other visualizers in Blender, the **Asset Browser** is an **Editor** and can be found in the editor selection, the first icon on the top left of the header of each view. For instance, we can replace the **3D Viewport** with an **Asset Browser**:

1. Click the **Editor Type** drop-down, the first icon on the top left of the viewport's header.
2. Select **Asset Browser** in the last column.

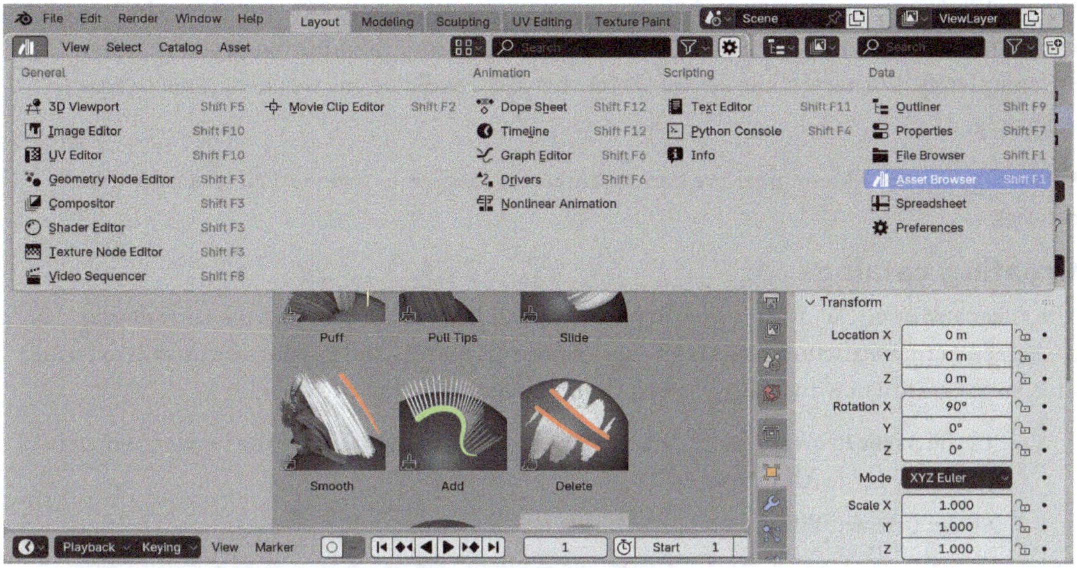

Figure 4.3: Selecting the Asset Browser

Blender comes with a few assets included, like brushes, hair, or geometric operations. The vertical bar on the left displays the available catalogs, which are arbitrary categories of assets.

If we click on the **Unassigned** catalog, we will find our `Crypt Blocking`. If we click on it and press *N* or click the cog icon on the top right, we will see the **Asset Properties**, such as **Description**, **Copyright**, and **Author**.

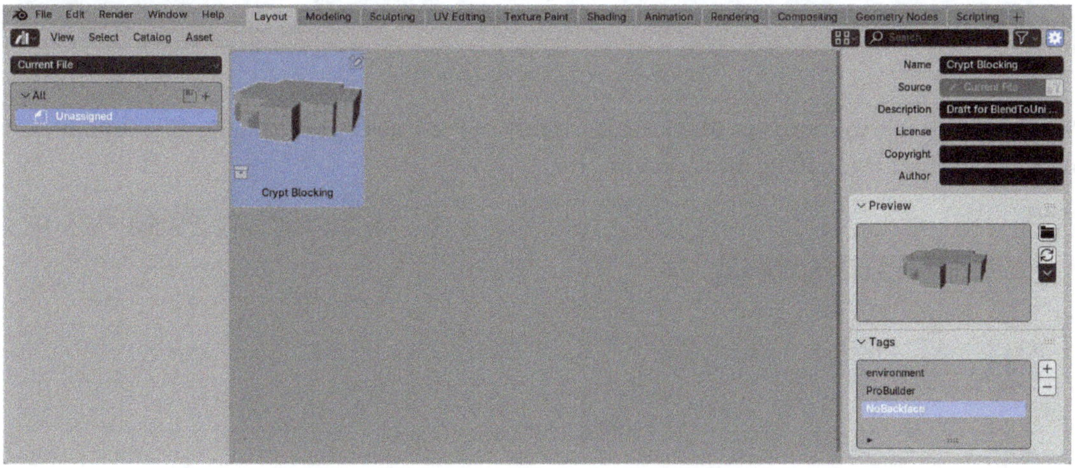

Figure 4.4: The Crypt Blocking asset

We can fill those properties as we like. For instance, we can type `Draft for BlendToUni level` as the **Description** and add **tags** for rapid search by pressing the **+** button in the **Tags** list. Tags are completely arbitrary; some keywords for this asset could be `environment`, `ProBuilder`, `NoBackface`.

While tags are not hierarchical, we can organize our categories in a vertical structure using *catalogs*.

Creating catalogs

The **Asset Browser** can display the content of multiple directories or just the current file, organized in tree-structured **catalogs**; we cannot edit objects and catalogs located in external files, so to create a new catalog, we must limit the display to the current file:

1. In the **Asset Browser**'s left bar, click the combo box right under the header, which is currently set to **All Libraries**.
2. Select **Current File**.

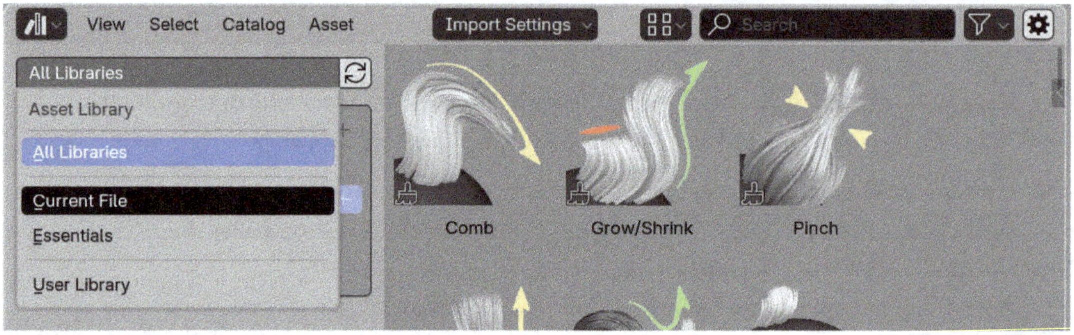

Figure 4.5: Switching to Current File

We should be able to see **Crypt Blocking**, currently in the **Unassigned** catalog. The thumbnail doesn't take backface culling into account.

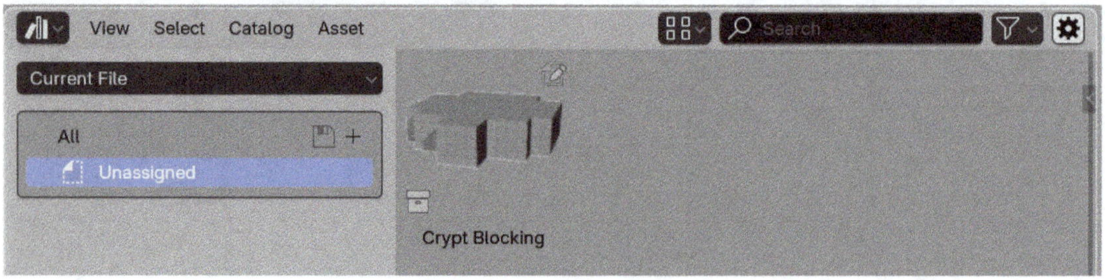

Figure 4.6: Crypt Blocking

We can create more catalogs for our project, and even nest them:

1. Click the **+** button beside the **All** category. `Catalog` is the default name.
2. Double-click on the new catalog and rename it `BlendToUni`.
3. Hover the mouse cursor on `BlendToUni` to display a **+** button. Press it to create a sub-catalog and rename it to `Blocking`.
4. Drag `Crypt Blocking` from the `Unassigned` catalog to **BlendToUni** | **Blocking**.
5. Save the scene.

Our scene now contains an asset and two catalogs. Blender will not display those yet when we work on other files; to do that, we need to add a new folder to the **Asset Libraries**.

Adding library folders

The **Asset Browser** looks for all the assets contained in specific directories on disk, like the assets folder of the Blender install. We can add more folders, though, which is very convenient as we can use different libraries for different projects.

To add our folder to the **Asset Libraries**:

1. From the top bar menu, click **Edit** | **Preferences...**
2. In the **Preferences** window, select **File Paths** in the navigation pane on the left.
3. Scroll down to **Asset Libraries** and click the **+** button to add a new folder.
4. Navigate to `BlendToUni_URP` | `_to_blender_` and click **Add Asset Library**.

The folder `_to_blender_` will be displayed among the **Asset Libraries**.

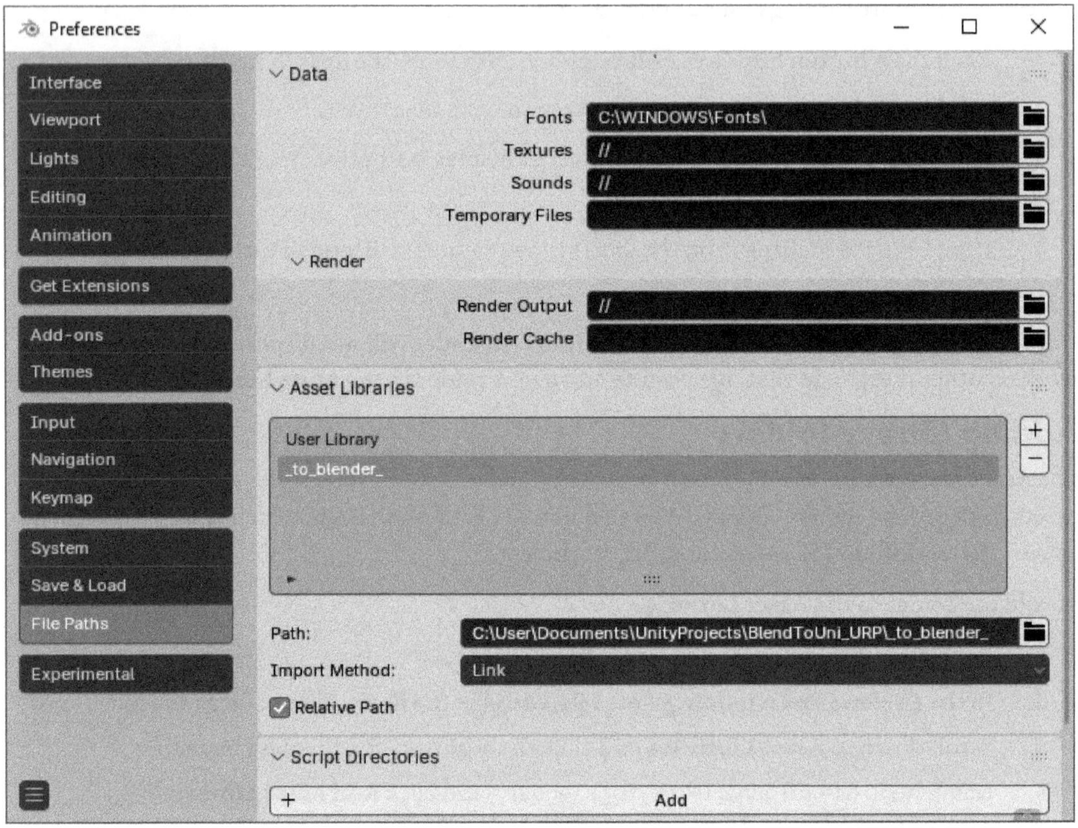

Figure 4.7: Adding asset libraries

Another important setting, **Import Method**, determines the preferred way for importing the assets from that specific library. There are three ways to import external files in Blender:

- **Link**: Reads the data from the asset and displays it in the current scene. Changes in the original asset will be propagated to all scenes where it is referenced.
- **Append**: Copies all data to the current scene. Imported elements are completely independent; changes in the original assets will not propagate to the scene that references them.
- **Pack**: Combines both methods; the asset is linked, but also included in the current file in case the original library is lost.

We want to import blockings as read-only references, so we set the **Import Method** to **Link** for this folder. At this point we can Crypt Blocking and work on our scene, but since we'll be working with the Asset Browser for the rest of the project, we might very well create a better interface around it.

Creating the asset workspace

The **3D Viewport** is the main component of Blender's default screen, the **Layout** workspace. To import assets with drag and drop, we need to split the layout between the browser and the viewport. No default workspace has that arrangement, so we will create a new one:

1. Start with a new scene by either restarting Blender or clicking **File** | **New** from the top menu.
2. Click the **+** button on the far right of the tab bar at the top of the window.
3. Select **General** | **Layout**. A new tab, **Layout.001**, will be added.
4. Double-click on **Layout.001** and rename it to `Assets`.

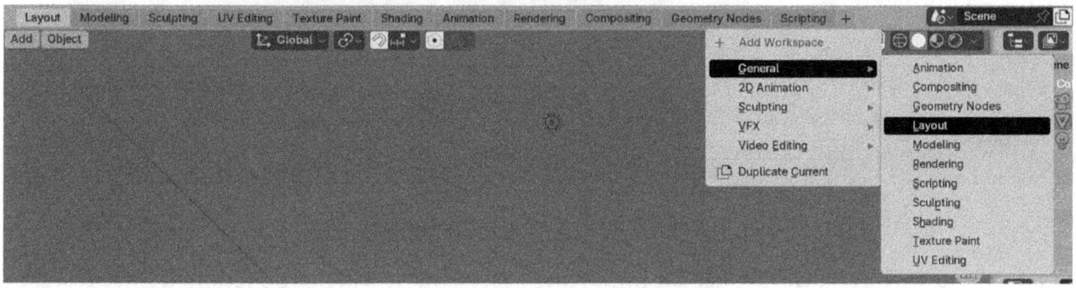

Figure 4.8: Creating a new Layout workspace

We will split this new layout to make room for the **Assets Browser**:

1. Move the mouse cursor to the viewport's upper or lower border: it will change to a bidirectional indicator for resizing the editor.
2. Right-*click* to bring up the **Area Options** menu and select **Vertical Split**. Move the split line to about one third of the viewport width.
3. Left-click to confirm the size of the new split: now there are two 3D viewports.
4. Click the **Editor Type** menu in the top left corner of the smaller viewport and switch to **Asset Browser**.

Figure 4.9: Asset Browser and viewport

At this point, we have a workspace for importing assets, but it will not be retained if we restart Blender. We can make our changes permanent by saving the current scene as the startup file.

Saving default settings

Blender loads its default settings from a startup file located in its installation folder. We can overwrite that file and retain our new workspace. Since we are going to work on game assets, it might be a good idea to activate **Backface Culling** in the **Viewport Shadin**g options, like in the *Passing models to Blender* section of *Chapter 3*.

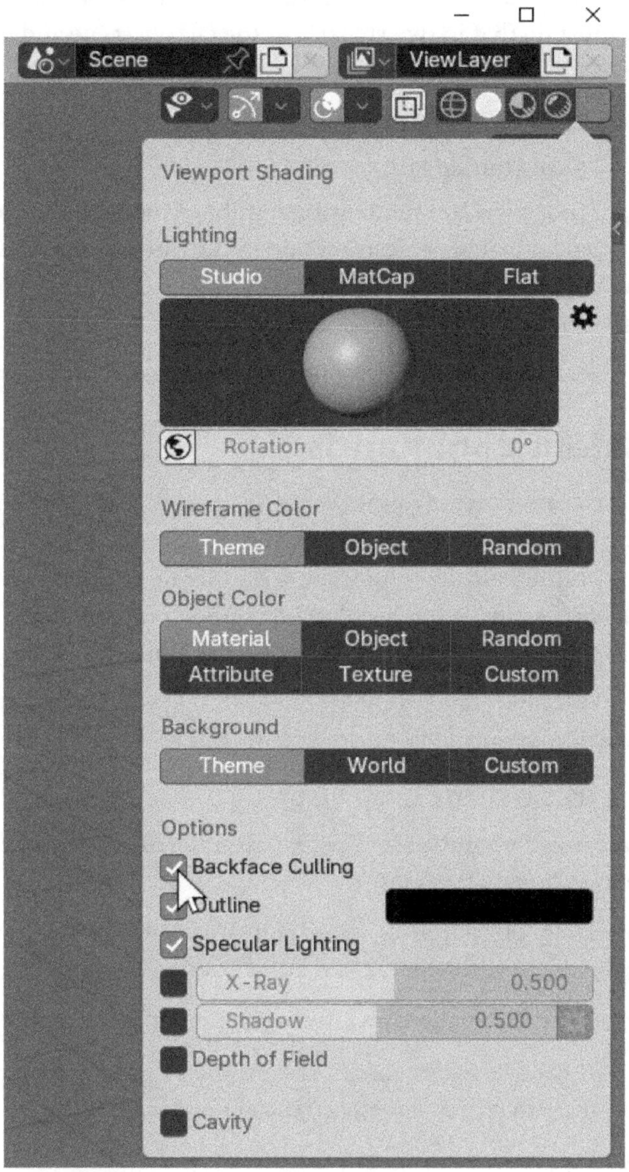

Figure 4.10: Activating Backface Culling

Then, we are ready to save our default arrangement:

1. Open the **File** menu from the top bar
2. Select **Defaults** | **Save Startup File**

From now on, Blender will load this scene at startup. If for any reason we want to roll back to the factory scene, we must do that in two steps: load the factory scene and save it as the startup file. From the menu bar:

- **File** | **Defaults** | **Load Factory Settings**
- **File** | **Defaults** | **Save Startup File**

Now we can import our prototype by dragging its thumbnail over the viewport. The action of drag and drop is designed for placing objects around in the three-dimensional space; in our case, we would rather reset the location with *Alt* + *G* (*Option* + *G* on Mac) and lock the transform channels to avoid accidental displacement.

We can bring customization to a further level and automate these kinds of tasks.

Creating custom commands

Working on a 3D project sometimes involves recurring operations: for instance, after we have dragged `Crypt Blocking` into the 3D space, we need to set its location to zero and lock the location, rotation, and scale channels—a procedure that we have already encountered in the *Working in Y-up in Blender* section in *Chapter 2*. It is common practice to *zero and lock* an object to avoid unwanted displacement, so it would be great to combine those two actions in one command.

This section covers the development of a custom command that performs these operations.

Automating zero and lock

Blender commands are called **operators** and can be executed manually by the user or invoked internally by the program or its extensions.

In extending the program for our purpose, we are going to create an operator and add it to a menu of the interface so that it can be invoked manually.

Custom operators are written in **Python**, an intuitive, modular programming language.

A Python program is also called a **script** since it is executed by an interpreter, in this case Blender's Python module, rather than directly by the operating system.

Blender provides a workspace for writing scripts.

Scripting in Blender

A layout arrangement for coding, the **Scripting** workspace, is located to the right among the top tabs. Scripts are typed in the **Text Editor**, the largest area at the center of the screen.

It is possible to write text files of any format, even simple text or programs written in other languages, although only Python scripts can be executed in the editor.

Working examples are a useful gist of how programming works, so it is worth having a look at the templates.

Writing "Lock at origin"

The **Text Editor** provides examples of the most common scripting necessities. In our case, we are interested in an operator template, like the one at **Templates** | **Python** | **Operator Simple** from the **Text Editor**'s top menu:

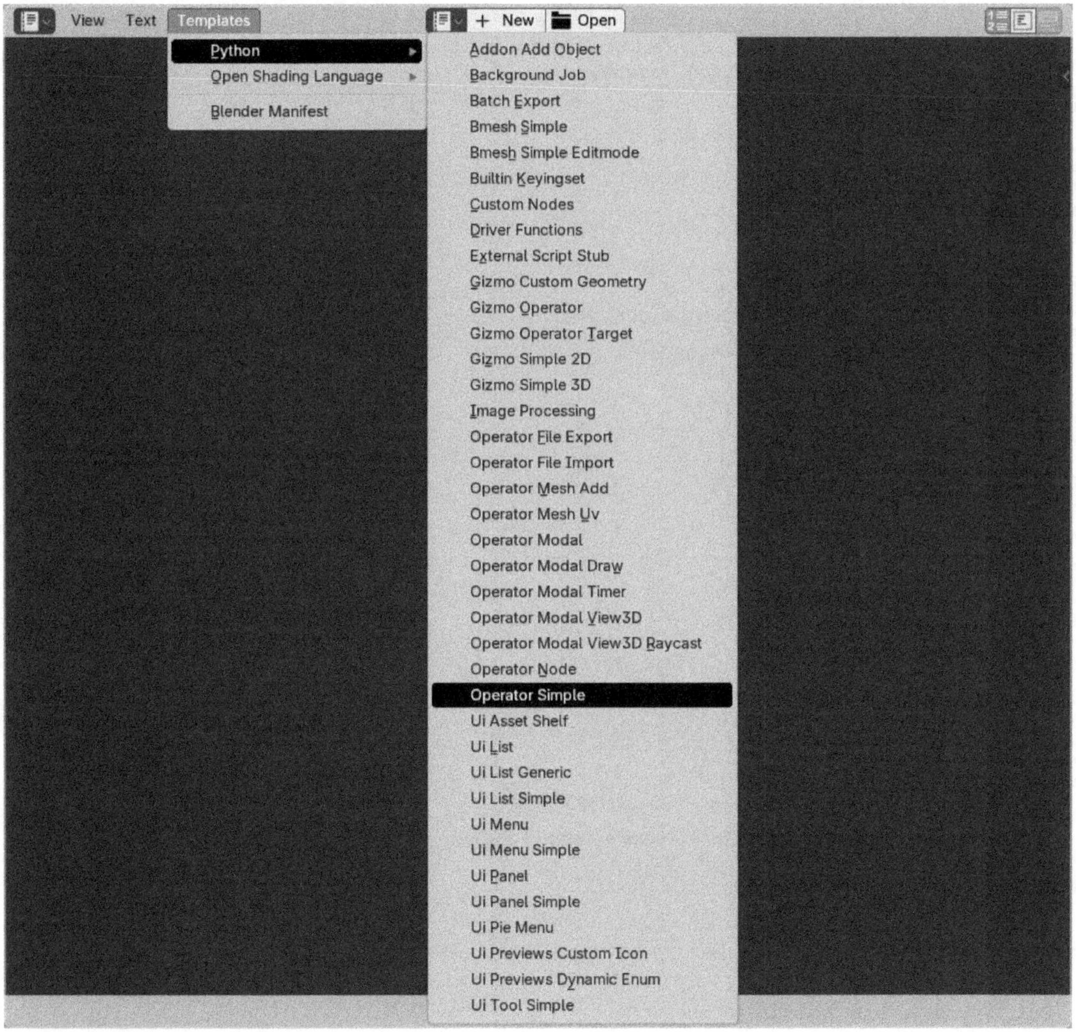

Figure 4.11: Opening the Operator Simple template

Clicking on the template creates a new text block, `operator_simple.py`, which consists of the following code:

```
import bpy

def main(context):
    for ob in context.scene.objects:
        print(ob)

class SimpleOperator(bpy.types.Operator):
    """Tooltip"""
    bl_idname = "object.simple_operator"
    bl_label = "Simple Object Operator"

    @classmethod
    def poll(cls, context):
        return context.active_object is not None
    def execute(self, context):
        main(context)
        return {'FINISHED'}

def menu_func(self, context):
    self.layout.operator(SimpleOperator.bl_idname,
                         text=SimpleOperator.bl_label)

def register():
    bpy.utils.register_class(SimpleOperator)
    bpy.types.VIEW3D_MT_object.append(menu_func)

def unregister():
    bpy.utils.unregister_class(SimpleOperator)
    bpy.types.VIEW3D_MT_object.remove(menu_func)

if __name__ == "__main__":
    register()
    # Test call.
    bpy.ops.object.simple_operator()
```

It can be a bit confusing at first, but Python templates are easier to read if we break down the sections of the code. The first statement, `import bpy`, loads Blender Python functionalities:

they must be *imported* from Blender's Python module, or they would not be available. Then a function is *defined*, using the `def` statement:

```
def main(context):
    for ob in context.scene.objects:
        print(ob)
```

A **function** is a sequence of instructions that can be executed by calling its name in other parts of the code: we can see that `main(context)` is *invoked* during the execution of the command, inside the `execute` function.

In this case, the function `main` displays the names of the objects using `print`, a built-in function that displays words in a text console. Python is almost human in some respects, as this code block, expressed in English language, would be approximately:

```
When I say "main":
    for each object of the scene:
        display its name in the text console
```

The command that we want, instead, would be something like:

```
When I say "main":
    for each object that is selected:
        clear its location
        lock its location
        lock its rotation
        lock its scale
```

So, we change this function to:

```
def main(context):
    for ob in context.selected_objects:
        ob.location.zero()

        for i in range(3):
            ob.lock_location[i] = True
            ob.lock_rotation[i] = True
            ob.lock_scale[i] = True
        ob.lock_rotation_w = True
```

Obviously, `ob.location.zero()` resets the object's location. In locking the transform channels, we take advantage of how this attribute is stored: it's a list of three elements, one element per axis, like `lock_location[0]` for x, lock_location[1] for y, and so on...

We can lock the 0, 1, and 2 indices at once using a `for` loop, that is, a repetition that counts to 3 (excluded), that is, `range(3)`.

We also lock the fourth rotation channel, available in **Quaternion** and **Axis/Angle** rotations, with `ob.lock_rotation_w = True`.

The `main` function is the core of our command: we only have to rename the entities in the rest of the script to finish our operator.

As pointed out earlier, in Blender a command is an *Operator*, and an *Operator* is a *class*. Python follows the paradigm of object-oriented programming, where a **class** is the definition of the information (data) and functionalities (functions) contained in a programmed object. We change the name of the class defined in this template, `SimpleOperator`, to `ZeroLockOperator`, and replace its description between triple quotes, so it becomes:

```
class ZeroLockOperator(bpy.types.Operator):
    """Clear objects' location and lock transforms"""
    bl_idname = "object.b2u_zerolock_operator"
    bl_label = "Lock at Origin"
    @classmethod
    def poll(cls, context):
        return context.active_object is not None
    def execute(self, context):
        main(context)
        return {'FINISHED'}
```

We change the values of `bl_idname` and `bl_label`, which are, respectively, the Python codename and the display text of this command. It's very important for `bl_idname` to be unique, as multiple operators with the same name will shadow each other.

The function `menu_func` adds the command to a menu of the interface. We replace any reference to `SimpleOperator` with the name of our class:

```
    def menu_func(self, context):
        self.layout.operator(ZeroLockOperator.bl_idname,
                             text=ZeroLockOperator.bl_label)
```

And then `register()`, a function that finally adds the new operator to Blender. Besides the name of the class, we change the menu from `VIEW3D_MT_object` to `VIEW3D_MT_object_context_menu`, which appears with a right mouse click in the viewport:

```
def register():
    bpy.utils.register_class(ZeroLockOperator)
    bpy.types.VIEW3D_MT_object_context_menu.append(menu_func)
```

Note

It's four the better!

A class or function defines a **scope**, that is, a part of the code that belongs to that entity. In Python, scopes are denoted with indentation—whitespaces at the start of a line of code—like:

```
This_is_a_class:
    and_this_is_a_function_of_the_class():
        and_this_is_a_line_of_the_function
```

Although any number of spaces (or tabulation) would work, conventionally, Python scripts are indented with *four* spaces.

Inconsistent indentation doesn't necessarily prevent a script from working, but it is unadvised for the sake of readability.

We also change the names in `unregister()`. This function is invoked when an extension is disabled and is added to the script only for symmetry, as it will not be used in our case:

```
def unregister():
    bpy.utils.unregister_class(ZeroLockOperator)
    bpy.types.VIEW3D_MT_object_context_menu.remove(menu_func)
```

The last bit, `if __name__ == "__main__"`, is a **namespace** condition that is executed only when the script is run on its own, as it could be imported by another script. We only keep the first line:

```
if __name__ == "__main__":
    register()
```

And remove the test call of `bpy.ops.object.simple_operator()` entirely. We rename the text block by clicking its name on the *Text Editor* header and changing it from `operator_simple.py` to `operator_zerolock.py`.

The full script can be found in this book's GitHub repo. To access the repository link, follow the steps in the *Download the example code files* section in the *Preface*.

Pressing *Alt* + *P* while in the **Text Editor** or selecting **Text** | **Run Script** from the editor menu bar will execute the script and add a new command to the right-click menu.

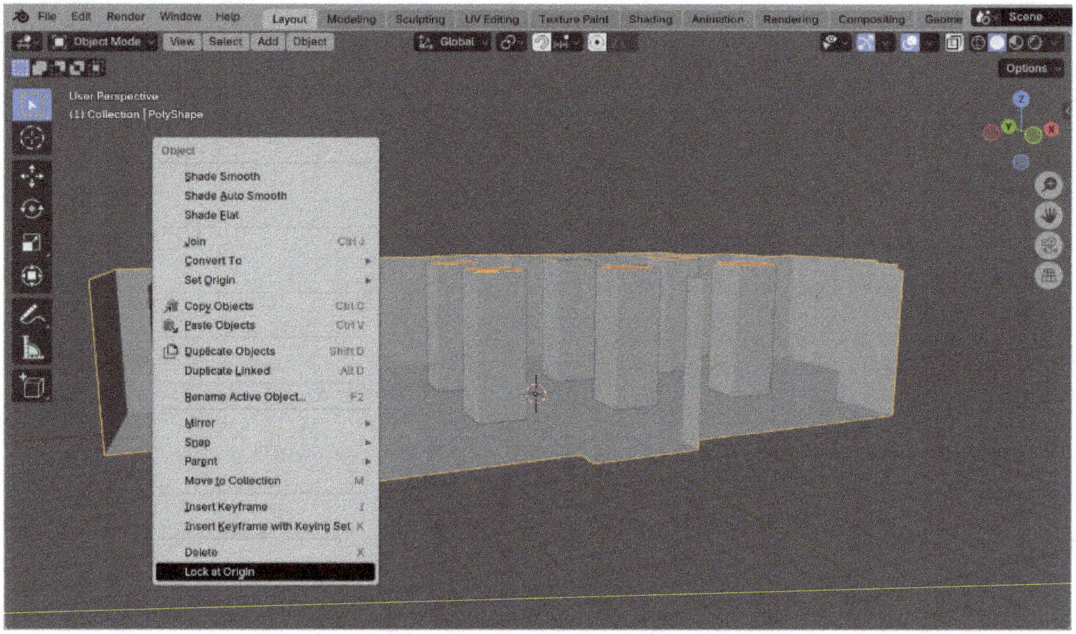

Figure 4.12: Lock at Origin in the Right-Click menu

The new command will zero the location of an object and lock its channels, but if restarted, Blender does not retain the scripts that were executed locally. We need to either install `operator_zerolock.py` as an extension, which is out of the scope of this book, or save it to a startup folder, which can be set up from the preferences.

Adding script folders

Blender comes with factory installed scripts, but we can create additional custom folders and add them to the list of script directories. Blender will search them for python files.

The process is similar to what we did with library folders:

1. From the top bar menu, click **Edit** | **Preferences...**

2. In the **Preferences** window, select **File Paths** in the vertical bar on the left.
3. Scroll down to the section **Script Directories** and click the **+ Add** button
4. In the browsing window, reach the folder `BlendToUni_URP` from the bookmarks. There, create a new folder named `_blender_scripts_`.

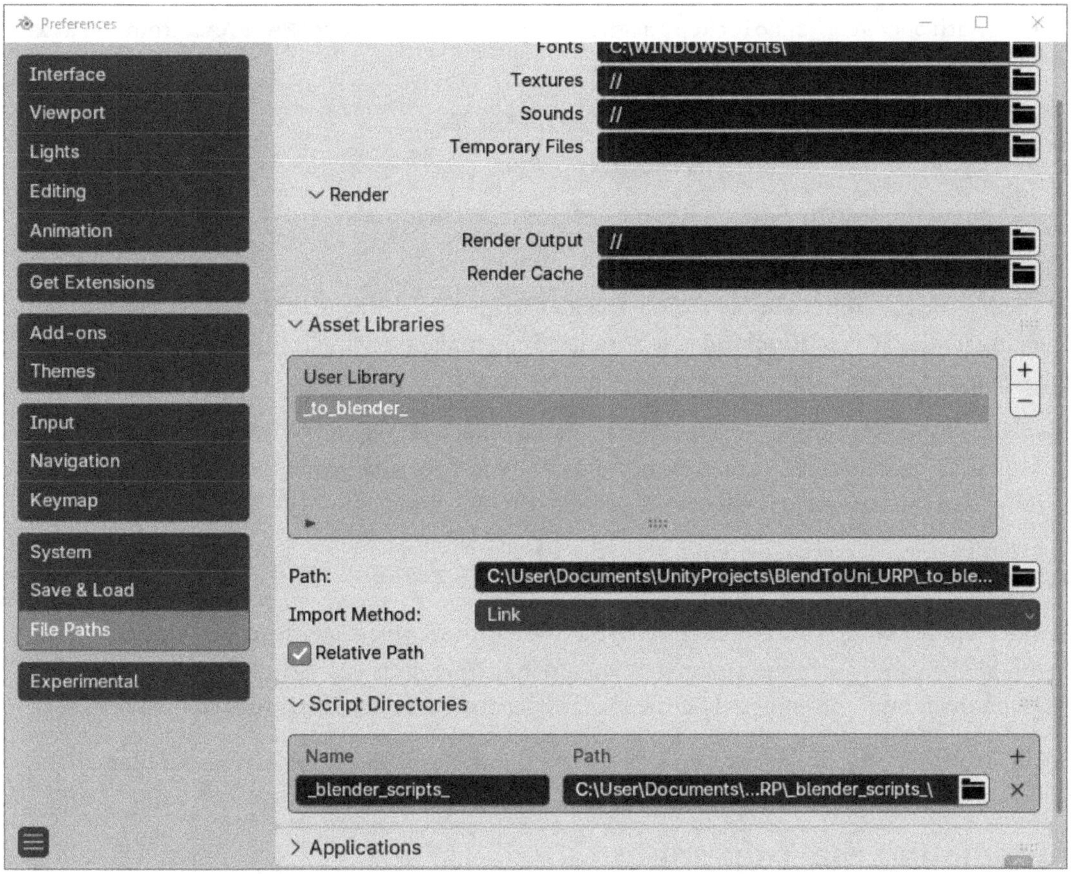

Figure 4.13: Adding Script Directories, just below the section Asset Libraries

Multiple script directories are useful as they can be added on a per-project basis and removed once a project is finished. We can proceed and save our script.

Saving startup scripts

We will save our script, `operator_zerolock.py`, so that it runs every time that Blender starts: this way, our command will be added to the context menu. To achieve that, we need to create a script sub-folder and name it `startup`:

1. With `operator_zerolock.py` as the current text, select **Text** | **Save As...** from the **Text Editor** menu.
2. Navigate to `BlendToUni_URP` | `_blender_script_`.
3. Create a new subfolder and name it `startup`.
4. Go to the **startup** folder and save `operator_zerolock.py`.
5. Restart Blender.

From now on, the command *right-click* | **Lock at Origin** will be available in **Object Mode**. By invoking it when **Crypt Blocking** is selected, we can make sure that it is placed at the center of the scene and locked to avoid accidental transformations.

Speaking of transformations, we created a rotated object in *Chapter 2* to mimic a Y-Up coordinate system in Blender. We are going to use that trick again, and now that we know how to script, we can automate the creation of our Y-Up object as well.

Automating object creation

Blender's programming interface allows you to create new objects with scripts; the procedure is only slightly more complex than what we did in the previous example, *Zero and Lock*, and relies on the module `object_utils`, meant for automating most object-related operations.

Again, in automating, we break a task down to its granular steps by reviewing our manual actions one by one.

Automating the Y-up setup

In *Chapter 2*, we have worked with Y-up coordinates in Blender by rotating an empty object and setting it as the parent of our geometries. We are going to use this trick again, so we can save time by making it a new command that:

1. Creates a new Empty
2. Rotates it by 90 degrees
3. Locks its transformation channels
4. Parents the selected objects to the new Empty.

This time, rather than starting with a template, we will create the script from scratch:

1. From the **Text Editor** menu bar, select **Text** | **New** to create an empty block of text.
2. The default name of the new text data is **Text**. Click on it and rename it to `operator_yup_add.py`.

We can write down our script: remember that the text editor must be in focus, i.e., the mouse cursor must be somewhere over the writing area, or our keystrokes will go to a different region of Blender!

Writing "Y up axis"

Python is a modular language: every script begins with an import of the ingredients required for the task. In our case we need:

- `bpy`: Blender's generic python interface
- `object_utils`: Blender scripting utilities for dealing with objects, which is part of the module `bpy_extras`.
- `AddObjectHelper`: A class for adding objects to the scene which is part of `object_utils`.

Translated to python, that reads:

```
import bpy
from bpy_extras import object_utils
from bpy_extras.object_utils import AddObjectHelper
```

After that, we leave two blank lines and declare our command, a class that we name `AddEmpty` and that contains functionalities from both `Operator` and `AddObjectHelper`. The code starts as follows:

```
class AddEmpty(bpy.types.Operator, AddObjectHelper):
    """Add a locked, rotated empty"""
    bl_idname = "object.b2u_y_up_add"
    bl_label = "Y-Up axis"
```

The description between triple quotes doesn't have a purpose beyond documentation, while `bl_idname` and `bl_label` are the Python identifier and display text of the new command.

As mentioned earlier, the four spaces of indentation before the properties are not purely visual: they inform Python that those attributes belong to `AddEmpty`. Blender adds those spaces automatically when we go to a new line. Incorrect indentation would prevent our Python script from working.

Now it's time to define the `execute` function, which is run when the command is executed. A function of the class is delimited by an additional level of indentation. The actions that we must perform are:

1. Add a new object by invoking the `object_data_add` function.
2. Switch its display type to `'ARROWS'` for a better display of the axis.
3. Rotate it by 90 degrees on its x axis.
4. Parent all the selected objects to it.

So, we must get a list of the selected objects and then create a new one. The python code is:

```
    def execute(self, context):
        selected_objects = list(bpy.context.selected_objects)
        ob = object_utils.object_data_add(context,
                                          None,
                                          operator=self,
                                          name='Empty')
        ob.empty_display_type = 'ARROWS'
        ob.rotation_euler.x = 1.5708
        ob.location.zero()
```

`90` degrees is `1.5708` in the wonderful language of math: rotations are expressed in **radians**, that is, in relationship with the length of a full circle. The circumference formula, $2 \times \pi \times$radius, becomes just $2 \times \pi$ if we are happy with a circle with a one-unit long radius. Ninety degrees is π divided in half, 3.14.../2, that is, 1.57...

We keep writing our function and lock the transform channels. As we have already seen in the *Writing "Lock at Origin"* section, location, rotation, and scale can be locked using a `for` loop:

```
        for i in range(3):
            ob.lock_location[i] = True
            ob.lock_rotation[i] = True
            ob.lock_scale[i] = True
        ob.lock_rotation_w = True
```

Again, we also lock the fourth rotation channel, `w`.

At the end of this function, we set the new object as the parent of the objects selected before the execution, then inform Blender that the command is finished:

```
        for sel_ob in selected_objects:
            sel_ob.parent = ob

        return {'FINISHED'}
```

We have declared our new operator. We write a menu function for the interface:

```
def menu_func(self, context):
    self.layout.operator(AddEmpty.bl_idname,
                         icon='EMPTY_ARROWS')
```

The `context` parameter is passed from Blender, and we must mention it even if we don't use it. We can add our menu function to the **Add Empty** menu.

Add Empty is part of the `bpy.types`, and its Python name is `VIEW3D_MT_empty_add`. We append our `menu_func` to it when we register the script:

```
def register():
    bpy.utils.register_class(AddEmpty)
    bpy.types.VIEW3D_MT_empty_add.append(menu_func)
```

We reverse those actions inside `unregister()`, which is invoked when an extension is disabled:

```
def unregister():
    bpy.types.VIEW3D_MT_empty_add.remove(menu_func)
    bpy.utils.unregister_class(AddEmpty)
```

With these functions, our script can be used as a Blender extension. We can register our script outside of the extensions system by invoking `register()` explicitly; we have seen in `operator_zerolock.py` how to avoid unwanted registrations by adding a namespace condition:

```
if __name__ == "__main__":
    register()
```

The full script, completed with comments, can be found in this book's GitHub repo. To access the repository link, follow the steps in the *Download the example code files* section in the *Preface*.

If we execute the script using *Alt* + *P* or **Text** | **Run Script** from the **Text Editor** menu bar, and then press *Shift* + *A*, we will see the entry **Y-Up Axis** in the **Add** | **Empty** menu.

Figure 4.14: The Y-Up Axis command

To make it permanent, we need to save it as a startup script:

1. With `operator_yup_add.py` as the current text, select **Text** | **Save As...** from the **Text Editor** menu.
2. Navigate to `BlendToUni_URP` | `_blender_script_` | `startup`.
3. Save `operator_y_up_add.py`.
4. Restart Blender.

Shift + *A* | **Empty** | **Y-Up axis** and **Viewport** | **Add** | **Empty** | **Y-Up axis** is now part of our copy of Blender.

With this command, we have automated the most common operation in a Blender to Unity workflow. Having a script that takes care of repetitive tasks lets us focus on the creative sides of our project. Besides, a better understanding of our software's architecture doesn't hurt at all in game development.

Summary

In this chapter, we looked at how we can make ourselves more comfortable with Blender by creating collections for sharing objects and marking assets for drag and drop. We also dived into Python and learned how to add functionalities to Blender.

Python scripting is a field of its own, and tool development is usually carried out by specialists, but it's important to know the basics of this discipline and have an idea of how it works.

Although the operations automated in this chapter can be performed manually, these additions to Blender will help in creating game assets for the rest of the book, starting with *Chapter 5*.

5

Modeling with Geometry Nodes

Modeling usually involves manual editing of the mesh components or sculpting techniques that resemble working with clay.

When it comes to architectural or industrial models, the structural constraints that affect their shapes may favor a procedural approach instead. Procedural models are created with geometric functions that produce different results with a change of parameters, allowing customization and editing.

As a downside, the creation process can be complex and sometimes too abstract, besides requiring parametric capabilities in the modeling application. Starting with version 4.2, Blender features **Geometry Nodes**, a way of generating three-dimensional models with a graph of geometric operations.

It is a remarkable feature of Blender and allows users to implement their own shapes or modifiers without coding. The application is not limited to architecture and design but also spans character animation, simulations, and special effects.

This introduction to procedural modeling with nodes presents a workflow for constructing the geometry of game levels, focusing on the open nature of the procedural approach.

This chapter covers the following topics:

- Modeling a shaft
- Modeling a capital
- Modeling an abacus
- Saving to Unity

Technical requirements

In this chapter, we will use *Blender 5.1,* which can be installed by following the instructions from *Chapter 1* or from the website `blender.org`.

You can download the example project and code for this book by following the instructions in the *Download the example code files* section in the *Preface* of this book.

This chapter's code files are included in the downloadable code bundle.

Planning the model

In *Chapter 3,* we created a blocking of the level with **ProBuilder**. That model is useful for production drafts, evaluating volumes, and early testing, but it is very far from the finished product.

Planning the visual outcome of a game involves visual research and sketches of the intended result, with the blocking often used as a reference for paint-overs. Our game is about the exploration of an ancient crypt, and the style of the level must match that theme. By painting over a screenshot of the blocking, we can use the grid texture as a perspective guide and sketch a vault and some columns, like in *Figure 5.1.*

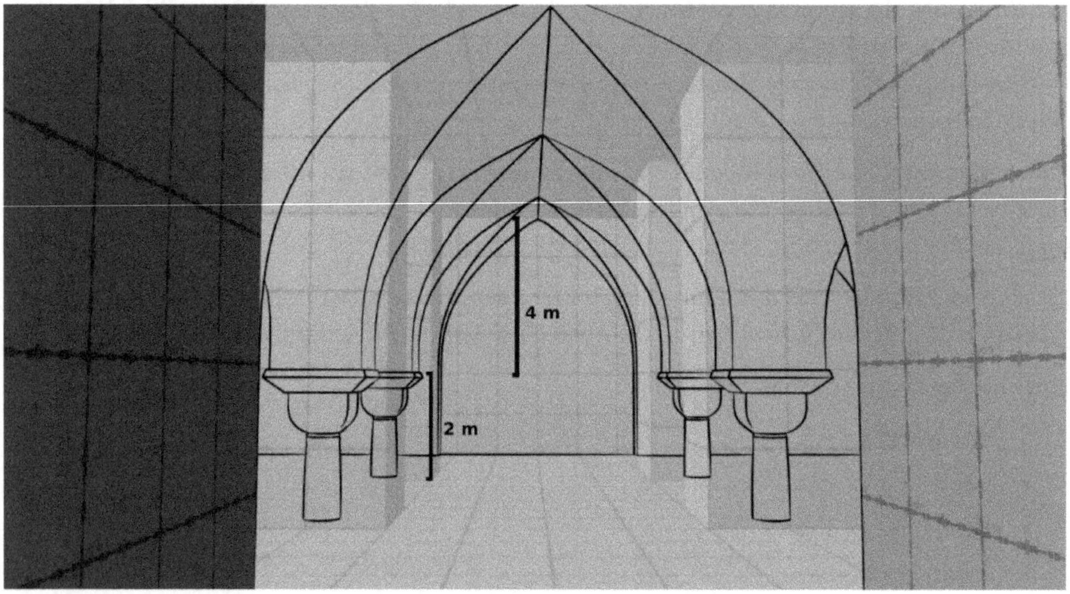

Figure 5.1: Sketch over the blocking; the squares are 1 meter wide

Once we have an idea of how our level would look like, we can plan the specifications of the models and devise a technique.

The squares of the grid textures are 1 m wide, so the columns in the sketch are 2 m tall and consist of three elements.

Understanding the separate parts of a model makes a difference to the task: welding all the elements into a single mesh increases the complexity with little to no benefit.

In this chapter, we will focus on creating the columns for this level, depicted in more detail in *Figure 5.2*.

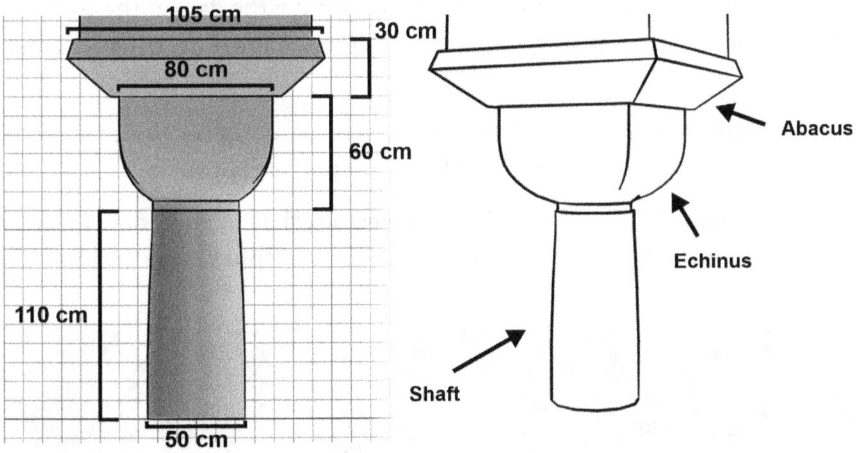

Figure 5.2: Detailed sketch of the column

As we can see, this column consists of three elements:

- The **shaft**, the main body of the column
- The **echinus**, a large cup-shaped block on top of the shaft
- The **abacus**, a flat slab placed above the echinus

Echinus and abacus form the **capital**, the upper part of the column.

Note

Blame the Romans!

Although those architectural elements date back to ancient Greece, the terminology used nowadays comes from the Latin spoken by ancient Romans: *capital* derives from *caput*, which means "head," while *echinus* had "bowl" among its meanings. *Abacus* is the Latin borrowing of *abax*, ancient Greek for "slab."

The shaft and echinus have a curved profile, which requires more polygons to represent: a mere interpolation of the face normals, which we used in *Chapter 2*, doesn't affect the silhouette.

Even if we handcrafted our models, we would require algorithmic subdivision to make them smooth enough. Subdivision would change the shape of the model, and we should account for that with additional geometry.

A procedural workflow, on the other hand, once implemented, allows increasing the mesh resolution without altering the overall shape.

Objects can be manipulated in Blender using **modifiers**, that is, interfaces for adding, removing, or displacing a model's geometry without affecting the data at the component level. They include operations like mirroring, duplication in rows, texture deformation, and much more.

To implement modeling operations in Blender, we resort to **Geometry Nodes**, a special modifier that mimics modeling operations and deformation of coordinates.

Each operation is contained in a node, a self-contained box that can take data through its input sockets and return its result from the output sockets. Every output can be the input of another node.

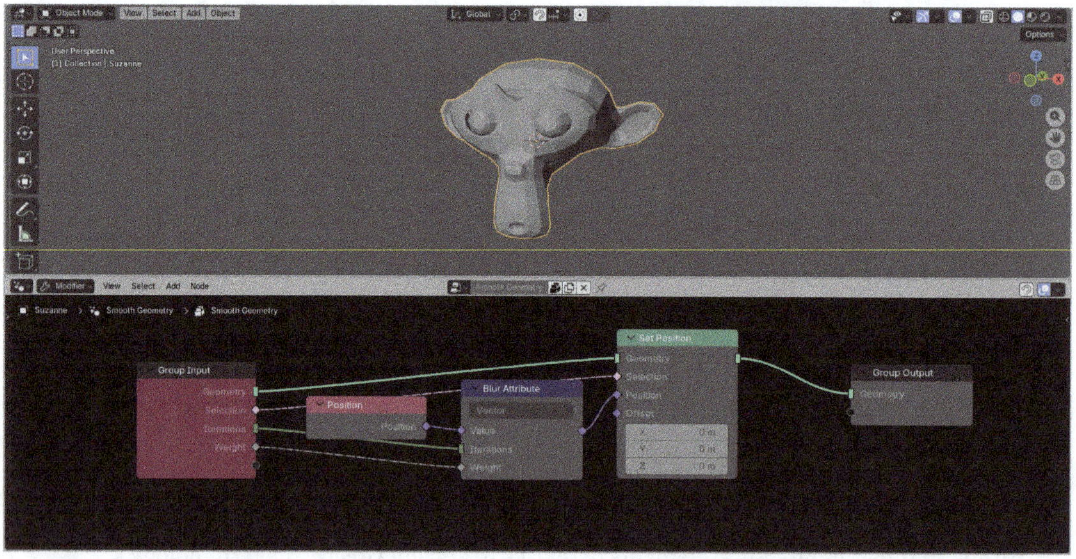

Figure 5.3: Example of geometry nodes, smoothing the model by blurring vertex positions

Nodes can be arranged in groups, which have input and output sockets and are displayed as a single node when compressed. All connected nodes make a node tree and are displayed as a graph in the **Node Editor**. The position of a node in the graph doesn't matter; only its place in the chain of inputs affects the result. Maintaining a visual layout of the connected nodes from left to right is advised for readability.

In the next section, we will model the shaft of the column using geometry nodes.

Modeling the shaft

The shaft is essentially a vertical pillar, but there's more to it than a pole: a slight bulge at approximately one third of its length, called **entasis**, compensates for perspective distortion and conveys structural strength. Toward its upper end, the curvature ends abruptly, leaving the **neck** of the shaft to rise vertically to the top. We will account for those features in designing the node tree.

Beginning the model

To create a model, we need to start with a mesh object. We don't care about its initial shape: it can be a cube, a plane, or anything else; our nodes will override the original components. If we haven't changed the content of the startup scene, we can use Blender's default Cube:

1. Open Blender or start a new scene.
2. Select the default geometry, **Cube**. If by any chance there are no geometries in your scene, press *Shift + A* | **Mesh** and select **Cube** or any other primitive, then press *Alt + G* to remove the location if any.
3. Press F2 or double-click the object in the **Outliner** to rename it, then type `Shaft` as the new name.

We are using **Geometry Nodes** to create our model, so we switch workspace:

1. From the workspace tabs on top, activate **Geometry Nodes**. The **Node Editor** is the wide area at the bottom.
2. Click the **+ New** button in the header of the *Node Editor* to create a new tree of geometry nodes. The default name is **Geometry Nodes**. We can see that a new item was created in the **Object Modifiers** properties to the right; that modifier connects our graph to the object.
3. Click on the name **Geometry Nodes** at the center of the **Node Editor**'s header and type the new name `GN-Shaft`.

A new node tree consists of just two nodes: **Group Input** contains the incoming geometry on which to operate, while **G**roup Output passes the result of the tree to the object modifier.

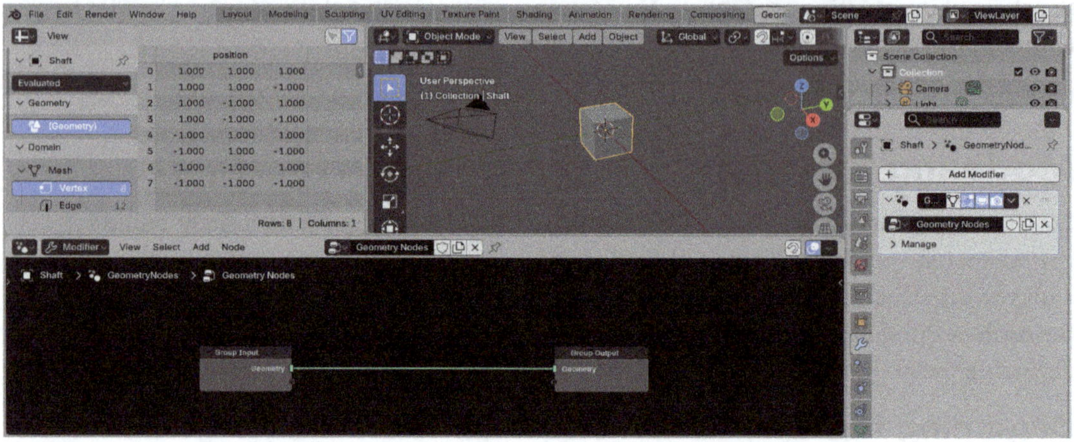

Figure 5.4: A geometry-to-geometry connection

A direct connection from **Group Input** to **Group Output** passes the mesh exactly as it is, so the model remains unchanged.

Processing the incoming geometry is useful for applying effects to the original model, but we don't need to retain the original mesh in this case: our goal is a cylindrical shape. We ditch the input and replace it with a cylinder:

1. In the **Node Editor**, select the node **Group Input** and press *X* or *Del*ete to remove it.
2. Press *Shift* + *A* or click the **Add** menu.
3. Select **Mesh** | **Primitives** | **Cylinder** to create a new node with mesh information; our node graph will start from here.
4. With the left mouse button, drag a connection from the **Mesh** socket of Cylinder to the **Geometry** socket of **Group Output**.

The model has changed to a cylinder. If we switch to **Edit Mode**, we can see that the mesh data is still a cube. That doesn't matter anymore; the geometry nodes took over.

In Object Mode, the result is the same as creating a cylinder mesh in the first place. The difference is that, even though we can't access the component, with Geometry Nodes we retain the primitive's parameters: *Width*, *Height*, etc.

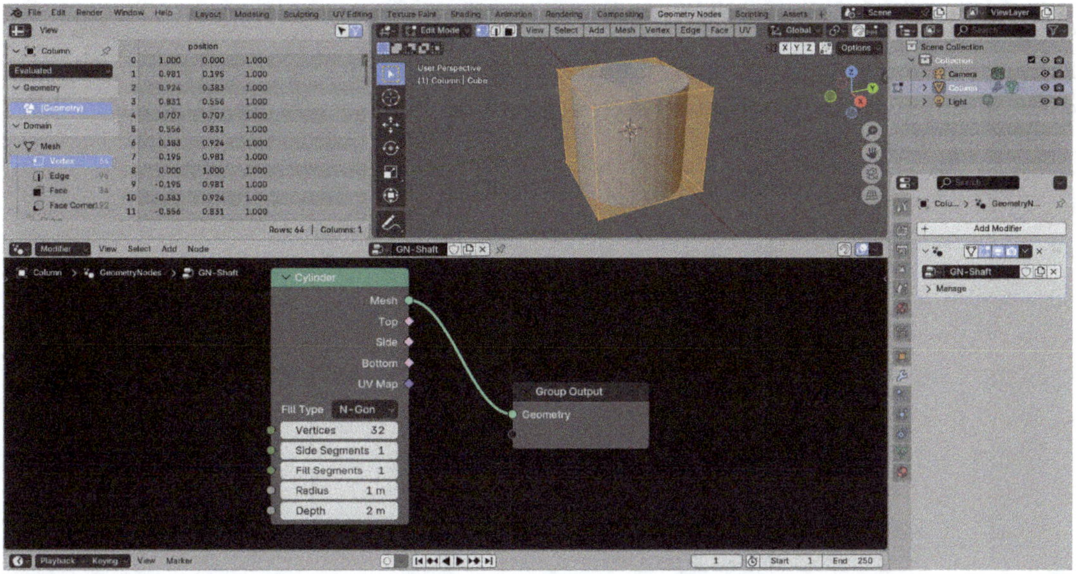

Figure 5.5: Edit Mode displays the original mesh, which is no longer in use

We will process the shape so that it looks like the element shown in *Figure 5.2*.

Setting up the graph

The attributes of the **Cylinder** node affect its **Mesh** output. The first step is changing its default values:

1. Set Vertices to 8 to get an octagonal section. That is enough for conveying a smooth surface, but not so many as to affect performance.
2. Set **Fill Type** to **Triangles** to use eight triangles, rather than one octagon, for the top and bottom caps. **N-Gon** creates polygons with more than four sides, which sometimes cause artifacts in game.
3. Set **Slide Segments** to 4 to create enough subdivisions for a curved profile.
4. Set **Depth** to `1.0`, a number that can be easily scaled to any value with multiplication.

Our model is a closed octagonal pipe. We would not rely on the attribute **Cylinder** | **Radius** for dimensioning the shaft, as that only produces a constant section size.

In contrast, we need to imprint a subtle curvature along the vertical span, altering the vertex positions with our node tree.

Adjusting width and height

Resizing or *scaling* a model multiplies its vertex coordinates by the same value. A uniform scale doesn't change the relative proportions. For instance, doubling the size of a model means multiplying all its coordinates by *2*.

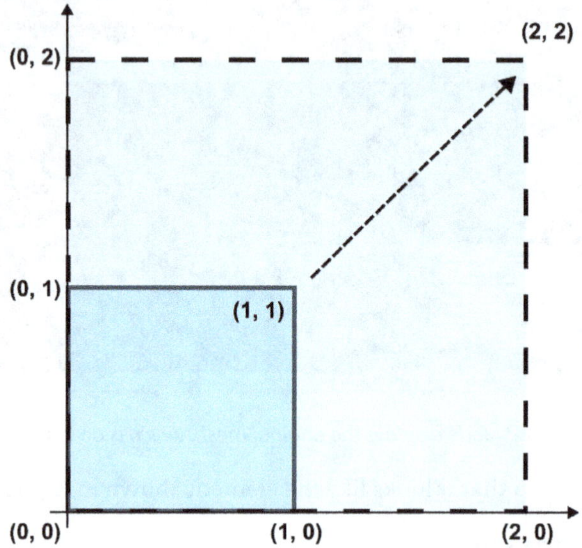

Figure 5.6: Doubling the size of a square by multiplying its coordinates by 2

Mathematically, coordinates are a **vector**, a collection of numbers, while the single number in a uniform scale is a **scalar**. The operation associated with uniform scaling is called **scalar multiplication**.

In contrast, doubling the width without affecting height and depth implies a different multiplier for each coordinate: *2* for the width, *1* for the height, and *1* for the depth. A collection of numbers itself, this multiplier is a vector as well. The operation for non-uniform scaling is an **elementwise multiplication** where two vectors produce a vector result, consisting of the products of each X, Y, and Z pair.

The visual outcome of scaling a model is the repositioning of its vertices based on the result of a multiplication. In *Geometry Nodes* we alter the vertex coordinates with the node **Set Position**:

1. In the **Node Editor**, press *Shift + A* and start typing `Pos`. This will activate a search filter.
2. Select **Geometry > Write > Set Position** and press the left mouse button. A new node is created, and until it is in insertion mode, it follows the movement of the mouse.

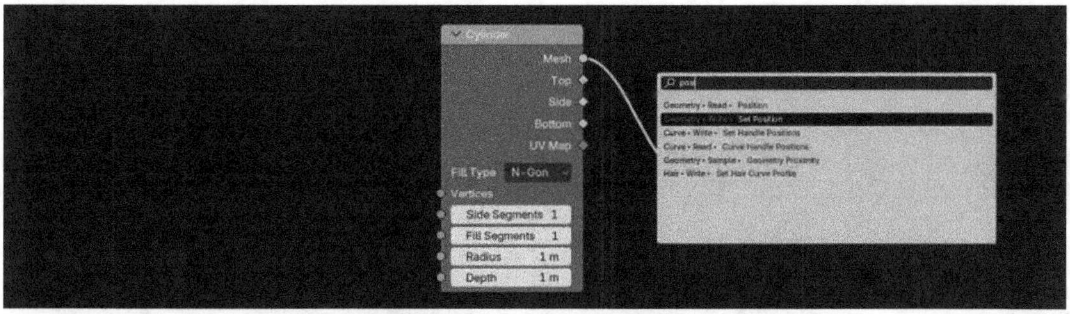

Figure 5.7: Search filter when adding a new node

3. Moving the new node over the link between **Cylinder** and **Group Output** highlights the connection between the two. By clicking the left mouse button, the new node is inserted between the two, offsetting the graph to make room and rewiring the existing connection through itself.

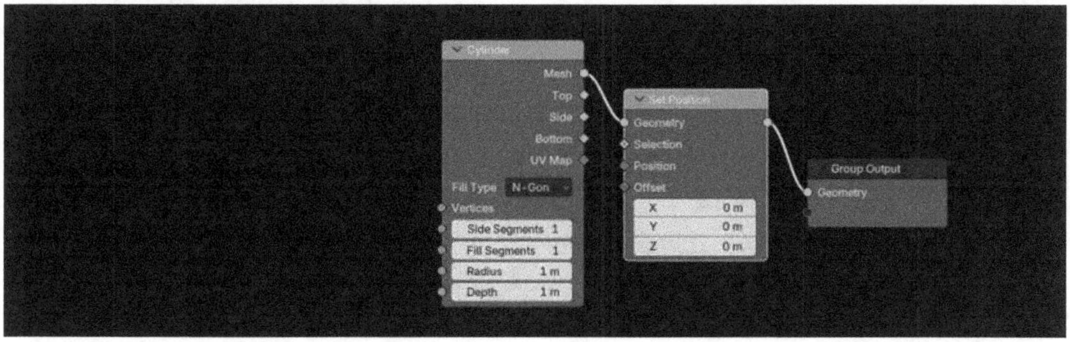

Figure 5.8: Cylinder mesh passing through Set Position

Set Position sets the location of the points to the value coming into its **Position** socket. Blue sockets indicate vector information, like three-dimensional coordinates.

The node **Set Position** alone can only offset the entire mesh; to displace a model in a more articulated way, we need an incoming **Position** input. To create a connection from the current vertex position:

1. With the *left mouse button*, click the socket **Set Position** | **Position** and, keeping the button pressed, drag a new connection and release the button over an empty area. A menu for selecting potential inputs will pop up.
2. Type pos to filter the results and select **Position** | **Position** to create and connect a new node.

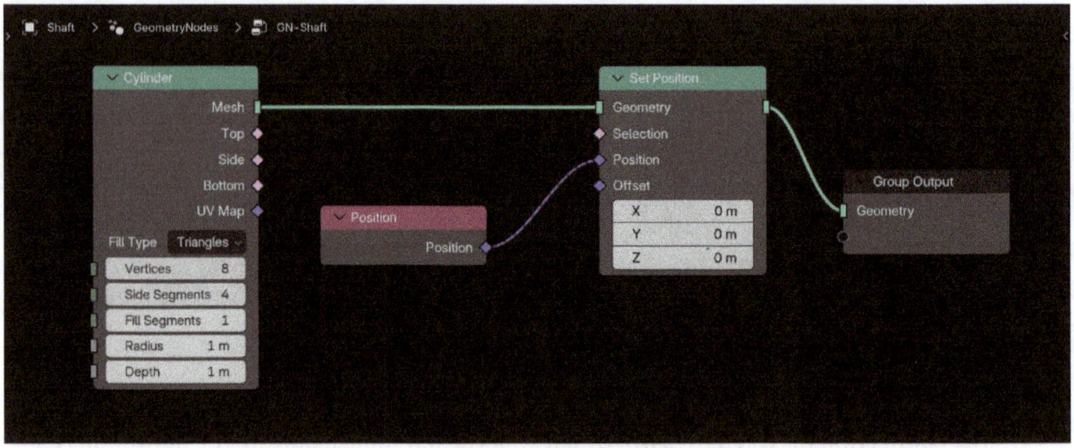

Figure 5.9: Incoming Position

Only nodes created with the *Add* menu auto-offset the existing nodes, so we might need to move Cylinder to the left to avoid overlapping. By acting on the **Position** input, we can alter the shape of the model.

As introduced when describing the math behind scaling, to resize the two horizontal coordinates but not the vertical one, we perform an element-wise product with a **Vector Multiplication** node:

1. Press *Shift + A* and start typing `mult vec`. From the search results, select **Utilities | Vector Math | Multiply**. The non-vector multiply will not work here, as we need *element-wise* multiplication.

   > **Note**
   >
   > **Type as you like**
   >
   > The filter search is very forgiving: we can find the node **Vector Math | Multiply** by searching `v mul`, `vec mul`, `mul v`, etc.

2. Drag the new node over the link between **Position** and **Set Position** and release it to form the chain **Position–Multiply–Set Position**. The model will disappear; all vertex coordinates, multiplied by zero, overlap at the origin.

3. We need to connect the coordinates of the multiplicator individually. Drag the free **Vector** socket of **Multiply** over an empty area and, typing xyz, search for the **Combine XYZ** node. That will create and connect a node with individual coordinate sockets.
4. Set all the coordinates of **Combine XYZ** to `1.0` to restore the geometry.

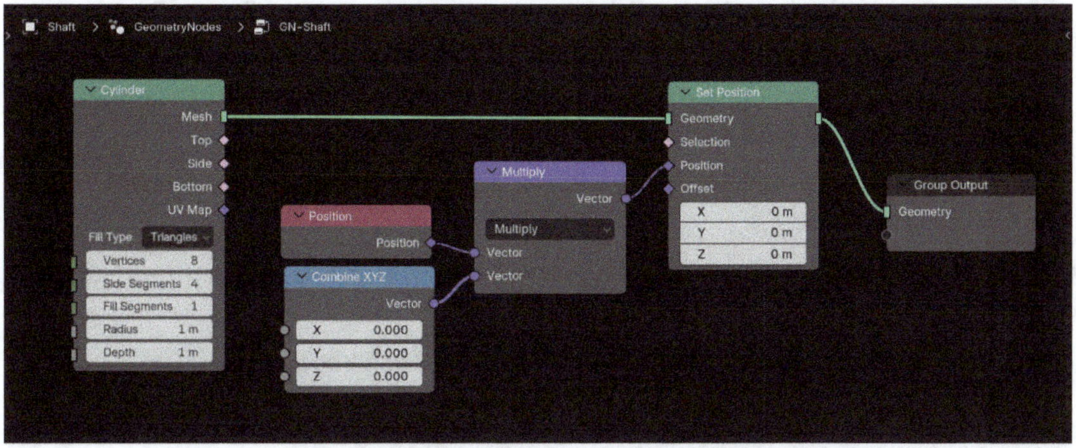

Figure 5.10: Multiplying vertex positions by (1.0, 1.0, 1.0) doesn't affect the model

The **X**, **Y**, and **Z** coordinates of **Combine XYZ** scale the cylinder along their respective axes. Scaling the horizontal size means that *X* and *Y* must have the same value, while the value of *Z* affects the height of the geometry.

We can compress the nodes for scaling width and height in a **Node Group** which takes care of that:

1. Select the nodes **Combine XYZ** and **Multiply**, either with drag selection or by clicking them while holding *Shift*.
2. Press *Ctrl* + *G* to create our new group. The editor will switch to the sub-graph of the single group. This is reflected in the header, which now reads **Shaft** | **Geometry Nodes** | **GN-Shaft** | **NodeGroup**.
3. Press `N` or click the expansion triangle on the right to display the *properties* panel if it is hidden.
4. In the **Group** tab, click the Name field, which is set to **NodeGroup** by default, and rename it **Scale Position**.

Since we want to set width and height through this node, we will create two inputs for those parameters:

1. The **Group Sockets** panel, always in the **Group** tab of the properties, displays a list of the node inputs and outputs. Rename the two **Vector** sockets to `Position`. That doesn't change the behavior of the group but makes our terminology consistent with Blender.
2. Press the + button and create a new **Input**, name it `Width`. The default type, **Float**, means decimal number and is good for our purpose. Scroll down to its **Default** value and set it to `1.0`; also set its **Min** to `0.0`, as we don't want negative width.
3. Press the + button and create a new float **Input**, name it `Height`. Set its **Default** value to `1.0` and its **Min** to `0.0`.

Group Sockets are displayed on the Group Input node, and they can be connected with the rest of the graph:

1. Connect **Group Input | Width** to **Combine XYZ**'s **X** and **Y** sockets.
2. Connect **Group Input | Height** to **Combine XYZ**'s **Z** socket.

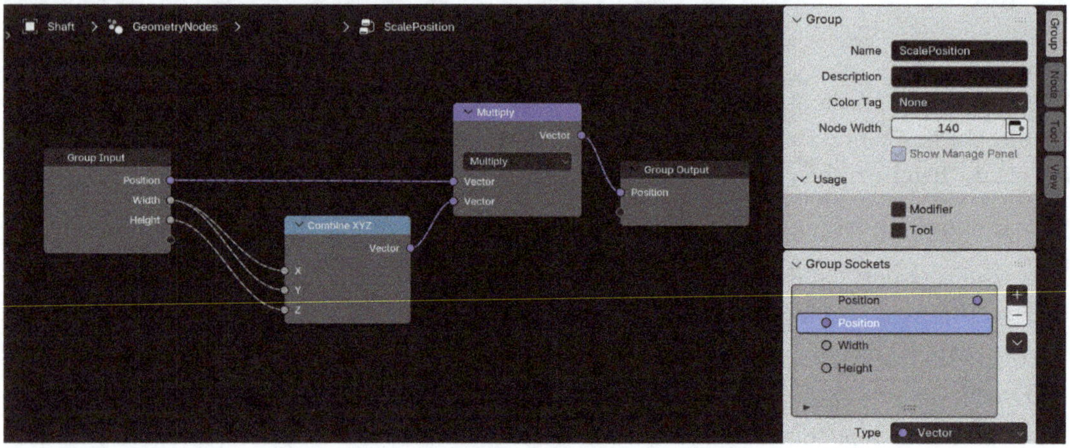

Figure 5.11: Creating a node group with inputs

3. Exit the group by pressing the *Tab* key. The nodes *Combine XYZ* and *Multiply* were replaced by our custom node, **Scale Position**. The model has collapsed again because **Width** and **Height** were created and set to **0.0** before we could set their default values. Set the attributes of **Scale Position** to `1.0` to restore the model.

The sliders displayed on **Scale Position** set the width and height of the model; to scale across the vertical length of the model, we connect **Position**'s *Z* to **Width**:

1. Drag the **Position** socket from the **Position** node and release it on an empty area, then select and create a **Separate XYZ** node. If necessary, make some room between **Position** and **ScalePosition** to accommodate the new node by dragging **Cylinder** and **Position** toward the left.
2. Connect **Separate XYZ | Z** to **Scale Position | Width**.

The result is not pretty: the *Z* coordinate of the lower half is negative, so the lower section is inverted, while the center, multiplied by *0*, is deformed like a candy wrap.

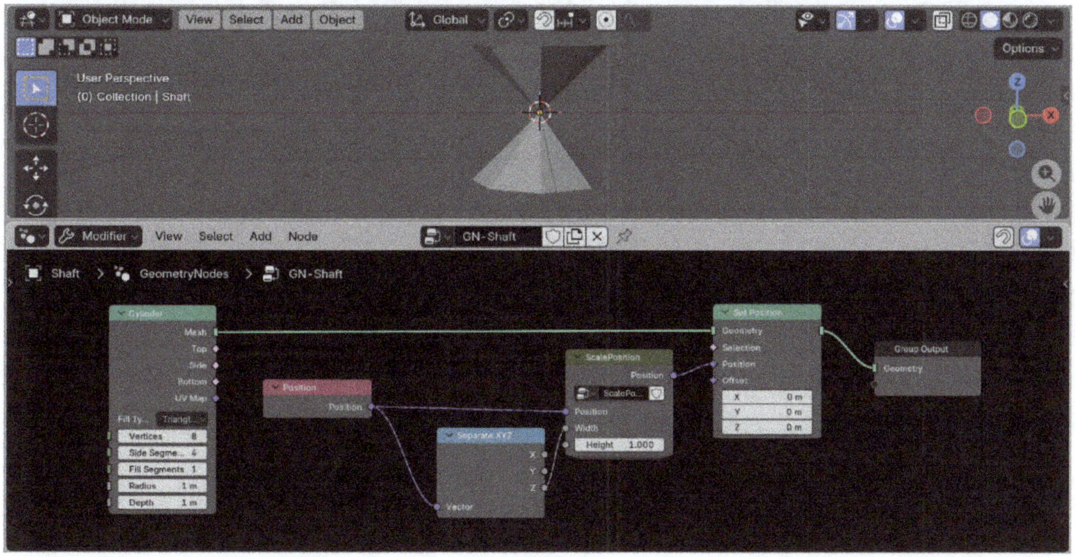

Figure 5.12: Negative values invert the points below the origin and wrap the center

Since the vertical coordinate of the points ranges from *–0.5* to *0.5*, we can offset that interval by 0.5 and fix it:

1. Press *Shift + A* and look for a *Vector Add* node, then insert the new node in the link between **Position** and **Separate XYZ**.
2. Since we have set **Cylinder | Depth** to `1.0` in the paragraph *Setting up the graph*, setting the third coordinate of **Vector Add**'s addend to 0.5 will set the range of the outgoing *Z* to the interval *0.0* and *1.0*. At this point, the model has a diamond shape, where the lower end is scaled by zero while the upper end, unaffected, is scaled by one.

3. We also connect the **Add** | **Vector** output to **Scale Position** | **Position**, replacing the previous connection. That will offset the model upwards so that, when it is not moved, it sits on the floor. That's the conventional approach in modeling, as zero is assumed to be the height of the floor.

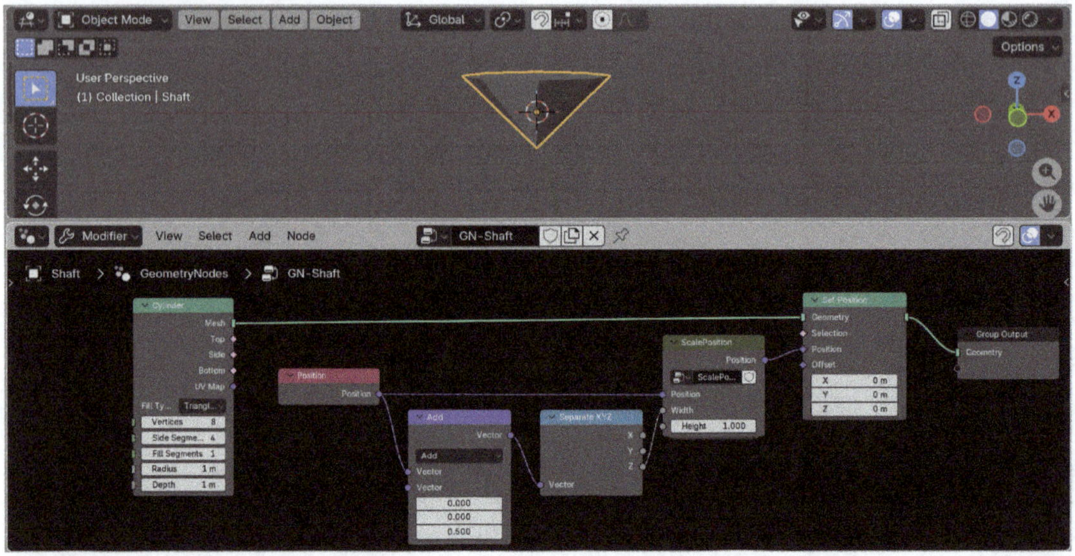

Figure 5.13: Collapsing the lower tip produces an inverted pyramid

With this setup, the width of each section is determined by its vertical coordinate.

We weren't looking for a diamond, though: we need to modulate **Separate XYZ** | **Z**'s value to achieve our intended result.

To ensure a smooth transition, we should pass the **Scale Position** | **Width** input through a *curve interpolation*

Press *Shift + A* and look for the **Float Curve** node, create it, and insert it between **Separate XYZ** | **Z** and **Scale Position** | **Width**.

Float Curve alters the input value based on the height of the curve on the node. The curve starts as a straight diagonal from the point (0, 0) to (1, 1). This curve has no effect, since all its points obey the rule that X equals Y, i.e., the output is the same as the input.

If we click the first control point at the bottom left corner and drag it to the upper region of the graph and then drag the top right corner below mid height, we get a truncated pyramid, as shown in *Figure 5.14*.

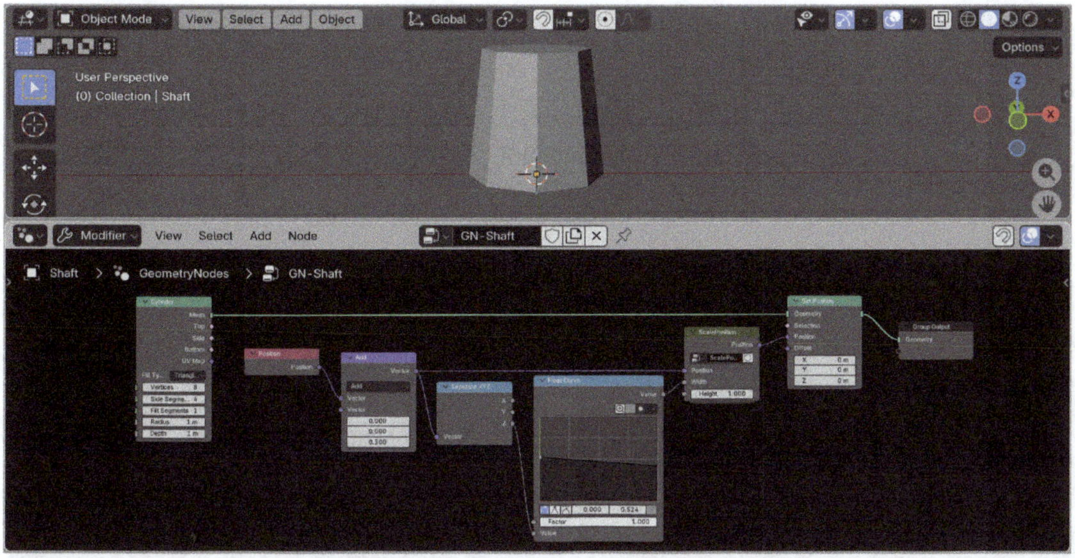

Figure 5.14: Modulating the width along the height

Clicking a point of the line where there are no control vertices will create a new one, so we can click the middle of the curve and drag the new point upwards: the graph bends and the shaft assumes a curved shape.

Although a *Float Curve* invites a visual approach, it is possible to enter exact values for the active control point by setting the two coordinates displayed under the curve:

1. Click the first control point, the one on the left; the node will display the *X* and *Y* coordinates just below the graph.
2. Set *X* to `0.0` and *Y* to `0.5`; the first control point will move exactly to the leftmost, mid-height point of the graph.
3. Select the second control point, the one in the middle, and set its *X* and *Y* coordinates to `0.33333` and `0.5`, respectively.
4. Select the end control point and set its coordinates to `1.0` and `0.45`. That will make the upper width of the shaft nine-tenths of the lower one.

Note

Control, but not too much!

Since the control vertices are so small, they are easy to miss, and a new point may be created by mistake. We can either undo that with Ctrl + Z or delete the active point with the X button at the right of the coordinates.

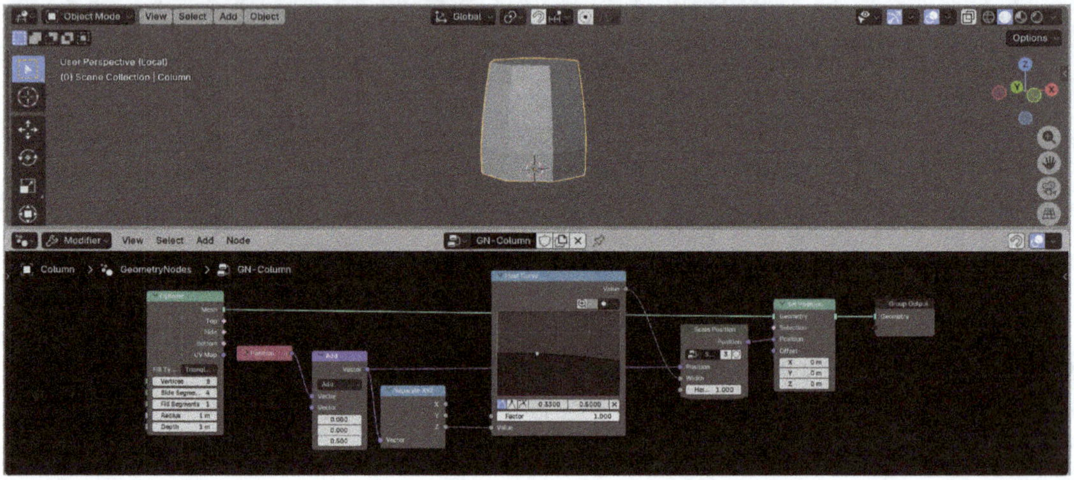

Figure 5.15: A column shaft bending smoothly

By editing the **Float Curve** graph at half height and connecting it to **Scale Position**, we have halved the cylinder width, which originally was 2 in diameter. That makes the resulting width equal to `1.0` in its wider section. As mentioned at the beginning of this section, *1.0* is a convenient size to start with because it can be resized to an exact value with a simple multiplication.

To make the size of the model easy to set, we must **expose** a few parameters so that they become properties of the modifier. This way, width and height can be set without editing the nodes.

Creating input attributes

Geometry Nodes can produce different results if given different parameters, like similar columns of a different size. That requires editable properties, which will be displayed as attributes of the modifier if we create new input sockets for the node tree. That is similar to creating the inputs of a *Group*, as the entire tree is considered a big group of nodes:

1. In the **Node Editor**, display the properties panel on the left by pressing the `N` key or clicking the small expansion triangle.
2. Select the **Group** tab, where the **Group Sockets** panel lets us create additional handles.
3. Select the last **Geometry** socket, then click the **+** button and select **Input** to add a new item: the sockets will not work properly if they precede the geometry in the list.
4. Double-click the new **Socket** in the list and rename it `Width`.
5. **Width** is a decimal number, so the predefined **Type**, **Float**, is correct; we need to scroll down to the **Default** value and set it to `1.0`.
6. Set the **Min** value to `0.0`, as our model cannot have negative width.
7. Add another input socket and rename it to `Height`. Set its **Default** value to `1.0` and its **Min** value to `0.0`.

The new sockets are displayed on the **Geometry Nodes** modifier and, if present in the scene, on the **Group Input** node.

We deleted **Group Input** at the start of our process. We could restore it by adding a new **Group | Group Input** node, but that's not necessary because we can connect specific input nodes.

By multiplying the output of **Float Curve** with the *Width* input, we can set the section size of the shaft in the modifier's property:

1. Press *Shift* + *A* and look for the **Math > Multiplication** node. Again, this is not a vector operation, but plain scalar math.
2. Insert the new **Multiply** node between **Float Curve** and **Scale Position | Width**.
3. Drag the **Multiply** free socket and release it to an empty area, type `width` as a search keyword, and select **Group Input > Width**.
4. The height parameter doesn't need additional nodes, just drag **Scale Position | Height** and release it to an empty area, search for `height`, and select **Group Input > Height**.

Again, even if we have set default values for the new *Width* and *Height*, we can see in the modifiers tab on the right that they were set to *0.0* when they were created. We can set them to `1.0` manually or right-click them with the mouse and click **Reset to Default Value**.

We can also set them to match the dimensions displayed in *Figure 5.2*, where the shaft is half a meter wide and, without considering the neck, one meter tall:

1. In the modifiers tab, set **GeometryNodes** | **Width** to `0.5`.
2. Set **GeometryNodes** | **Height** to `1.0`.

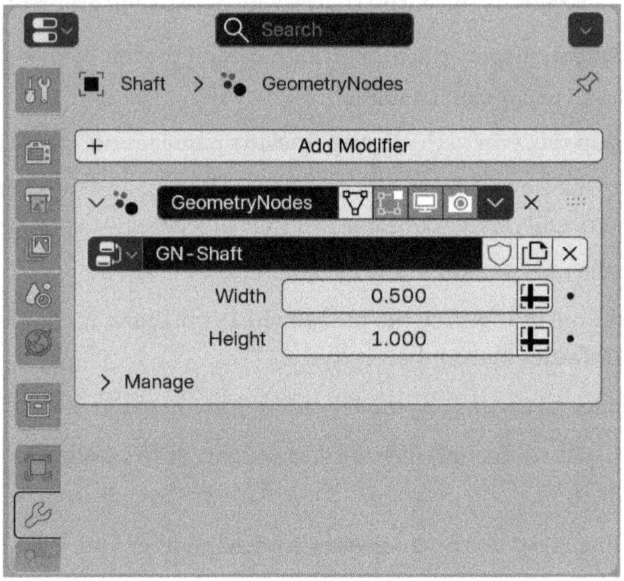

Figure 5.16: Setting dimensions in the modifier tabs

We can rearrange the nodes for better readability. The flow should proceed from left to right and minimize overlapping between nodes and links. Nodes can also be minimized to optimize the available space:

1. Select the **Group Input** node connected to **Scale Position** | **Height**, press *F2*, and rename it to `Height`. Minimize the node by clicking the commutation arrow, a symbol resembling a *V* that precedes the node name. It switches to a > when the node is reduced.
2. Select the **Group Input** connected to **Scale Position** | **Width**, press *F2*, and rename it to `Width`. Minimize the node.
3. Minimize all the nodes except **Cylinder** and **Float Curve**.

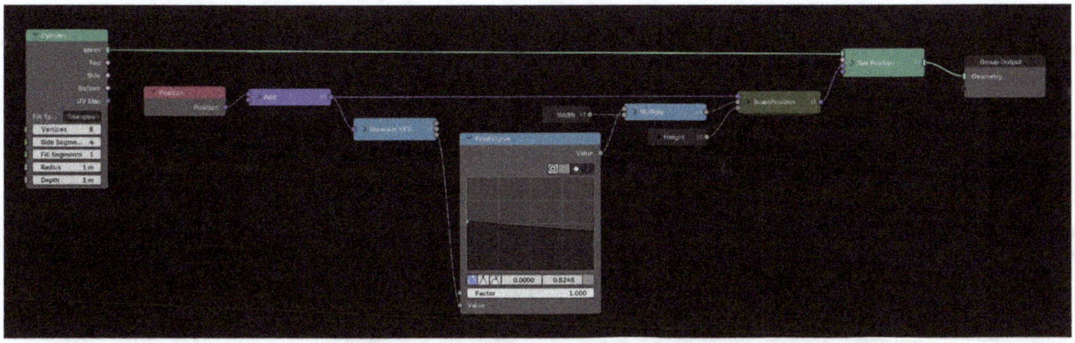

Figure 5.17: Minimizing nodes in the graph

To finish the first piece of our column, we need to add a *neck*, that is, the vertical end of the shaft.

Finalizing the shaft

The last section of the shaft should go upwards straight. We will add a section on top by extruding faces of the upper cap:

1. Press *Shift + A* and look for **Extrude Mesh**. Create this new node and insert it between **Set Position** and **Group Output**.
2. We only want to extrude the top face, so connect the pink socket **Cylinder** | **Top** to **Extrude Mesh** | **Selection**.
3. We want to extrude the section as one, so we uncheck the **Individual** checkbox of the node.

We can set the height of the new section by changing **Extrude Mesh** | **Offset Scale**. We connect that attribute to a new property of the modifier. *Offset Scale*, a float, gray socket, should not be confused with *Offset*, which is a blue vector:

1. In the properties (`N` key to display if hidden), create a new input in **Group Sockets** and enter `Neck` for its name. Set its **Default** and **Min** values to `0.1`; zero is unadvised because a zero extrusion creates overlapped surfaces, which is bad for rendering.
2. Drag the socket **Extrude Mesh** | **Offset Scale**, release it to an empty area, and look for **Neck**. Select **Group Input > Neck**.
3. Press *F2* to relabel the new **Group Input** socket to `Neck`.
4. Set a value of *0.1* in the **Geometry Nodes** modifier for a ten-centimeter-long neck.

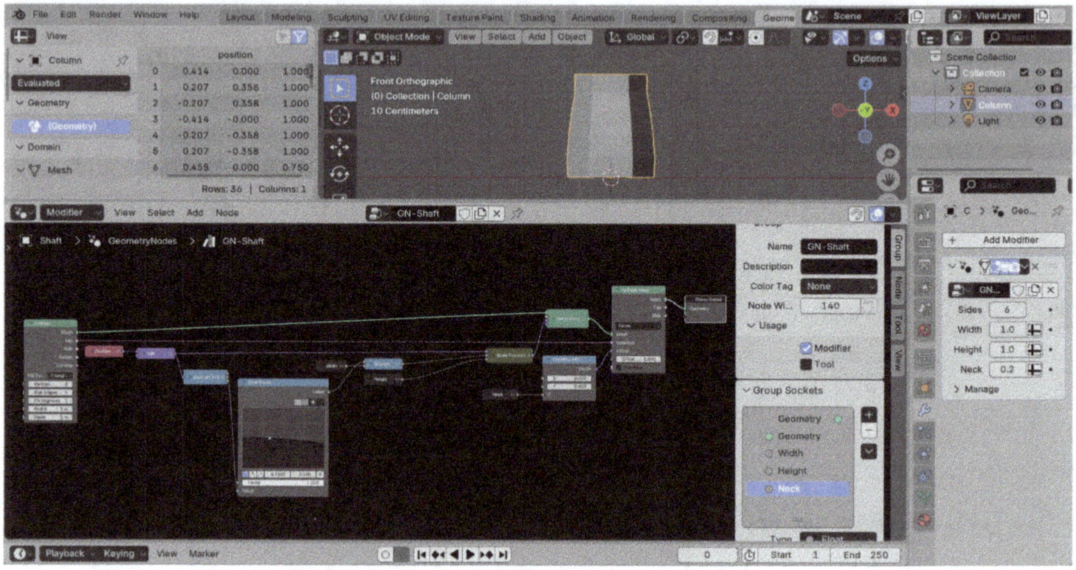

Figure 5.18: Modifier properties affecting the node tree

The shaft is almost finished: we must smooth the faces to remove the polygonal look. We cannot use the *Shade Smooth* command like in *Chapter 2*, as it doesn't affect procedural geometry. We need to add a smooth node to the tree:

1. Press *Shift + A* and create a **Smooth by Angle** node, then insert it between **Extrude Mesh** and **Group Output**.
2. Set the **Angle** value to `50`: that's enough for shading the edges between the sideways faces, while setting a value higher than *90* would smear the normals with the top and bottom triangles.

Smoothing by angle preserves a sharp edge where adjacent faces change direction abruptly: failing to do so would produce a dark smear toward the ends of the shaft.

Since we are creating for Unity, we may want to follow its coordinate orientation for this model. We can use the *Y-Up axis* command from *Chapter 4*:

1. Select the *Shaft*.
2. Press *Shift + A*, then click **Empty** | Y-Up Axis from the **Add** menu.

The shaft will be rotated, as the mesh was modeled according to Blender's orientation, but that is fixed easily:

1. In the **Node Editor**, press *Shift + A* to create a **Transform Geometry** node and insert it between **Smooth by Angle** and **Group Output**.
2. Set **Transform Geometry** | **Rotation** | **X** to `-90` to rotate the geometry.

The shaft is finished. Since Geometry Nodes reproduce the operations of traditional modeling, we could have modeled our shaft manually, but thanks to this node tree, we can change the dimensions easily and keep a clean, uniform model.

Some of the nodes from the **GN-Shaft** tree will be reused in the other two elements.

Modeling the capital

The *capital*, or head, of this column doesn't have decorations or refinements that are present in more elaborate designs.

Its first element, the *echinus*, is more challenging because of the transition from a square to a round section, while the abacus is quite simpler. The varying width of their sections can be achieved with the **Scale Position** node that was implemented for the shaft.

Modeling the echinus

We'll create another object and a new node tree graph for the echinus. Like with the shaft, the actual mesh components don't matter, so we can start with any shape:

1. In the **3D Viewport**, create a new object with *Shift + A* | **Mesh** | **Cube** or any other mesh primitive. If, for some reason, the new object is not centered on the origin, press *Alt + G* to zero its location.
2. Press *F2* and rename it to `Echinus`.
3. Keep *Shift* pressed and select the Y-up **Empty** so that both are selected.
4. Press *Ctrl + P* and choose **Object (Without Inverse)** to avoid relative transformations. Now the object's upper axis is *Y*.
5. Press *G*, then press *Z* to move the object vertically, then type `1.1` to move its center above the column, and finalize by pressing *Enter*.

Even if we have moved *Echinus* along the global *Z* axis, the affected local coordinate is *Y*, as we can check from the transform channels. We start modeling and create a node tree for this object:

1. Select the new object, **Echinus**.
2. In the **Geometry Nodes** workspace, click the **New** button in the **Node Editor** to create a new graph and modifier.
3. Rename the new *Node Tree* from **Geometry Nodes** to `GN-Echinus`.

An object which is part square and part circle must have enough vertices to convey a round shape. For that reason, we'll start with a cylinder:

1. Delete **Group Input**
2. Press *Shift + A* to create a **Cylinder** node and connect its **Mesh** output to **Group Output | Geometry**.
3. We set the default attributes of **Cylinder**:
    - **Fill Type** to **Triangles** to avoid exportation issues.
    - Set **Vertices** to `8` to have enough geometry for shaping a circle but not so much that it would make it harder to square.
    - **Slide Segments** to `8` as well to produce enough sections for shaping the profile.

The cylinder extends horizontally because of its Y-up orientation. We do not want that, so we rotate the mesh with a transform node:

1. Press *Shift + A*, look for the **Transform Geometry** node, create it, and insert it between **Cylinder** and **Group Output**.
2. Set **Transform Geometry | Rotation | X** to `-90` to align the cylinder along the vertical axis.

Now it's time to work on the shape of the model.

Squaring round shapes

Our section has eight sides, and a circle split at multiples of four is morphed into a square by a power of two. That might sound weird, but it follows from planar geometry, as the power of two is a *quadratic* operation, i.e., it produces squares.

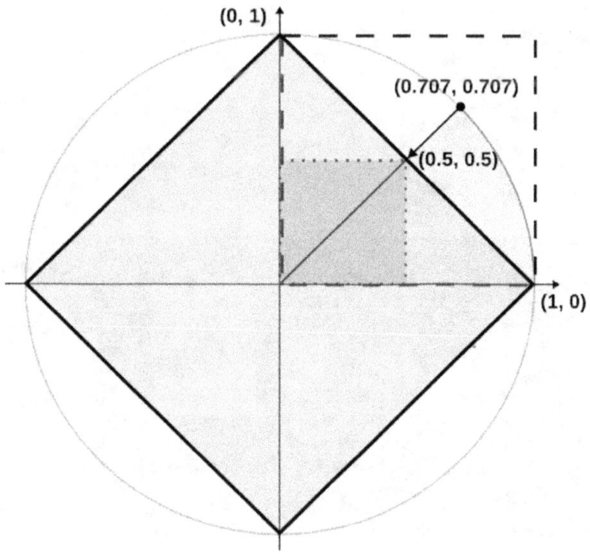

Figure 5.19: Squaring the coordinates of the circle at each fourth gives the inscribed square.

It helps if we see for ourselves what happens when we multiply the cylinder points by themselves, using element-wise multiplication:

1. Press *Shift + A* to create a **Set Position** node and insert it between **Cylinder** and **Transform Geometry**.
2. Create some room between **Cylinder** and **Set Position**, drag the **Position** socket to an empty area, and create a **Position** node: it will be auto connected.
3. Press *Shift + A* to create a **Vector Multiply** node and insert it between **Position** and **Set Position**.
4. Connect **Position** to the other socket of Multiply so that both are connected, multiplying each position vector by itself.

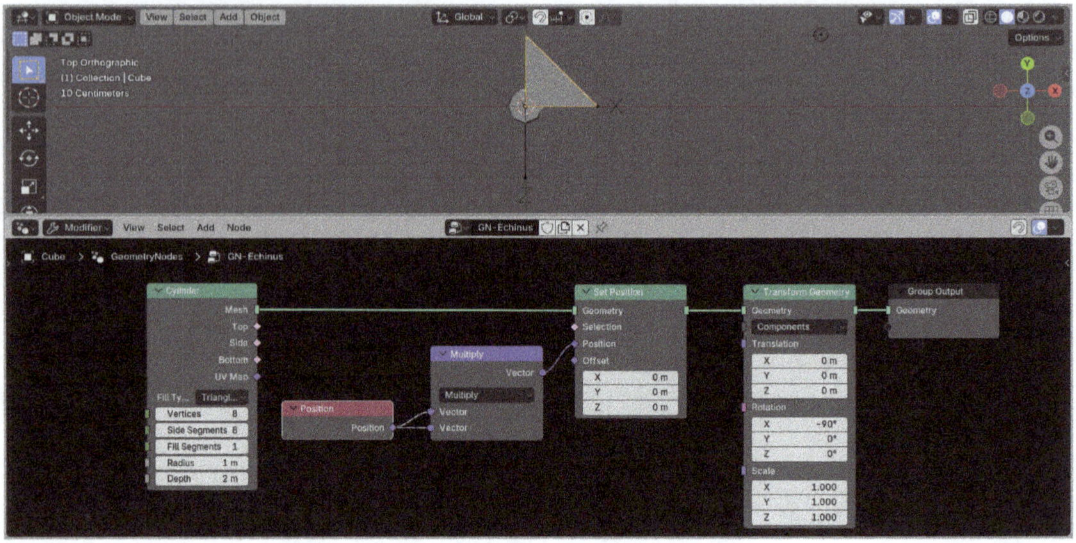

Figure 5.20: Squaring the position moves all the geometry to the first quadrant.

That has produced a triangular slice rather than a square, because all powers of two are positive and are pushed to the first quadrant. To leave their sign unaffected, we must replace one of the multiplicands with its *absolute value*:

1. Press *Shift* + *A* to create a *Vector Absolute* node and insert it between **Position** and **Multiply**. It must be the vector type; *Math* and *Integer Math* don't work correctly with Position. That will change the geometry to a squared section model, although misaligned.
2. To fix the diagonal orientation of the model, set **Transform Geometry** | **Rotation** | **Y** to 45 degrees.

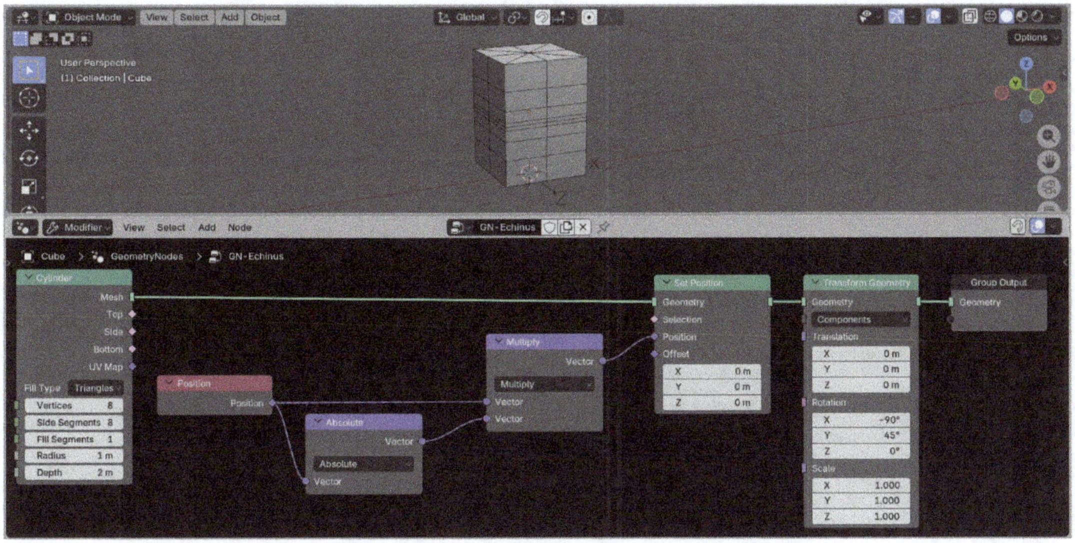

Figure 5.21: Absolute square power deforms a cylinder into a parallelepiped.

We have straightened our model, but squaring the vertical coordinate is causing an uneven vertical distribution, which can be seen in wireframe mode, displayed in *Figure 5.22*. That would create uneven deformations, which we can prevent by setting the multiplier's *Z* to `1.0`:

1. Press *Shift* + *A* to create a **Separate XYZ** node and insert it between **Absolute** and **Multiply**.
2. Press *Shift* + *A* to create a **Combine XYZ** node and insert it between **Separate XYZ** and **Multiply**.
3. Connect **Separate XYZ** | **Y** to **Combine XYZ** | **Y**.
4. Set **Combine XYZ** | **Z** to `1.0`.

An inscribed square is obviously smaller than the circle in which it's contained: we can see from the **Dimensions** properties displayed by pressing *N* in the *3D Viewport* that our model is **1.41** meters wide.

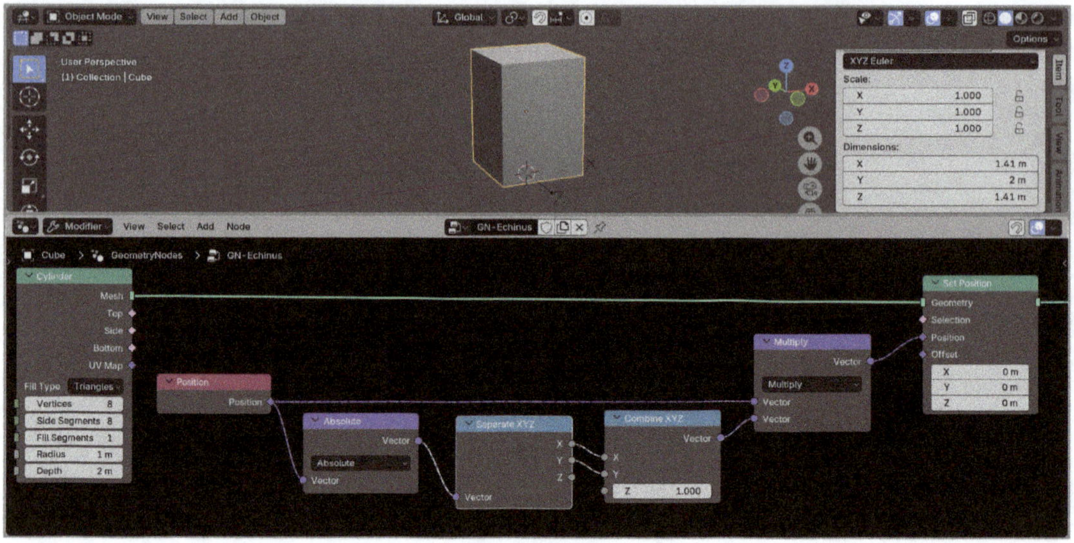

Figure 5.22: A circle with a diameter of 2 units becomes a parallelepiped with a width of 1.41 units

That is not a random number, but an approximation of the *square root of 2*, about 1.4142. It's much easier to work with discrete values, so we will restore this geometry to the former *2 x 2 x 2* volume.

> **Note**
>
> **Pythagoras rules!**
>
> The square root of 2 has been an important number in technology since ancient times: it measures the diagonal of a square whose side is 1 unit long and is ubiquitous in architecture, art, and geometry in general. It is also named **Pythagoras's constant** because it can be extrapolated from the dude's theorem.

Adjusting the square proportions

The width of the model was reduced to *1.414* since we have squared and rotated its coordinates. We can restore the two-units width with a horizontal scale of *1.414*:

1. Press *Shift + A* and create a **Vector Multiply** node. Insert the new node between **Multiply** and **Set Position**.
2. Set the **X** and **Y** values of the free multiplicand to `1.414` and the **Z** value to `1.0`.

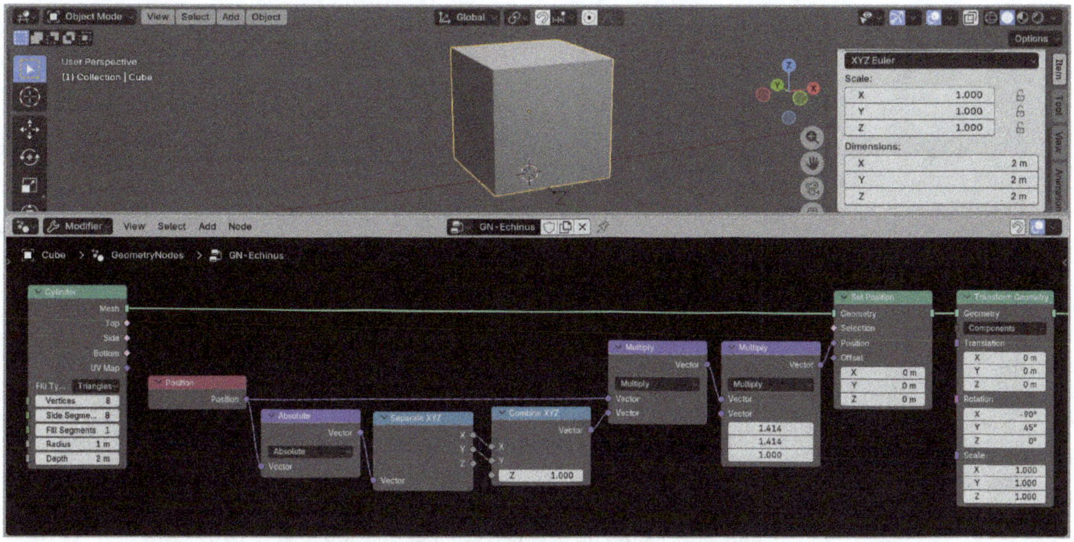

Figure 5.23: A 2 x 2 x 2 cylinder becomes a 2 x 2 x 2 cube

It's important that the model's boundaries are the same as the original cylinder, as we want to transition between the two shapes. To morph between cylinder and cube, we mix the initial position with the results of the last multiply:

1. Press *Shift* + *A* and create a **Mix Vector** node. Insert the new node between the last **Multiply** and **Set Position**
2. To display a cylinder when the factor is *0.0*, the cuboid must be connected to the second socket, so we connect **Multiply** | **Vector** to **Mix** | **B**.
3. Connect **Position** | **Position** to **Mix** | **A**, replacing the first incoming link from **Multiply**.

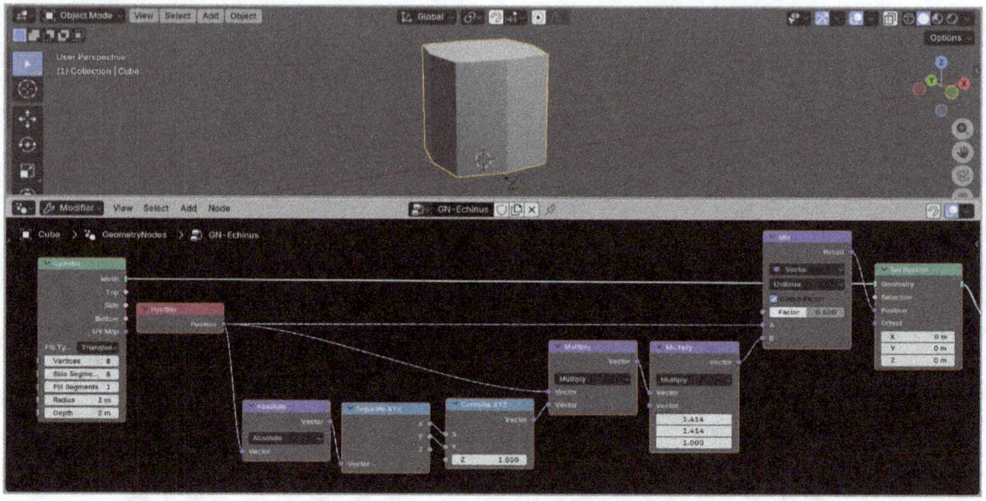

Figure 5.24: Morphing between cylinder and cube.

Moving the slider **Mix** | **Factor** switches gradually between a cylinder and a cube; both have dimensions `2.0` x `2.0` x `2.0`, but we want our results to measure 1.0 along each dimension, so we add a *Scale* node:

1. Press *Shift* + *A* and look for a **Vector Math > Scale** node; insert it between **Mix** and **Set Position.**
2. Set the **Scale** attribute of the new node to `0.5`.

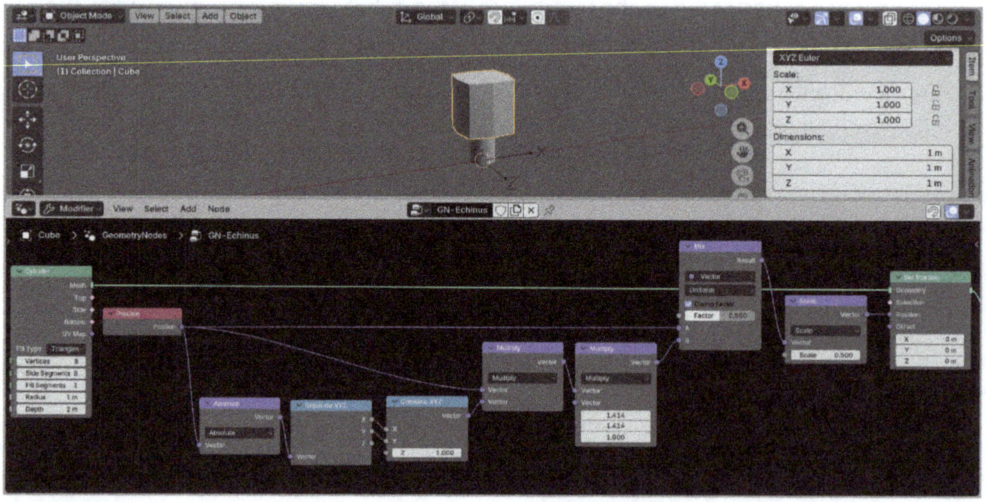

Figure 5.25: Our model was scaled to a 1 × 1 × 1 volume

Creating the Cubify node

We have implemented a formula that generates a cylindrical or cubic shape based on the **Mix** | **Factor** parameter. We can enclose those operations in a new group:

1. Select all the nodes between **Cylinder** and **Set Position**: Absolute, Separate XYZ, Combine XYZ, two vector **Multiply**, **Mix**, and **Scale**.
2. Press *Ctrl + G* to create a new group.
3. Click the group name in the **N properties** and name the new group `Cubify`.
4. Rename both **Vector** handles from the **Group Sockets** properties to `Position` to match Blender's terminology.
5. Create a new input and name it **Factor**, set its **Default** value to `1.0`, **Min** to `0.0`, and **Max** to `1.0`.
6. Connect **Group Input** | **Factor** to **Mix** | **Factor**, so that it can be set from outside the group.

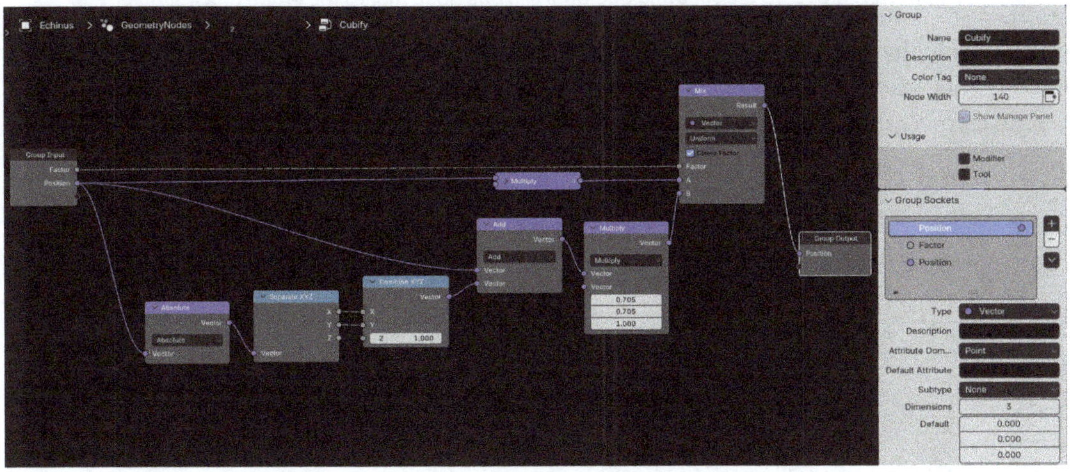

Figure 5.26: The Cubify node group

7. Press *Tab* to exit the group.

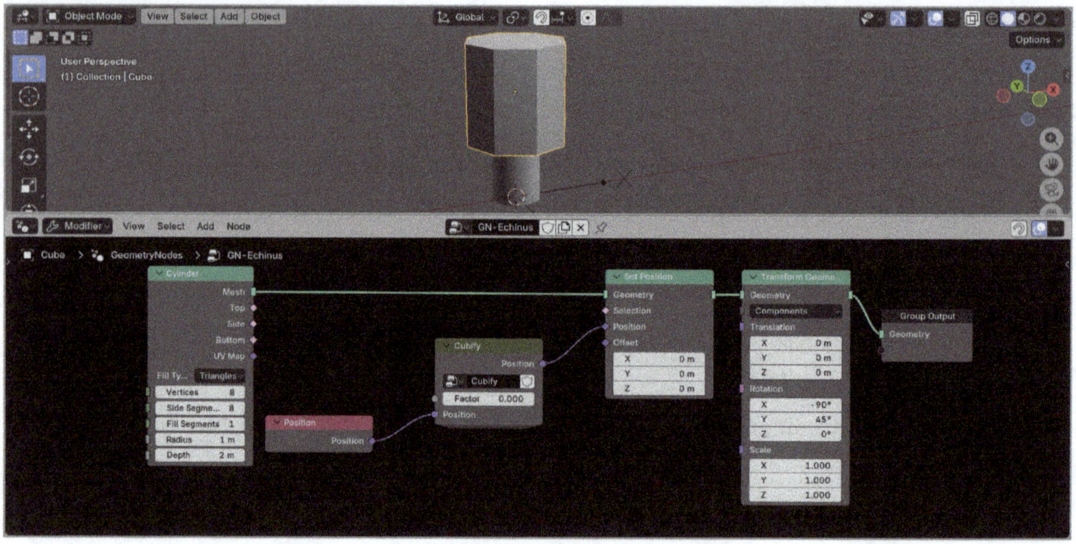

Figure 5.27: Grouping the squaring operations in one node makes the graph much simpler

Once outside the group, we can morph our model from cylinder to cube with the slider **Cubify | Factor**. This was the hardest part of the process, as we have learned in *Modelling the shaft* that we can connect the section's vertical coordinates to a factor attribute.

Finishing the echinus

Our model should be round at its base and square at the top, so we need to connect the vertical coordinate to *Cubify*'s factor. In the **Node Editor**:

1. Drag the **Position | Position** socket and release it over an empty area to create a **Separate XYZ** node.
2. Connect **Separate XYZ | Z** to **Cubify | Factor**.

Since the *Cylinder* geometry is centered at its middle, the points below the center have negative *Z*. The model is 2 units tall, so we shift *Z* by *1.0* to make it always positive:

1. Press *Shift + A* to create a **Vector Add** node and insert it between **Position** and **Separate XYZ**.
2. Set the free **Add | Vector**'s **Z** to 1.
3. Also connect **Add | Vector** to **Cubify | Position** to offset the geometry above the object's pivot.

Now the sections transition smoothly from a circular base to a square top.

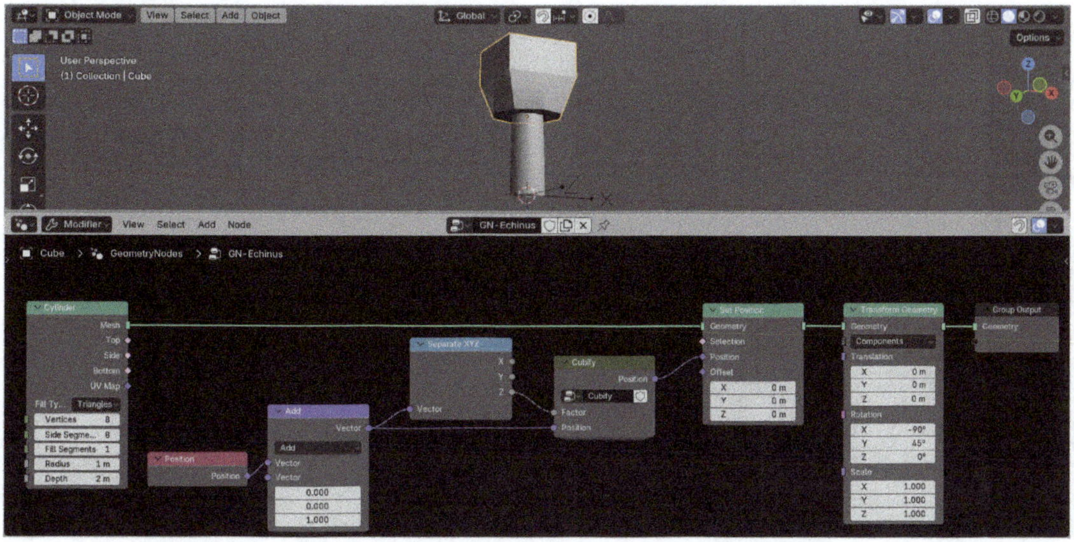

Figure 5.28: The shape's section transitions from round to square along the model's height

We need to modulate the profile of the shape and match the concept art in *Figure 5.2*. We can use our custom node for scaling width and height:

1. Press *Shift + A* and type *Scale Pos* to create a new **Scale Position** node. Insert the new node between **Cubify** and Set Position.
2. Connect **Separate XYZ** | Z to **Scale Position** | **Width**, and the model will assume a diamond shape.
3. Press *Shift + A* to create a **Float Curve** node and insert it between **Separate XYZ** and **Scale Position** | **Width**.

We bend the profile by shaping the curve graph:

1. Click on the first control point of the **Float Curve** graph and raise it to mid height by setting its coordinates, listed under the graph, to `0.0` and `0.5`.
2. Click the middle of the curve and drag it upwards to bend the graph. Set the coordinates of the new control point to `0.25`, `0.55`.
3. Click the middle of the curve again and drag a new control point upwards. Set the new coordinates to `0.6`, `0.9`.

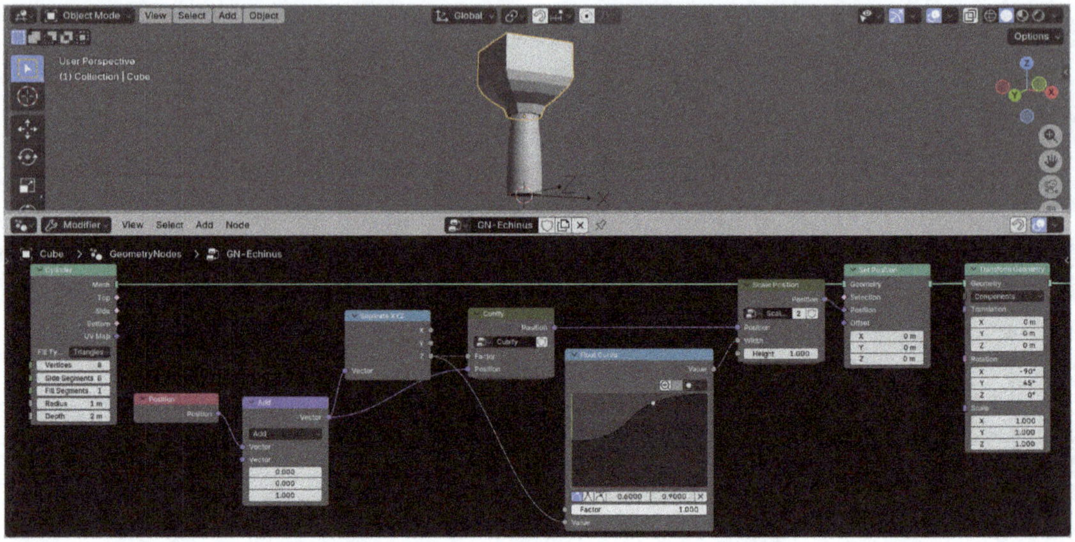

Figure 5.29: Shaping a smooth profile with a Float Curve node

This wine-glass shaped curve conveys the bowl shape of our architectonic element; we can finish this object by adding width and height controls on the modifier:

1. In the **Group Sockets** properties (*N panel*), create two input attributes and name them `Width` and `Height`.
2. Set the new attributes **Default** to `1.0` and **Min** to `0.0`
3. Set the desired height in the modifier properties: based on *Figure 5.2*, we need to set **Width** to `0.8` and **Height** to `0.6`.

With the width and height properties in place, we can use them to multiply the vector that is passed to **Scale Position**:

1. Press *Shift + A* and create a **Math > Multiply** node, then insert it between **Float Curve** and **Scale Position**.
2. Drag the new **Multiply**'s free socket and release it over an empty region; look for **Group Input > Width** to create a connection to the modifier property.
3. Drag **Scale Position**'s **Height** socket and release it over an empty region; look for **Group Input > Height** to create a connection to the modifier property.

With those connections in place, the model will be resized to fit the dimensions from the concept art.

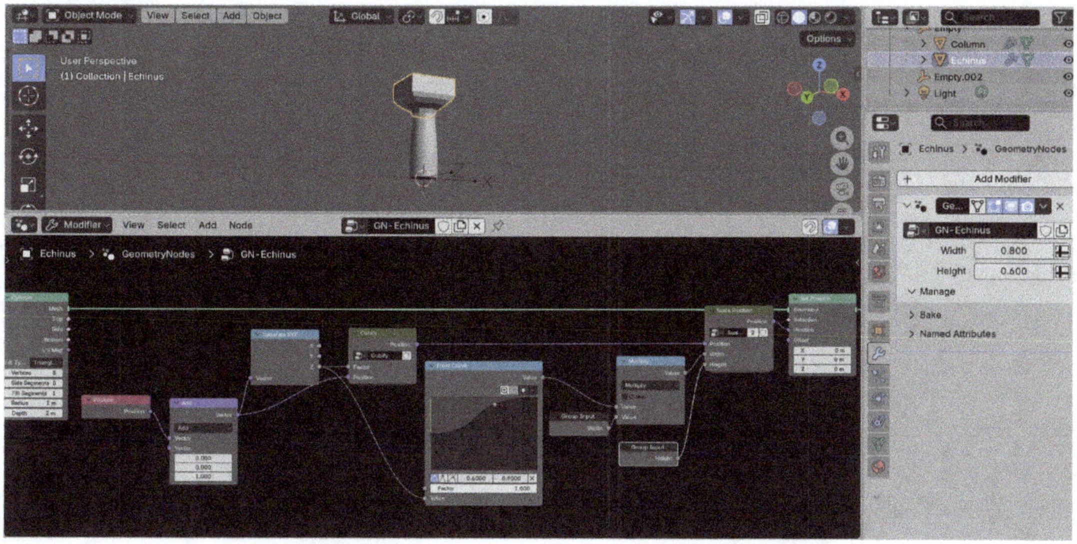

Figure 5.30: Setting width and height from the modifier properties

We are almost done; all that is left to do is to offset and smooth the geometry:

1. We want the surface to look smooth in the lower section and sharp at the top, so we press *Shift* + *A* and look for a **Smooth by Angle** node. We create it and insert it between **Set Position** and **Transform Geometry**.
2. Enable the **Ignore Sharpness** checkbox on **Smooth by Angle**, since the primitive faces are sharp.
3. Set **Smooth by Angle** | **Angle** to `60` degrees; that will smooth the round regions but not the hard edges at the top.

The peculiar shape of this model offered a bit of a challenge, but some notions of geometry and our *Scale Position* setup made it possible to lay a generative algorithm. Reusing existing solutions and implementing topological concepts are the main advantages of a geometric approach.

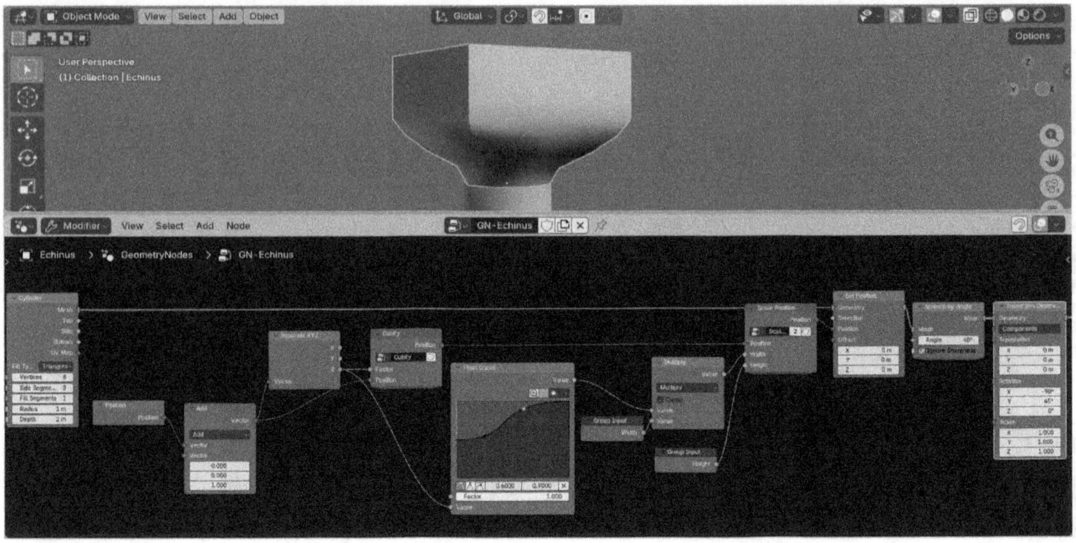

Figure 5.31: Finished model of the echinus.

The next architectural element, the *abacus*, is much simpler and can be derived from the *echinus*.

Modeling the abacus

The abacus is the most basic shape in this asset: it's a rough, tapered block for which we would not bother with geometry nodes, if not for the fact that we already have a setup for it. A squared model like this can be derived from the echinus:

1. In the **3D Viewport**, select the `Echinus`.
2. Press *Shift + D* to duplicate the model, press *Z*, and type `0.6` to offset it vertically.
3. Press *Enter* to finalize the duplication.
4. Press *F2* to rename the new object `Abacus`.
5. In the modifier properties, reset **Width** and **Height** to `1.0`.

Even if this new object is a copy, the node tree is still shared with *Echinus*; any changes in the graph would affect the other object as well.

We can see that in the header of the **Node Editor**, where the **2** on the user buttons indicates how many objects are using the same graph.

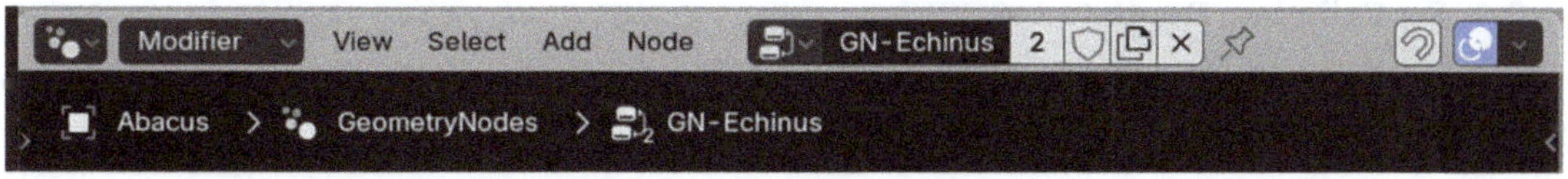

Figure 5.32: The Node Editor shows that Abacus is the second user of GN-Echinus.

We will duplicate the node tree as well to edit it independently:

1. In the **Node Editor**'s header, next to the name, click the button indicating the number of users, currently **2**. That will duplicate the node tree.
2. Rename the node tree from **GN-Echinus.001** to `GN-Abacus`.

Now we can make changes and, since we don't need that many nodes for a simpler shape, simplify the tree:

1. All the sections of this model are the same, so we select **Cubify** and press *Ctrl* + *X*. That will remove the node and rewire the connections.
2. We set **Cylinder** | **Vertices** to 4 to make the model a parallelepiped.
3. We can lower the density by setting **Cylinder** | **Side Segments** to 2.

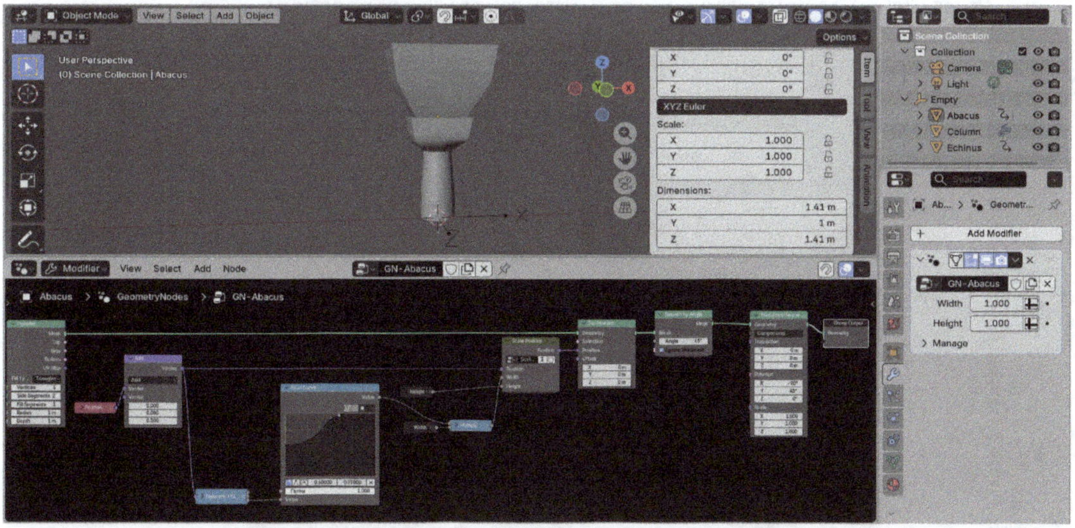

Figure 5.33: The node graph of Abacus generates a blocky shape

With the *Cubify* node gone, the width of the model is back to 1.414. We already know how to deal with that by multiplying by the square root of 2:

1. Click **Cylinder** | **Radius**. We can insert the value `1.414` manually, but we can also type the formula for the square root of 2: `sqrt(2)`, then press *Enter*.

2. Set **Cylinder | Depth** to `1.0`.
3. Set **Add | Z** to `0.5` as we only compensate for a one-unit tall mesh.

The curvature of the model is simpler, as its profile is not smooth. The graph of **Float Curve** will be a segmented line, with one intermediate control point:

1. Select one of the two intermediate control points of the **Float Curve** and delete it by clicking the **X** button below the graph, to the right of the coordinates.
2. Select the remaining median point and change it to a linear interpolator by clicking the second button below the graph, to the left of the coordinates, i.e., *Vector handle*.

With three control points interpolated linearly, we can set a tapered shape for the abacus:

1. Set the first control point coordinates at `0.0`, `0.4`.
2. Set the middle control point coordinates to `0.6`, `0.55`.
3. Set the end control point coordinates to `1.0`, `0.5`.

We don't want to smooth the faces of this model, as all the edges are sharp:

1. Select the node **Smooth by Angle** toward the right end of the Node Tree.
2. Press *Ctrl* + *X* to delete the node and auto-rewire the connections.

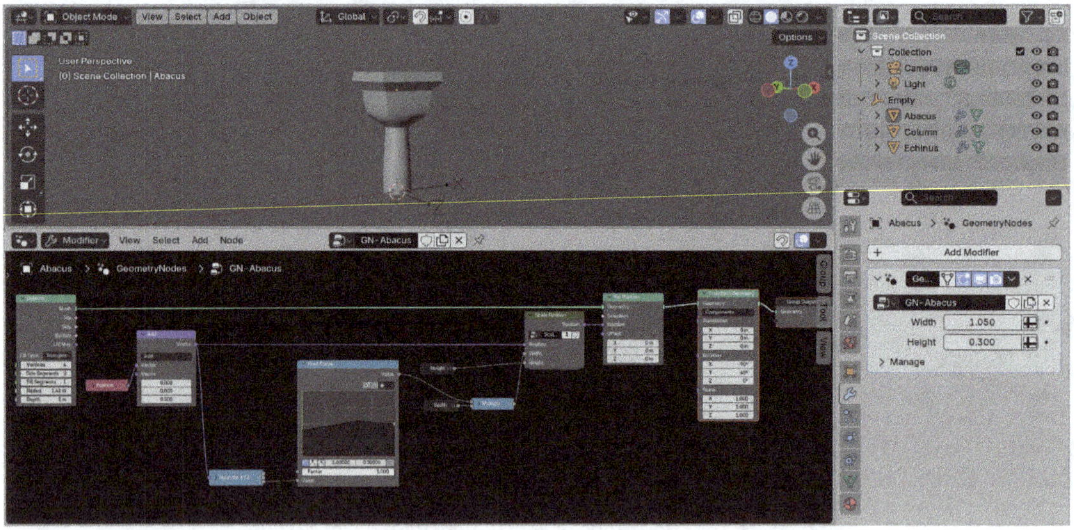

Figure 5.34: The full column in Blender.

We can insert the dimensions of the model in the modifiers' properties, based on *Figure 5.2*:

1. In the object modifiers properties, set the **GeometryNodes' Width** to `1.05`.
2. Set the modifier's **Height** to `0.3`.

Our model is complete. It reflects the specifications from the concept, and we can change its dimensions and density if needed. We are ready to save the scene in the game folder.

Saving to Unity

When we started to model, we didn't delete the *Light* and *Camera* objects, which are part of Blender's default scene. We don't want to export them to Unity, as this should be a mesh-only asset.

> Note
>
> **Unticking is not enough!**
>
> We can uncheck the **Import Cameras** and **Import Lights** settings in Unity. That would leave the Camera and Light data-blocks out of Unity, but they would still clutter the asset as top-level objects. They would also prevent Unity from skipping the Y-up axis Empty when the file is imported, adding a step to the hierarchy and an explicit rotation inside the asset.

Disabling objects with collections

We could very well delete **Camera** and **Light** and fix the issue, but sometimes we want to keep objects in the scene without exporting them.

Camera and lighting might be useful for tests, screenshots, and other production materials.

Collections can help, as we can move objects to a collection that will be disabled:

1. Select both **Camera** and **Light**, either by keeping *Shift* pressed while clicking them in the **Viewport**, or *Ctrl* if using the **Outliner**.
2. Press `M` to move them to a new collection.
3. Type `LookDev` as the new name and press `Enter` or the **Create** button.
4. The **Outliner** displays a checkbox beside every collection. Disable the **LookDev** checkbox to turn it off.

Even if **Camera** and **Light** are still part of the scene, only **Shaft**, **Echinus**, and **Abacus** are displayed.

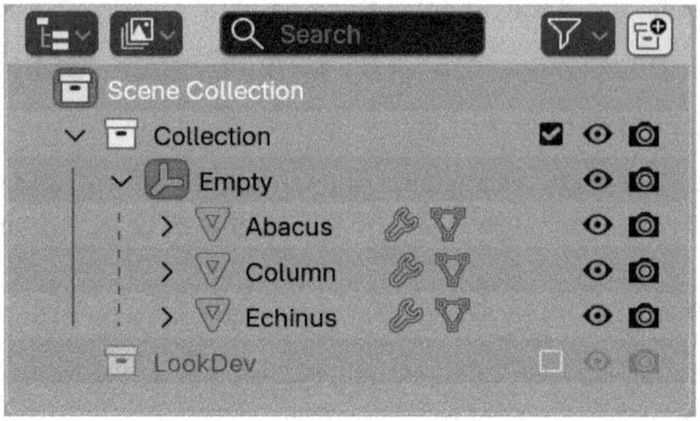

Figure 5.35: LookDev is disabled in the Outliner

We can go on and save the scene as a new asset.

Saving the asset

The **GeometryNodes** modifier is converted to plain geometry when Unity imports the .blend file, so we can just save our scene to the game folder:

1. From the top bar menu, select **File** | **Save As** to open the save dialog.
2. Go to the BL2Uni_URP directory and navigate to the `Assets` | `Arts` | `Models` folder.
3. Type Column as the filename and click **Save As**

If we open our game project in Unity, we will see the new asset in the **Project Browser**.

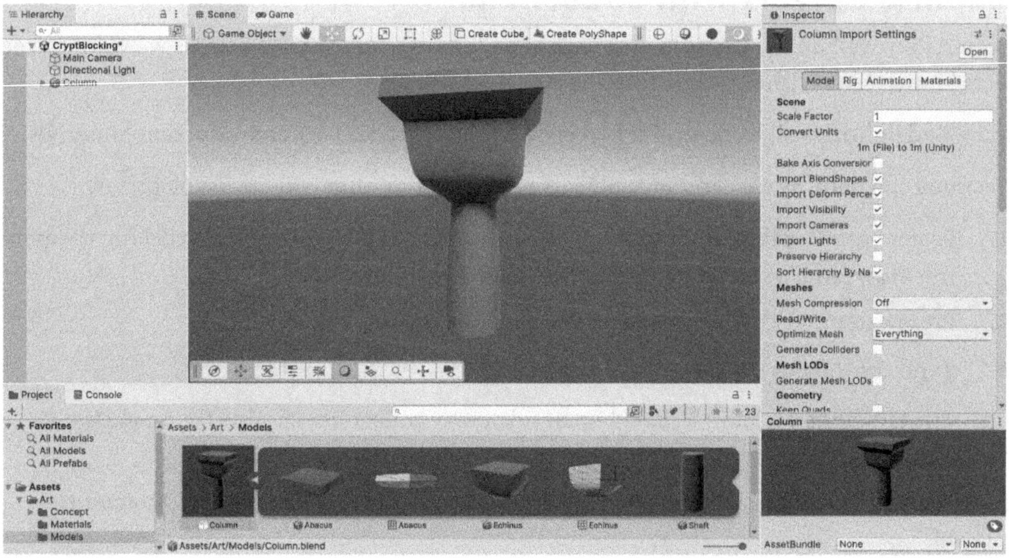

Figure 5.36: Our column displayed in Unity

The asset is not final, as this chapter is focused on modeling, and textures and materials are still missing. Our geometry made it to the project, though, and that is the first step in creating actual game content.

The node trees created in this chapter will be useful for creating other elements of the environment, like walls and roofs, in the upcoming steps of the book. After all this work, Geometry Nodes are part of our arsenal and will help with the next steps of the project.

Summary

In this chapter, we have generated an architectural model using Geometry Nodes. The process is not always straightforward, as it involves the development of an algorithm capable of producing a three-dimensional model that matches a specific design.

Modelling with Geometry Nodes can be counterintuitive at first, as it sometimes introduces algebraic thinking in lieu of artistic craftsmanship, but it essentially involves the same operations performed in manual modeling, like extrusion and displacement, laid down in the form of an operations graph.

Although we lose access to the generative parameters once the models are imported, the asset can be opened and edited with a few clicks of the mouse.

In *Chapter 6*, we will finish our environment and bring it into Unity.

Get this book's PDF copy, code bundle, and more

Scan the QR code (or go to `packtpub.com/unlock`). Search for this book by name, confirm the edition, and then follow the steps on the page.

UNLOCK NOW

Note: Have your invoice handy. Purchases made directly from the Packt website don't require an invoice.

6

Assembling the Level

The previous chapters paved the way to level development, as we created a rough prototype, implemented custom features, and created procedural models. Working on games demands a balance between planning and execution, and we put the Unity project on hold as we get the pipeline ready.

Asset creation takes up a large portion of the time budget, so exploring a viable workflow before venturing straight into it is a good idea. As we get ready to jump back to Unity, we will strengthen the integration with Blender by implementing import-time commands and extend our usage of Blender's **Asset Browser** by adding **Geometry Nodes** to it.

The first task relies on Python for checking if Blender is exporting a scene. Then, we will model the remaining element of the map by taking advantage of the work done in the previous chapters. Finally, we will put everything together in the game engine.

This chapter covers the following topics:

- Running scripts when Unity imports
- Sharing Geometry Nodes
- Assembling the level

Technical requirements

We will use *Blender 5.1* and *Unity 6.3*, which can be installed by following the instructions from *Chapter 1* or from their respective websites.

You can download the example project and code for this book by following the instructions in the *Download the example code files* section in the *Preface* of this book.

This chapter's code files are included in the downloadable code bundle.

Running scripts at import time

In *Chapter 5*, we modeled a column and disabled a collection to prevent some objects from being imported.

It is a useful trick, but a fragile element of our pipeline: if we edit that .blend file, enable the collection, and save it, we will find unwanted objects in our game when Unity re-imports the asset.

Python comes to the rescue, allowing us to execute operations at the import stage.

Detecting Unity's commands

As seen in *Chapter 2*, Unity launches a hidden session of Blender when it imports `.blend` files. The export command has the following structure:

```
blender -b scene.blend -P Unity-BlenderToFBX.py -- temp.fbx
```

These arguments run a Python script in Blender and export a temporary `.fbx` file.

We can check the command line arguments with Python and turn off a collection only when `Unity-BlenderToFBX.py` are present in the command.

Writing the turnoff script

We have learned how to write Python scripts in *Chapter 4*:

1. Start a new scene in Blender.
2. Go to the **Scripting** workspace.
3. Create a new text block in the **Text Editor**.
4. Name the new text `exclusion.py`.

We will need the Blender python module to affect collections, so the first line will be:

```
import bpy
```

We can write a function to change the state of a given collection. It will take two arguments: `name` and `exclude_it`. If the collection is found, its status is set:

```
def exclude_collection(name, exclude_it):

    layer = bpy.context.view_layer.layer_collection
    try:
```

```
        coll = layer.children[name]
    except KeyError:
        # collection not found, exit
        return
    # set the exclude flag
    coll.exclude = exclude_it
```

The `try/except` combination is Python's way of saying, "*If something goes wrong, never mind.*" It's a common approach, and we are going to use it again later. We just must be careful and explicit about which error we expect: `KeyError` is what happens when an item's name is not found.

The finished script can be found at:

`https://github.com/PacktPublishing/3D-Game-Development-with-Blender-5-and-Unity-6/blob/main/_blender_scripts_/modules/exclusion.py`

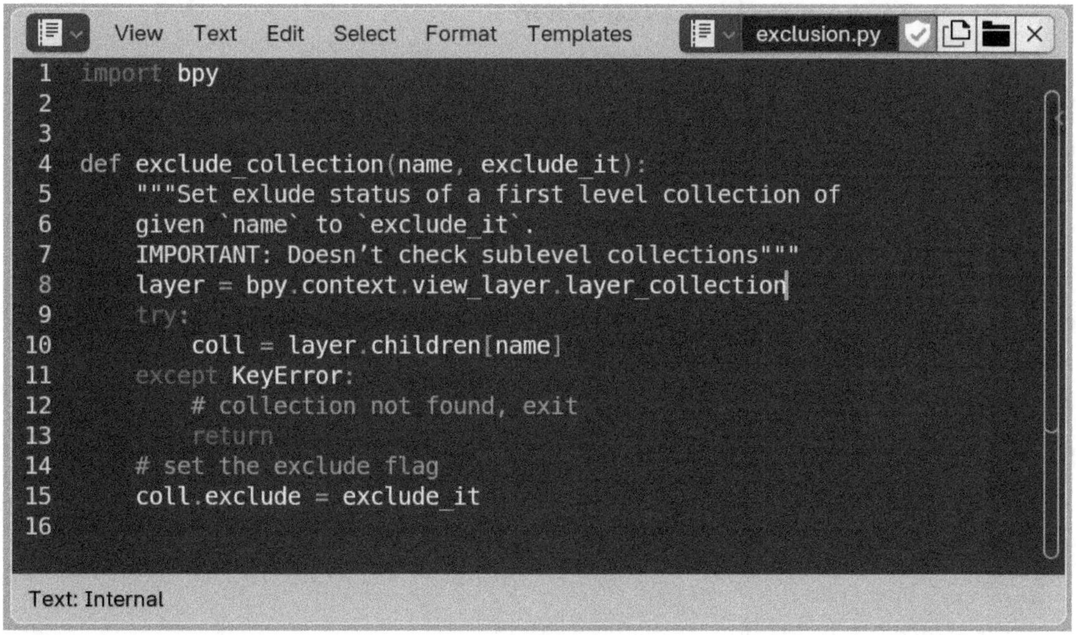

Figure 6.1: The exclusion.py script

This script only acts on the first-level collections, that is, those directly under **Scene Collection**, but that works for us. We can save the new script to the `modules` subfolder of our script path and it will work for every scene:

1. From the **Text Editor** menu bar, click **Text** | **Save As**

2. Reach the folder `BlendToUni_URP` | `_blender_scripts_`.
3. Create a new folder with *right-click* | **New Folder** or the **Create New Directory** button, and type `modules` as the new folder's name.
4. Enter the new folder and click **Save As**.

Now our function can be called in every script running inside Blender. We will write an event script that runs `exclude_collection` in the asset scenes.

Excluding collections on scene load

We want to invoke `exclude_collection` when a scene is exported to Unity, so we set up a script in the scene for automatic execution:

1. Open the scene `BlendToUni_URP` | `Assets` | `Art` | `Models` | `Column.blend`, either from Blender or by double-clicking in Unity's **Project Browser**.
2. Go to the **Scripting** workspace.
3. Create a new text block in the **Text Editor**.
4. Name the new text `on_scene_load.py`.

We will rely on our script `exclusion.py` and check the command line arguments, handled by the `sys` module, so the first lines of this new script are:

```
from exclusion import exclude_collection
import sys
```

Our code looks for the name `Unity-BlenderToFBX.py` in the command-line arguments. The "*never mind*" keyword used when something is not found while scrolling for the next element is `StopIteration`.

If the script name is part of the command line, we set the exclusion flag of a collection named `_NO_EXPORT_` to `True`:

```
script_name = 'Unity-BlenderToFBX.py'
try:
    next(a for a in sys.argv if script_name in a)
except StopIteration:
    pass
else:
    exclude_collection("_NO_EXPORT_", True)
```

We can save the file so that it can be used in other scenes too:

1. From the **Text Editor**'s menu bar, click **Text** | **Save As...**.
2. Reach the folder `BlendToUni_URP` | `_blender_scripts_`.
3. Create a new folder and name it `events`.
4. Click **Save As**.

We enable the **Registered** checkbox for running this script when the scene is loaded:

1. From the **Text Editor**'s menu bar, click **Text**.
2. Enable the **Register** checkbox.

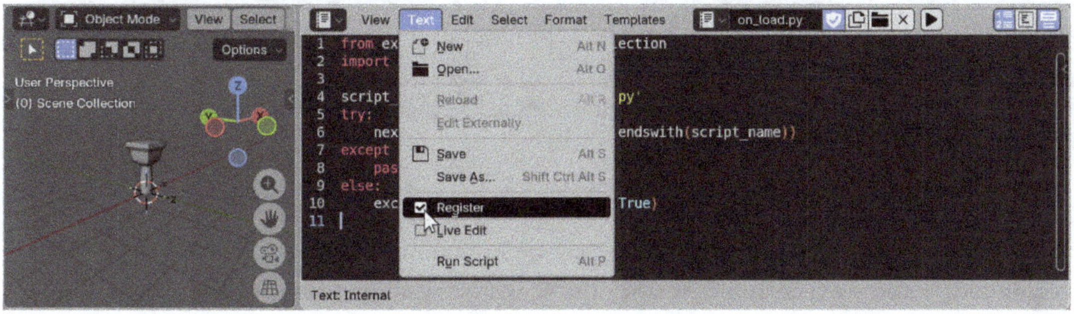

Figure 6.2: Registering the script execution

Last, we create the collection `_NO_EXPORT_` and place **LookDev** under it:

1. In the **Outliner**, *right-click* on the top-level **Scene Collection** and select **New Collection** from the menu.
2. Double-click on the new collection with the left mouse button and rename it to `_NO_EXPORT_`.
3. Enable the collection **LookDev**, drag it with the left mouse button, and release it over **_NO_EXPORT_**.
4. Save the scene with `Ctrl + S` or **File** | **Save** from the top bar.

After saving the scene, the script won't run yet because of security reasons. If we reopen the scene using **File** | **Revert** from the top bar and confirm with the **Revert** button, Blender displays a warning:

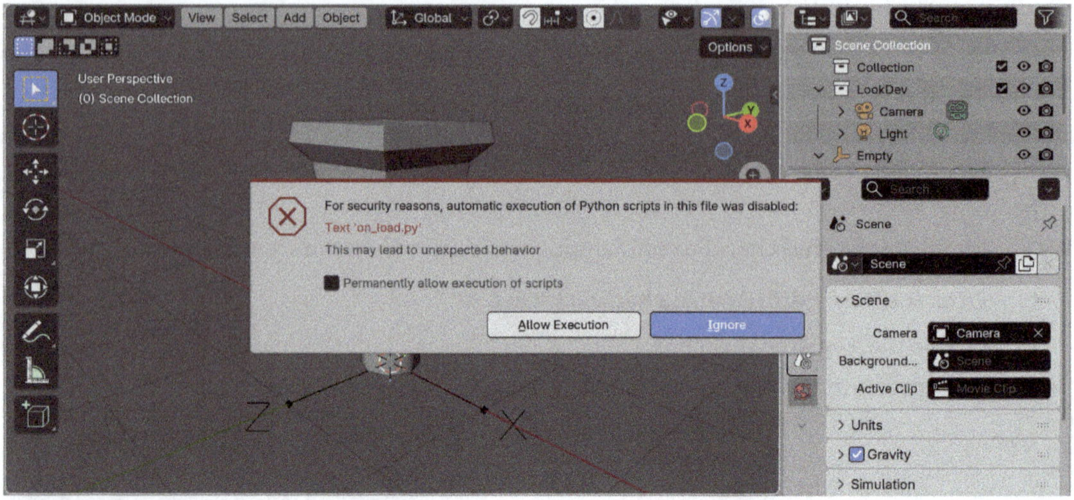

Figure 6.3: Blender warning about our script

Automatic execution can be dangerous, as a malicious actor might hide harmful code in a `.blend` file. We will enable permanent execution from now on by checking the box **Permanently allow execution of scripts** and clicking the **Allow Execution** button. We will see that, in Blender, the collection is not turned off, and the **Camera** and **Light** are present.

Check that **Auto Run Python Scripts** is enabled in the **Edit** | **Preferences...** | **Save & Load** section, which can be accessed from the menu bar, and that no other instances of Blender are running. Then close Blender to make sure that the preferences are saved.

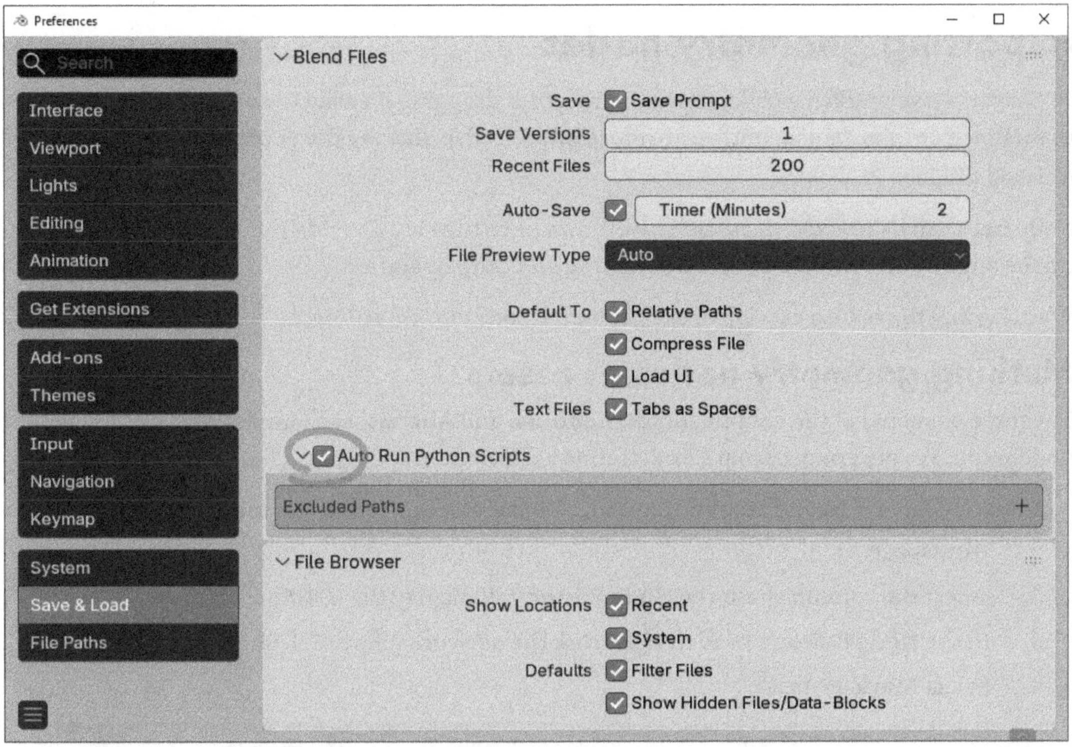

Figure 6.4: Auto Run Python Scripts allows Blender to run on_load.py.

Note

Safe or trusty?

Although a legitimate concern, preventing the execution of scripts can be limiting on articulate projects. Security settings can be tweaked in the **Edit** | **Preferences...** dialog, in the **Save & Load** section, where we can revoke the **Auto Run** permission and create a list of excluded paths for unsafe scenes.

If we switch back to Unity, the asset `Art` | `Models` | `Column` is reimported. Even if this time the **LookDev** collection is not disabled, the asset is clean of **Camera** and **Light**.

This technique is useful for improving the conversion from Blender to Unity. Our level requires other models besides the columns, and since we can reuse some elements of `Column.blend`, we are going to mark some of its content for Blender's **Asset Browser**.

Importing geometry nodes

In *Chapter 4*, we marked a collection as an asset for dragging it easily to any scene. We could do the same in `Column.blend`, but we are more interested in sharing the geometry nodes than the finished models.

Node trees can be marked as assets as well, and once they are listed in the **Asset Browser**, they can be applied directly to a model with a drag and drop operation.

We are going to create a catalog of the geometry nodes for this project.

Marking geometry nodes as assets

The three elements of the column, **Shaft**, **Echinus**, and **Abacus**, each implement a different node setup. We are going to mark each tree as a different asset:

1. In Blender, stay in the scene `Column.blend` and move to the **Geometry Nodes** workspace.
2. Select the column shaft; the **Node Editor** will display the **GN-Shaft** tree.
3. In the **Node Editor**'s header, *right-click* the network name, **GN-Shaft**.
4. Select **Mark as Asset**.

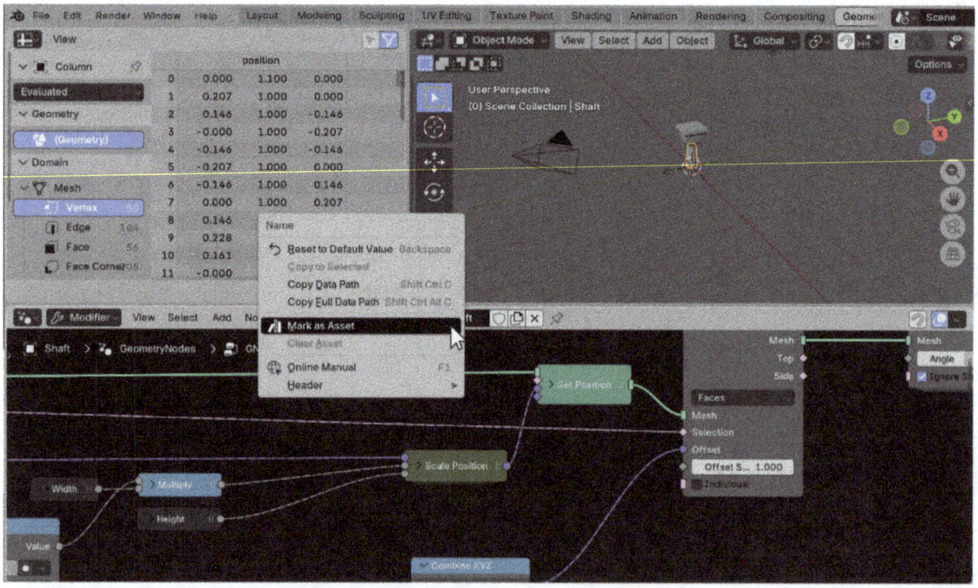

Figure 6.5: Marking Geometry Nodes as assets

A bookshelf icon will be displayed in the **Node Editor**'s header. We repeat the same steps for the other two pieces:

1. Select `Echinus`.
2. Mark **GN-Echinus** as asset
3. Select `Abacus`.
4. Mark **GN-Abacus** as asset

Our three node groups are now Blender assets; we can set their properties in the **Asset Browser**.

Setting up the geometry nodes assets

We can switch to the **Assets** workspace created in *Chapter 4*, or, if that's not available, change the **Spreadsheet** in the **Geometry Nodes** workspace to an **Asset Browser**.

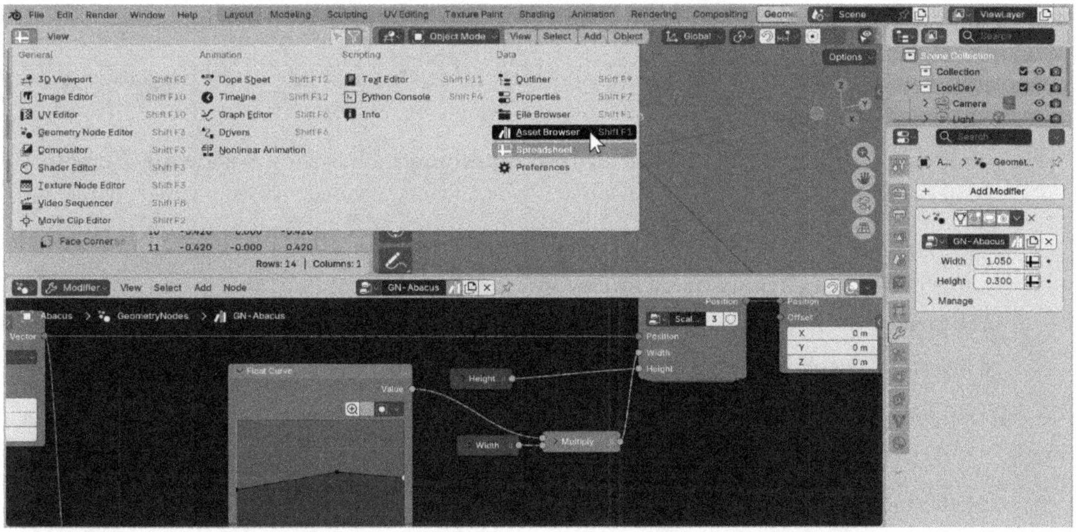

Figure 6.6: Changing from Spreadsheet to Asset Browser

In the **Asset Browser**, we can see our new assets in the **All Libraries** | **All** catalog; their icon represents two stylized nodes on a sheet.

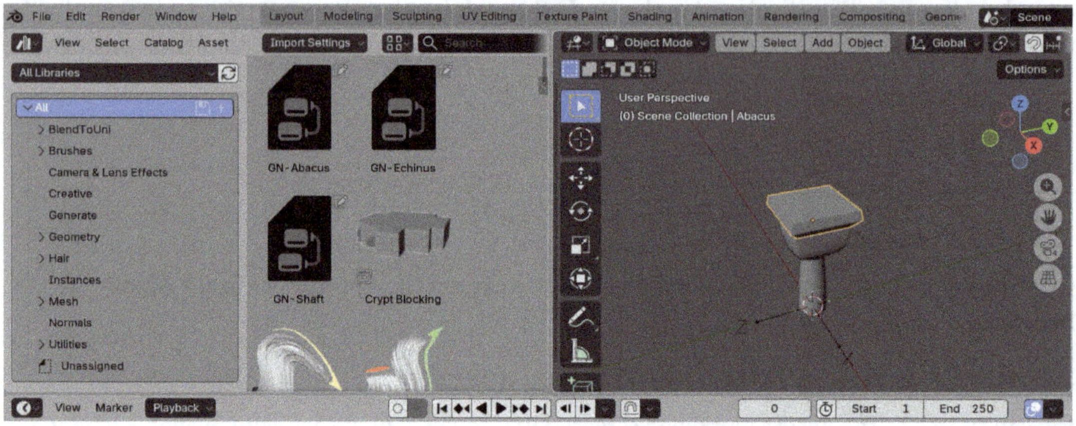

Figure 6.7: Our geometry nodes among the assets

We can only create catalogs in the current file, so we must change the view to proceed:

1. In the **Asset Browser**, switch from **All Libraries** to **Current File** in the dropdown box in the top-left corner.
2. Only two catalogs are displayed: **All** and **Unassigned**. Click the **+** beside **All** to create a new catalog.
3. *Double-click* the new catalog name and change it from **Catalog** to `BlendToUni`. It's the same name that we have used in *Chapter 4*, and the two catalogs will merge when **All Libraries** are displayed.
4. Click the **+** beside **BlendToUni** to create a sub catalog and name it `Modeling`.

We will put all the modeling-related assets in this catalog, so we drag and drop the new assets there:

1. Click the **Unassigned** catalog to display the new assets.
2. Select **GN-Abacus**, **GN-Echinus**, and **GN-Shaft** either with rectangular selection or by pressing *Ctrl + click*.
3. Drag the three of them with the left mouse button pressed and release them over the **Modeling** catalog.

Unlike the asset created in *Chapter 4*, these new ones were not assigned a thumbnail automatically; we will create their preview pictures manually.

Creating asset thumbnails

Node groups are not intrinsically associated with any object: they are recipes for geometry rather than finished models, so Blender does not create a thumbnail automatically. We still have two ways of creating preview images manually: **Render Active Object** and **Capture Screenshot**.

To create a **Render Preview** for the abacus nodes:

1. Select the **Abacus** element in the **3D Viewport**.
2. In the **Asset Browser**, select the asset **GN-Abacus**.
3. Press the *N* key to display the properties panel on the right.
4. Click the *down arrow button* in the **Preview** panel and select **Render Active Object**.

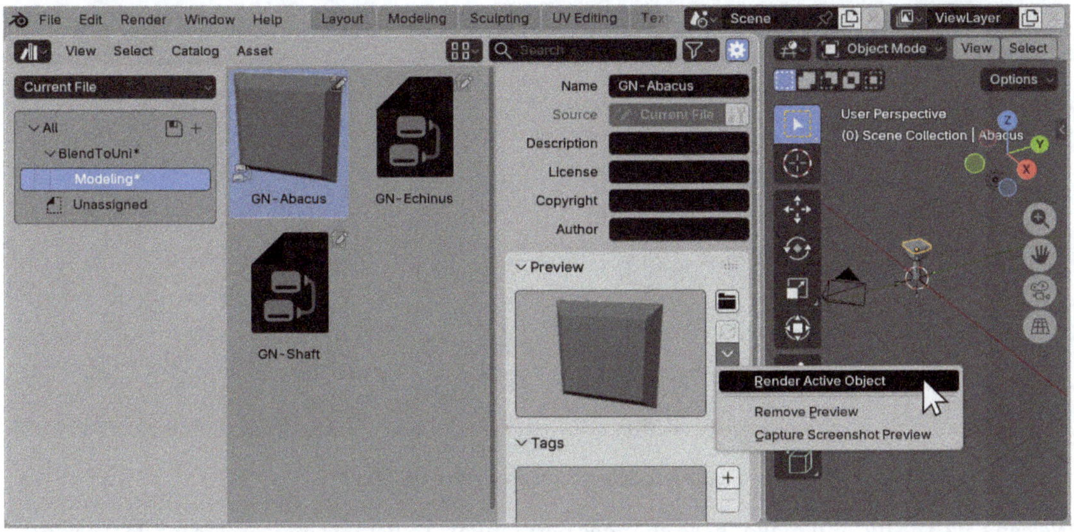

Figure 6.8: Rendering GN-Abacus preview

A **Render Preview** is relative to the object's transformation, so **Abacus**, which follows Unity's *Y-Up* orientation, is rendered from above rather than frontally. We can repeat the process with **Echinus**, and the result will be the same:

1. Select **Echinus** in the viewport.
2. Select **GN-Echinus** in the **Asset Browser**.
3. Click the *down arrow button* in the **Preview** panel and select **Render Active Object**.

Since the shaft spans vertically, picturing from above is not helpful for its preview. We are going to do something and capture a screenshot:

1. In the **3D Viewport**, select **Shaft** and press the *dot* key on the numeric pad or **View** | **Frame Selected** from the **Viewport** header. Orbit the view to get a good shot of the pillar.
2. In the **Asset Browser**, select **GN-Shaft**, click the down arrow button, and select **Capture Screenshot Preview**: screenshot mode will be activated in the viewport.
3. In the **Viewport**, drag a rectangle around the pillar with the *left mouse button* pressed, and release when finished: a thumbnail will be created.

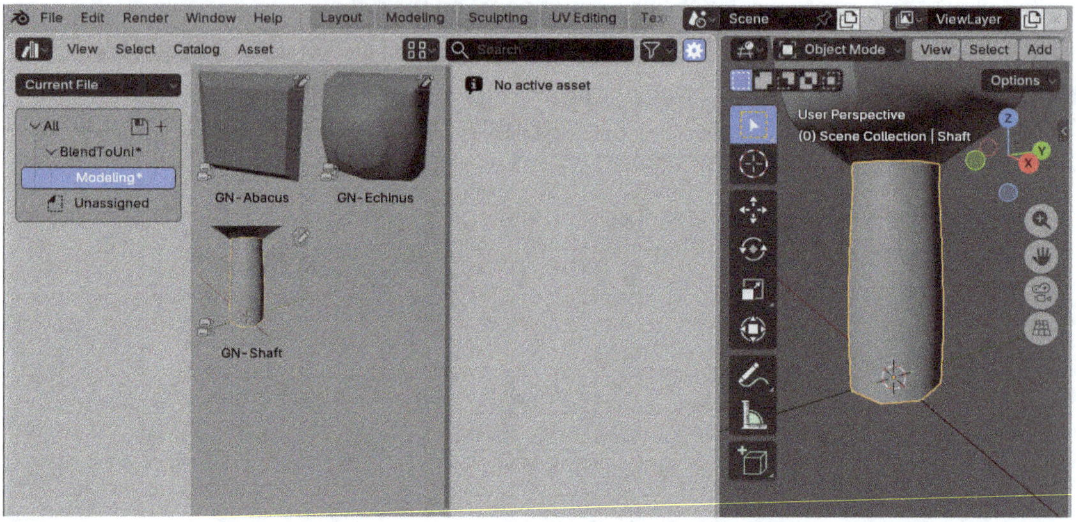

Figure 6.9: Screenshot preview of GN-Shaft

We can save the file and make these changes permanent. To list our new assets while working on other scenes, we need to add their folder to the file paths.

Adding the asset folder

`Column.blend` is saved in the Unity project and, since Blender scans the library paths periodically, we will limit the lookup to the `Assets` | `Art` | `Models` folder:

1. From Blender's top menu bar, click **Edit** | **Preferences** to open the settings
2. Scroll the navigation list on the left and select **File Paths**.
3. In the **Asset Libraries** panel, click the **+** button to open the folder dialog.
4. Navigate to the folder `BlendToUni_URP` | `Assets` | `Art` | `Models` and click **Add Asset Library** to confirm.

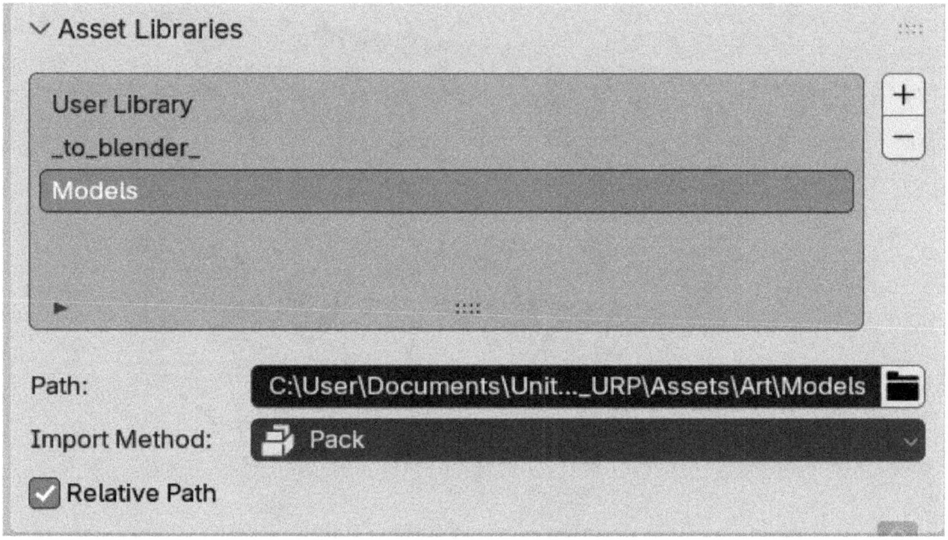

Figure 6.10: Asset Library paths for the project

Models was added to the **Asset Libraries**, but it is a generic name. Also, the import method was set to **Pack**, the default setting, which keeps the link to the original scene on import. In this case, it is better for the imported node tree to be imported independently:

1. Double-click **Models** in the **Asset Library** list and type `BlendToUni Models` as the new name.
2. Click the **Import Method** drop-down choice and change it from **Pack** to **Append**.

Those Geometry Nodes now can be dragged from the Asset Browser to new objects; this way, we will be able to model the roof of our level.

Modeling the vault

The concept picture from *Figure 5.1*, in *Chapter 5*, depicts a vaulted roof. A vault is an architectural form where the arches sustain the weight of the structure. *Figure 6.11* provides a view of how the ceiling of our level should look.

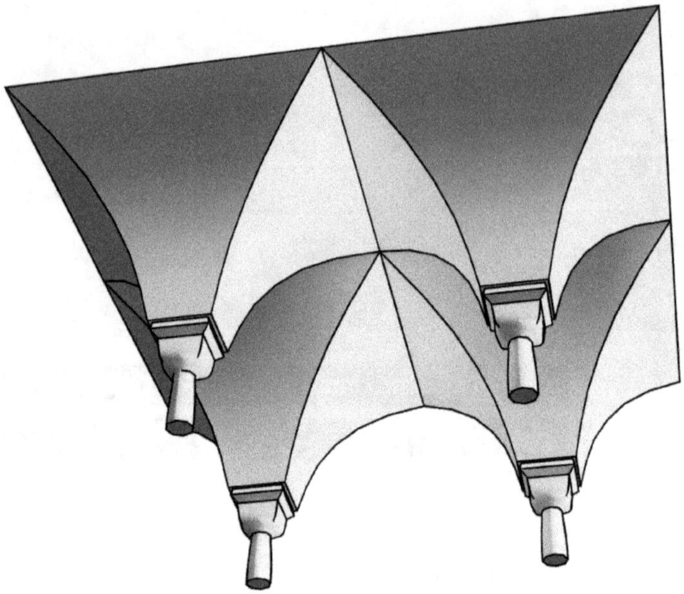

Figure 6.11: Vaulted ceiling viewed from below

At first, one could think of such a figure as unrelated to the work carried out so far: our Geometry Nodes generate columns, not arches. Still, an arched vault can be built with adjacent, smoothly tapered blocks, so we can model the ceiling using the nodes that were just marked as assets.

Creating smooth arches

We can drag our nodes from the **Asset Browser** and override a model geometry. We will use the **Abacus** setup, which is simpler:

1. Start a new Blender scene. If the default **Cube** is not present for some reason, create a new one with **Add | Mesh**.
2. Move to the **Assets** workspace created in *Chapter 4*, or alternatively, arrange the layout so that both **Asset Browser** and Viewport are displayed.
3. In the **Asset Browser**, switch to the catalog **BlendToUni**, drag **GN-Abacus** onto the **Viewport**, and release it over the **Cube**.
4. The object will assume the tapered shape of **Abacus**, which follows the Unity orientation. Select the cube and use the command **Add | Empty | Y-Up Axis** from *Chapter 4* to orient it properly.
5. Rename the object to `Vault` for clarity.

The arches of the vault are rather big as they take most of the upper space. We can set the size of a single block using the exposed modifier attributes:

1. Switch to the **Geometry Nodes** workspace.
2. In the modifier's properties, set **Width** to `6.0` and **Height** to `4.0` to match the size from the concept.

The shape generated by **GN-Abacus** is too blocky, so we will refine its curvature:

1. In the **Node Editor**, rename the node tree from **GN-Abacus** to `GN-Vault`. If the node tree is grayed out and not editable, it means that it was linked rather than appended. In that case, clicking any of the *Chain*, *Pack*, or *Duplicate* buttons in the header localizes the tree.
2. Look for the node **Float Curve** and select its control point in the middle. Change the interpolation mode to Auto Handle by clicking the first button on the left, beneath the curve, as in *Figure 6.12*.

Now the curve interpolates the width smoothly along the height of the model. We'll leave the control point on the right at the position (`1.0`, `0.5`) to ensure that the top of the model fits the Width set in the modifier, but we will reposition the other two:

1. With the central point still selected, set its X and Y coordinates to `0.6` and `0.25`, respectively.
2. Select the first control point and set its coordinates to (`0.0`, `0.1`).

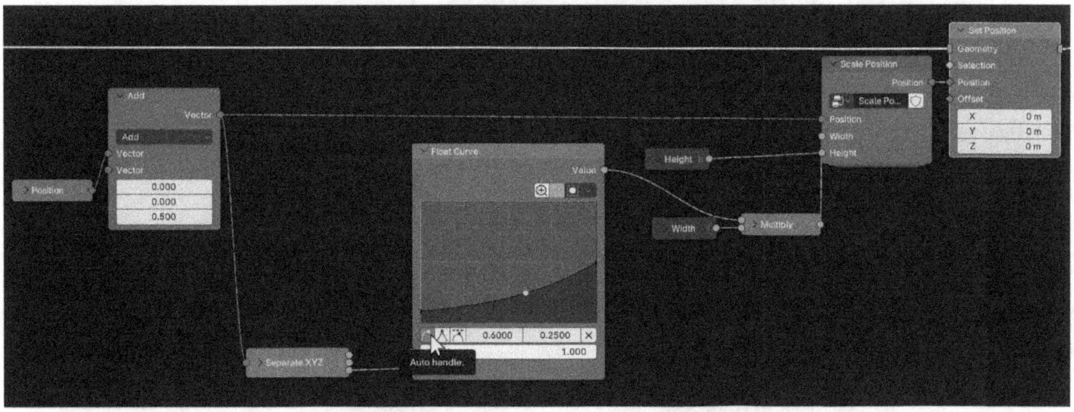

Figure 6.12: Smooth curvature for the arches

This curve will increase the section width gradually as the model reaches the roof, but we need more sections to get a smooth arc:

1. Select the **Cylinder** node; it's the first node of the tree.
2. Set the attribute **Side Segments** to 8.

We have modeled the building block of the vault, a quadrilateral shape with a half arch on each side. By repeating this shape, we will cover the entire colonnade.

Extending a model with arrays

Repeated patterns are not uncommon in models; for instance, chains or stairs can be broken down into identical links or steps. In Blender, we can repeat a model along a direction using an **array**, a modifier which creates rows of duplicates:

1. Select the model and click the **Add Modifier** button in the Modifiers panel on the right.
2. In the **Add Modifier** menu, select **Generate** | **Array** to create a new modifier.

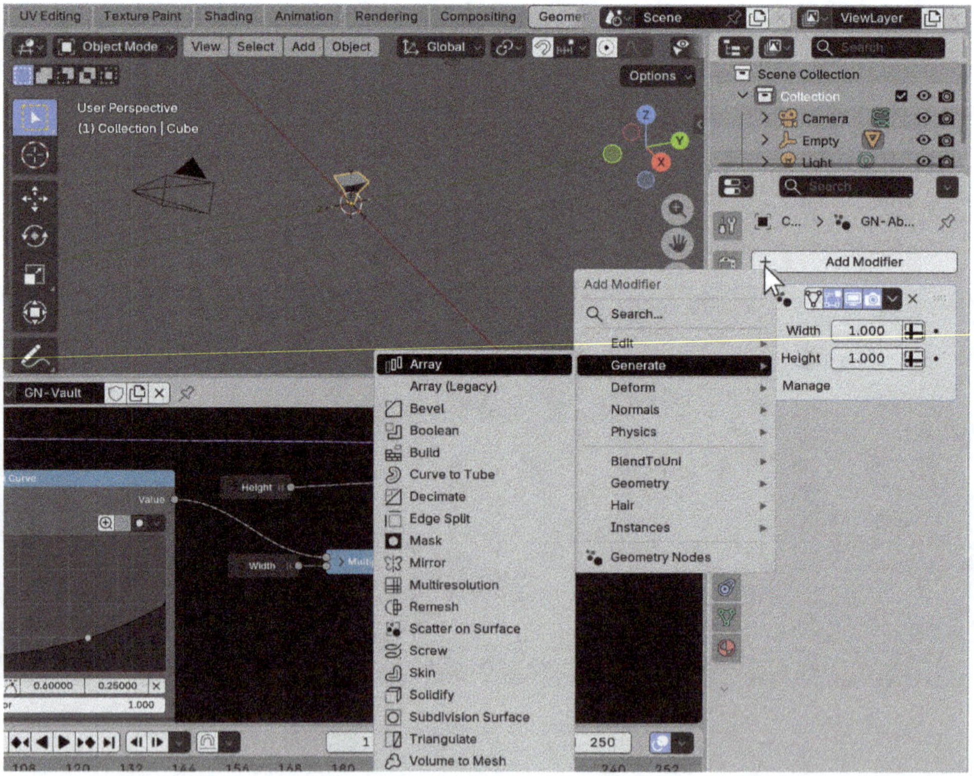

Figure 6.13: Adding an Array modifier

By default, *array* repeats the geometry three times along the *X* axis. Our map features two rows of four columns each, plus one arch per side to cover the walls, so we need to change the parameters of the modifier:

1. The **Modifier** panel displays the **Array** attributes. Set **Count** to 6.
2. Adjacent copies means that the duplicate vertices of the borders overlap at each junction. We don't want that, so we enable the **Merge** checkbox in the **Array** properties.

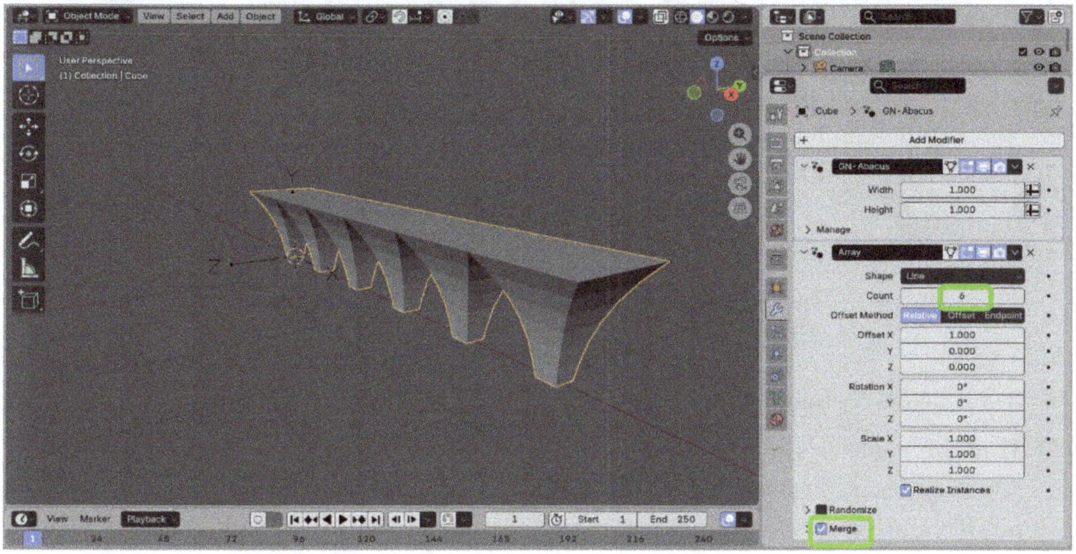

Figure 6.14: Forming five arches with no double vertices

To create the second row of columns, we will add another array:

1. In the **Add Modifier** menu, select **Generate** | **Array** to create a second **Array** modifier. It will duplicate the entire row generated by the previous modifier.
2. The new array should span towards the *Z* axis of the model, not *X*, so we set **Offset** | **X** to `0.0` and **Offset** | **Z** to `1.0`.
3. Set **Count** to 4: two rows for covering the columns and two for leaning against the wall.
4. Enable **Merge** to weld adjacent vertices.

The result of chaining two Array modifiers is four adjacent rows of five arches, as we can see in *Figure 6.15*.

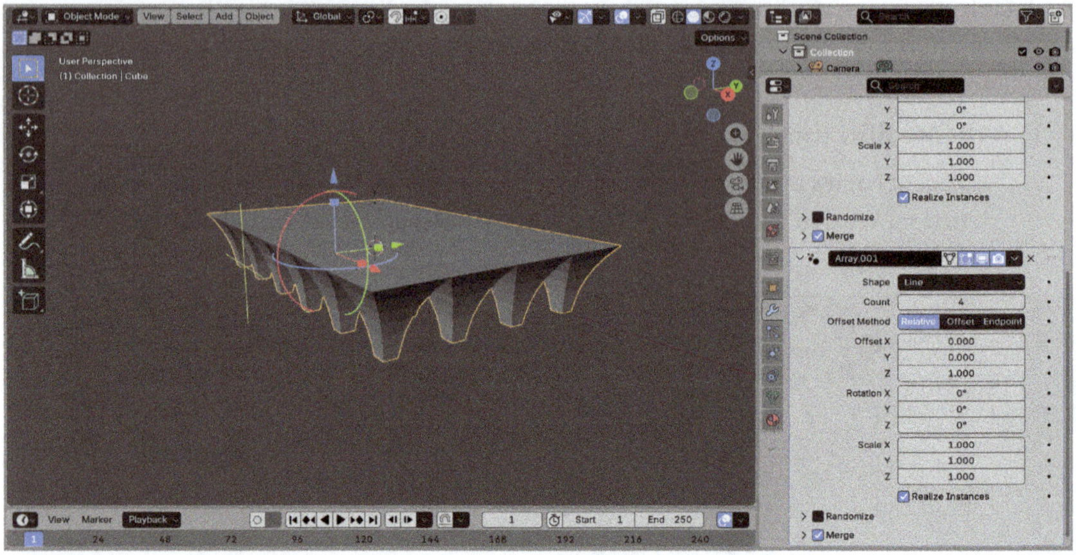

Figure 6.15: Generating a colonnade with two Array modifiers

> **Note**
>
> **It was Geometry Nodes all the time!**
>
> The **Array** modifier is implemented using Geometry Nodes, only this time Blender takes care of setting up the graph: the **Node Editor** displays the **Array** node tree when the modifier is selected. A legacy option that does not rely on geometry nodes is available for compatibility.

We have generated a colonnade for our level, but it doesn't match the position on the map. We need to place it so that it fits the level blocking.

Positioning the geometry

The building block of our arrays is centered at the origin, so the generated model spans through the positive *X* axis. We need to center the colonnade instead, so we are going to offset the mesh. It helps if we check the placement with the blocking created with **ProBuilder**. We made it an asset in *Chapter 4*, so it is easy to bring into our scene:

1. From the **Asset Browser**, drag and release **Crypt Blocking** into the **3D Viewport**.
2. The object is positioned at the drop point, so we must clear its location. Rather than *Alt + G*, we can use the viewport command *right-click* | **Lock at Origin**, created in *Chapter 4* as well.

We can see that our vault is displaced; we should move it toward the left on the *X* axis.

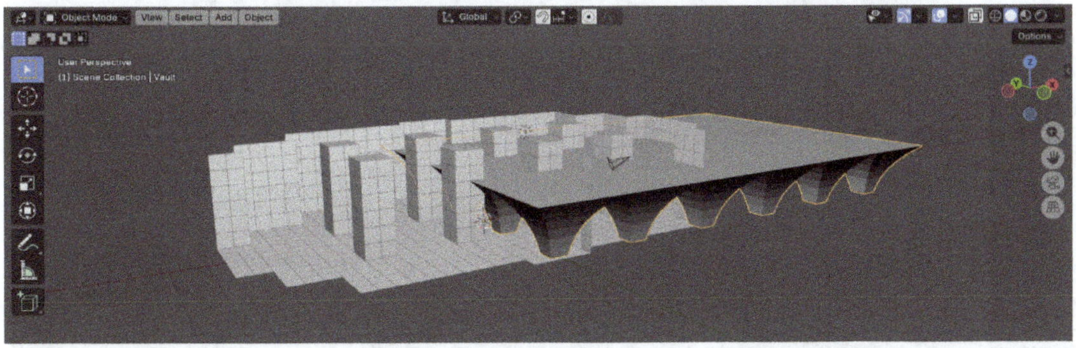

Figure 6.16: Our roof is out of place with respect to the map

We don't want to change the transform channel of the vault, as the `Roof` asset should be in place without any transformations; we will change the placement in the `GN-Vault` node tree:

1. Make sure that `Vault` is selected; the **Node Editor** will display the node tree of the last `Array`, not `GN-Vault`.
2. In the **Modifiers** panel, click the first modifier at the top. The **Node Editor** will display `GN-Vault`.
3. Reach the **Transform Geometry** node at the right end of the graph. Click the channel **Translation** | **X** with the *left mouse button* and keep it pressed while moving the mouse sideways to move the model.
4. Keep the *Ctrl* key pressed too to enable stepped values while scrolling until the vault matches the columns from the blocking; the exact value is `-15`.
5. Likewise, change the value of **Translation** | **Z** until the inner arches match the columns from the blocking. The exact value is `-9`.
6. Set **Translation** | **Y** to `2` to match the height of the columns and roof.

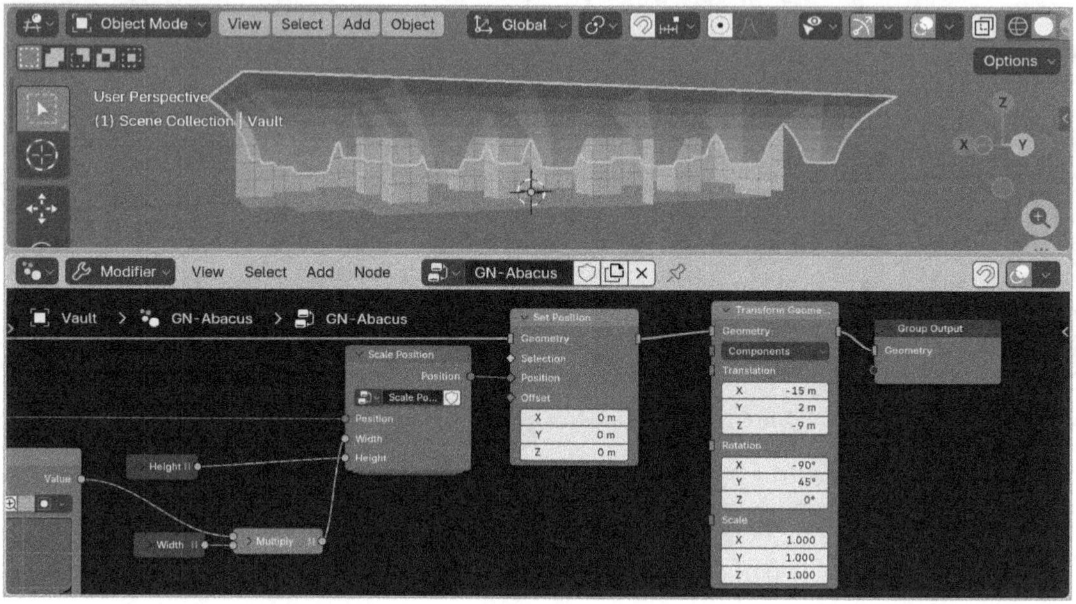

Figure 6.17: Placement of the colonnade

The roof is almost finished; now we must account for the entrance and exit corridors.

Extruding the corridors

Although the wall created during blocking is a closed room, the game requires a way in and a way out of the level.

We can create a roof for the two corridors with a new **Geometry Nodes** modifier:

1. With the `Vault` selected, in the modifiers panel, click **Add Modifier** and choose **Geometry Nodes**, the last entry in the menu.
2. Click the **New** button in the **Node Editor**'s header to create a new node tree.
3. Rename the tree to `GN-Corridors`.

To create the entrance, insert an extrusion operation in the graph:

1. In the **Node Editor**, bring up the **Add** menu with *Shift + A* or from the menu bar, then type ext and click **Extrude Mesh**.
2. Insert the new node between **Group Input** and **Group Output**. The result will be a bit messy, but we are going to fix it.
3. Disable the **Extrude Mesh | Individual** checkbox, as we want the extruded faces to stick together.

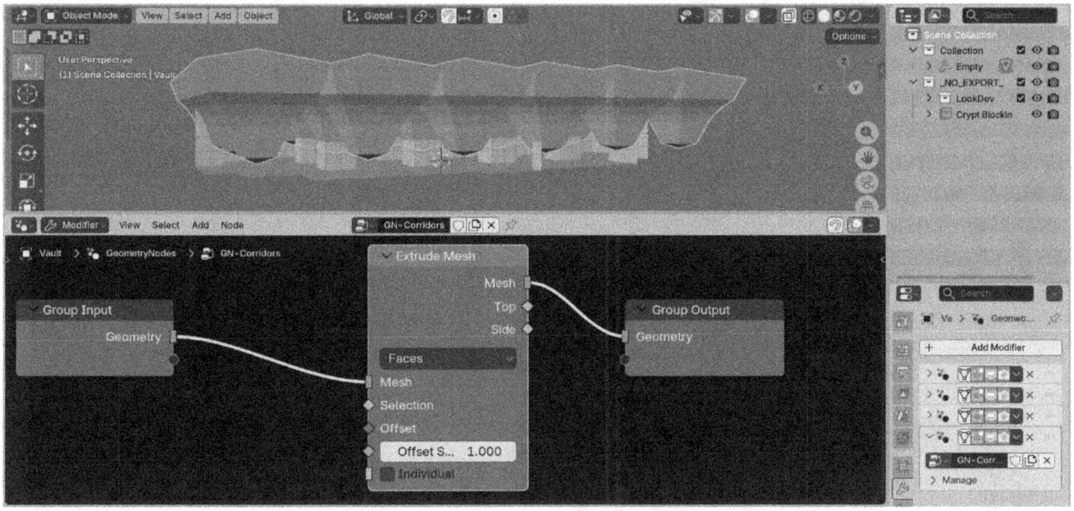

Figure 6.18: Extruding through an additional modifier

We only want to extrude the border polygons on the long sides, so we add a condition to the extrusion:

1. Add a **Position** node to the graph (*Shift* + *A*, type `pos`, and click **Position**).
2. Drag the **Position** | **Position** socket and release it on the clear area, then click **Separate XYZ** in the menu.
3. Now drag and release the **Z** from **Separate XYZ**, then create a **Greater Than** node.
4. Connect **Greater Than** | **Result** to **Extrude Mesh** | **Selection**.
5. The default value of **Greater Than** | **B** is `0.0`, so only the positive side of the mesh is extruded. Set it to `9.0` since the entrance is ten meters from the center.

This way, we extrude only the faces at more than nine meters right of the origin. The default behavior extrudes along the face normals, but we just want to push the new faces horizontally. We create an input vector for the offset:

1. Drag the socket **Extrude Mesh** | **Offset** and release it on the clear. Select **Combine XYZ**.
2. Connect **Separate XYZ** | **Z** to **Combine XYZ** | **Z** to set the corridor length.

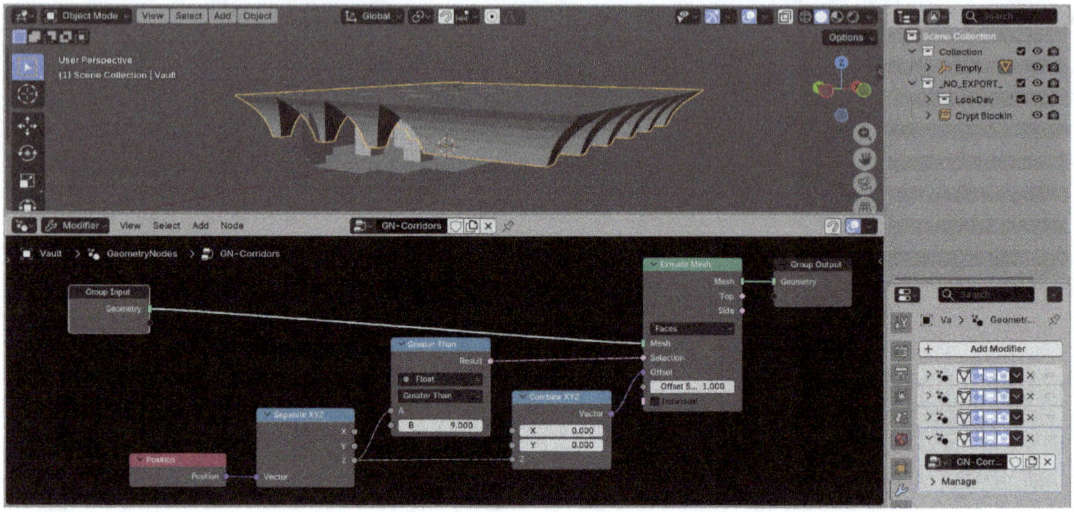

Figure 6.19: Creating corridors by extruding one side

Now the corridor is as long as the distance between the entrance and the origin. We could duplicate this setup and extrude the other side, but a smarter approach makes the same nodes work in both directions:

1. In the **Node Editor**, press *Shift + A* and add a **Math | Absolute** node.
2. Insert the new node between **Separate XYZ | Z** and **Greater Than | A**: now the extrusion affects both sides of the model, positive and negative *Z*.

The node **Absolute** makes all values positive, so that the arches are extruded on the negative and positive *X* coordinates: we have created five corridors per side.

We do not need so many, but the model is good to go: the wall closes the extra corridors, as we are going to open only two "doors" in the middle.

We finalize the model by smoothing its surface:

1. In the **Node Editor**, press *Shift + A* and add a **Smooth by Angle** node.
2. Insert the new node between **Extrude Mesh** and **Group Output**.
3. Enable the **Ignore Sharpness** checkbox for smoothing. The default value of `30` degrees is already good.

The model is ready; we will make sure that no object other than `Vault` is exported:

1. Select *Vault* and the *Empty*, then press *Ctrl + I* to invert the selection. **Light**, **Camera**, and **Crypt Blocking** will be selected.

2. Press *M* to invoke the **Move** menu and select **New Collection**.
3. Type `_NO_EXPORT_` for the name and press *Enter* or the **Create** button.

With all the extra objects inside `_NO_EXPORT_`, we can use the same script as in `Column.blend` to exclude them from the Unity import:

1. Switch to the **Scripting** workspace.
2. Click the **Open** button in the **Text Editor**'s header.
3. Reach the folder `BlendToUni_URP` | `_blender_scripts_` | `events`.
4. Select the file `on_scene_load.py` and press *Enter* or the **Open Text** button.
5. Enable the **Register** checkbox in the **Text** menu.

We can finally save the scene for the Unity project:

1. Click **File** | **Save As...** from the top bar menu.
2. Reach the folder `BlendToUni_URP` | `Assets` | `Art` | `Models`.
3. Type `Roof.blend` in the filename and press `Enter` or the **Save As** button.

Now that the `.blend` file is in the game folder, Unity will load it and display a new entry in the **Project Browser**.

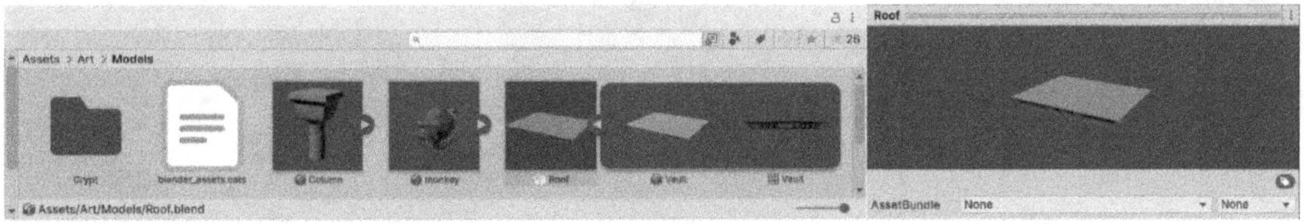

Figure 6.20: The Roof asset in Unity

We assemble the actual game level by starting with the blocking created in *Chapter 3*.

Assembling in Unity

Finishing the models is only the first part of the job: we need to place them in the game editor and make sure that they match the level design. We will use the existing white-box models as placeholders.

Placing the models

When modeling **Column** and **Roof**, we have accounted for the measurements from the concept art and the blocking, so the models fit the level design.

We can start with the map created with *ProBuilder* and place the new assets there:

1. Open the Unity project `BlendToUni_URP`.
2. With the **Project Browser**, navigate to the folder `Assets` | `Level` | `Scenes`.
3. *Double-click* the scene **CryptBlocking** to open it.

Unity will load the white-box version of the crypt and display it in the viewport. We will replace the pillars with the column modeled in Blender:

1. Select all the columns in the level. This can be done easily in the **Hierarchy** by selecting the first object named `Cube` with a *left mouse click* and, while keeping *Shift* pressed, selecting the last one.
2. With all eight columns selected, *right-click* one of them in the **Hierarchy** and, in the menu, click the **Prefab** | **Replace...** entry.

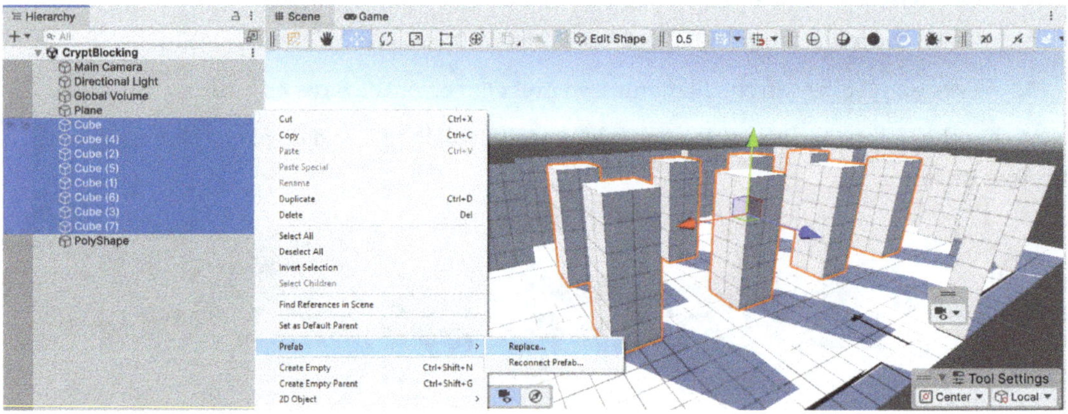

Figure 6.21: Replacing the rough pillars with a different asset

3. In the selection dialog, select **Column** to replace the ProBuilder shapes with the Blender model.

While ProBuilder blocks have their center of coordinates at their middle, our columns have their pivot at the origin, so they will be floating three meters above the ground after the switch, as we can see from their **Position** | **Y** in the **Transform** panel.

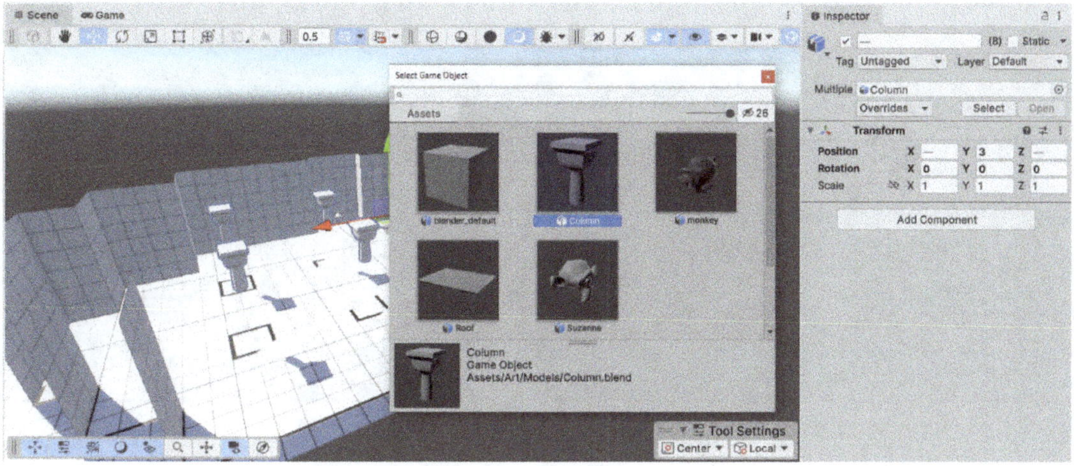

Figure 6.22: Our columns inherited the coordinates of the blocks

We can fix that in their **Position** coordinates:

1. With all columns still selected, click the **Position** | **Y** field in the **Transform** panel on the right
2. Set the value to `0.0` and press *Enter*.

Now that all the columns are positioned, we can place the ceiling:

1. In the **Project Browser**, reach the folder `Assets` | `Art` | `Models`.
2. Drag the asset `Roof` with the *left mouse button* and drop it on the **Viewport**.
3. Set the roof **Position X**, **Y**, and **Z** values to `0.0` manually or, in the **Viewport**, use *right-click* | **Transform** | **Reset Property** | **Position** to place it at the origin.

The ceiling covers the view if we look at the scene from above, but by taking a tour inside the room, we will see how our location has improved.

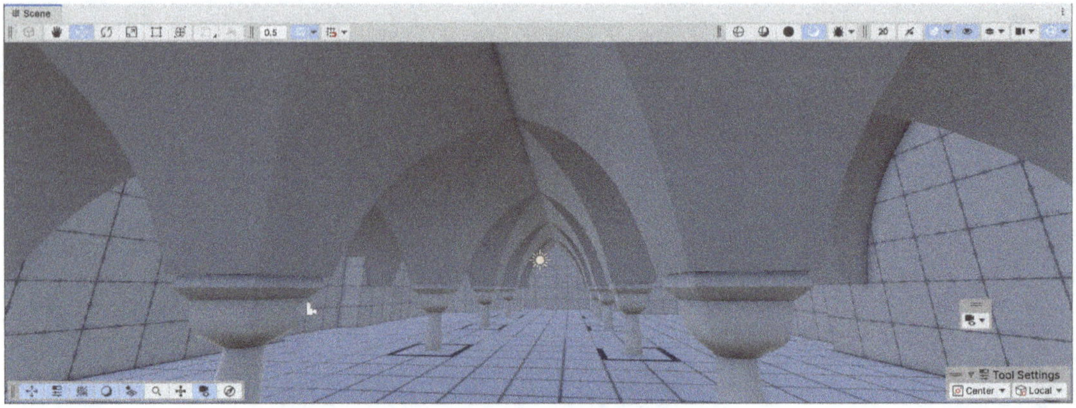

Figure 6.23: Visiting our model in Unity

We are keeping the **PolyShape** room modeled in ProBuilder, as it serves its purpose quite well, but we need to carve the corridors for entering and exiting the level.

Editing the polyshape

When drawing the room in *Chapter 3*, we haven't accounted for the in and out corridors, but we can push the **PolyShape** walls to create an entrance and an exit:

1. Select the room, either with a *left mouse click* on the walls in Unity's **Scene** viewport or by selecting **PolyShape** in the **Hierarchy** view.
2. Click the **Active Context** drop-down button, the first on the left in the **Viewport**'s header, change it from **Game Object** to **ProBuilder**.

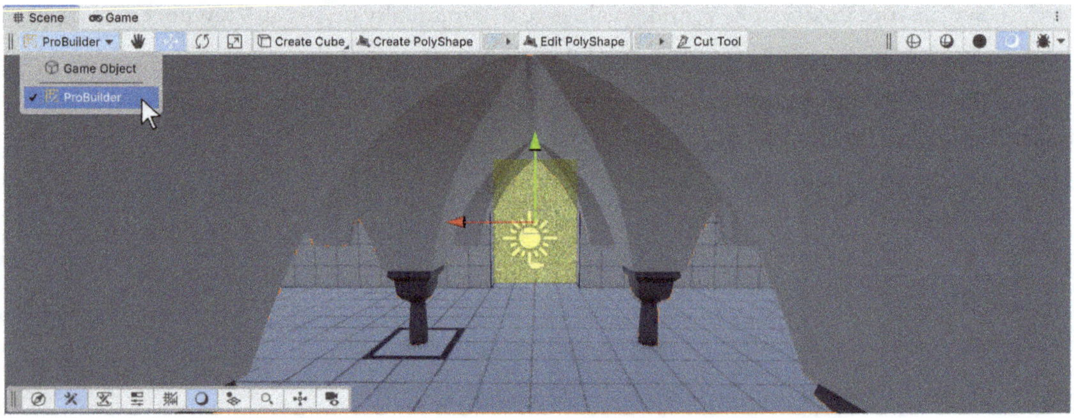

Figure 6.24: Selecting faces in the ProBuilder context

The *ProBuilder* context allows us to select and displace the faces of *PolyShape*. This way, we can push the walls to make way:

1. Select the central face of the crypt wall, where the exit is supposed to be, with a *left mouse click*, like in *Figure 6.23*.
2. The extrude manipulator appears. Press *F* to focus on the selection and rotate the view so that you can drag it along the *Z* axis.
3. Keep *Ctrl* pressed to enable grid snapping, grab the blue arrow (*Z*) with the left mouse button, and pull it out for nine units to extrude a corridor until it matches the length of the roof, as shown in *Figure 6.24*.

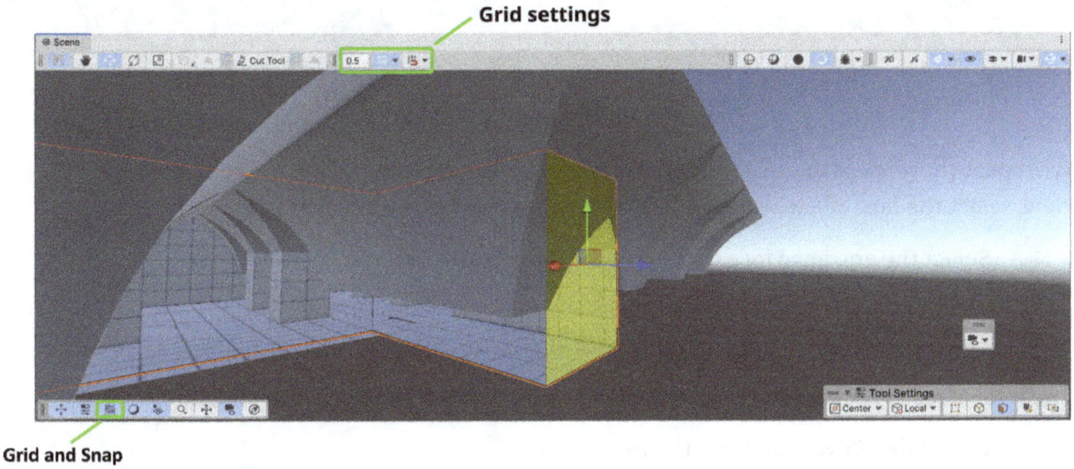

Figure 6.25: Extruded corridor and grid tools buttons

We must also adapt the corridor to the arch width, which is one unit wider than the distance between walls. We need to push the two side walls by half a unit each to match the width of the arches, so we change the step in the **Grid and Snap** settings.

The **Grid Size** can be set in the **Grid and Snap** toolbar on the **Viewport** header. If it is not visible, it can be enabled with the **Grid and Snap** toggle on the lower-left bar, highlighted in *Figure 6.25*.

To enlarge the corridor and fit the arc:

1. Change the **Grid Size** from **1** to `0.5` in the **Grid** settings.
2. Rotate the view and select one of the long walls of the corridor.
3. Keeping the *Ctrl* key pressed, snap it by `0.5` units on the *X* axis and match its side to the arch.
4. Do the same with the opposite wall of the corridor.

As a result, the walls will stay behind the vaulted arch, as in *Figure 6.26*.

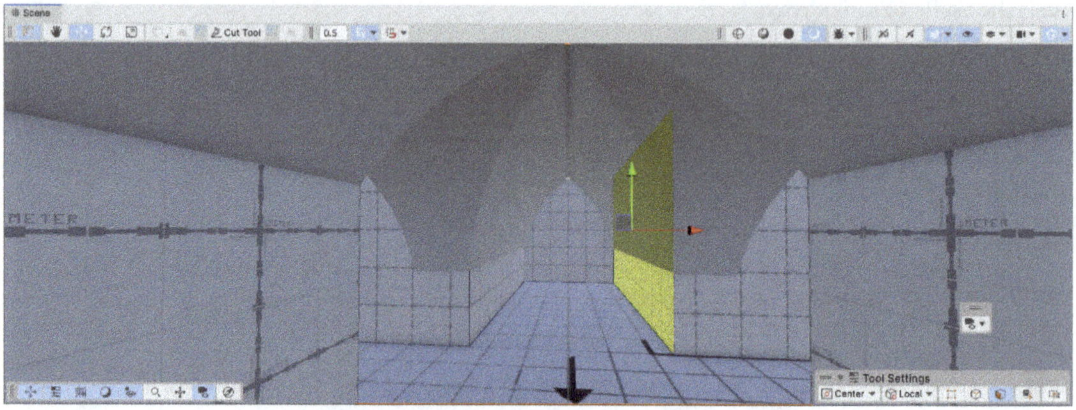

Figure 6.26: Fitting the width of the corridors

We repeat those steps to create the corridor at the opposite side of the room, so we rotate the view, select the face of the walled entrance, and perform the same actions:

1. Select the entrance face in the middle and press *F* to focus.
2. Push it back by 9 units along the *Z* axis to match the border of the roof.
3. Move the lateral walls aside by half a unit each to match the width of the vault.

The level is ready for exploration; we will save a new scene alongside *CryptBlocking*:

1. Click **File** | **Save As...** from the top menu.
2. Reach the folder **Level** | **Scenes** in the `Assets` directory.
3. Type `Crypt` as the filename and press the **Save** button.

The materials are still missing, but we can play around with this map and get a glimpse of how the level looks. The overlap between the concept map Plane and the floor causes some artifacts, as Unity can't tell for sure which polygons should be rendered. We will keep it for now, as it can still be useful to mark the starting point of the game.

Summary

In this chapter, we have automated the asset clean-up in a safe way, reused and expanded the Geometry Nodes from the previous chapter, and finally brought everything back to Unity by assembling the level.

The elements of our map come together naturally, and the level starts looking more like a game scene and less like a placeholder; we will finalize the environment and make it explorable in *Part 3, Shading and Playing*.

In *Chapter 7*, we will create the materials for this location.

Part 3

Shading and Playing

Now that we have modeled and placed our assets, we need to finalize our project by creating materials and addressing the hardware input. Materials are created in Unity, as it is the end application, but we will still generate the texture maps and the playable character in Blender.

In the next two chapters, you will learn how to merge Blender and Unity physically based rendering (**PBR**) systems. In the last chapter, you will create a very simple character and play it in Game mode using the new input system.

This part of the book includes the following chapters:

- *Chapter 7, Shading the Models*
- *Chapter 8, Baking Detail Maps*
- *Chapter 9, Creating Gameplay and Animation*

7

Shading the Models

The visual development of a game involves artistic choices of color and appearance, applied to 3D models using shaders—that is, recipes for translating polygons to colors on the screen.

Working on the look entails the definition of materials, the application of textures, considerations about the workflow, the adoption of specific software, the exchange of surface properties, and ultimately the imaging workflow.

Allocating the detail between geometry and shading is part of the task. Modern systems can reproduce the behavior of light realistically but, to a certain degree, look development delivers an illusion of reality through visual tricks, like painted details and optical effects.

We will bring color to our game by creating shaders and textures for our models. This chapter covers the following topics:

- Creating textures for Unity in Blender
- Creating shaders and material properties
- Texturing generated models

Technical requirements

We will use *Blender 5.1* and *Unity 6.3*, which can be installed by following the instructions from *Chapter 1* or from their respective websites.

You can download the example project and code for this book by following the instructions in the *Download the example code files* section in the *Preface* of this book.

This chapter's code files are included in the downloadable code bundle.

Creating textures for PBR shaders

The appearance of real-world objects is conditioned by many factors, like microscopic features of the surface, composition, exact shape, and consistency. Three-dimensional models don't contain that much information, so algorithms called sh**aders** define how they look according to a set of parameters.

In *Chapter 2,* we created materials for *Suzanne,* the monkey head model included with Blender. In 3D, a **material** attaches a shader to one or more objects. Besides connecting shaders and objects, materials pass information like color and other properties, allowing real-time editing of the shader parameters. Blender materials are part of the scene file, while in Unity they are assets of the project.

Both systems take into account the physical properties of light and surfaces.

Understanding physically based rendering

Almost all modern renderers implement **physically based rendering** (**PBR**), an approach that relies on the study of reflectance and optics.

Physically based shaders are versatile and can produce realistic or stylized outputs. The concept is that rough surfaces absorb more light than smooth ones, and metallic objects reflect more light than insulators.

The usual steps in PBR materialing involve setting up the base color of a surface, its roughness, metallicity, and additional parameters such as opacity and light transmission.

As we learned in *Chapter 2,* Blender and Unity provide Node Editors for setting up the shaders. There are exchange formats for shaders, but generally it is better to create them in the final application, in this case the game engine, which is what the players are going to see. We can use Blender for creating textures and details.

Before starting, a rough painting of the desired look can help you figure out the intended result. It doesn't need much detail and can be a paint-over, like the one in *Figure 7.1.*

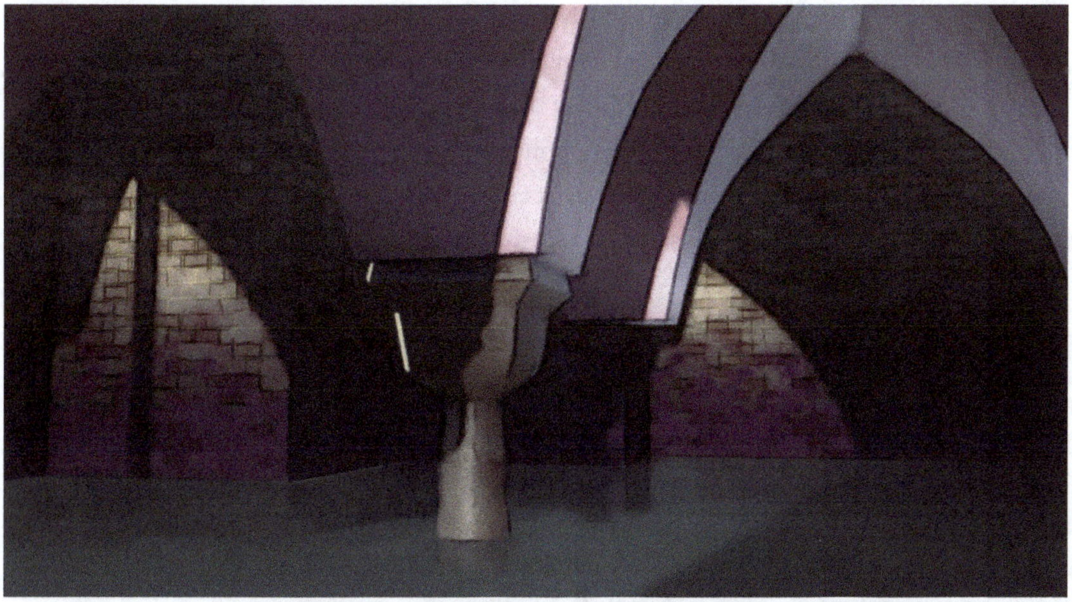

Figure 7.1: Concept illustration of the colors

The vault and the columns have a plastered look, while the walls have visible bricks; we are going to create images for texturing these details.

Creating textures in Blender

Geometry alone cannot contain all visual information. Textures are images or patterns attached to the surface of an object, like a sticker or wrapping would do in real life.

They can contain color but also geometric features like surface normals, where three axes of displacement are stored as the red, green, and blue channels of an image.

Image textures can be painted manually with Blender's *Texture Paint* or other painting applications, or generated procedurally, and are displayed on objects by projecting them onto a plane, the two axes of which are named **U** and **V**—that is, the UV plane.

We can create the textures for our brick wall in Blender, using a plane for displaying and capturing the images:

1. Start a new scene in Blender.
2. Delete the **Cube** from the default scene.
3. Press *Shift + A* and create a new **Mesh | Plane**.

Then we need a material for assigning the texture:

1. Switch to the **Shading** workspace using the tabs at the top.
2. Select the *Material* tab at the bottom of the properties panel on the left.
3. Click the **+ New** button to create a new material.
4. Double-click the new material in the list and rename it `Bricks`.

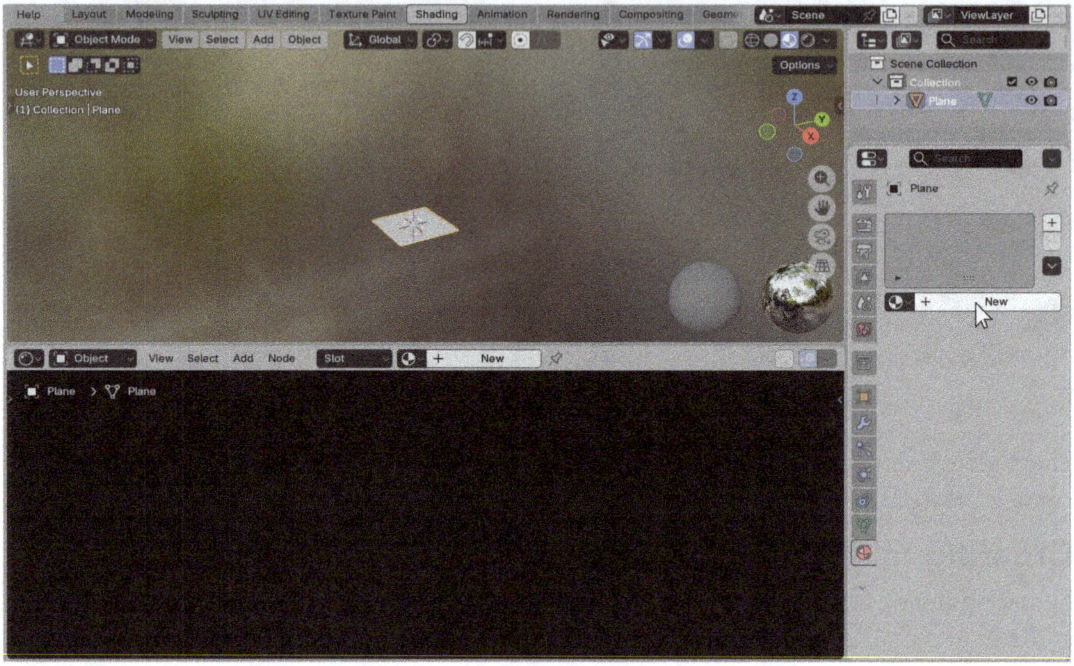

Figure 7.2: Assigning material to plane

The **Node Editor** will display a new material graph. It resembles the **Geometry Nodes** editor and operates similarly, but most nodes are different. The initial setup is a Principled BSDF connected to the Material Output.

The letters **BSDF** stand for **Bidirectional Scattering Distribution Function**. That name describes the two directions of incoming and reflected light rays spreading across the surface of an object.

Principled is an all-purpose shader, useful for many kinds of surfaces; we are not rendering in Blender, so we are only using it for creating image textures.

The default base color is light gray, almost white, and we will replace it with a texture of bricks. Textures are nodes and can be created with the **Add** menu or the *Shift + A* combination, but we can also create and connect inputs in the **Material** tab:

1. The material properties display the parameters of the shader. Click the **yellow dot** on the **Base Color** to select an input.
2. Textures are in the second column of the pop-up menu. Click **Brick Texture** to connect a texture of bricks.

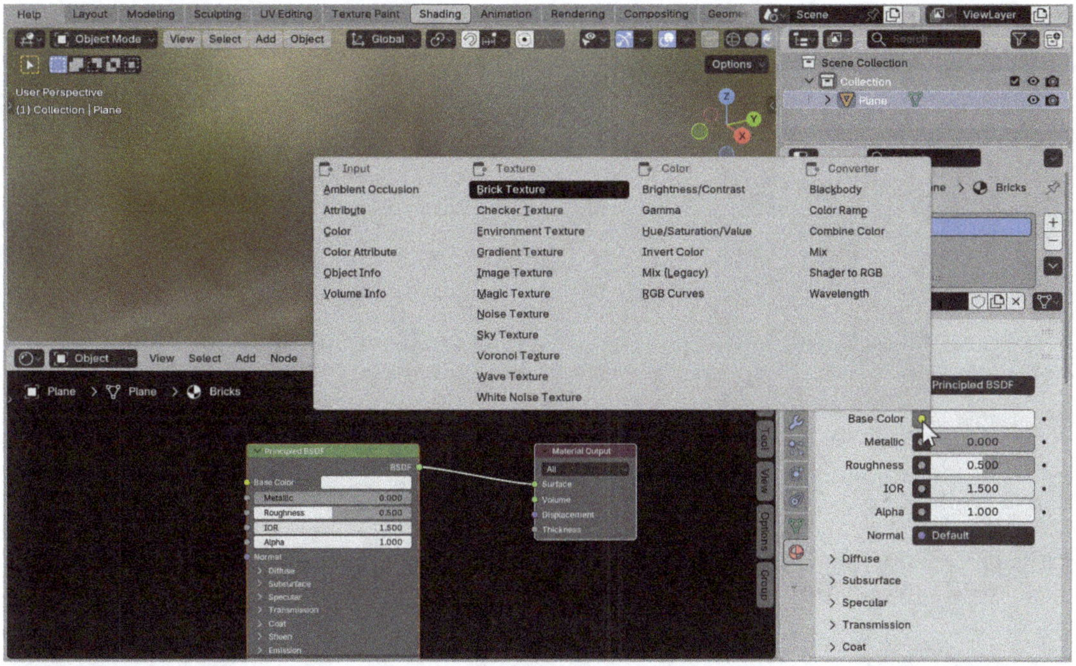

Figure 7.3: Creating bricks in Blender

A **Brick Texture** was connected to the shader, as we can see by looking at **Viewport**. We can get a better view by looking directly at our plane:

1. In the **3D Viewport**, press *7* on the numeric keypad or select **View** | **Viewpoint** | **Top** from the header to look at the scene from above.
2. The **Top** view switches to **Orthographic** mode, where perspective and some of the shading are disabled. Press *5* on the numeric keypad or select **View** | **Perspective / Orthographic** to enable perspective.
3. Make sure that the plane is selected and press the dot (.) on the numeric keypad or **View** | **Frame Selected** from the header to zoom closer.

Brick Texture has three parameters for the color of the bricks and one for the grout lines in between; we are going to set up a red/brown pattern:

1. Click **Color 1** and pick a light orange from the color wheel or, in HSV mode, set **Hue**, **Saturation**, and **Value** to `0.05`, `0.3`, and `0.9`, respectively.
2. Click **Color 2** and pick a mid-brown from the wheel or, in HSV mode, set its **Hue**, **Saturation**, and **Value** to `0.02`, `0.3`, and `0.65`, respectively.
3. Click the **Mortar** color and pick a light beige, or set **Hue**, **Saturation**, and **Value** to `0.1`, `0.3`, and `0.8`, respectively.

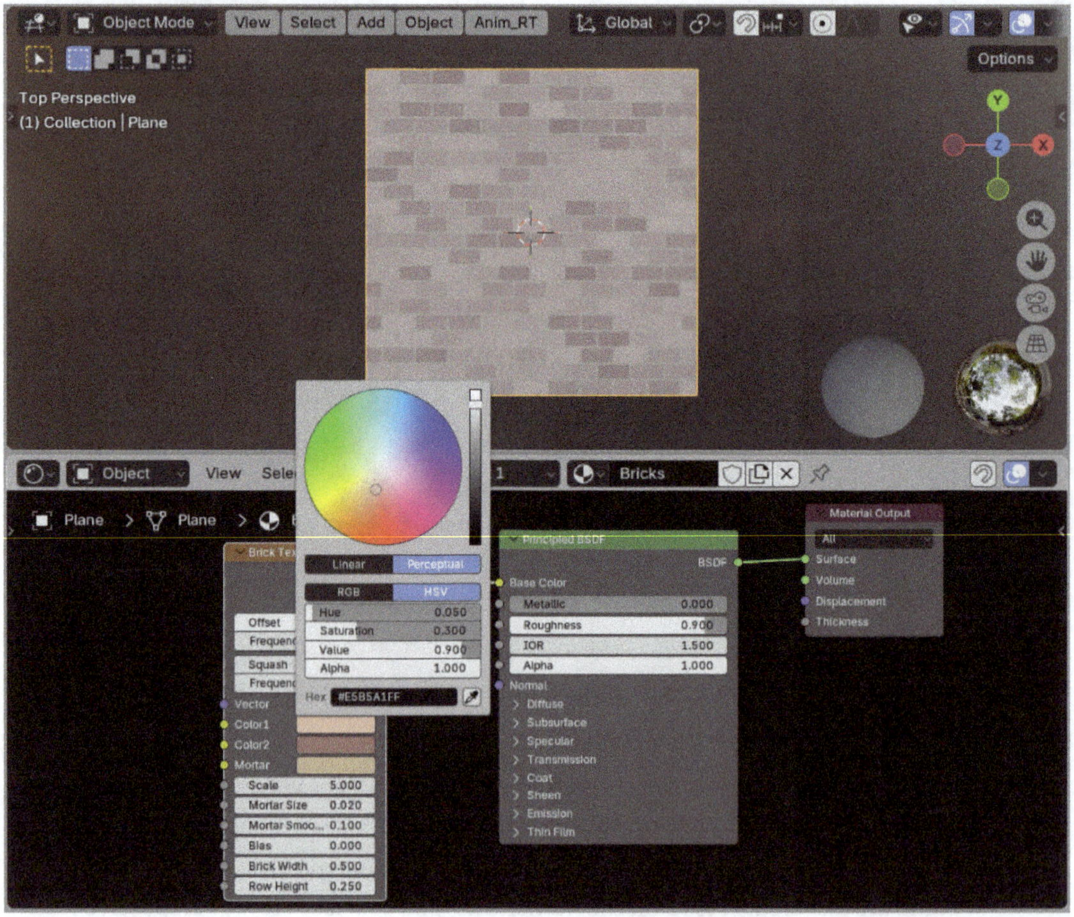

Figure 7.4: Procedural bricks in Blender

We can't translate this node to Unity as it is; we will export its colors to an image.

Baking textures to image files

In computer graphics, **baking** refers to storing the results of a computational process as static data. In this case, we are baking a procedural texture into an image. **EEVEE**, Blender's real-time renderer, doesn't support texture baking, so we switch the render engine to **Cycles**:

1. In the **Properties** on the right, click the **Render** tab, which is the second from the top and has a camera icon.
2. Set the **Render Engine** to **Cycles** with the drop-down box, like in *Figure 7.5*.

Cycles performs a full render when baking a map. It's not a real-time engine, so the process might take a few minutes; we are only exporting the input colors, not full renders, so we can decrease a few expensive parameters and settle for lower render quality:

1. In the **Sampling** properties, set **Render | Max Samples** to 8. It's way too low for rendering, but is good for baking color channels.
2. Disable the **Denoise** checkbox, as noise is not a concern.

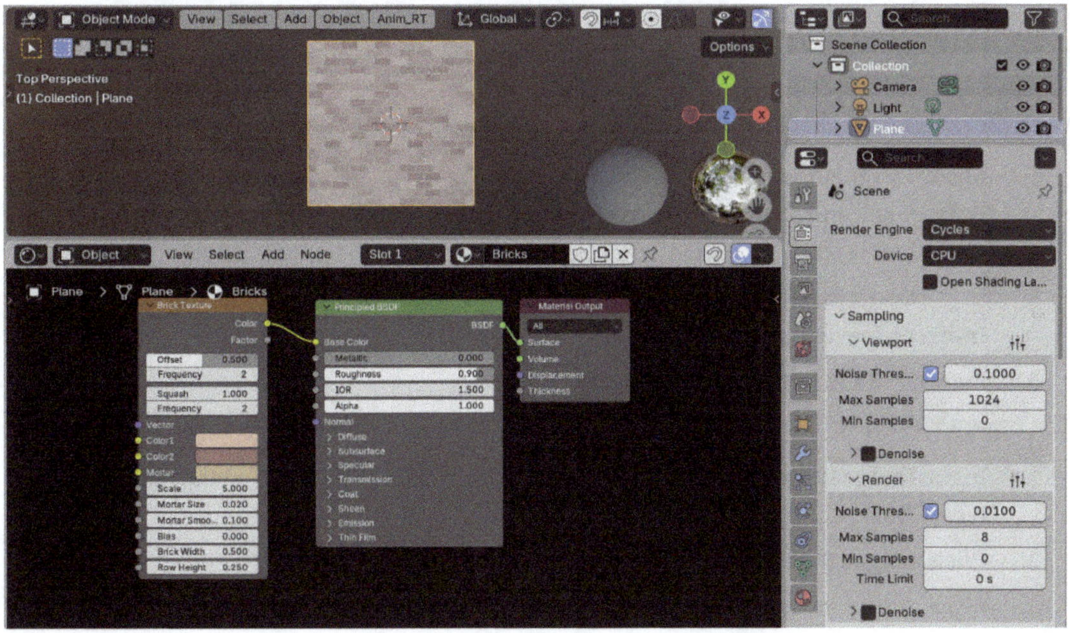

Figure 7.5: Cycles settings for fast baking

Those settings would produce ugly renders, but the baking of input channels will work just as well and take only a few seconds.

We need an image to bake to; it doesn't have to be connected, but it must be the active node of the shader graph:

1. In the **Shader Editor**, use *Shift + A* to add a **Texture | Image Texture** node.
2. The **Image Texture** doesn't point to any data yet: click its **New** button to create one.
3. The **Create a New Image** dialog asks for a **Name**: type `Bake Image` to recognize the new picture.
4. The default setting of **1024** pixels per side is fine, along with blank and the other parameters. We can click the **New Image** button to create it.
5. Click the **Bake Image** node to make it active. The black image will be displayed in the **Image Editor** on the left.

> Note
>
> **Focus on the picture!**
>
> Bakes are saved to the active image node of the graph, which is outlined. If a non-image node is active, baking will fail with an error.

With the image data allocated and active, we can bake the base color input:

1. Make sure that the plane is selected, scroll down in the **Render** properties, expand the **Bake** panel, and change the **Bake Type** from **Combined** to **Diffuse** with the drop-down box.
2. In the **Contributions | Contributions** settings, uncheck the channels **Direct** and **Indirect**, leaving only **Color** active.
3. Press the **Bake** button to start the process.

The **Image Viewer** will display the baked pattern that we can save directly to the game project:

1. In the **Image Editor**, click the "**hamburger**" button to display the menu, as shown in *Figure 7.6*.
2. Click **Image | Save As...**
3. Reach the folder `BlendToUni_URP` | `Assets` | `Art`, create a new directory with the header button or right-click | **New Folder**, and name it `Textures`.

4. Enter the `Textures` folder, set the filename to `bricks_base`.
5. Make sure that the **File Format** is set to **PNG (.png)** in the dialog preferences, set **Color** to **RGB**, and click **Save As**.

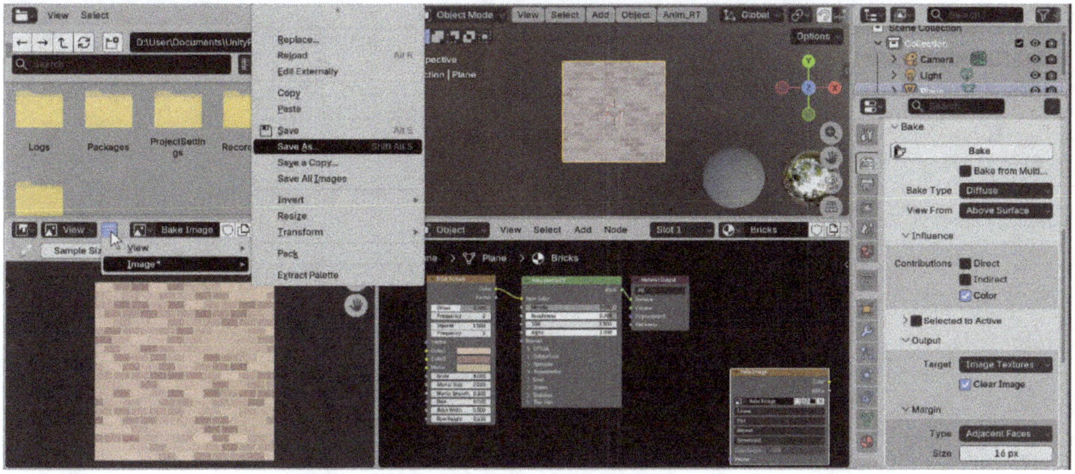

Figure 7.6: Baking and saving the brick colors

Besides the color, we can export other information like *roughness*. For rough surfaces like bricks, a value of `0.9` would be appropriate; the mortar lines should be slightly rougher, so we use the **Factor** output of the *Brick texture*, which is white on the mortar and black on the bricks:

1. In the **Node Editor**, connect **Brick Texture** | **Factor** to **Principled BSDF** | **Roughness**.
2. That makes the bricks too shiny. Press *Shift + A*, type `ramp`, and create a **Color Ramp** to adjust the black/white ratio of the input.
3. Insert the new node between **Brick Texture** | **Factor** and **Principled BSDF** | **Roughness**.
4. The first handle is selected. Click the black color and, in **HSV** space, set **Value** to `0.9`.

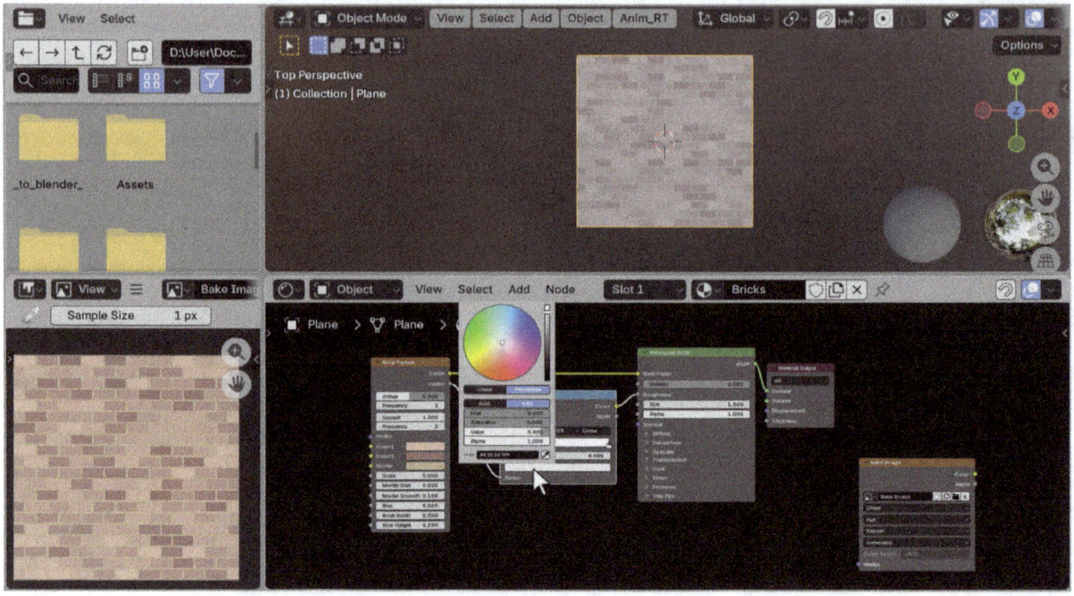

Figure 7.7: Using the brick factor for roughness

The difference is very subtle and only slightly noticeable under default lighting, but it conveys some variation to the unnatural flatness of 3D surfaces.

We can add more details with a height map, a gray texture where dark areas represent valleys and lighter shades are lit as bumps. We will use the *Factor* socket again:

1. In the **Node Editor**, with the *left mouse button*, drag the **Brick Texture** | **Factor** socket to a clear area, release, and type `bump`.
2. Select Bump | Height to create a connected **Bump** node.

A bump map pushes the lighting outwards where it is white and inwards where it is black. **Factor** is white on the mortar and black otherwise, the opposite of what we need since we want to carve the mortar, not the bricks. We can reverse the bump using the node settings:

1. Click the **Invert** checkbox on the **Bump** node to enable it.
2. Connect **Bump** | **Normal** to **Principled BSDF** | **Normal**.

A bump map is gray where it is neutral, i.e., where it doesn't affect the original surface. We have inverted the bump so that black (the bricks) means higher, so our white-to-black input should become white-to-gray. We can use another **Color Ramp** node:

1. In the **Node Editor**, press *Shift + A*, type `ramp`, and create a new `ColorRamp`.
2. Insert the new ColorRamp between **Brick Texture | Factor** and **Bump**.
3. Click on the black color and raise its value to `0.5`.

The effect is barely visible under the default lighting, although it can be noticed by looking at the plane very closely. We could tweak the **Bump** parameters and make it more evident by increasing **Distance** and **Strength**, but we don't need to—we will create the actual shader in Unity after exporting the textures.

Exporting multichannel textures

Roughness and Height are one-dimensional parameters, while RGB images can store three channels and potentially a fourth with alpha. Exporting two gray textures, for instance `roughness.png` and `height.png`, would waste two channels in each image.

Note

It's not all black and white

We can save a black and white picture to save space on disk, but Unity would still load it as an RGBA image: it's optimized for colorful pictures.

Storing multiple attributes as the Red, Green, Blue, and Alpha of one image is common practice in games: it saves precious memory, and dealing with fewer assets sometimes makes creating the shader easier.

Blender is not designed for that kind of workflow, but we can combine more inputs into one and connect the result to a color channel. In our case, we can use the **Emission** socket to bake height, softness, and occlusion into a single texture:

1. In the **Node Editor**, expand the **Principled BSDF | Emission** attributes.
2. Drag **Principled BSDF | Emission | Color** with the *left mouse button*, release it on the clear, type `comb`, and create a **Combine XYZ > Vector** node.
3. Connect the first **Color Ramp**, the one between **Brick Texture** and **Principled BSDF | Roughness**, to **Combine XYZ | X**.

4. Unity shaders have an Occlusion parameter for the regions that are less exposed to light. We can use the grout lines for that: connect **Brick Texture | Factor** to **Combine XYZ | Y.**
5. Connect the **Color Ramp** between **Brick Texture** and **Bump** to **Combine XYZ | Z.**

We have combined three different attributes into a color channel that we can bake.

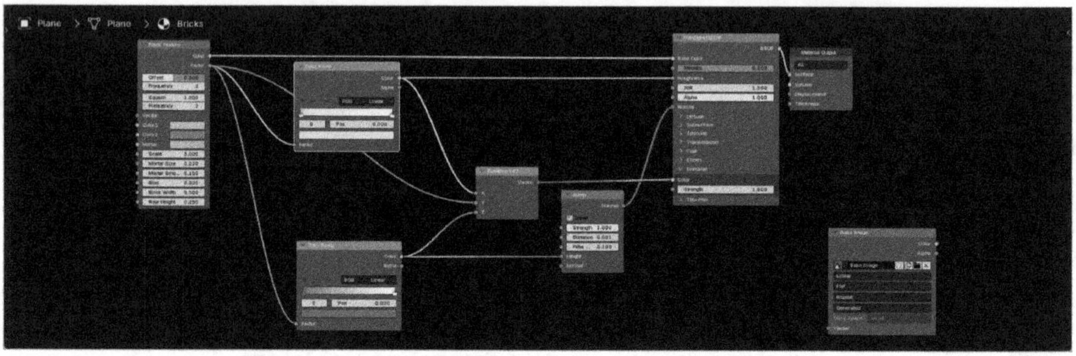

Figure 7.8: Combining roughness, occlusion, height into emission

> Note
>
> **Color or vector?**
>
> The node Combine XYZ joins three inputs into a three-dimensional vector; Combine Color is similar, and its output socket is a color, so both have a three-dimensional output and are exchangeable to some degree.
>
> The main difference is that colors can be subject to screen perceptual correction (sRGB), while vectors are left unchanged.

The emission color is not considered if the emission strength is **0.0**, so we increase that value before baking:

1. In the **Node Editor**, set **Principled BSDF | Emission | Strength** to `1.0`. That changes the material to a weird pink; it's not a problem, since the individual channels are baked correctly.
2. Select the **Bake Image** node to make it active.
3. In the **Render | Bake panel**, set **Bake Type** to **Emission.**
4. Press the **Bake** button

We will see a purple result in the **Image Editor**. Before saving, we make a few considerations:

- We enable **Bump** | **Invert** because our height input is inverted.
- Blender shaders have a **Roughness** parameter, but Unity shaders have a **Smoothness** parameter, which is the inverse.
- The **Occlusion** texture should be dark where the light does not reach, but **Brick Texture** | **Factor** is white on the mortar so, again, it should be inverted.

All three channels work better in Unity if they are inverted; a color operation in the shader graph would apply perceptual correction, so we use the image editor instead:

1. In the **Image Editor**, press the **"hamburger"** button and click **Image** | **Invert** | **Invert Image Colors**. The image will shift to a green picture.
2. Expand the same menu again and click **Image** | **Save As...**
3. Reach the folder **BlendToUni_URP** | **Assets** | **Art** | **Textures**
4. Set Color Space to **Non-Color** in the saving options.
5. Set the filename to `bricks_SOH.png` and save. **SOH** stands for **Softness**, **Occlusion**, **Height**.

> Note
>
> **A color or not?**
>
> The same image looks different on different devices, like projectors, standard displays, or professional high-range monitors, so applications manipulate the image data rather than displaying their raw colors.
>
> To store the correct information as an RGB image, we must be careful not to apply any color management, hence the *non-color* space.
>
> We inverted the colors in the Image Editor rather than in the shader to prevent the color correction from altering the RGB values.

We have generated all the images for shading the wall. This Blender scene is not a game asset, but we can still save it along with its textures so that it can be readily opened from Unity:

1. Open Blender's save dialog with **File** | **Save As...** and navigate to the folder `BlendToUni_URP` | `Assets` | `Art` | **Textures**.
2. Set the file name to `bricks_gen.blend` and press **Save As**.

We can finally close Blender and switch to Unity to create the game shaders.

Connecting the shader graph

The Project Browser in Unity will display the textures saved from Blender in the folder **Assets | Art | Texture**.

Unity assumes **bricks_SOH** to be a color texture, so it applies an sRGB correction to it. We must disable that in the **Inspector**:

1. In Unity's **Project Browser**, select **bricks_SOH** from the **Assets | Art | Texture** folder.
2. In the **Inspector** on the right, disable the **sRGB (Color Texture)** checkbox, which is the third attribute from the top.
3. Click the **Apply** button at the bottom of the **Inspector**. The image colors will change slightly, as the correction is off.

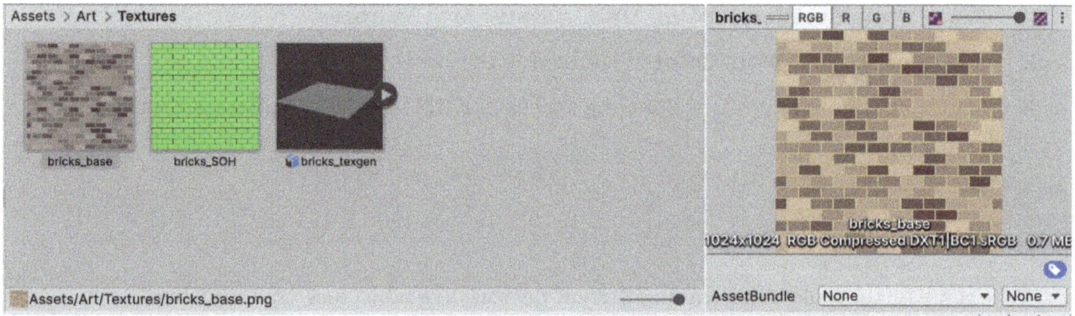

Figure 7.9: Bricks textures imported into Unity

There's more than one way to create shaders in Unity, but the **Shader Graph**, which we have already used in *Chapter 2*, is very similar to the Blender shader editor and offers high flexibility without coding.

Using the color map

We can create a new graph for the shader of the wall:

1. In the **Project Browser**, reach the folder `Assets` | `Art` | `Materials`.
2. From the **Asset** menu on the top bar, or from the **Project Browser** *right-click* menu, select **Create | Shader Graph | URP | Lit Shader Graph**.
3. Name the new asset `Bricks_Graph`.
4. *Double-click* **Bricks_Graph** to open the **Shader Graph** editor.

The graph displays the shader outputs, that is, **Vertex** and **Fragment** PBR attributes, a tall blackboard panel for the custom properties, the inspector, and the material preview.

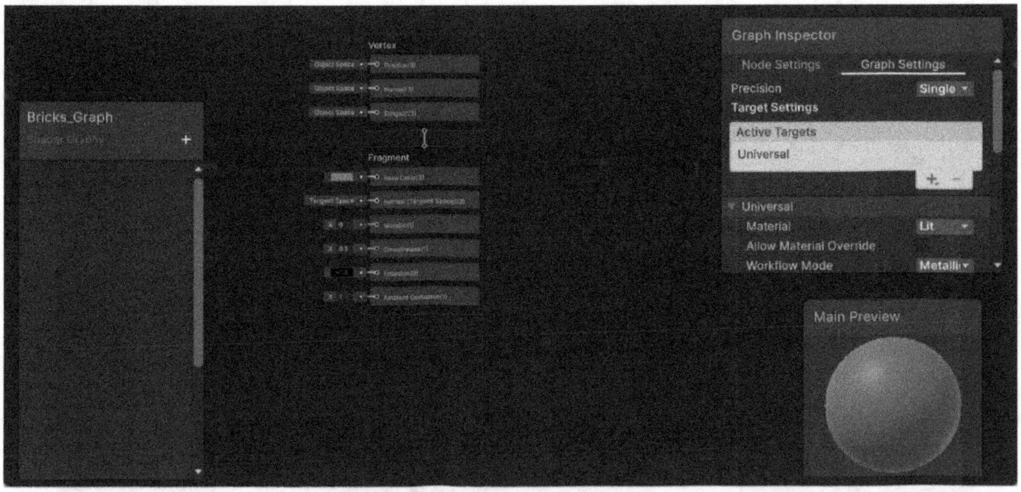

Figure 7.10: The Shader Graph editor's blackboard, shader sockets, inspector, and preview

We can import our textures with drag and drop:

1. From the **Project Browser**, navigate to the folder `Assets` | `Art` | `Textures`.
2. Select the texture **bricks_base** with the *left mouse button* and drag it to the shader graph. That creates a **Sample Texture 2D** node, with **Texture** and **UV** connections.
3. Drag the socket **Sample Texture 2D** | **RGBA** with the *left mouse button* and release it over **Fragment** | **Base Color** to create a connection.

We can see the preview mesh in the bottom-right corner changing to a brick pattern. We can connect the other attributes to add more detail.

Using the smoothness, occlusion, and height map

The R, G, and B channels of our second texture contain, respectively, *smoothness*, *occlusion*, and *height*. We can connect the first two right away:

1. Drag and drop the texture **bricks_SOH** onto the **Shader Graph** to create another **Sample Texture 2D** node.
2. Connect the **R** socket of the new **Sample Texture 2D** to **Fragment** | **Smoothness**.
3. Connect the **Sample Texture 2D** | **G** socket to **Fragment** | **Ambient Occlusion**.

Height maps must pass through a **Normal From Height** node to become three-dimensional:

1. Drag the **B** socket of the `bricks_soh` sampler with the mouse left button and release it on an empty area, type `height` to search, and select **Normal From Height**: In.
2. Connect **Normal From Height** | **Out** to **Fragment** | **Normal**.

The bricks in the **Main Preview** panel have gained depth, as normal mapping affects lighting.

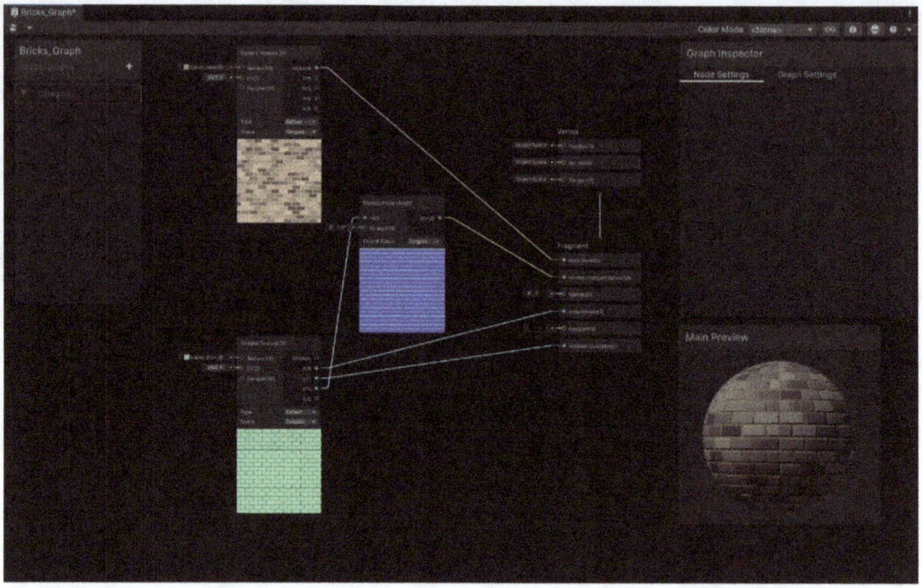

Figure 7.11: Connecting the textures to the fragment shader

Connecting the textures to their respective outputs looks great in the preview; we may want to add a new node to control tiling, the scaling factor, and a property for editing that value.

Exposing the tiling property

Textures are painted on 3D models using UV mapping, a planar representation of the polygons. We can see that the default input, **UV0**, is connected to the **Simple Texture 2D | UV** inputs.

The brick textures are tileable, that is, they can repeat infinitely along the surface of large objects. That allows us to paint the walls of our level with a relatively small texture, but we can do even better and add a control for changing the size of the bricks by adding a tiling node:

1. In the **Shader Graph**, *right-click* on a clear area and select **Create Node**.
2. Type `offset` to search and click **Tiling and Offset**.
3. Move the new node to the left of the graph.

Now we are going to replace the **UV** input with the output of **Tiling Offset**:

1. Connect **Tiling Offset | Out** to the first **Sample Texture 2D | UV** input.
2. Connect **Tiling Offset | Out** to the other **Sample Texture 2D | UV** input.

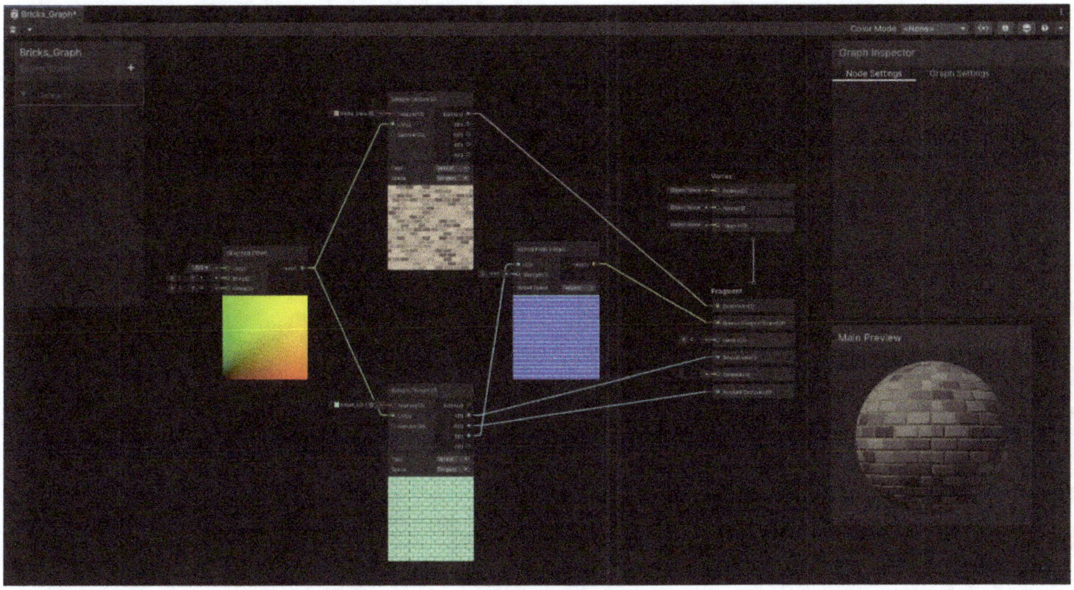

Figure 7.12: Using a tiling UV for both textures

We can change the **Tiling** parameter in the graph to enlarge and reduce the texture, but our shader will be much more useful if we expose the **Tiling** property to allow real-time editing:

1. Click the **+** button on the **Bricks_Graph** blackboard on the top left. If it is not visible, it can be toggled with the **<x>** button on the top right.
2. Tiling is a bidimensional attribute, but we can use a single value to set its coordinate, so we click **Float** in the pop-up menu asking for the type.
3. Enter `Tiling` as the name of the new property.

`Tiling` will be displayed as a material property in the **Inspector**. We can set its default value and connect it to the graph:

1. Select **Tiling** in the **Bricks_Graph** blackboard; the **Graph Inspector** at the top right will display the property in the **Node Settings**.
2. Set the **Default Value** to `1`.
3. Drag `Tiling` from the **Bricks_Graph** blackboard with the *left mouse button* and release it to the left of the **Tiling and Offset** node.
4. Connect Tiling to **Tiling and Offset | Tiling**

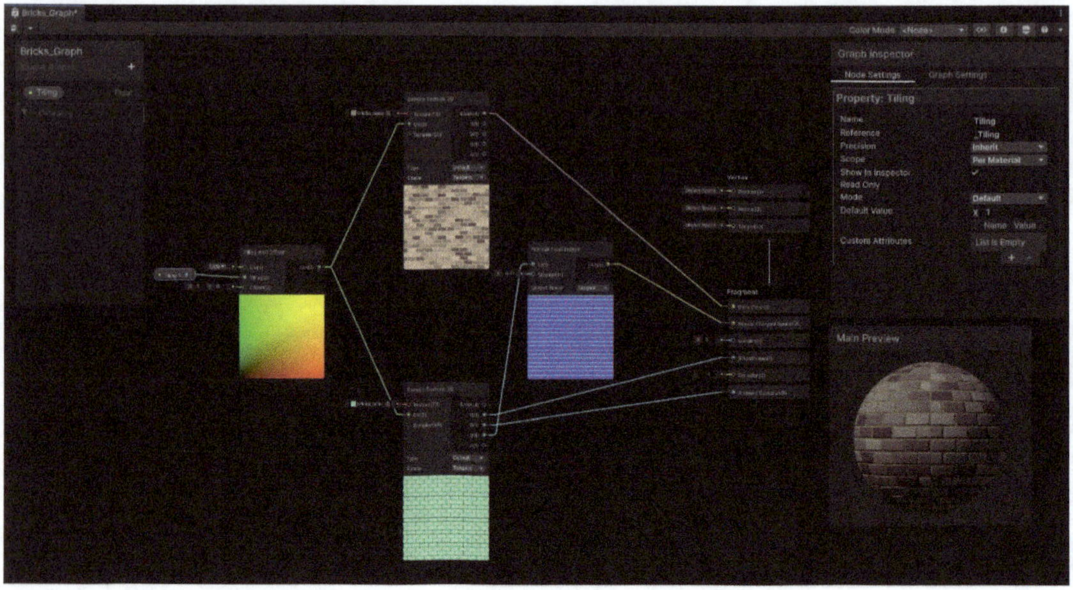

Figure 7.13: Connecting the Tiling property

With this setup in place, tiling becomes a property that can be set on every material that references this shader.

Blending the occlusion input

The Occlusion from our **SOH** texture ranges from black to white, which is a bit too heavy. We can create a property to modulate its blending:

1. In the **Shader Graph** editor, drag the HSO **Sampler Texture 2D** | **G** with the *left mouse button* and release it on the background. Type `blend` to search and click **Blend**: Blend **(1)**.
2. Set the **X** input of **Base** to `1`, which is white and the default value for **Occlusion**.
3. Set **Mode** to **Multiply** so that the black of the texture darkens the **Base**.
4. Connect **Blend** | **Out** to **Fragment** | **Ambient Occlusion**, replacing the previous connection.

The **Blend** | **Opacity** attribute controls the amount of occlusion coming from the texture. We can create a material property for it:

1. Click the **+** button on the properties Blackboard.
2. Select **Float** and name the new attribute `Occlusion`

3. Select **Occlusion** in the blackboard and, in the **Graph Inspector**, set its default value to `0.5`.
4. Drag the **Blend | Opacity** socket and release it on the background, type `occlusion`, and click **Property : Occlusion : Occlusion**.

With those properties, the bricks shader is ready for our walls.

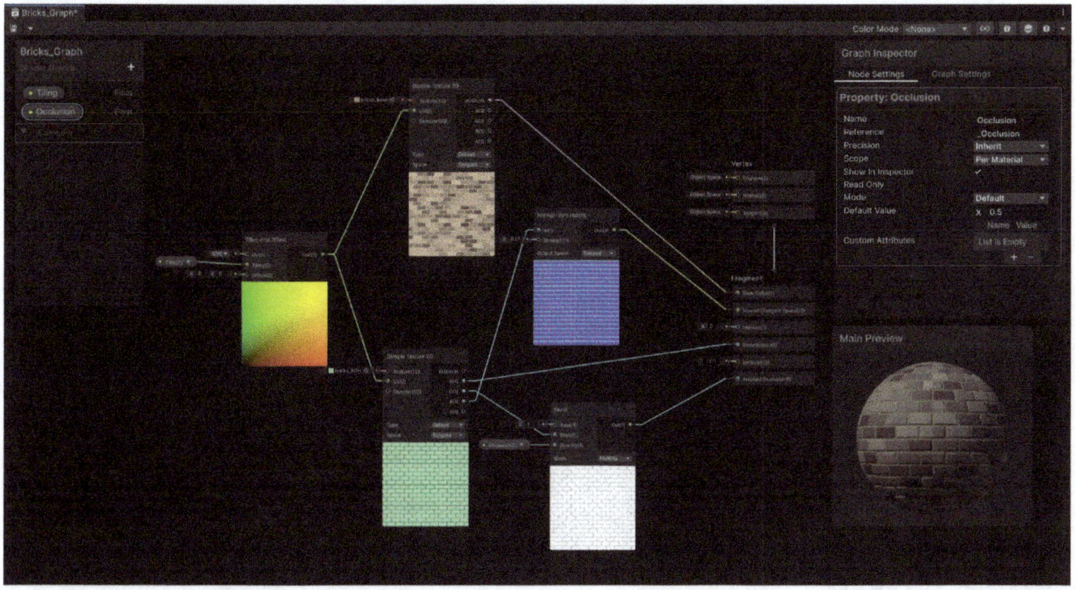

Figure 7.14: The bricks shader graph

We can save the graph using the **save icon** on the top left or the *Ctrl + S* combination. Now we need to create a material to apply this shader to a model.

Applying the material

Like in Blender, shaders are applied to models through a material. A material can be created directly in the project browser:

1. In the **Project** browser, go back to the folder `Assets | Art | Material`.
2. *Right-click* the **Bricks_Graph** asset and select **Create | Material**
3. Enter `Bricks` as the name of the new material. The thumbnail will display a sphere covered with bricks.
4. With the *left mouse button*, drag the new material from the **Project Browser** and release it over the wall of the crypt in the **Scene** viewport.

The walls are now entirely covered with bricks, but they are too small compared to the sketch from *Figure 7.1*. We need to adjust the *Tiling* property:

1. Select the **Bricks** material in the **Project Browser**; the **Inspector** on the right displays its properties.
2. **Tiling** is in the **Surface Inputs**; we set it to `0.3` to increase the dimensions of the bricks.

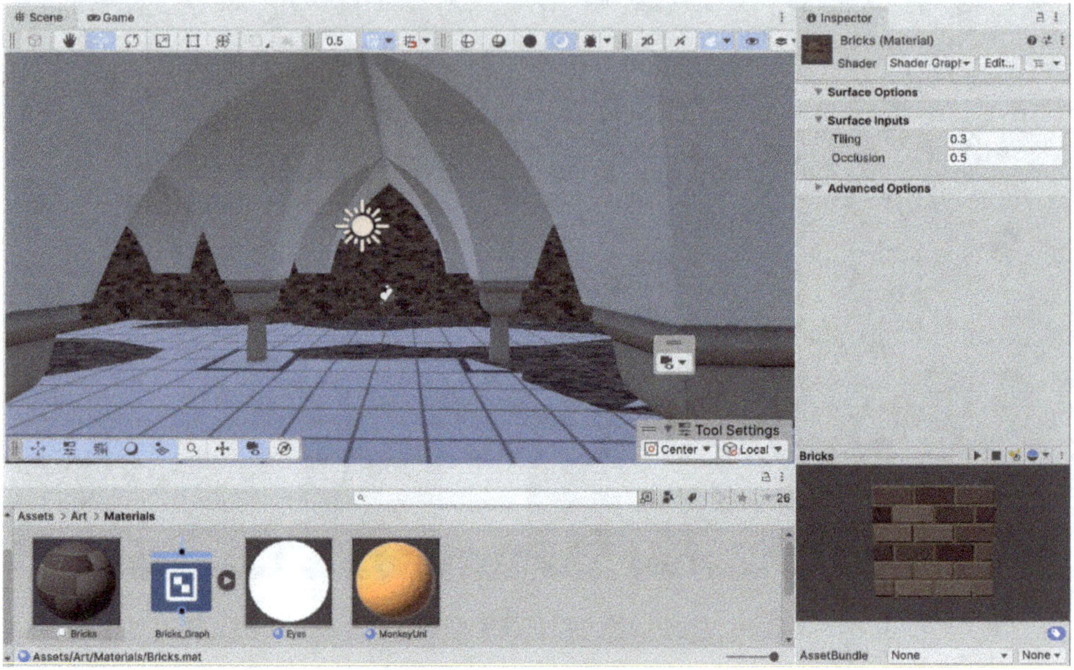

Figure 7.15: Applying the Bricks material

The wall has become more convincing. The bricks do a good job of covering the walls, but we will need a different material for the ceiling, which looks like a rough plaster in the concept:

1. In the **Project Browser**, in the folder `Assets` | `Art` | `Material`, show the **Create** menu, either from **Assets** in the top bar or from the right-click menu of the folder.
2. Click **Create** | **Shader Graph** | **URP** | **Lit Shader Graph** to start a new shader.
3. Type `Plaster_Graph` as the name of the shader.
4. *Right-click* Plaster_Graph in the **Project Browser** and select **Create** | **Material.**
5. Type `Plaster` as the name of the new material.

We are not setting up this material yet, as at present, our model lacks the UV coordinates required by the textures.

Texturing generated models

We have created the walls with ProBuilder, which assigns default texturing coordinates. Blender geometry nodes don't do that automatically; we must add them explicitly with nodes.

Creating UVs for the vault

We will create UVs for the ceiling in Blender:

1. In Unity's **Project Browser**, reach the folder `Assets` | `Art` | `Models` | `Crypt` and *double-click* **Roof** to open it in Blender.
2. Go to the **Geometry Nodes** workspace, make sure that **Vault** is selected, and select the first **Geometry Nodes** modifier in the **Modifiers** panel.

The **Node Editor** will display the graph created in *Chapter 6*. The first node of the tree, **Cylinder**, provides a UV output, but it is not connected and those coordinates are lost. We need to store the UV in a mesh attribute:

1. In the **Node Editor**, press *Shift + A*, type `store` as a search key, and create a **Store Named Attribute** node.
2. Insert the new node between **Cylinder** | **Mesh** and **Set Position**.

Store Named Attribute stores information of the geometry nodes into attributes of the mesh. UV coordinates require a specific **type** and **domain**:

1. Click the first dropdown box of **Store Named Attribute** and change the *type* from **Float** to **2D Vector**, since UVs are two dimensions.
2. Click the other dropdown box and change the *domain* from **Point** to **Face Corner**, as UVs are associated with vertices.
3. Set an attribute name in the **Name** field and type `UVMap`, Blender's default name for texture coordinates.
4. Connect **Cylinder** | **UV** to **Store Named Attribute** | **Value** to pass the UV mapping to the object.

We can switch the top left editor from *Spreadsheet* to **UV Editor** to see the planar projection of the geometry.

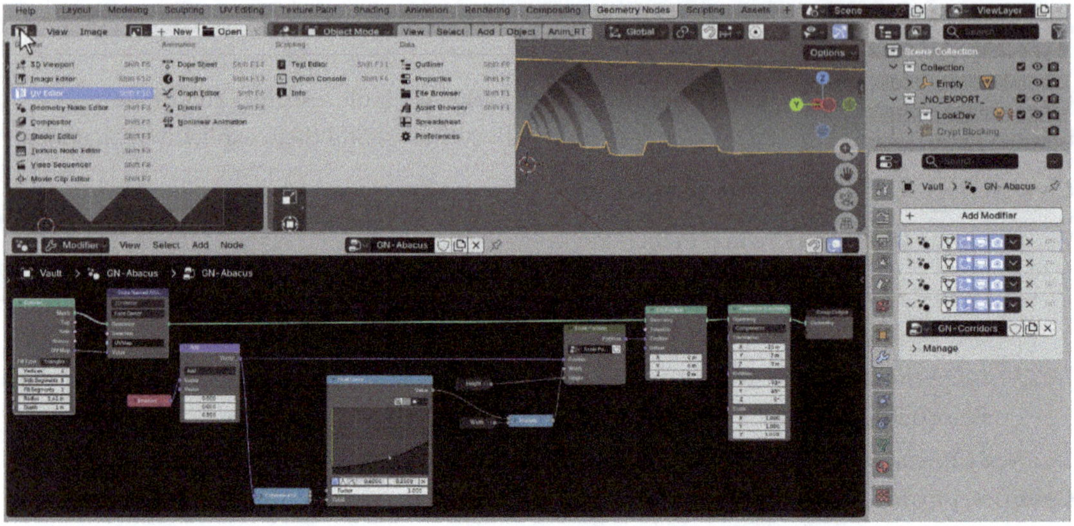

Figure 7.16: The second node from the left stores the UVMap attribute

The ceiling was modeled by duplicating the same block repeatedly, with the UV coordinates of every duplicate overlapping the original ones. That's usually discouraged, and it would be a problem if we were to paint textures manually, but such an arrangement works in our case: the texture will repeat across the model.

The side corridors present a different issue: we created them with extrusions and that process stretches the texture coordinates, creating artifacts. We should account for that after the extrusion node:

1. In the **Geometry Nodes** editor, select our **Store Named Attribute** node and press *Ctrl + C* to copy it to the clipboard. That will save us the trouble of setting up a new node from scratch.
2. Select the last **Geometry Nodes** modifier in the **Modifiers** panel. The **Node Editor** will display the graph of **GN-Corridors**.
3. Press *Ctrl + V* to paste an already set **Store Named Attribute** node into the current graph.
4. Insert the new node between **Extrude Mesh** and **Smooth by Angle**; the UVs will disappear from the UV Editor.

The last **Store Named Attribute** node has no input and overwrites **UVMap** with empty coordinates, but it will integrate the existing UVs if we connect it properly:

1. We only want to map the extruded walls, so connect **Extrude Mesh | Side** to **Store Named Attribute | Selection**; the previous UVs will be back.

2. Create a projection of the corridors by adding an unwrap node with *Shift + A*, type `unwrap to`, and select **UV Unwrap** from the search results.
3. Connect **Extrude Mesh** | **Side** to **UV Unwrap** | **Selection** to limit the unwrapping to the new polygons
4. Connect **UV Unwrap** | **UV** to **Store Named Attribute** | **Value** to add the new coordinates to the UV layout

The new UV will appear in the **UV Editor**, but they are very small if compared to the UVs created previously. We can set their dimensions by scaling the UV vector:

1. Press *Shift + A* and type `multiply add`, then create a **Utilities** | **Vector** | **Vector Math** | **Multiply Add** node.
2. Insert the new node in the connection between **UV Unwrap** and **Store Named Attribute**.
3. Set **Multiply Add** | **Multiplier** to `7.5`, `7.5`, `1.0` to match the relative size of the corridors with respect to a single element of the Vault.
4. Set **Multiply Add** | **Addend** to `1.0`, `0.0`, `0.0` to avoid overlapping between vaults and corridors.

> Note
>
> **Not thinking U-dimensionally!**
>
> Normally, UV coordinates are limited to the first quadrant, so they don't exceed the 0 to 1 range. Outside of this range, textures are either repeated, like in our case, or not displayed at all.
>
> It's not within the scope of this book, but a sequence of textures, known as UDIM, can be assigned to different quadrants of the UV plane. The offset in **Multiply Add** makes the **Vault** model ready for UDIM.

Those coordinates allow us to use textures, but we need to assign a material as well.

Setting up materials and remapping

Assets with no materials would be a minor concern in this case, because we can assign Unity materials with drag and drop; assigning a material in Blender is still useful, though, as that makes it possible to set up **On Demand Remap** in Unity.

Our model is generated entirely with **Geometry Nodes**, so we need to assign materials in the node graph:

1. Click the **Materials** tab in the properties on the right, then click the **+ New** button to create a new one.
2. *Double-click* the new material in the list and rename it to `Plaster`.
3. In the **Node Editor**, press *Shift* + *A*, type `material`, and create a **Set Material** node. Insert it between **Smooth by Angle** and **Group Output**.
4. Click the **Material** field and select **Plaster** from the drop-down menu.

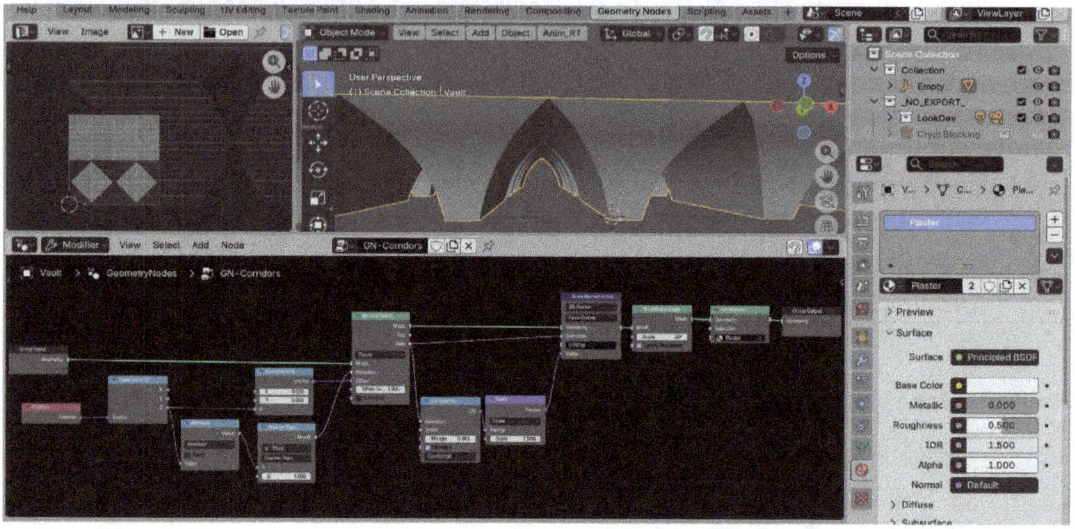

Figure 7.17: Assigning UVs and material to the ceiling

We can save the scene, close Blender, and switch back to Unity. The **Roof** asset will be reimported, and this time it contains the **Plaster** material. We can also select the **Vault** mesh and check **UV Layout** in the inspector to make sure that the data was imported.

Figure 7.18: Vault UVs in Unity

We will use the **Plaster** material created in Unity, so we set up a remapping rule for this model:

1. In Unity's **Project Browser**, navigate to the `Assets` | `Art` | `Models` | `Crypt` folder and select **Roof**.
2. In the **Inspector**, select the **Materials** tab.
3. Click the expansion triangle of **On Demand Remap** to display the remapping rules.
4. Click the **Naming** drop-down box to change it from **By Base Texture Name** to **From Model's Material**: that will look for materials with matching names.
5. Click the **Search** drop-down box to change it from **Local Materials Folder** to **Recursive-Up**: this way Unity will search in the `Materials` folder of upper directories.
6. Click the **Search and Remap** button; Unity will fill the **Plaster** field with its *Plaster* material.
7. Click the **Apply** button to confirm.

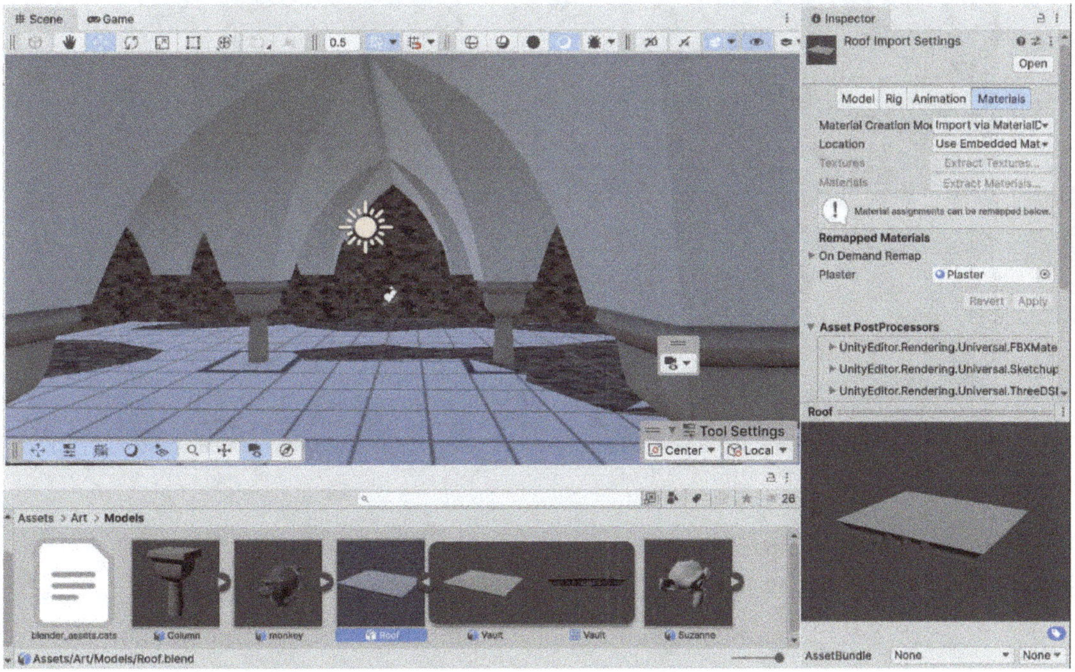

Figure 7.19: On-demand remap for Plaster

The **Ceiling** material is no longer displayed in the asset, even if it is part of the `.blend` scene; it was replaced with the Unity material.

We can set up this shader in the **Shader Graph** and check how it looks in our level.

Creating the plaster shader

We are not using image textures for the ceiling and rather use Unity's nodes for it:

1. In the **Project Browser**, reach the folder `Assets` | `Art` | `Materials` and *double-click* **Plaster_Graph** to open the **Shader Editor**.
2. *Right-click* on the graph editor's background and select **Create Node**
3. Type `noise` as a search keyword and select **Simple Noise.**

Simple Noise is a grayscale irregular pattern that we can use for bumps on the surface:

1. Drag the socket **Simple Noise** | **Out** and release it on the **Graph Editor** background.
2. Type `normal` as the search key and select **Normal From Height : In** to create and connect a normal conversion node.
3. Connect **Normal From Height** | **Out** to **Fragment** | **Normal.**

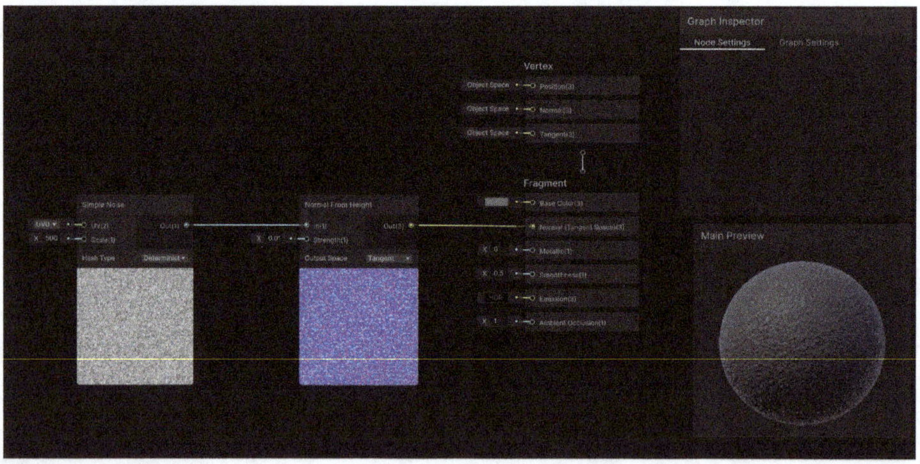

Figure 7.20: Noise bump for the plaster shader

Using noise as a height map conveys irregularity and a less artificial look to the model. We can use another noise texture to add some variation by blending two colors:

1. *Right-click* on the **Simple Noise** node, click **Duplicate**, and move the new node upwards.
2. Drag the **Out** socket of the new **Simple Noise** node and release it on the background, type `blend` to search and select **Blend : Opacity**. This way, the noise becomes the blending factor between the **Base** and **Blend** colors.

3. Connect **Blend | Out** to **Fragment | Base Color**.
4. By default, the mixing mode is set to **Overlay**: click the drop-down box on the **Blend** node and change it to **Overwrite** (the last entry). This way, the second color replaces the **Base** color entirely where the noise input is white.

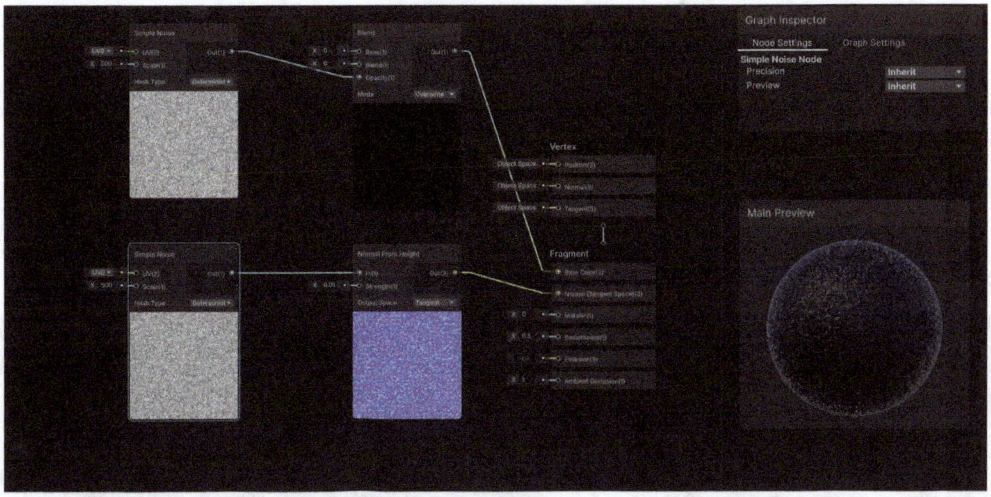

Figure 7.21: Using Simple Noise for color and normal variation

By default, **Base** and **Blend** inputs are set to `0`, so both are black. We can create graph properties and then set the colors on the material:

1. Click the **+** on the **Plaster_Graph** blackboard at the top left to create a new property.
2. Choose **Color** and enter `Base` as the name of the new property.
3. Create another **Color** property and name it `Blend`.
4. We may want to adjust the size of the noise too, so click the **+** button again to create a **Float** property and name it `Color Scale`.

These properties handle the parameters for adjusting the color, so we can connect them to the **Blend** node and its **Simple Noise** input:

1. Drag the **Blend | Base** socket and release it on the background, type `prop` to search, and select **Property: Base: Base**.
2. Drag the **Blend | Blend** socket and release it on the background, type `prop` to search, and select **Property: Blend: Blend**.
3. Drag the **Scale** input socket of the **Simple Noise** connected to Blend, release it on the background, type prop, and select **Property: Color Noise: Color Scale**.

The default values of these properties are usually `0`, or black, which are not very useful even for preview, so we'd better set their default values:

1. Select the **Base** property by either clicking the input of **Blend** in the graph or its entry on the blackboard on the top left.
2. In the **Graph Inspector** on the top right, click the color in the **Default Value** field to pop up a picker.
3. **HSV** is the default mode for the picker. Bring the **Value** to `80` by adjusting the slider, or just select a very light gray in the picker.
4. Select the **Color Scale** input and set its default value to `30`.

We can see the gray spots in the preview; there might be a seam on the sphere in the material preview, but that effect won't be noticeable on our model.

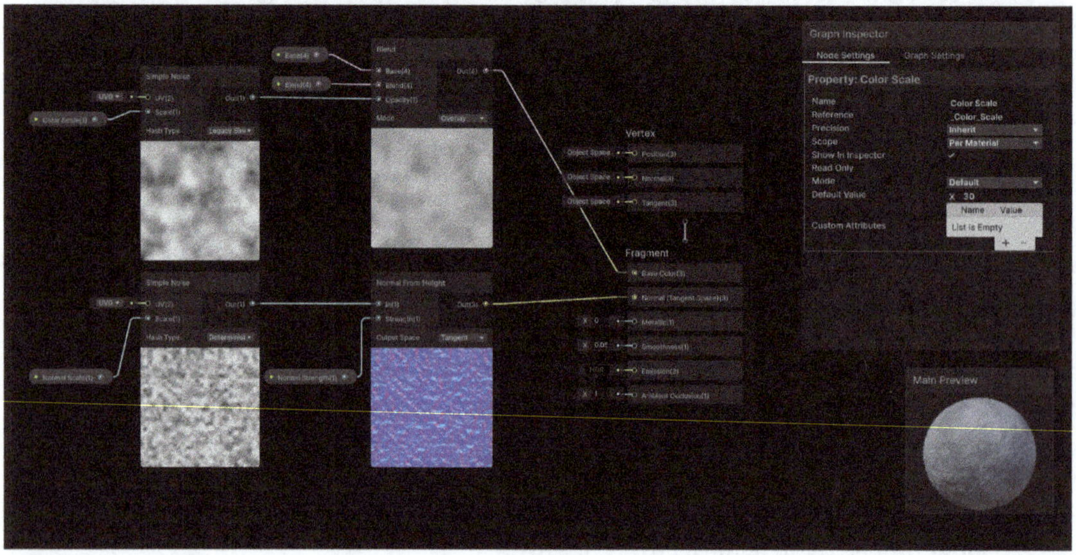

Figure 7.22: Color inputs of the Plaster shader

Now that the **Base** color is lighter, we can see the dark spots in the **Main Preview**. We are setting the final colors in the material rather than in the shader, so that we can have immediate feedback. We can create input parameters for the normal textures too:

1. Click the **+** button on the **Plaster_Graph** blackboard, create a new **Float** property, and name it `Normal Scale`.
2. Create another **Float** property and name it **Normal Strength**.

Those properties will regulate the bump noise and strength, respectively, so we connect them to their sockets:

1. Drag the **Scale** socket of the **Simple Noise** connected to **Normal From Height**, release it on the background, and type `prop`, then select **Property: Normal Scale: Normal Scale**.
2. Drag the **Normal From Height | Strength** socket and release it, type `prop`, and select **Property: Normal Strength: Normal Strength**.

Once connected, our properties will override the previous node settings, so we set their default values:

1. Select the **Normal Scale** property and, in the **Graph Inspector**, set its **Default Value** to `100`.
2. Select the **Normal Strength** property and, in the **Graph Inspector**, set its **Default Value** to `0.05`.
3. Our plaster is not smooth: set **Fragment | Smoothness** to `0.05`; we will not expose this property to the material.

We can save the **Plaster_Graph** shader and close the *Shader Graph* editor. The **Viewport** will compile the shader and update the ceiling.

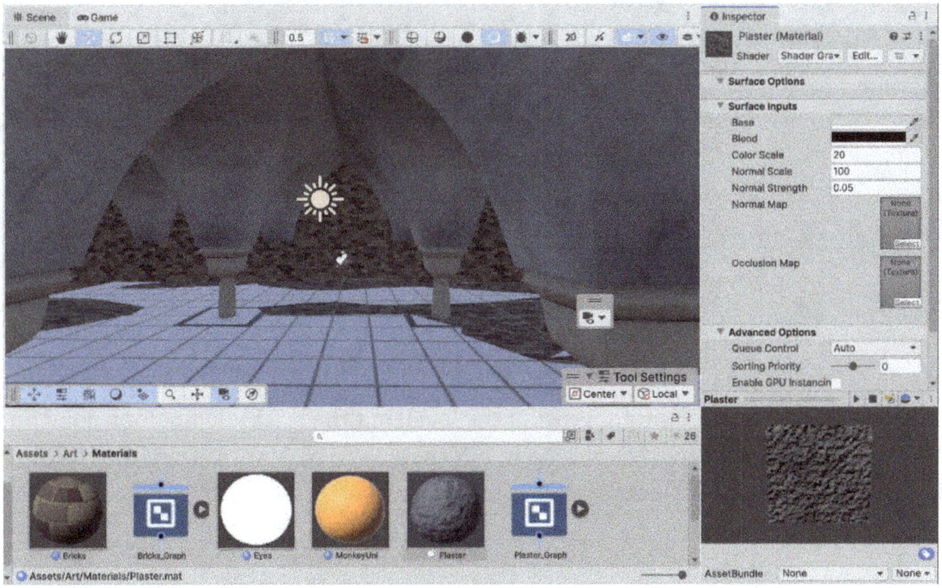

Figure 7.23: The Plaster shader with default parameters

By default, our plaster is gray, so we change its parameters to something more colorful:

1. In the **Project Browser**, select the **Plaster** material, not the **Plaster_Graph** shader.
2. The **Inspector** will display the **Surface Inputs**. Click the **Base** color to pop up the picker and, in **HSV** space, move the **Saturation (S)** slider to `10`. The result is pale pink.
3. Click the **Blend** color and set its saturation to `10` and the **Value (V)** to 60; the result is slightly darker than the **Base** color.

We can observe the effects of changing the **Surface Inputs** instantly, while changing values in the graph requires recompiling, so it is generally advised to expose visual properties to the material rather than hard-coding them in the shader.

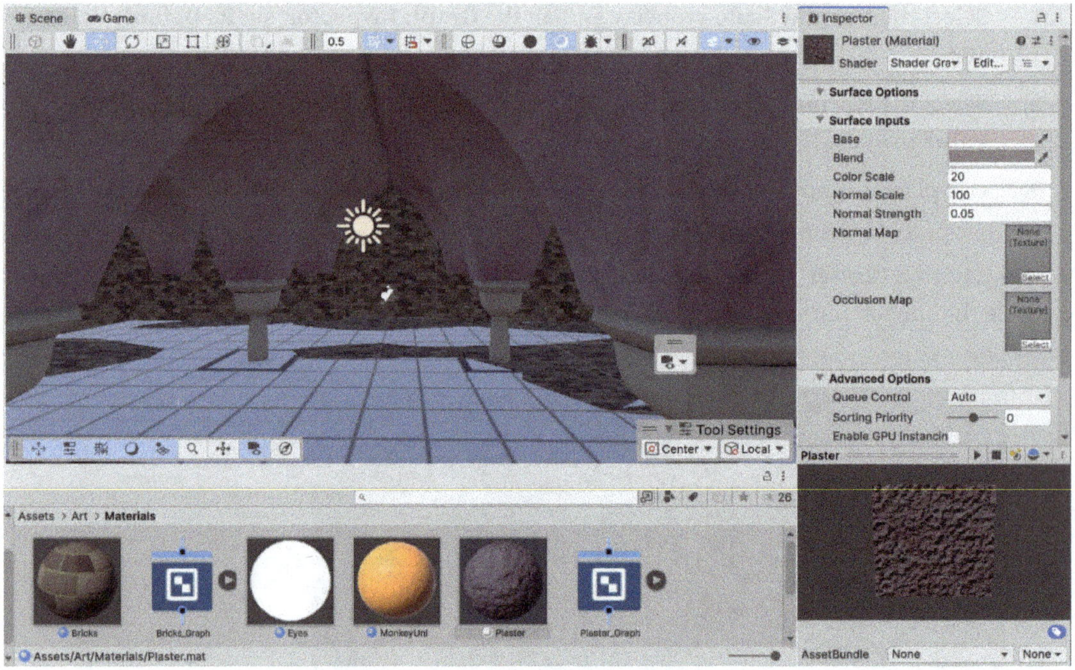

Figure 7.24: The final material for the ceiling

The walls and the ceiling account for most of the level, but the bricks do not look good on the floor. We could assign a different texture to it, but there is no need to, as from the concept in *Figure 7.1*, we can see that the floor is covered by water.

Creating the water plane

Fluid water is not easy to implement, but we only need a layer of water to cover the floor. In such cases, we can convey the illusion of a water surface by using a simple plane:

1. From Unity's top bar menu, click **GameObject | 3D Object | Plane**. A plane will be added to the scene.
2. The **Inspector** will display the new plane properties. Change its name to `Water` in the **Name** field on top.
3. Set its **Position** coordinates to `0`, `0.2`, `0`.
4. Enable the "chain" lock on the **Scale** and set it to 4, 4, 4 to cover the entire location.

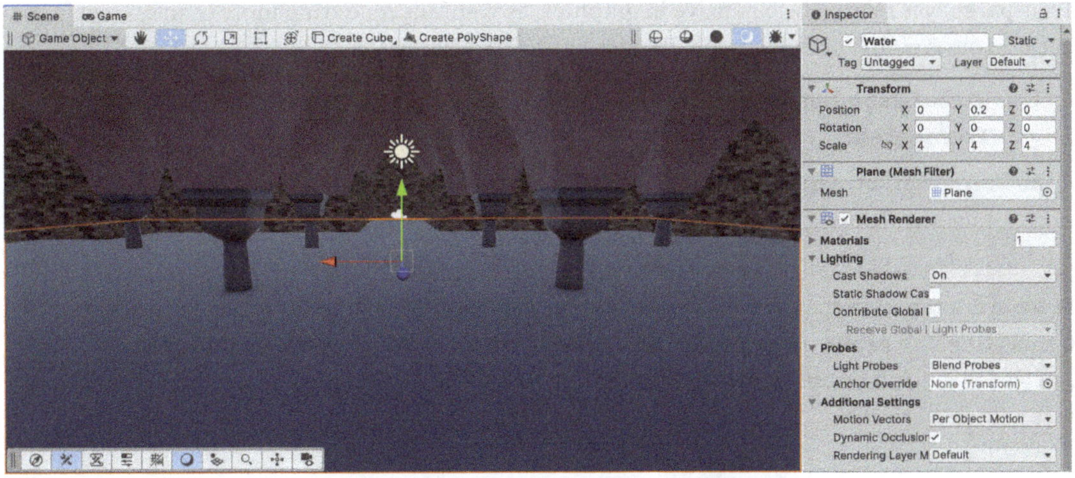

Figure 7.25: Adding a water plane to our level

Covering the bricks on the floor is already an improvement, but we can create better water with a proper shader. To convey the right look, we will focus on three properties of water:

- **Transparency**: We can see through water, although not from any angle.
- **Depth**: Deep water is darker than shallow water.

It is possible to reproduce those features using the **Shader Graph** nodes:

1. In the **Project Browser**, *right-click* in the **Assets | Art | Materials** folder and select **Create | Shader Graph | URP | Lit Shader Graph**.
2. Name the new asset `Water_Graph`.

We are going to create and assign the material right away, so that we can check our progress while creating the shader:

1. *Right-click* on **Water_Graph** in the **Project Browser** and select **Create | Material**. Name the new material `Water`.
2. Drag the **Water** material from the **Project Browser** and drop it onto the **Water** plane in the **Scene** viewport.
3. Double-click the new asset to open the **Shader Graph** editor.

Unlike the bricks and the plaster, water is transparent, so we will enable transparency for this shader.

Creating transparent shaders

Transparency is relatively expensive in graphics, as it entails rendering more than one surface in the same region. For that reason, it must be enabled explicitly:

1. In the **Graph Inspector | Graph Settings**, change the **Surface Type** from **Opaque** to **Transparent**.
2. A new input, **Alpha**, appears on the **Fragment** node. Drag its socket with the *left mouse button*, release it, and type `fresnel`. Click **Fresnel Effect : Out** to connect a `fresnel` node.

Fresnel is a function that simulates a change in the direction of light as it travels inside a solid. Connecting it to **Alpha** imitates the transparency of water, which is transparent when we look straight through it but becomes increasingly opaque as the surface becomes parallel to the view.

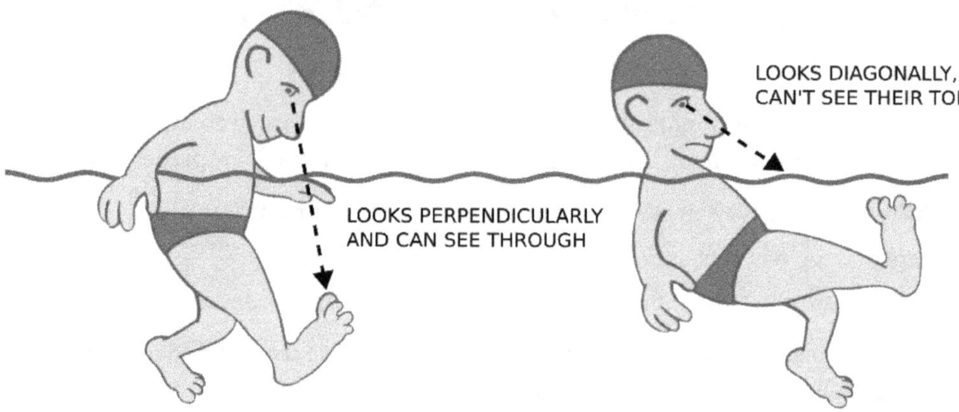

Figure 7.26: The swimmer on the left can look at their toes, the one on the right can't.

We can save the shader and see how it looks in the scene. While uniform transparency would be unrealistic, varying the *alpha* according to the view angle helps create the illusion of looking through a body of water.

Figure 7.27: Water becomes opaque as it approaches the horizon

While directional transparency can be achieved with a single node, the illusion of depth requires a bit more effort.

Blending depth colors

Our water is not volumetric, but we can affect the color of the surface with the depth of the underlying geometry, conveying the illusion of depth:

1. In the **Shader Graph** editor, *right-click* on a clear area on the left and select **Create Node**. Type `depth` to search and click **Scene Depth**.
2. Click the **Scene Depth | Sampling** drop-down box to change it from **Linear 01** to **Eye**, as we are using the distance from the viewpoint to darken the shader.
3. *Right-click* on a clear area below **Scene Depth**, select **Create Node**, type screen to search, and click **Screen Position**.
4. We will compare the scene depth to the rendered position of the surface relative to the screen, so we change **Screen Position | Mode** from **Default** to **Raw**.

Screen Position's output is four dimensional; its last coordinate, `W` in vector convention and `A` (alpha) in color representation, is the distance of the water surface from the camera. **Scene Depth** is the distance of the floor from the camera. The difference between the two is the depth of the water at some point. We can use that result to change the color of our plane, based on what is underneath.

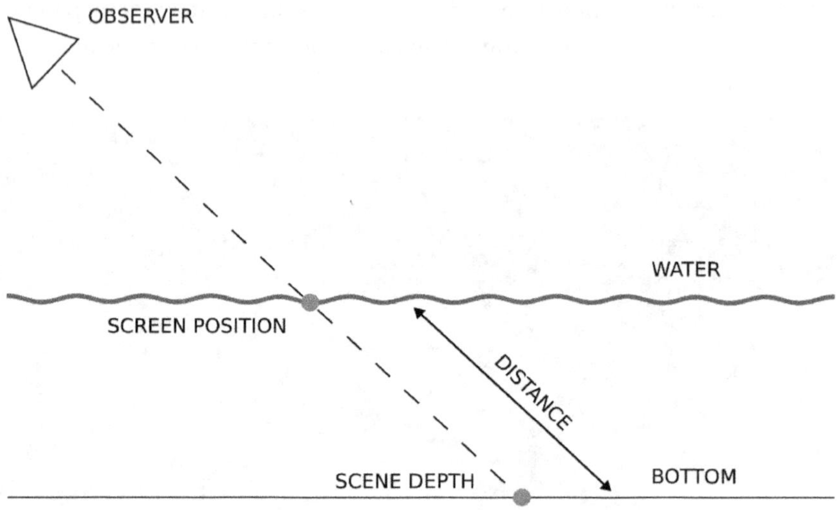

Figure 7.28: Difference between Screen Position and Scene Depth

We can implement depth blending with a **Subtract Node**:

1. In the **Shader Graph** editor, drag the **Scene Depth** | **Out** socket with the left mouse button and release it over an empty area, type `sub`, and select **Subtract : A(1)**.
2. That will create and connect a **Subtract** node. We need to connect **Screen Position**'s `W` to it, so drag **Screen Position** | **Out** and release it, type `split`, and select **Split : In(1)**.
3. The *Split* node follows the color naming convention, **RGBA**. Connect **Split** | **A** to **Subtract** | **B**.

The subtraction's result is the value that we need for blending shallow and deep color. This value will exceed the 0 to 1 range, so we must clamp it before using it:

1. In the **Shader Graph** editor, drag the **Subtract** | **Out** socket with the left mouse button and release it over an empty area, type `clamp`, and select **Clamp : In(1)**.
2. The default min/max values for clamping are already set to 0 and 1. Drag the **Clamp** | **Out** socket, type `blend`, and select **Blend : Opacity(1)** to create and connect a **Blend** node.
3. Connect **Blend** | **Out** to **Fragment** | **Base Color**.

Again, the default inputs of **Blend** are set to `0`, but we will replace them with input properties:

1. In the **Water_Graph** blackboard, press **+** and select **Color**. Type `Shallow` as the name of the new property.

2. Select **Shallow** in the blackboard and, in the **Graph Inspector**, click the **Default Value** color. Pick a white color in the picker.
3. We need another color for blending. In the **Water_Graph** blackboard, press **+** and select **Color** again. Type `Deep` as the name of this property.

The color properties are ready to be connected:

1. Drag the **Blend | Base** socket and release it on the background. Type `surface` and select Property: **Shallow: Shallow (4)**.
2. Drag the **Blend | Blend** socket and release it on the background. Type deep and select Property: Deep: Deep (4).
3. Set the blending **Mode** with the drop-down box on the **Blend** node and change it from **Overlay** to **Overwrite**.

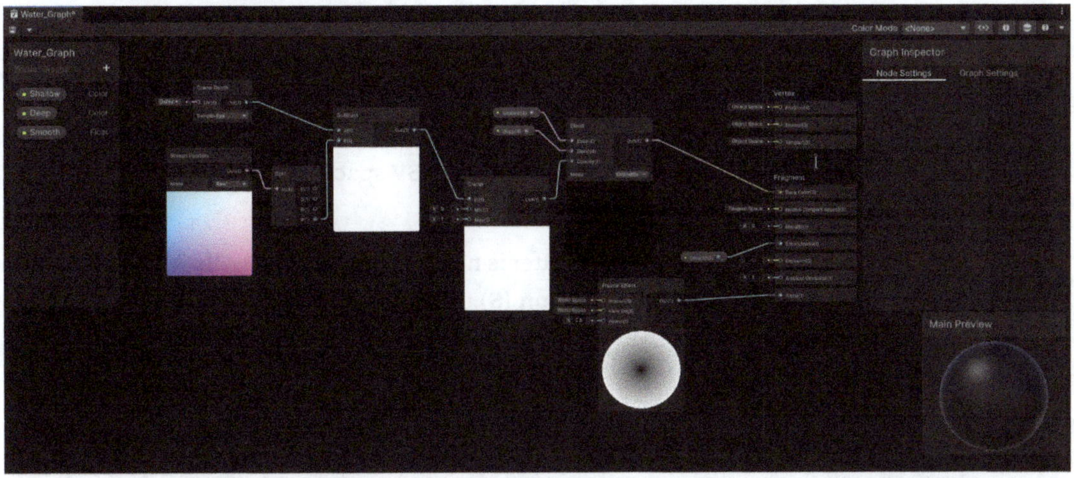

Figure 7.29: Clamped relative depth and Fresnel to mimic depth and transparency of water

The setup for transparency and color is finished. We may want to expose the **Smoothness** attribute to adjust it in the material:

1. In the **Water_Graph** blackboard, press **+** and select **Float**. Name the new property `Smooth`.
2. Drag **Fragment | Smoothness** and release it on an empty area, type `smooth`, and select **Properties: Smooth: Smooth**.

We can save **Water_Graph** and have a look at the scene. We will see that the water is white where there are surfaces underneath, and black otherwise.

Figure 7.30: Depth blending of colors in the scene

With our shader ready, we can set the colors of our water:

1. Select the **Water** material in the **Project Browser**.
2. Set the **Smooth** value to `0.2`, as dirty water reflects less light.
3. Click the **Deep** color to display the picker and, in **HSV** space, set **Hue** (**H**) to `140`, **Saturation** (**S**) to `70`, and **Value** (**V**) to `30`.
4. We will use a lighter color where the water is not deep. Click the **Shallow** color and, in HSV space, set **Hue** (**H**) to `140`, **Saturation** (**S**) to `70`, and **Value** (**V**) to `100`.

The result is a flooded crypt, where our poorly textured floor is conveniently covered with muddy water.

Figure 7.31: Final look of water and walls

There are many ways to refine those shaders, as water is a complex material and the wall is much too regular. As the scene has gained color through a combination of images and procedural textures, the game looks closer to its final look.

Summary

In this chapter, we have used Blender as a texture generator, taking advantage of its bake feature to create images for our shaders. We have also accounted for texture coordinates and material assignment so that remapping and tiling could work correctly.

Shader development is both a technical and visual task, and not an easy subject, but having a clear goal in mind can help make it simpler.

In *Chapter 8*, we will complete the look dev stage of our project and create high-resolution normal maps for our models.

Get this book's PDF copy, code bundle, and more

Scan the QR code (or go to `packtpub.com/unlock`). Search for this book by name, confirm the edition, and then follow the steps on the page.

UNLOCK NOW

Note: Have your invoice handy. Purchases made directly from the Packt website don't require an invoice.

8

Baking Detail Maps

Modern hardware and game engines can render high-resolution models in real time, but it is still advisable to keep the polygon count low when it comes to game assets. Using lighter models frees up resources for bigger environments, a larger number of characters and effects, and higher render quality. Also, a game with a smaller footprint can be ported easily to mobile and web platforms and fit the specs of lightweight devices.

On the other hand, low-resolution models lack the detail that comes with denser geometry and can look unrealistically sharp. A common trick for bypassing such limitations is to work on a high-resolution copy of the mesh, where density can be increased at will and details can be adjusted with component editing or digital sculpting.

Then, the high-resolution features are transferred to the initial mesh by baking the properties of one model onto the other. Although consolidated, this workflow presents challenges, as some shapes might prevent a correct match between low and high resolution.

Most issues related to texture generation can be countered by paying attention to the settings, with some help from geometry nodes.

This chapter covers the following topics:

- Creating high-resolution models and details
- Transferring model features via baking
- Blending the exported maps in Unity

Technical requirements

We will use *Blender 5.1* and *Unity 6.3*, which can be installed by following the instructions from *Chapter 1* or from their respective websites.

You can download the example project and code for this book by following the instructions in the *Download the example code files* section in the *Preface* of this book.

This chapter's code files are included in the downloadable code bundle.

Creating detailed geometry

In *Chapter 7*, we generated image textures by baking the shading channels of an object, in that case a plane. To use image textures, we need to set up the UV coordinates of our models so that a planar image can be wrapped around a three-dimensional solid.

Complex models are usually broken into multiple objects so that they are easier to model and keep track of. In that case, we fit the texture coordinates of all the parts in a single UV quadrant so that one image can cover the entire group.

In our case, the column modeled in *Chapter 5* contains three models generated with geometry nodes.

While the UV of multiple static objects can be fit in one quadrant using the Pack Islands operator, the most convenient way to fit generated models together is by merging them using Geometry Nodes. As a bonus, that reduces the content of the Unity assets to a single geometry.

Joining objects with geometry nodes

Our column consists of three objects: *Shaft*, *Echinus*, and *Abacus*. By default, Unity maintains that division when the .blend file is imported as a *prefab*.

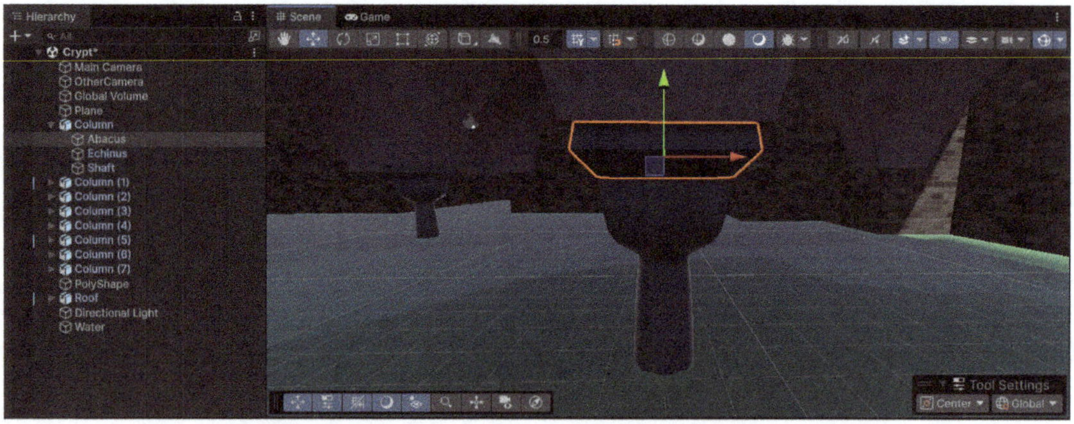

Figure 8.1: The three components of column in Unity

This partition is convenient when modeling, but not so much for texturing, since we want our textures to cover the entire column. Working on a single object makes that easier, so we will combine those elements into one. We start by moving the models to a different collection:

1. In Unity's **Project Browser**, navigate to the folder **Assets** | **Art** | **Models** | **Crypt** and *double-click* **Column** to open it in *Blender*.
2. In Blender, go to the **Geometry Nodes** workspace and select the three objects: **Abacus**, **Echinus**, and **Shaft**.
3. Press the `M` key and, in the **Move to Collection** menu, select **_NO_EXPORT_** | **New Collection**.
4. Type `Components` as the name of the new collection.

Thanks to the `on_load.py` script created in *Chapter 6*, those models will not be imported into Unity. The **Components** collection is only for storage, and we can hide it safely; the models are still listed in the default collection, although grayed out, because they belong to *Empty* in the hierarchy. That's distracting and no longer useful, as those objects are not going to Unity anymore, so we remove their parentage and hide the collection:

1. Press *Alt + P* and select **Clear Parent and Keep Transformation** to remove them from **Empty**
2. In the **Outliner**, click the "eye" and "camera" icons beside the **Components** collection to hide it in **Viewport** and renders.

With the original components now hidden, we will create a new object to import the models into the game. We will parent this new mesh to **Empty** to account for the difference in orientation between Blender and Unity.

1. In the **Outliner**, select the default **Collection** to make it active.
2. In the **Viewport**, press *Shift + A* and, from the **Add** menu, select **Mesh** | **Plane**. It could be any other mesh, as we will replace the mesh data with geometry nodes, but a plane is the simplest shape.
3. Always in the **Viewport**, use the operator *right-click* | Lock at Origin, added in *Chapter 4*, or press *Alt + G* to zero the location.
4. This object will be exported to Unity, so we place it under the *Y-Up* Empty: in the *Object* properties (orange square icon), expand the **Relations** panel, click the **Parent** field, and select **Empty**.

Usually, Blender counters the inherited transformation when the parent object is assigned, which is why we set it in the Relations properties; it's the same result as using **Object** | **Parent** | **Make Parent without Inverse**.

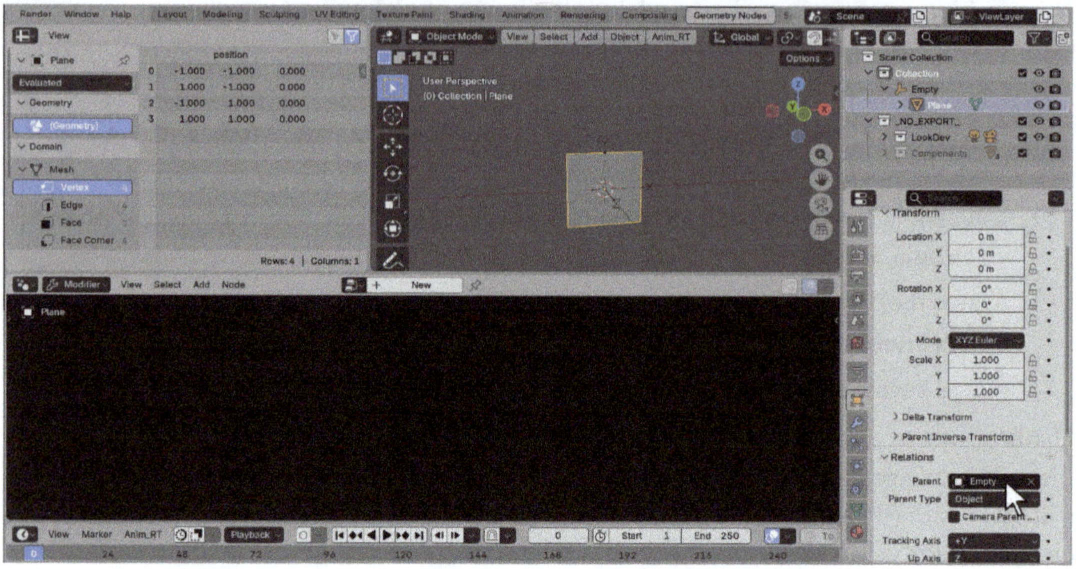

Figure 8.2: Replacing column elements with a plane

The new object was rotated by the parent, but that's no concern as we will replace the mesh data with geometry nodes:

1. *Double-click* the new object in the **Outliner** and rename it `Column`.
2. In the **Node Editor**, click the **New** button to create a new node tree.
3. The button is replaced by the new graph: click it and rename it from **Geometry Nodes** to `GN-Column`.

Geometry nodes can access the objects contained in a collection and pass them through the modifier:

1. In the **Node Editor**, select the **Group Input** node and press `Delete` or `X` to delete it.
2. Press *Shift + A*, type `coll` to search and create an `Input | Scene | Collection Info` node.
3. Connect the output `Collection Info` | `Instances` to `Group Output`.

We set the collection attribute of the new node so that it reads the column elements:

1. Click the **Collection Info** | **Collection** field and select `Components` from the dropdown menu.
2. Click the **Collection Info** | **Relative** button to maintain the current positions of the components.

With this setup, we can merge multiple objects into one, which is easier to unwrap procedurally.

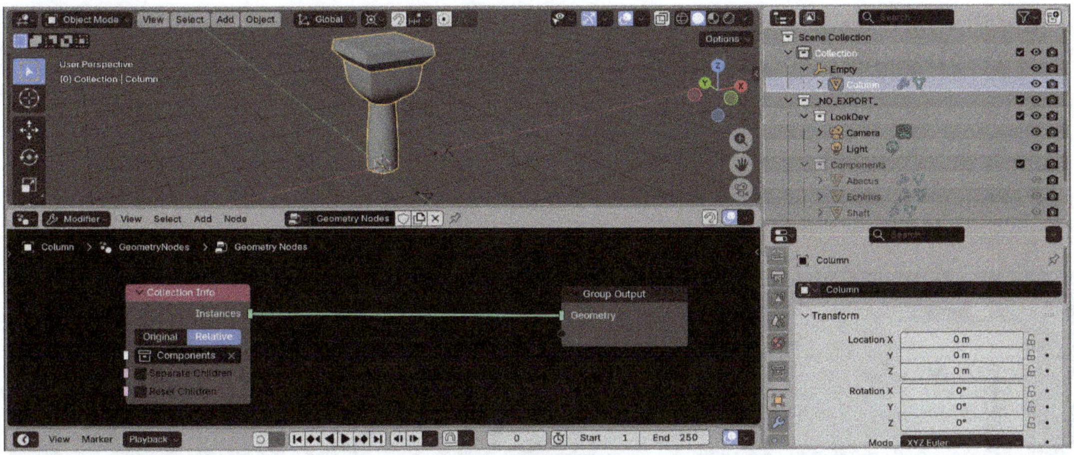

Figure 8.3: The three elements from the Components collection as a single object

The model imported by Unity now consists of only one object, so it is easier to unwrap.

> Note
>
> **Y-Up them all**
>
> We have modeled for Unity since the beginning, so our models were aligned to Unity's Y-up reference all along, but collection instancing is a good way to bring any object under a rotated parent without altering its mesh or object transformation, in case such an operation is needed for models that were not created for Unity in the first place.

Unwrapping instanced meshes

The output of *Collection Info* consists of object instances. Instances are read-only, but we want to store new UV data, so we need to convert them to real data:

1. In the **Node Editor**, press *Shift + A*, type `real`, and click **Instance** | **Realize Instances**; insert the new node between **Collection Info** and **Group Output**.
2. Press *Shift + A*, type `store`, and create an **Attribute** | **Store Named Attribute** node; insert the new node between **Realize Instances** and **Group Output**.

We know from *Chapter 7* that we must set the named attribute's type and domain according to the format of the texture coordinates:

1. Click the first drop-down attribute of **Store Named Attribute** and change it from **Float** to **2D Vector**.
2. Change the second drop-down attribute from **Point** to **Face Corner**.
3. Click the **Name** field and set it to `UVMap`.

By combining **Realize Instances** and **Store Named Attribute**, we can create UVs for the instanced models.

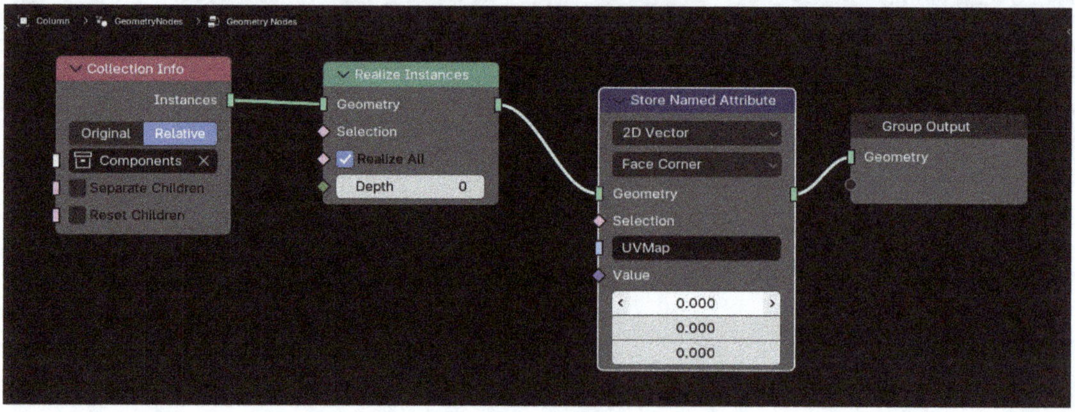

Figure 8.4: Storing UVs on instanced geometry

Store Named Attribute requires valid coordinates as input. Unwrapping objects manually follows a cardboard analogy, where we create seams on the edges where a real-life paper model would be cut. On generated geometry, we need to specify explicit criteria for placing the seams. For instance, we can discriminate the width of the face angles at each edge:

1. Drag the **Store Named Attribute |Value** input with the left mouse button and release it on an empty area, type `unw`, and select **UV Unwrap | UV**.
2. Press *Shift + A*, type `edge` and select **Mesh | Read | Edge Angle**. Place the new node to the left side of the graph.
3. Drag the **Edge Angle | Unsigned Angle** with the left mouse button and release it over an empty area, type great and select **Compare | Greater Than**
4. Connect **Greater Than | Result** to **UV Unwrap | Seam**.

This setup cuts the model into pieces to generate two-dimensional islands. We can display the result and refine the node settings:

1. Click the *Editor Type* button on the *Spreadsheet* header at the top left and select **UV Editor** to display the UV plane.
2. In the **Node Editor**, set **Greater Than | B** to *0.7* to minimize the cuts
3. Set **UV Unwrap | Margin** to *0.08* to leave some room between the UV islands.

UV coordinates make it possible to attach textures to a model, but we must also assign a material for Unity to remap:

1. Click the **Material** tab in the properties, and click the **+ New** button to create a new material.
2. *Double-click* the new material in the list and rename it **Column**.

Materials must be assigned to the generated mesh through geometry nodes:

1. In the **Node Editor**, press *Shift + A*, type `mat`, and click **Geometry | Material | Set Material**. Insert the new node between **Store Named Attribute** and **Group Output**.
2. Click the material drop-down box under the list and select **Column**.

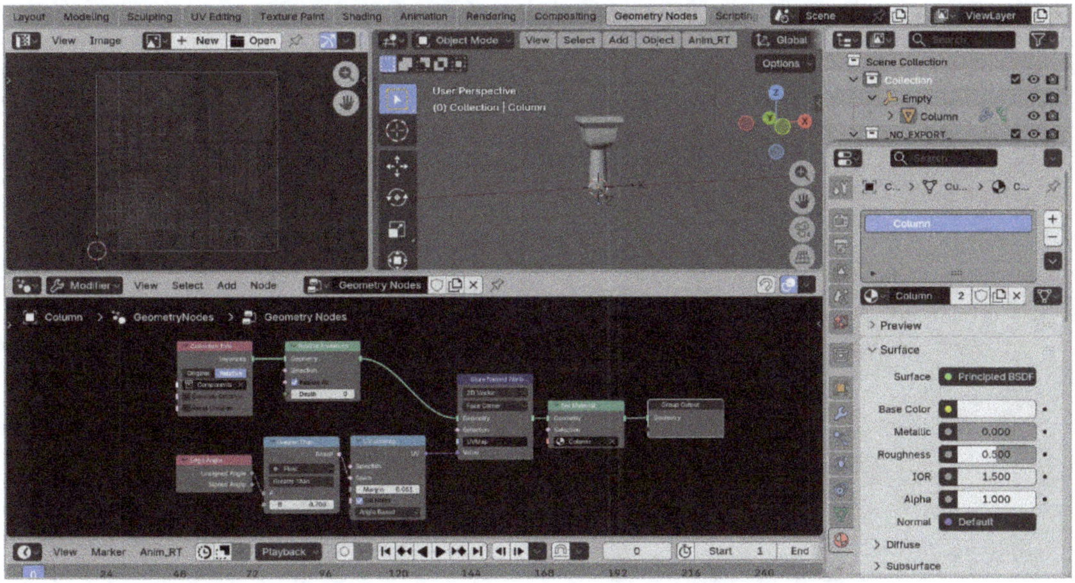

Figure 8.5: Geometry nodes for merging, unwrapping, and shading models

This material will be replaced in Unity, so we don't care about what the shader does in Blender. We will use it for baking the textures, but first we need to create the reference models.

Creating high-resolution duplicates

Our models are very simple, and that makes them easier to edit and exchange, but they are not very realistic, as they have very sharp edges, which are unusual in the real world.

A smoother look requires more density in terms of polygons, so we will create a collection for high-resolution models:

1. In the **Outliner**, *right-click* on the **Components** collection and select **Duplicate Collection**.
2. Double-click the collection **Components.001** and rename it `HighRes`.

The new collection is automatically made visible, even if it's a copy of a hidden one. The duplicates were given a `.001` suffix to their names, so we rename them at once using **Batch Rename**:

1. In the **Outliner**, *right-click* the **HighRes** collection and click **Select Objects** to select all three duplicates.
2. In the top-bar, click the **Edit** menu and then **Batch Rename....** A dialog pops up.
3. Using the default options, **Selected** – **Objects** | **Find/Replace**, type `.001` in the **Find** field and `_HR` in the **Replace** field, then press **OK**.

Working on just three objects, we could have renamed them individually, but *Batch Renamer* ensures that our naming remains consistent.

Being part of the **_NO_EXPORT_** collection, the *HighRes* models will not be imported either; we will polish them only for the purpose of texturing.

Figure 8.6: Batch renaming objects in Blender

Increasing the detail

We can hide the *Column* model for now and focus on the duplicates. Also, since we don't need the **Node Editor**, we will move to a different workspace:

1. Click the **Layout** workspace, the first tab at the top.
2. In the **Outliner**, click the eye icon beside **Collection** to hide it.

We start by cutting a bevel on the abacus, using object modifiers:

1. Select **Abacus_HR**, which at this point is the only abacus displayed in the **Viewport**.
2. Press the dot (`.`) on the numeric pad, or **View** | **Frame Selected** in the **Viewport** top buttons to frame the view to the selected object.
3. In the properties, select the **Modifiers** tab and click the **+ Add Modifier** button.
4. In the menu, select **Generate** | **Bevel**.

The *Bevel* modifier cuts each edge on a slant, creating new faces on top of the edges of the original model. We can tweak the bevel parameter to adjust the shape.

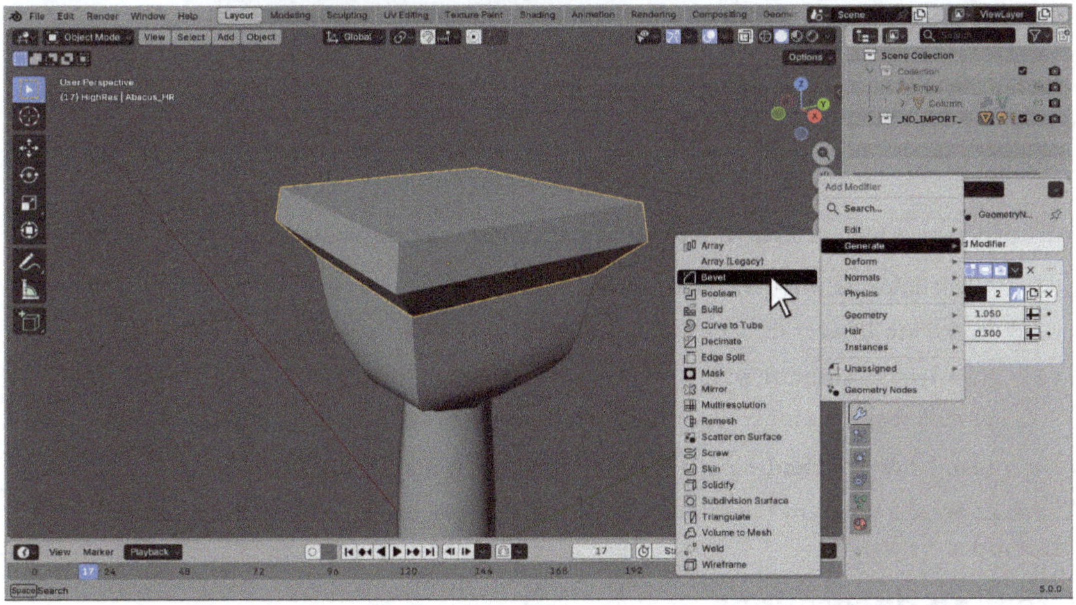

Figure 8.7: Creating a Bevel modifier

We limit the bevel to a tiny amount, just enough to remove the unnatural sharpness:

1. In the **Modifiers** tab, change the bevel **Amount** from `0.1` to `0.015` m.

2. Scroll down to the **Shading** properties of the modifier and expand them.
3. Enable **Harden Normals** to keep the orientation of the original faces.

Beveling increased the polygon count of the mesh but removed the "razor cut" look.

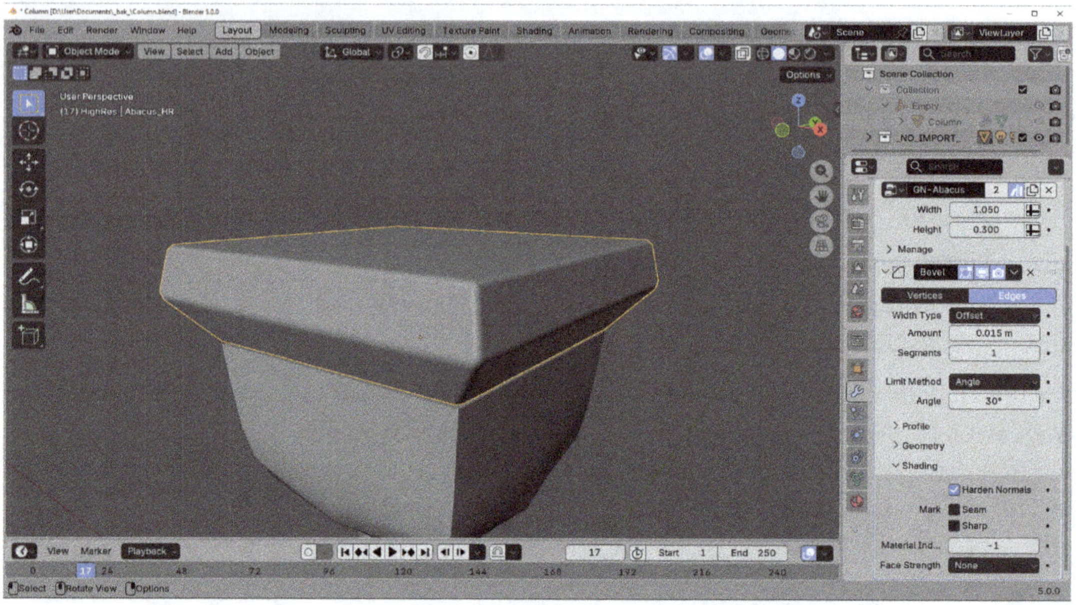

Figure 8.8: A smooth-edged abacus

We can do something similar with the other square piece of the column:

1. Click **Echinus_HR** to make it active.
2. In the **Modifiers** tab, click **+ Add Modifier**, then select **Generate | Bevel**.
3. The default **Amount**, `0.1`, works for this model, but to remove overlapping on the circular base, we must lower the limiting angle to `28`.
4. Scroll down to **Shading** and check **Harden Normals** to smooth the bevel.

The shaft doesn't need any bevel, so rather than increasing its density, we can add some decorations.

Creating decorations

In *Chapter 5*, we have modeled a "neck," a slightly thinner section, on the upper end of our shaft. We can mark the separation between the neck and the main body with a notch, so we fit a ring around the top of the shaft:

1. In the **Viewport**, press *Shift + A* or the **Add** button from the top, and select **Mesh | Cone**.

2. Set Vertices to `8` to match the shaft's octagonal section.
3. Set **Radius 1** to `0.207`; that's the width of the shaft at the neck.
4. Set **Radius 2** to `0.21` to make it slightly larger.
5. Set **Depth** to `0.02` because the notch is supposed to be narrow.
6. Set **Location** | **Z** to `1.01` to place it at the height of the neck.

We have used a cone because the difference in slopes will make the texture more noticeable.

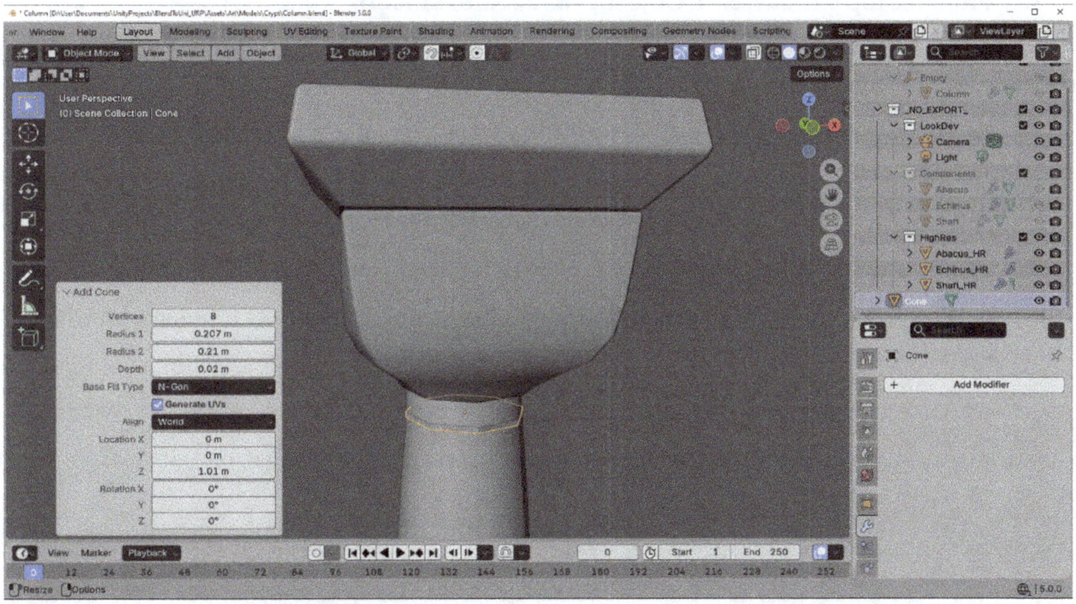

Figure 8.9: Creating a conical notch

As a detail, this cone should belong to the **HighRes** collection and should be smooth:

1. In the **Viewport**, press the `M` key and in the menu select **_NO_EXPORT_** | **HighRes**.
2. From the top buttons, click **Object** | **Shade Auto Smooth** to smooth the surface. The default value of `60` is good for this mesh.

We can decorate the pillar with the low-relief sculpture of a face by placing a monkey head above the surface of the shaft:

1. In the **Viewport**, press *Shift* + *A* or the **Add** button on top, and select **Mesh** | **Monkey**.
2. Expand the **Add Monkey** operator properties at the bottom left corner of the **Viewport** and set **Size** to `0.2`.
3. Set **Location** | **Z** to `0.85` to raise it to the upper half.

4. Set **Location** | **Y** to `-0.14` to bring it forward.
5. Set **Rotation** | **X** to `-8` degrees to match the slope of the shaft.

The monkey must fit the cylindrical shape of the column and have a smooth surface:

1. With the monkey head still selected, in the **Modifiers** properties, click **+ Add Modifier** and select **Deform** | **Cast**.
2. In the modifier's properties, change **Shape** to **Cylinder**.
3. From the top buttons, click **Object** | **Shade Auto Smooth**

We can remove the faces hidden inside the column, which are not required and would be troublesome during baking:

1. In the Modifiers properties, click **+ Add Modifier** and select Generate > Boolean.
2. We subtract the shaft from the monkey head, so the default operation, **Difference**, is the right setting. Click the **Object** field and select `Shaft`.
3. Press `M` and move the model to **_NO_EXPORT_** | **HighRes.**

The models resulting from boolean operations are often prone to incorrect topology, but that's not a concern here as we will not use this model in the game.

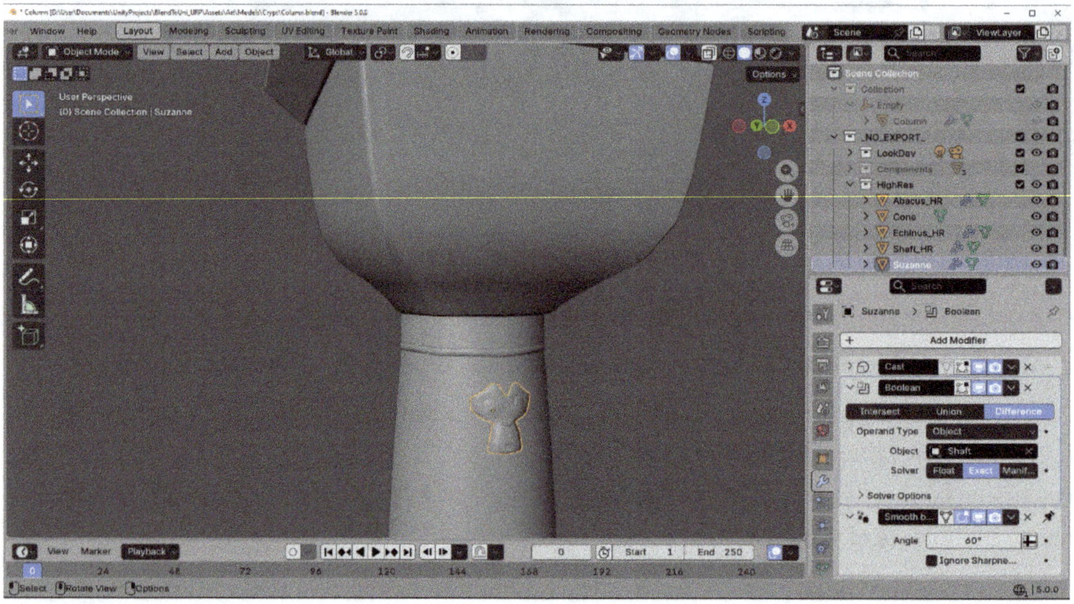

Figure 8.10: A face emerges from the shaft

We can add the same decoration to the other sides of the column:

1. Select the monkey head and press *Alt + D* to invoke **Duplicate Linked**. This operator reuses the same mesh data and doesn't add weight to the scene.
2. Press the dot (`.`) on the keyboard to choose the *Pivot Point*, then click **3D Cursor**.
3. Press **Shift + C** and click **Cursor to World Origin**. This way, the objects are rotated around the origin point.
4. Press `R` to rotate the model, then `Z` to lock on the vertical axis, then type `90` and press `Enter` to finalize the transform.

At this point, there are two monkey faces in relief, watching the south and east sides; we add another pair to finish the job:

1. With the two heads still selected, press *Alt + D* to duplicate again.
2. Press `R`, then `Z`, then type `180` to position the new models and press `Enter` to confirm.

Now there is a head at each cardinal direction, covering the four sides of the column.

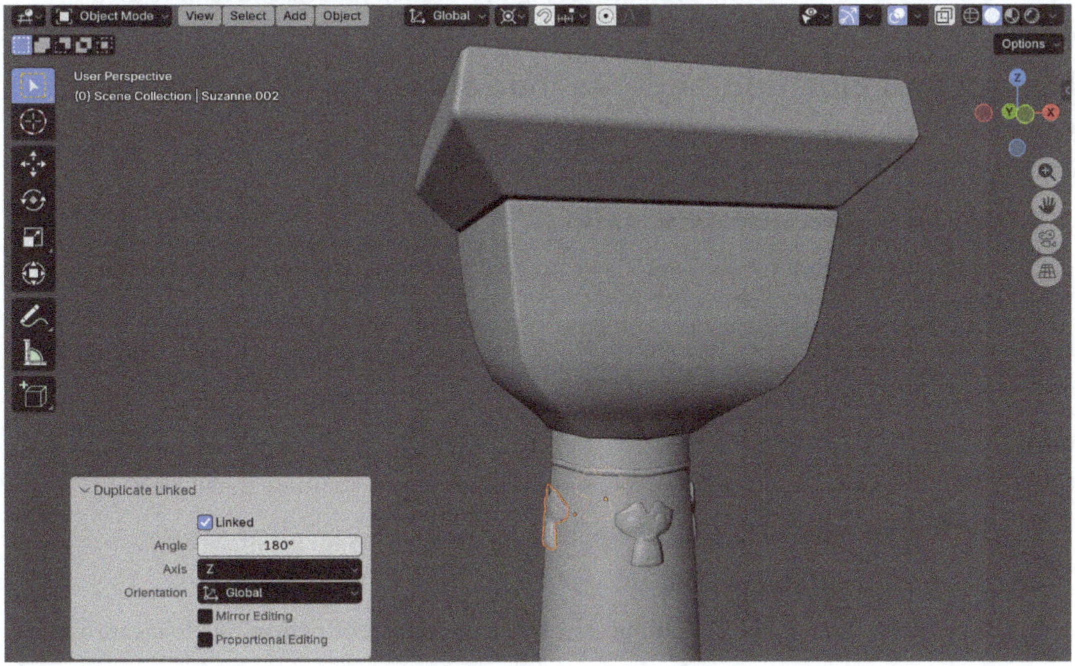

Figure 8.11: Four monkey faces in relief

We didn't edit the geometry of the shaft, so the model Shaft_HR is not needed:

1. Select **Shaft_HR**, either in the **Outliner** or by clicking it in the **Viewport**.
2. Press `X` and click **Delete** to remove it.

Now that the high-resolution models are ready, we can bake their features to textures.

Baking detail maps

We have used texture baking in the section *Creating Textures for PBR Shaders* of *Chapter 7*, and generated images from the channels of a shaded plane. To generate detail maps, we must project the geometry of another model. While the game asset was merged into one object in the paragraph *Joining objects with geometry nodes*, the high-resolution models are still separated.

It's not uncommon for detailed models to be split into multiple objects, so Blender allows baking from a multiple selection, but that can be problematic if there are overlapping faces between two models, like *Abacus* and *Echinus* in our scene.

To avoid texture artifacts, we will combine the high-resolution models and remove their interior faces.

Joining and cleaning high-res models

We will start in the same way as we did for *Components*, reading the geometry from the collection info:

1. Move to the **Geometry Nodes** workspace.
2. In the **3D Viewport**, press *Shift + A* or the **Add** button at the top, and click **Mesh | Plane**.
3. Rename the plane to `Column_HR`.
4. Press `M` and move *Column_HR* to `_NO_EXPORT_`.

We have moved the new object to the *_NO_EXPORT_* collection to prevent it from going to Unity, but it MUST NOT be part of *HighRes*, since it is going to instantiate that collection:

1. In the **Node Editor**, click the **New** button and rename the graph `GN_Column_HR`.
2. Delete the **Group Input** node.
3. Press *Shift + A* and type `coll`, then click **Input | Scene | Collection** Info to create a new node.
4. Click on the **Collection Info | Collection Field** and select **HighRes** from the list.

5. Connect **Collection Info | Instances** to **Group Output Geometry**.
6. In the **Outliner**, click the eye icon beside the **HighRes** collection to hide it and avoid confusion.

This is the same configuration used at the beginning of the graph *GN_Column*; we can display the inner geometry by pressing the Z key and selecting **Wireframe**.

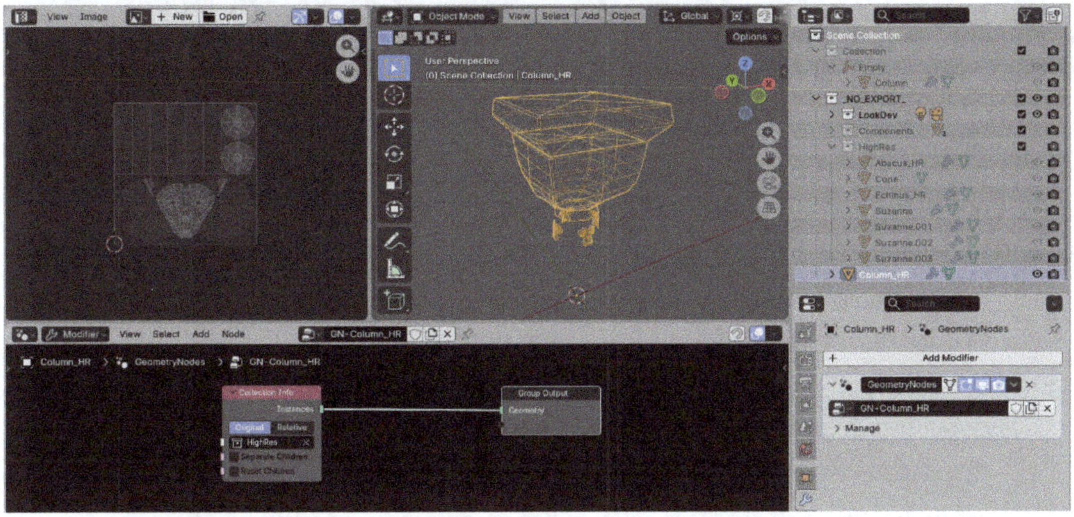

Figure 8.12: The wireframe displays the inner polygons of the high-resolution mesh

We want to remove the internal polygons, so we will use *Delete Geometry*:

1. In the **Node Editor**, press *Shift + A*, type `reali`, and click **Instances | Realize Instances**. Insert the new node between **Collection Info** and **Group Output**.
2. Press *Shift + A*, type `del`, and click **Geometry | Operations | Delete Geometry**. Insert the new node between **Realize Instances** and **Group Output**.
3. Change **Delete Geometry**'s first attribute, the *domain*, from **Point** to **Face**.

This setup is quite nasty and deletes our geometry entirely!

Figure 8.13: All Column_HR is gone with Realize Instances and Delete Geometry.

We can discriminate which geometry should be deleted using the **Delete Geometry | Selection** socket. To determine which faces qualify as inner, we can use raycasting, an algorithm that looks for neighbor polygons by casting rays from a position toward a direction:

1. Move **Collection Info** and **Realize Instances** to the left side of the graph, and **Delete Geometry** and **Group Output** to the right side to make room.
2. Press *Shift + A*, type ray, and click **Geometry | Sample | Raycast**.
3. Connect the output of **Realize Instances** to **Raycast | Target Geometry**.
4. Connect **Raycast | Is Hit** to **Delete Geometry | Selection**.

We can see in the **Viewport** that face deletion has become more selective.

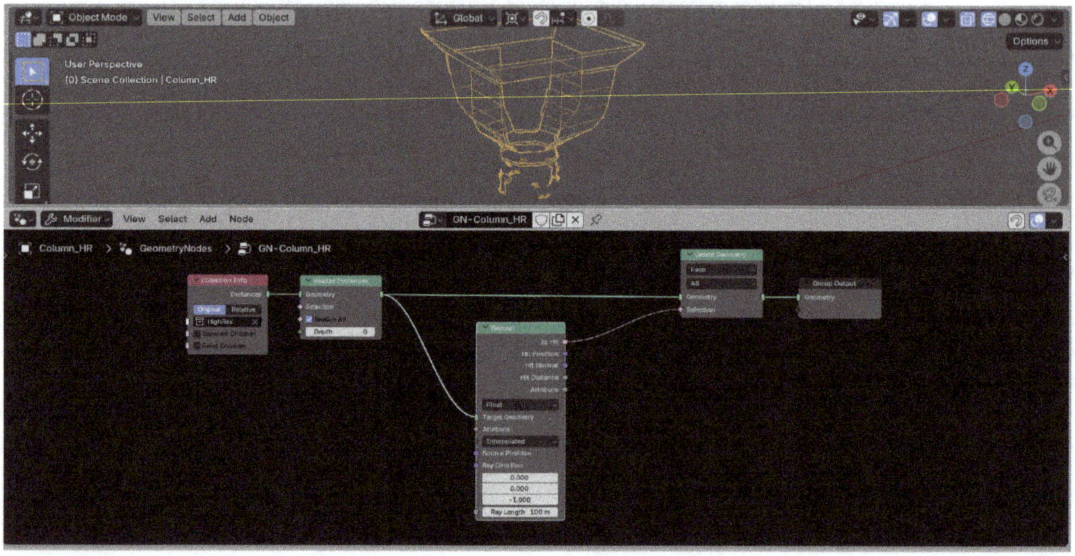

Figure 8.14: Selecting faces with Raycast

We need to adjust the raycast to delete only the faces on the inside:

1. In the **Node Editor**, press *Shift + A*, type `pos`, and connect a **Geometry | Read | Position** node to **Raycast | Source Position**. The point position is the default value of this socket, so this connection doesn't affect the outcome.
2. Press *Shift + A*, type `nor`, and create a **Geometry | Read | Normal** node. Connect **Normal | Normal** to **Raycast | Ray Direction**

Casting from each point towards the direction of its normal catches the geometry in the middle, but the criterion is still too permissive and needs refinement:

1. Drag the **Position | Position** socket with the left mouse button, release it on the background, and select **Vector Math | Add**; insert the new node between **Position** and **Raycast | Source Position**.
2. Connect **Normal | Normal** to the second socket of **Add**; this way, we inflate the point positions and cast rays from outside the model. All the faces of the model are back in the **Viewport**.
3. Press *Shift + A*, type `scal`, and select **Utilities | Vector | Vector Math | Scale**. Insert the new node between **Normal** and **Add**.
4. Set **Scale | Scale** to `0.09` to reduce the displacement.

We can see that the faces between abacus and echinus were removed.

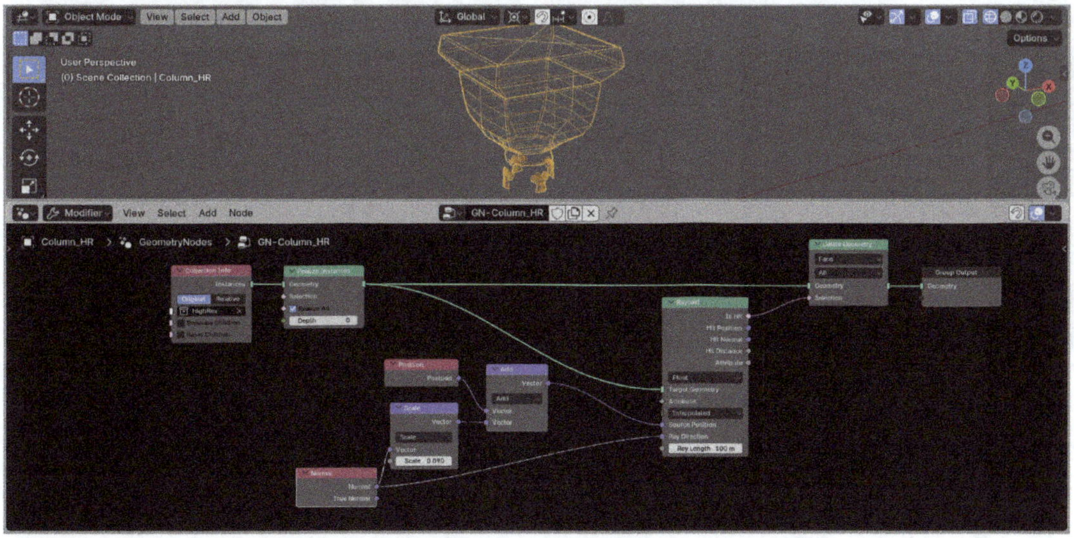

Figure 8.15: Removing inner faces with Raycast

Our setup is working almost as intended: some polygons of the monkey decorations were removed. The easiest way to fix that is by limiting the deletion above a certain height:

1. In the **Node Editor**, press *Shift + A*, type and, click **Utilities** | **Math** | **Boolean Math** | **And**, and insert the new node between **Raycast** | **Is Hit** and **Delete Geometry**.
2. Drag the free **And** | **Boolean** input socket with the left mouse, release it on the background, type pos, and click **Position** | **Position** to connect a new **Position** node. *Position* is not a boolean type, so we must insert a comparison node.
3. Drag the new **Position** socket with the left mouse button, release it on the background, type great, and click **Compare** | **Greater Than**. Insert the new node between **Position** and **And**.
4. Set the three components of **Greater Than** | **B** to `-1000`, `-1000`, and `1.0`, respectively.

The default comparison is elementwise, so our nodes will only delete the points whose *Z* is above the threshold of `1.0`. Using such low values for the first two components ensures that no points are excluded because of negative *X* or *Y*.

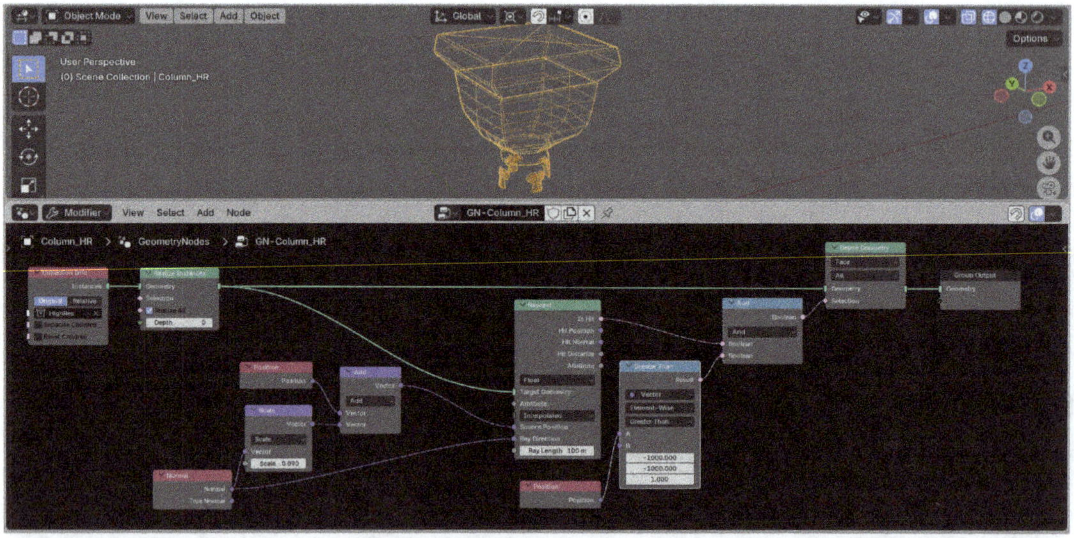

Figure 8.16: Deleting inner faces with Z above 1.0.

This setup could become more generic if we use group inputs, but it's good as it is for our purpose. Now that our high-resolution model is ready, we can bake the normal map that we will use in the game.

Setting up the model for baking

The Bake operator doesn't account for generated coordinates, so we should apply the **Geometry Nodes** modifier before creating our textures. When a modifier is applied, its result is moved into the actual mesh data and the modifier itself is deleted. We don't want to lose our procedural workflow, and since our nodes override the geometry, we can apply a duplicate and keep our modifier:

1. In the **Outliner**, click the "closed eye" icon beside **Collection** to make it visible again.
2. Select **Column**, always in the **Outliner**, as in the **Viewport** there might be confusion with *Column_HR*, which is also visible and overlaps at the top.
3. In the **Modifiers** tab, click the expansion button with the options to the left of the Geometry Nodes modifier, just before the **X** button.
4. Click **Duplicate** from the drop-down menu.

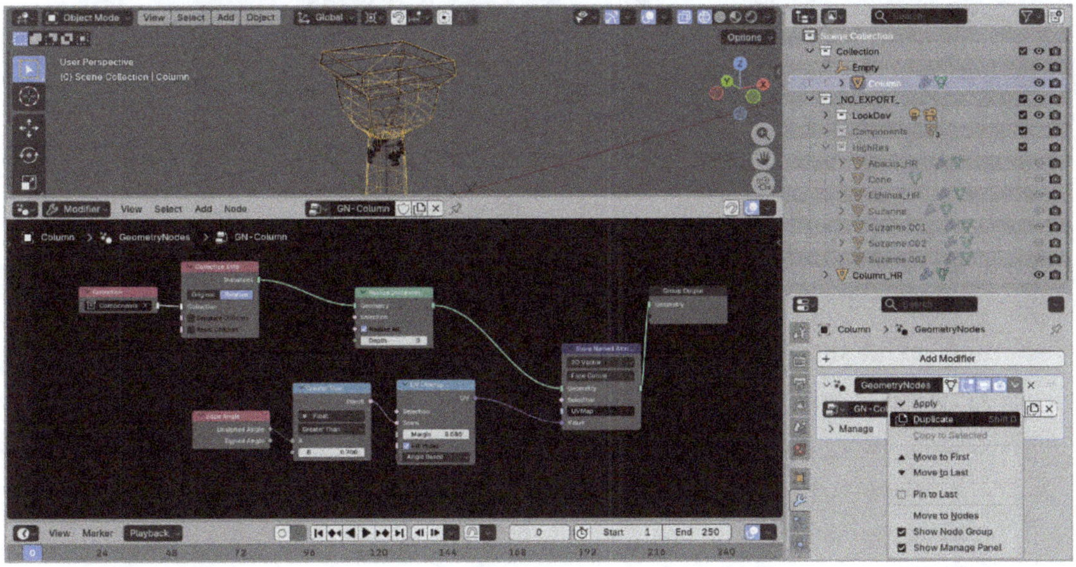

Figure 8.17: Duplicating a modifier

Now there are two identical modifiers on our column. The result is unchanged, as the second modifier overwrites the first. We can apply one of them. It's not important which one, as they are equivalent, the only difference being a .001 suffix at the end of the second modifier's name, `GeometryNodes.001`:

1. Click the Options button of the new **Geometry Nodes** modifier.

2. Click **Apply** to pass its result to the mesh data.
3. The **Bake** operator doesn't like the remaining modifier: uncheck the camera button to disable it during renders and bake operations.

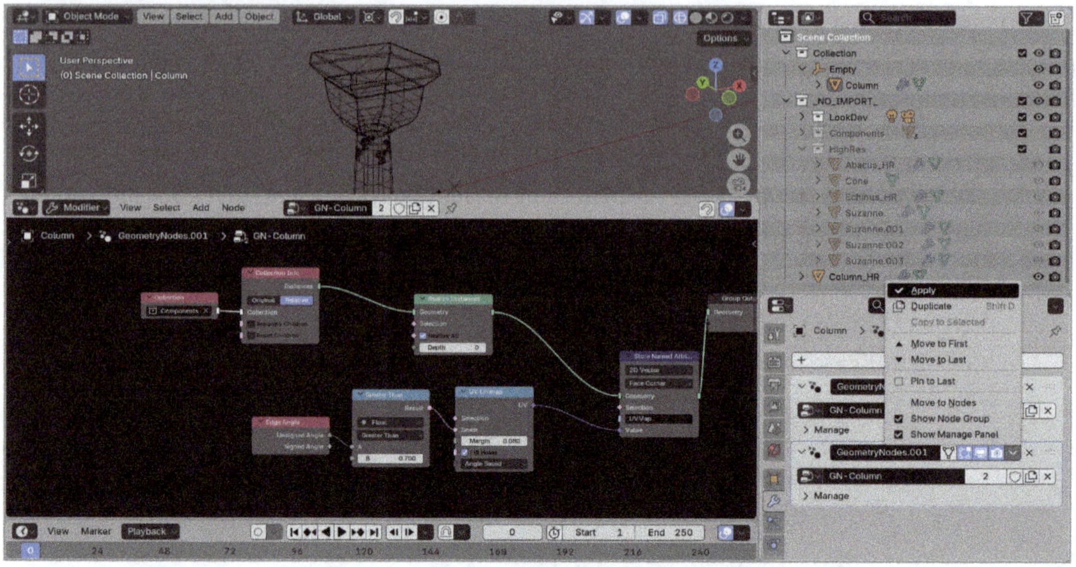

Figure 8.18: Applying a duplicate of our modifier

This solution is suboptimal, and we must apply the modifier again every time we make changes to the column, but at least it will allow Blender to bake texture images.

We can move to the **Shading** workspace and set up the material:

1. Click the **Shading** tab in the workspace top bar.
2. Select the **Material** properties on the right; the list will be empty after the application of the **Geometry Nodes** modifier.
3. Expand the material drop-down button to the left of the **+ New** button and select **Column**.

Figure 8.19: Setting the object material of the column

Now we can see our material in the **Shader Editor**, and create an image for baking:

1. In the **Shader Editor**, press *Shift + A* and select **Texture** | **Image Texture**.
2. Place the texture in the graph and press the **New** button.
3. Type `Column_normal` as the name of the new map.
4. Set both **Width** and **Height** to 4096, as normal maps require higher resolutions, then press the **New Image** button.
5. Set the **Color Space** of the new image to **Non-Color**, or the color profile will mess up the normals.

The model and its material are ready, and we can proceed with baking.

Baking the normal map

We know from *Chapter 7* that baking requires the *Cycles* render engine, so we change that in the render properties:

1. Select the **Render** tab in the properties panel on the right.
2. Click the **Render Engine** drop-down box and change it from **EEVEE** to **Cycles**.
3. Set **Render** | **Max Samples** to 8 and uncheck **Denoise** to reduce time.

First, we will bake the normal map, to mimic the lit surface of the detailed model:

1. Scroll down the *Render* properties and expand the **Bake** section. Set **Bake Type** to **Normal**.
2. We are baking from one model to another, so check **Selected to Active** and expand its options panel.
3. Set **Extrusion** to `0.02` to probe the neighboring faces from slightly above the surface; that helps capture the normals of the relief.
4. Set **Max Ray Distance** to `0.03` to limit the search distance of matching geometry.
5. Set **Margin | Size** to `0`, or the texture will bleed where no high-resolution geometry is present, e.g., around the monkey heads.

Selected to Active requires selecting the high and low resolution models together:

1. In the *Outliner*, click **Column_HR** with the left mouse button to select it.
2. Keep the `Ctrl` key pressed, either one, and click **Column** with the left mouse button to select it too.
3. Click **Bake** to start the process.

After a while, we should see that `Column_normal` is baked; normal maps have a distinguishing purple trait.

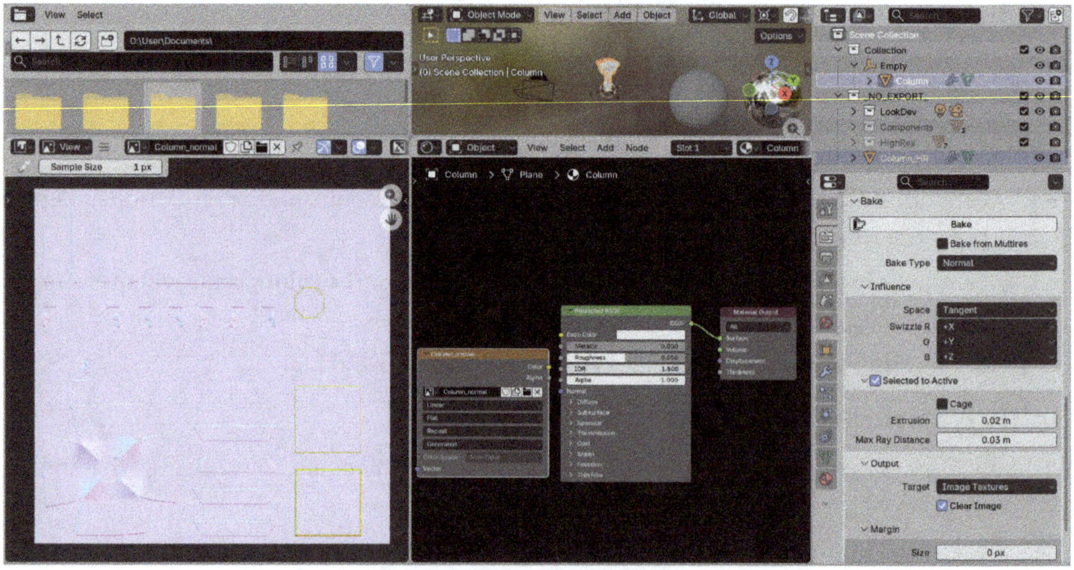

Figure 8.20: Normal map of the column

We can save this texture to the Unity project, using the Image Editor:

1. Click the "hamburger" menu of the *Image Editor* and select **Image** | **Save As...**
2. Reach **BlendToUni_URP** | **Assets** | **Art** | **Textures** in the file dialog.
3. The image name is already set to `Column_normal.png`. Click the **RGB** button since this texture doesn't have *Alpha*, but leave the **Color Space** set to **Non-Color**.
4. Press **Save As Image** to write the file to disk.

Using this texture in Unity will display the smooth edges and decorations on the base model of the column. To help the illusion of detail, we can generate an occlusion texture as well.

Baking the occlusion map

Unity can generate screen space ambient occlusion, but having that information in a texture is helpful for creating effects in our shaders.

There is a useful Blender node for occlusion shading, which accounts for normal maps:

1. We don't need the high-resolution model anymore: in the *Outliner*, disable the eye and camera buttons beside **_NO_EXPORT_** to exclude it from rendering, or it will cause unwanted occlusion.
2. In the *Shader Editor*, press *Shift + A* and create an **Input** | **Ambient Occlusion** node.
3. Connect **Ambient Occlusion** | **Color** to **Principled BSDF** | **Base Color**.

To evaluate the normal map occlusion, we need a connection from *Column_normal*:

1. Drag the socket **Column_normal** | **Color** and release it on the background, type `nor`, and click **Normal Map** | **Color**.
2. Connect **Normal Map** | **Normal** to **Ambient Occlusion** | **Normal**.

The effect is very faint under the default lighting, but by zooming in on the column, we should see the "dirt" caused by the decorations.

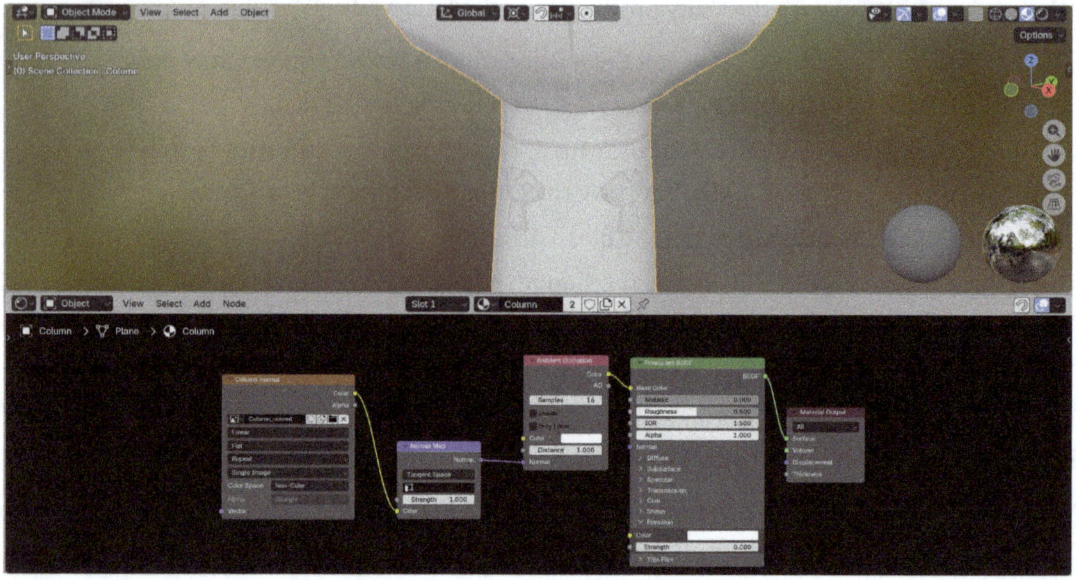

Figure 8.21: Ambient occlusion from the normal map

We will create another image for baking this texture to Unity:

1. In the Shader Editor, press *Shift + A* and select **Texture** | **Image Texture**.
2. Place the texture in the graph and press the **New** button.
3. Type `Column_occlusion` as the name of the new map.
4. Set **Width** and **Height** to `4096`: occlusion maps might not need as much detail as normal maps do, but sticking to one format for all textures is convenient.
5. Set the **Color Space** to **Non-Color**, as this is not a color map either.

With the `Column_occlusion` image node active, we can write a diffuse texture:

1. In the **Bake** properties on the right, set **Bake Type** to **Diffuse**.
2. In the **Influence** properties, uncheck **Direct** and **Indirect**.
3. Uncheck **Selected to Active** as we are not baking from another model.
4. Set **Margin** | **Size** to 8: that avoids sampling artifacts around the seams for non-normal maps.
5. Click the **Bake** button to create the texture.

The *Image Editor* will display the black and white texture of the occlusion.

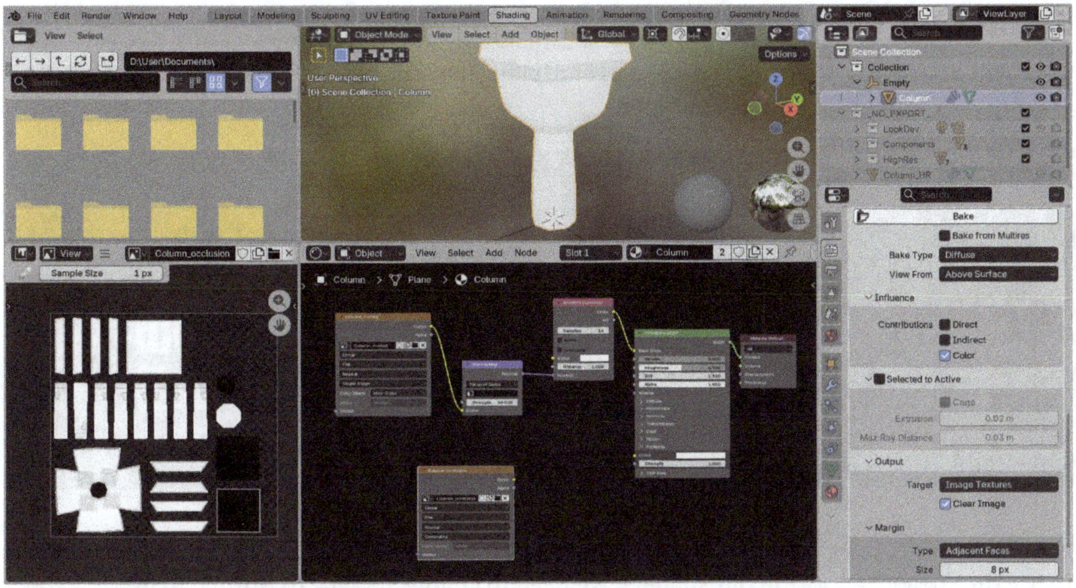

Figure 8.22: Baking the occlusion texture

We can save this new image to the game project:

1. In the *Image Editor*, click the "hamburger" menu and select **Image** | **Save As...**
2. The file dialog should already point to **BlendToUni_URP** | **Assets** | **Art** | **Textures**. Click the **BW** button for the **Color** format and press **Save As Image** to write `Column_occlusion.png`.
3. Save the `Column.blend` file using **Ctrl + S** or **File** | **Save** from the top menu bar.

Now that we have generated the textures for our column, we can switch to Unity and create the material.

Mixing the textures in Unity

Once the textures are exported to image files, the Blender part of our shading process is done. We can connect our textures to Unity's shaders right away, but we can also include them in our current workflow and integrate texture properties into our existing shaders. We will start by setting the correct image type for our new assets.

Setting up the texture type

If we switch to Unity or open the project `BlendToUni_URP`, the project browser will display the new files in `Assets` | `Art` | `Textures`.

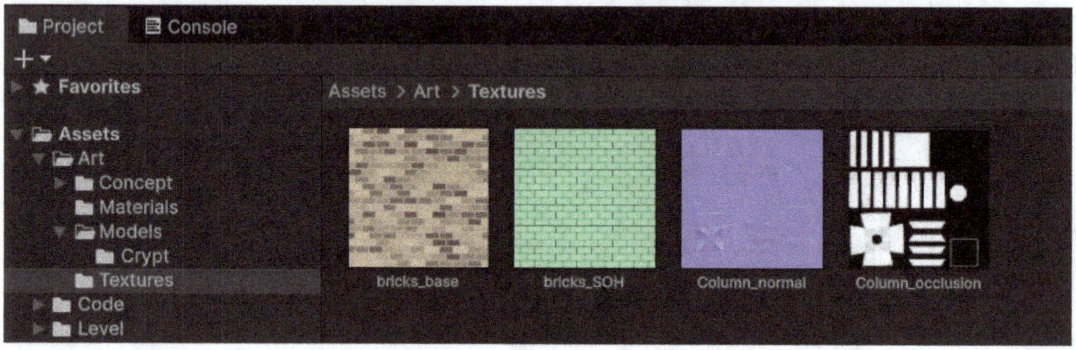

Figure 8.23: Column textures in Unity

To use the `Column_normal` in our shaders, we need to change its type to Normal map:

1. In Unity's **Project Browser**, navigate to the folder **Assets** | **Art** | **Textures** and select the image **Column_normal**.
2. In the **Inspector** on the right, set **Texture Type** to **Normal Map**.
3. Click the **Apply** button in the *Inspector* to apply the change.

The *Occlusion* texture works correctly with the default image type, but we must disable the *sRGB* correction since it was saved as *Non-Color*:

1. In the **Project** browser, select the texture **Column_occlusion**.
2. In the **Inspector**, uncheck the **sRGB (Color Texture)** box.
3. Click the **Apply** button.

To attach those textures to the columns, we will need a shader and a material.

Blending the normal map

We can extend the shader created for the plaster, with its variation in color and porosity, and add two texture parameters to use the same graph for the column's material:

1. In the **Project Browser**, navigate to the folder **Assets** | **Art** | **Materials** and *double-click* **Plaster_Graph** to open the shader editor.
2. The **Fragment**'s **Normal** of Plaster_Graph is already connected, so we insert a normal texture using a blending node. Drag the **Normal From Height** | **Out** socket with the

left mouse button and release it on the background, type `blen`, and click **Normal Blend: A** to create a blend node.

3. Connect **Normal Blend** | **Out** to **Fragment** | **Normal**.

Normal Blend mixes two normal inputs, so we can set a normal property for the graph:

1. In the **Plaster_Graph** blackboard, click **+** to create a new property, and select **Texture 2D**.
2. Name the new node `Normal Map`.
3. Select the **Normal Map** property on the blackboard. In the **Graph Inspector** | **Node Settings**, change **Mode** from **White** to **Normal Map**.

We can connect the **Normal Map** to **Normal Blend**, passing through a *Sample* node:

1. Drag the input socket **Normal Blend** | **B** with the left mouse button and release it, type `samp`, and click **Sample Texture 2D : RGBA**.
2. On the **Sample Texture 2D** node, change **Type** from **Default** to **Normal**.
3. Drag the input socket **Sample Texture 2D** | **Texture** with the left mouse button and release it on the background, type `nor`, and click **Property: Normal Map: Normal Map T(2)**.
4. Set the **Mode** on the **Normal Blend** to **Reoriented** for a correct recalculation of the normals, as the default averaging might cause artifacts.

The default value of *Normal Map* is a neutral blue, so leaving it unset doesn't alter the output of the **Normal From Height** node.

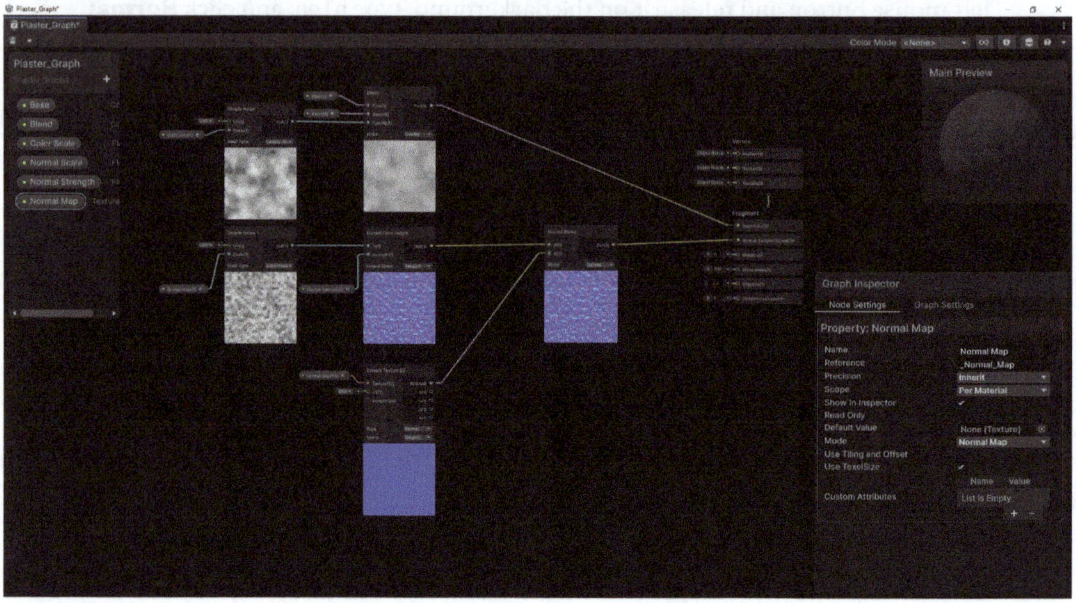

Figure 8.24: Adding Normal Map to the Plaster_Graph shader

We can do the same for the *occlusion* map and create another texture property.

Blending the occlusion map

Occlusion is a shading technique where a surface gets darker if surrounded by other polygons. It is not strictly photorealistic, as it is determined by the shape of an object rather than by the properties of light, but it is a good representation of how closed corners get less lighting. In Unity, the white areas of an occlusion map indicate where a model receives full environment lighting, while black areas indicate no indirect lighting.

In our case, `Column_occlusion` will limit the indirect lighting that reaches the notch and carvings.

1. In the **Plaster_Graph** blackboard, click **+** to create a new Texture 2D property.
2. Name the new node **Occlusion Map**
3. Drag the socket **Fragment** | **Occlusion** with the left mouse button, release it, and type `samp`. Double-click **Sample: Texture 2D: R(1)**, as occlusion is a grayscale map.
4. Drag the new **Sample Texture 2D** | **Texture** socket with the left mouse button, release it, and type `occ`, then *double-click* **Property: Occlusion Map: Occlusion Map(T2)**.

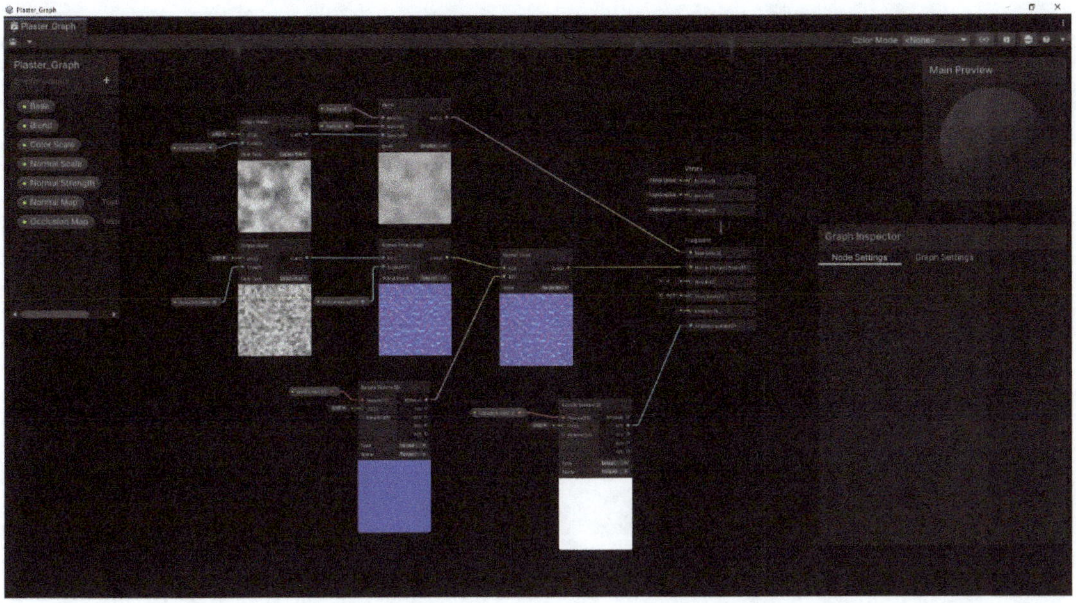

Figure 8.25: Plaster_Graph with both texture inputs

The default value of a new **Texture 2D** input is white, so if left blank, our new property doesn't affect the **Plaster** material. Now we can create a material for the columns.

Shading the columns

We have put together the `Plaster_Graph` so that it works for textured and untextured models. While we leave the texture slots empty on the material assigned to the roof, we create a new material that uses the column textures:

1. In the **Project** browser, *right-click* on **Plaster_Graph** and click **Create | Material** from the menu.
2. Type `Column` and press `Enter` to name the new material.

This material is a different variant of **Plaster**, on which we set the texture properties in the inspector:

1. Select the **Column** material. In the **Inspector**, click the **Select** button on the **Normal Map** thumbnail.
2. In the **Select Texture** dialog, select the **Column_normal** texture.
3. Click the **Select** button in the **Occlusion Map** thumbnail and select **Column_occlusion**.

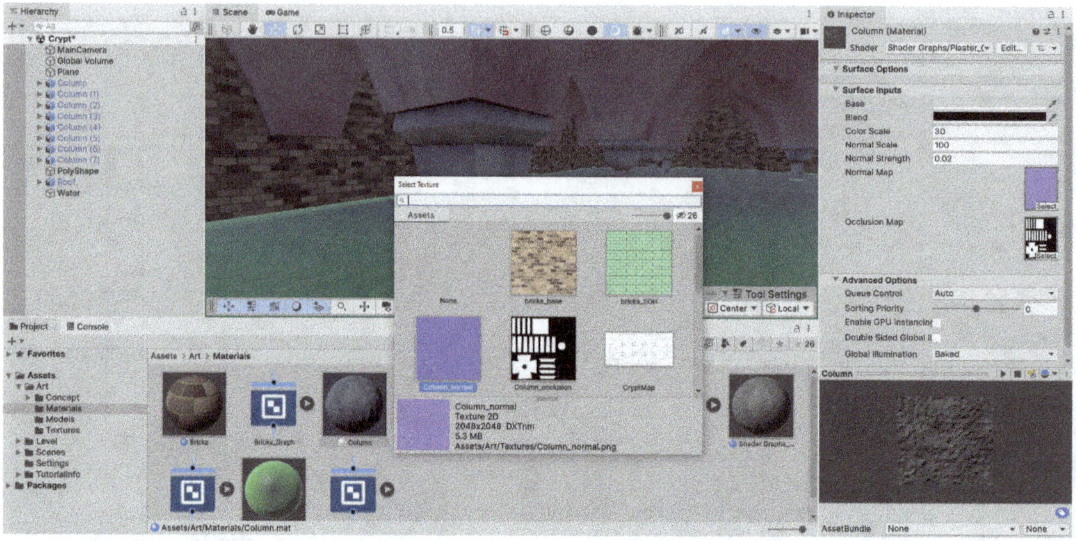

Figure 8.26: Setting the textures of Column

With an entry in the `Materials` folder, we can set up a remap policy for the column:

1. In the **Project** browser, navigate to the folder **Asset** | **Art** | **Models** | **Crypt** and select the asset **Column**.
2. In the **Inspector**, click the **Materials** button and expand the **On Demand Remap** options.
3. Make sure that **Naming** is set to **From Model's Material** and **Search** is **RecursiveUp**, then press the **Search and Remap** button.
4. The remap entry of **Column** will be set to the **Column** material, then press the **Apply** button.
5. Unity replaces the material imported from Blender with the one in `Asset` | `Art` | `Materials`. In the **Viewport**, we will see the baked details on the columns.

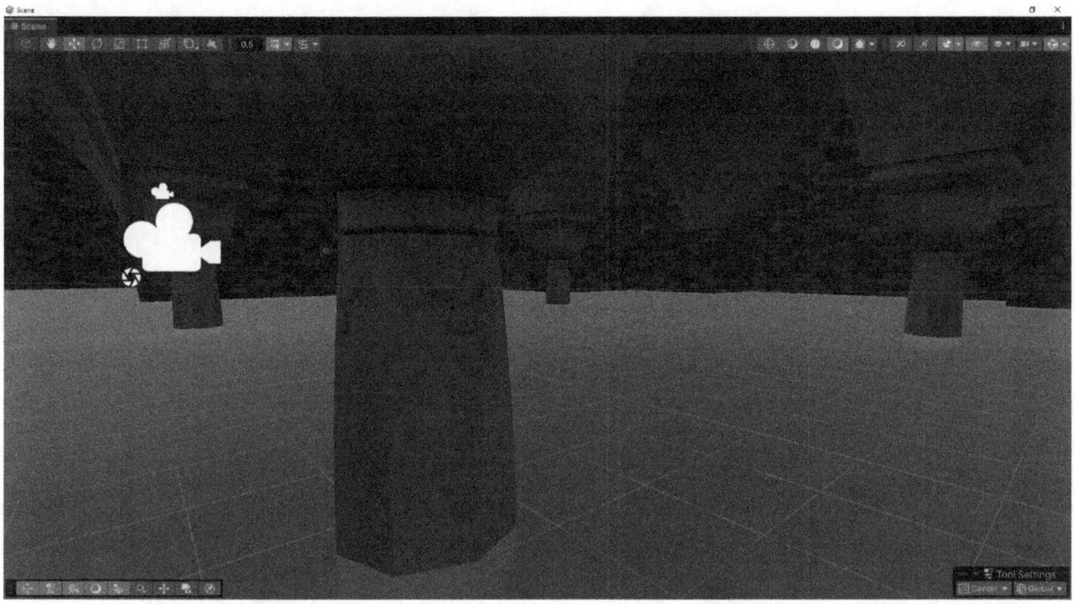

Figure 8.27: The textured columns in Unity - we can see the details from the normal map

The column's edges became more visible, but it's not our texture's fault: it's due to the plaster noise being more evident around the seams. Adjusting the color parameters will make it less noticeable:

1. In the **Project** browser, select the **Column** material in `Assets | Art | Materials`.
2. Click the **Base** color and, in the picker, set its **H**, **S**, and **V** values to `30`, `15`, and `90` respectively.
3. Click the **Blend** color and set its **H**, **S**, and **V** values to `25`, `30`, `50`.
4. Set **Color Scale** to `5.0` for larger marbling.

With the column shading in place, our materials are finished, and our scene is ready.

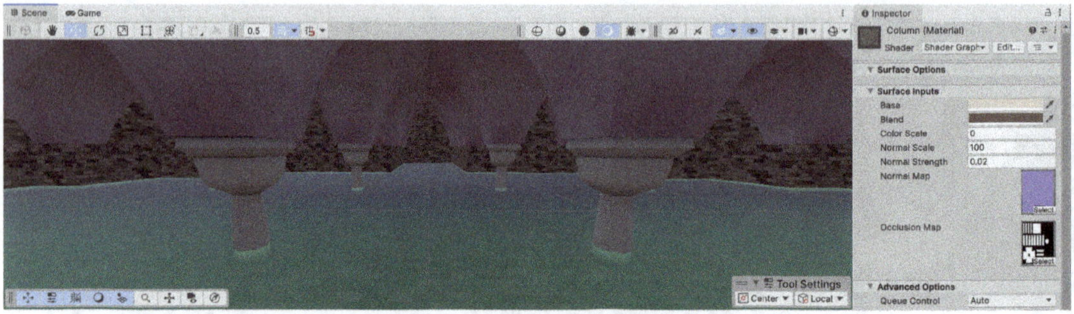

Figure 8.28: Final shading of the level

Blending images with editable parameters helps integrate our models organically and confers some variability to an otherwise too regular look. Even in such an unlit environment, textures help give character to our models.

Summary

Texturing is an essential part of the shading process, and it is even more prominent in videogames, where there are constraints that force aesthetic and topological choices on models and materials.

Blender provides more advanced techniques, like texture painting and digital sculpting, which cannot be covered in a generalist book. Still, the steps illustrated in this chapter complete the workflow for image map extraction from Blender to Unity and bridge the texturing tools of the first with the shading system of the latter.

In the next chapter, we will finally bring some action to our game.

9

Creating Gameplay and Animation

We have created assets and materials, and our level is ready for exploration, so we need a character that can move in the game. The implementation of controls and interactivity is mostly technical, but it's not devoid of creativity in devising the point of view and the aesthetic of the experience: in a visual medium, movement and animation are part of the narrative.

A first-person perspective, like the one used in this project, doesn't require a full character model, but it still requires some work in positioning the camera and props, which can be carried out in Blender and transferred to Unity.

At the same time, we need to define the actions that will be available to the player and make our character able to perform them within the constraints enforced by the game. The three elements of input, performance, and control can be stacked together using Unity's component system.

Unity provides a scripting programming interface that allows developers to instruct the behavior of game objects; some programming is inevitable when it comes to games, which are programs after all. The coding elements will be introduced gradually for the purpose of integrating the asset workflow presented in the book.

Topics like character setup and animation are separate disciplines that are treated in specific books, but the present work would be incomplete without an introduction to character articulation and an example of animation.

This chapter will cover the following topics:

- Creating a first-person character
- Implementing the input system
- Game character animation

Technical requirements

We will use *Blender 5.1* and *Unity 6.3*, which can be installed by following the instructions from *Chapter 1* or from their respective websites.

We will also use a programmer text editor: any editor would do, but here are a few lightweight options:

- Notepad++ for Windows, downloadable from `https://notepad-plus-plus.org`
- *CotEditor* for Mac, available at `https://coteditor.com`
- *xed*, or the default text editor for most Linux distributions

Readers already versed with scripting are encouraged to keep using their editor of choice, usually an advanced tool like *Visual Studio Code* or *JetBrains Rider*. Those are better equipped for production game development, but their extra functionalities are not a must-have for our simple project.

You can download the example project and code for this book by following the instructions in the *Download the example code files* section in the *Preface* of this book.

This chapter's code files are included in the downloadable code bundle.

Creating the character

In games, a character is the focus of impersonation, even more than in traditional media; the amount of characterization in a game protagonist ranges from incredibly detailed backstories to a barely noticeable presence. It is an apparent contradiction, but it is how game designers balance the player's attachment between narrated knowledge and direct experience. In our case, we are not building a character at all: we will implement a first-person perspective.

Creating the first-person scene

In a first-person game, we cannot see the protagonist except for the hands or a handheld object, so we will start with a Camera:

1. Open Blender and press *A*, then `X` and confirm **Delete** to remove all objects.
2. Press *Shift + A* and select **Camera** to create a new camera.

Cameras in Blender are created with a look-down rotation, but this one will be our point of view, so we want it to look straight ahead inside the Unity coordinate system.

1. Select the **Camera** and press *Alt + R* to reset its rotation.
2. Press *Alt + G* to clear the translations.
3. Press *Shift + A* and select **Empty** | **Y-Up Axis**, our utility created in *Chapter 4*, to align it with Unity's axis.

We also move the camera to an average person's height and rotate it to face the forward axis, *Z* in Unity:

1. With Camera still selected, press *G* to move the object, then *Z* to lock the vertical axis, type `1.7`, and press *Enter* to confirm.
2. Press *R* to rotate, then *Z* to lock the vertical axis, type `180` to orient it toward the *Empty*'s *Z* axis.

It's time to save our scene to the game project; we will use the Level folder as this is a level navigation asset:

1. Press *Ctrl + S* or **File** | **Save** to open the **File** dialog.
2. Reach the folder `BlendToUni_URP` | `Assets` | `Level`, create a new directory, and name it `Prefabs`.
3. Type `FirstPerson` as the filename and click **Save Blender File**.

Our blender scene is now part of the project, and can be used as a game object:

1. Open the Unity project and, in the **Project** browser, navigate to the folder `Assets` | `Level` | `Prefabs`.
2. Drag the asset **FirstPerson** and release it in the **Crypt** level.
3. With **First Person** selected, in the **Inspector**, set **Position**'s `X` and `Y` to `0`, and **Position Z** to `12`.
4. Orient the character toward the level by setting **Rotation Y** to `180`.
5. Now that our character is in the scene, we don't need the plane with the concept map anymore. Select **Plane** in the **Navigation** view and press `Delete`.

If we switch to the **Game** tab, we will look at the level from **FirstPerson**'s camera and notice that something is wrong.

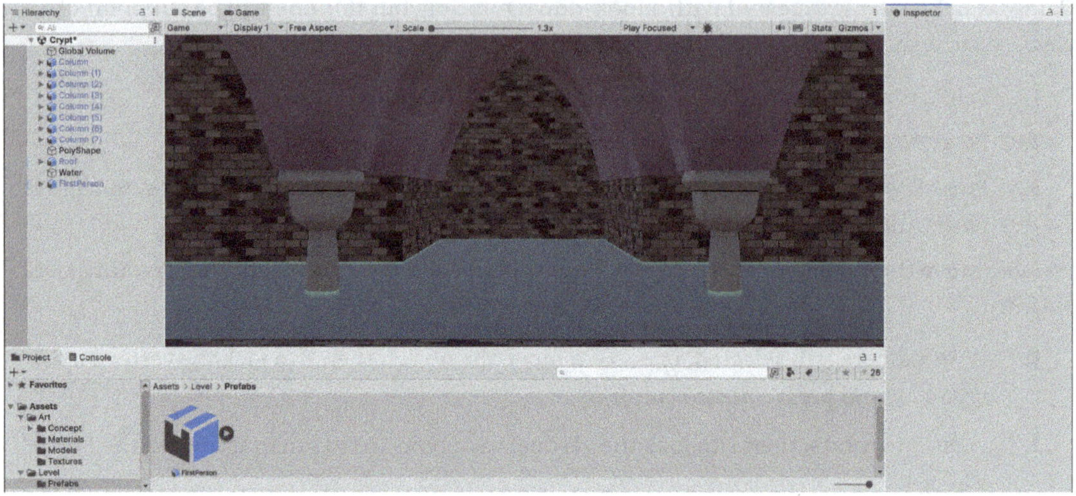

Figure 9.1: Looking through the FirstPerson's camera

First, because of Blender's default focal length, our character doesn't see the first two columns; also, the water plane is cut because of the default near clip setting. We can fix those properties in Blender:

1. Switch back to Blender and open `FirstPerson.blend`. Make sure that **Camera** is selected.
2. Select the *Camera* tab in the properties panel on the right.
3. Change **Lens Unit** from **Millimeters** to **Field of View**, the metric used in Unity.

Field of View is an angular measure of how wide the view of a camera is: a `180`-degree field of view allows a person to see what happens at their sides; the optimal field of view for a first-person camera depends, besides considerations about human perception, on the target screen (mobile, computer screen, etc.) and the size of the game window. Here we will set a value large enough for viewing the environment, and lower the *Clip Start* to prevent the view from cutting through geometries:

1. With *Camera* still selected, in the *Camera* properties, set **Field of View** to `90` degrees.
2. Set **Clip Start** to `0.001` to display close geometries.

We can save the `FirstPerson.blend` and switch back to Unity. The numeric values will be translated to the Unity metrics, so if we select **FirstPerson** | **Camera** in our scene, we can see that **Field of View** is approximately **67.38** and **Clipping Planes** | **Near** amounts to `0.1`. That's fine, as the camera works as intended.

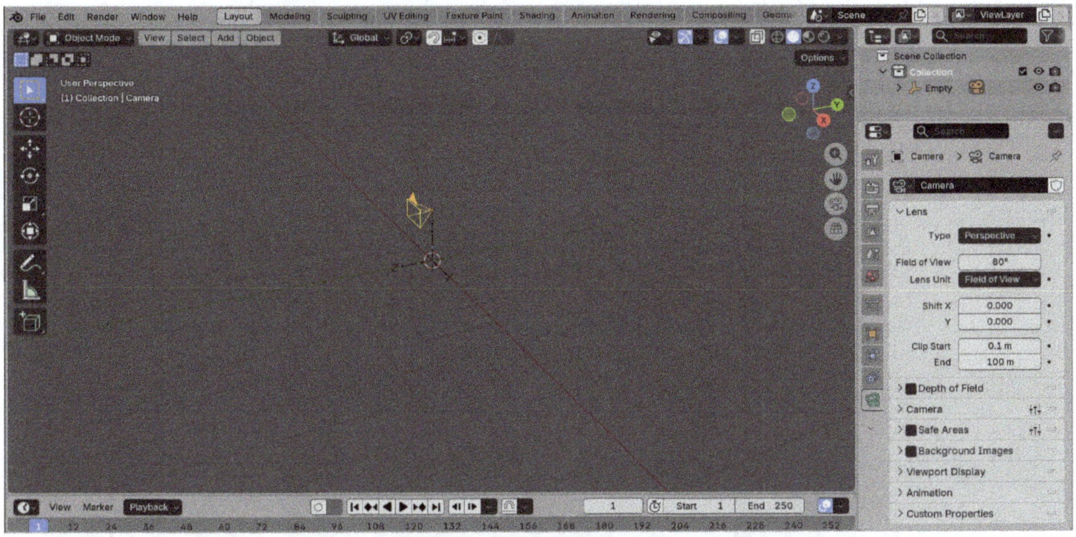

Figure 9.2: Setting the camera

Our character is ready for action, but we need to set up an input system to control it in the game.

Adding game inputs

In Unity, all objects belong to the same type and are differentiated by adding specific components. A camera is an object that contains a Camera component, a model is an object containing a Mesh component, and so on. All of this is in accordance with the Entity Component System (ECS), a development pattern used in videogames.

More information about the *ECS* architecture can be found on *Wikipedia* at `https://en.wikipedia.org/wiki/Entity_component_system`. The Entity Component System allows us to add functionalities to our assets, independently from their origin; to be controlled in game, our character needs three components:

- **Player Input**: This component allows a game object to receive signals from keyboard, mouse, gamepad, and other input peripherals
- **Character Controller**: This component moves the character in the game by acting on its transformations, taking collisions into account. Many developers use a **Rigidbody** instead, which simulates motion using physics.
- **Script**: for coding the response of the *character controller* to input events.

We start by adding the *player input* so that we can define the game controls:

1. In the Unity level, make sure that **FirstPerson** is selected.
2. In the **Inspector**, click **Add Component** and type `input` to narrow the search.
3. Select **Player Input** from the list.

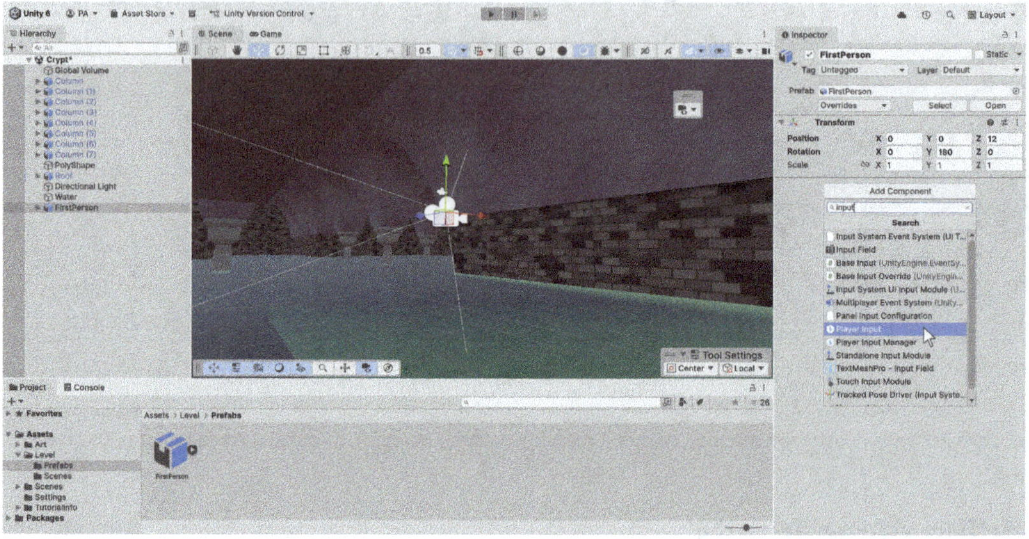

Figure 9.3: Adding Player Input

A new component is attached to *FirstPerson*; at creation, a Player Input component refers to the project-wide actions, which affect the entire game. Since the gameplay controls might differ from those of the initial screen or change during the game, it's a good practice to create specific controls for our first-person exploration, so we will create our *Input Actions* from scratch.

Creating input actions

Input Action is an asset type for binding inputs from a physical device to actions in the game. Every game can have different kinds of actions and inputs; for instance, a platform game usually doesn't implement mouse input, or a rail game doesn't feature free movement. In our case, we will create an action for moving the character and one for looking around.

Creating the Move action

In our game, we want to connect the pressure of the `WASD` keys to the traditional navigation setup: *forward*, *left*, *back*, and *right* directions.

To do that, we create an Input Action for our first-person movement:

1. In the **Project** browser, *right-click* in the **Assets | Level | Prefabs** folder and click **Create | Input Actions** in the menu. **Input Actions** is one of the last entries down in the **Create** menu.
2. Type `FP_Actions` as the name of the new asset.
3. In the **Project** browser, *double-click* **FP_Actions** to open the Input Actions editor.

The **Input Actions Editor** is a window consisting of three columns, where we can define, respectively, input categories, actions, and bindings:

1. The first column, **Action Maps**, is for creating a typology of actions, typically one for gameplay and one for the User Interface. Press the **+** button beside **Action Maps** and type `Player` as the name of the new mapping.
2. A new action is created automatically in the second column. *Double-click* the **New action** and rename it to `Move`.
3. In the third column, **Action Properties**, we can set the actual interaction. Movement is a directional input, so we change the **Action Type** from **Button** to **Value**.
4. A new property allows us to set the data type of *Move*. We have two axes of movement, horizontal and vertical, so we change **Control Type** from **Any** to **Vector2**.

Once we have defined the nature of our game action, we can bind it to a physical event like the pressure of a key. The editor has a quick utility to set up four directions controls:

1. In the central column, **Actions**, click the **+** button beside **Move** and select **Add Up\Down\Left\Right Composite**.
2. A **2D Vector** group is created; select **Up** and, in the **Binding Properties** column on the right, click the **Path** field.
3. Type `W` and select **W [Keyboard]** to bind the *Up* direction to the `W` key.

The Up entry is decorated with an icon representing a button pressure; we do the same with the remaining three buttons:

1. Select **Down** in the central column, click **Path** in the third column, type `S`, and select **S [Keyboard]**. There are many events starting with `S`, so the **Keyboard** entry is down in the list.
2. Select the **Left** entry in the **Actions** column, type `A` in the **Path** field of the **Binding Properties** column, and select **A [Keyboard]** from the list.
3. Select the **Right** entry, type `D` in the **Path** property, and select **D [Keyboard]**.

With all four directions assigned, the keyboard can be used as the input device for the *move* action.

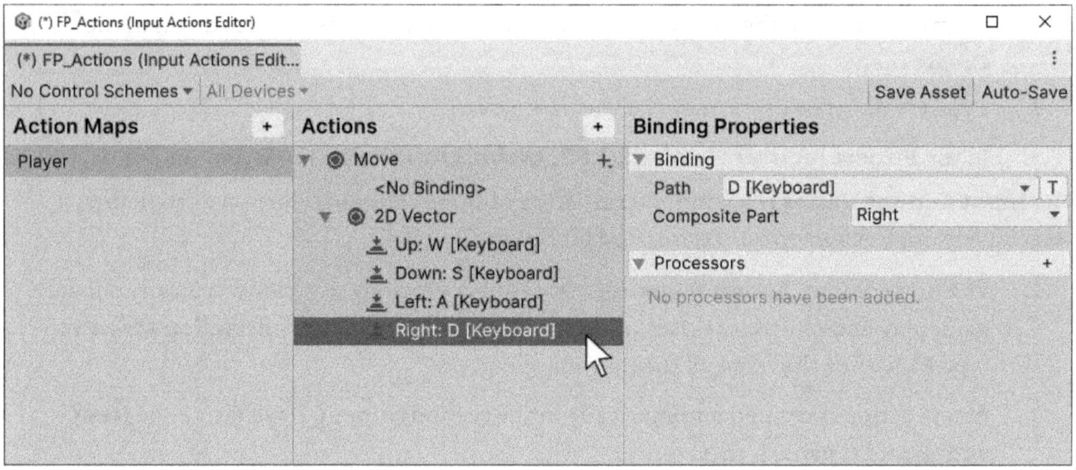

Figure 9.4: Key bindings for first-person movement

> Note
>
> **More controls**
>
> The point of action mapping is the possibility to connect different inputs to the same action, so that we can bind movement to the arrow keys and the gamepad input at the same time.
>
> Input peripherals can be selected by clicking the Path drop-down box and are quite straightforward; we will limit ourselves to setting the WASD keys in exploring the workflow.

Once we have sorted out the *move* input, we can proceed with implementing an action for looking around.

Creating the Look action

In our first-person game, the player will be able to look around in the level by moving the mouse, so we create another action for that:

1. Click the **+** beside **Actions** in the central column and type `Look` as the new action name.
2. In the action properties on the right, set **Action Type** to **Value**.
3. This action is a **Delta** type, that is, it's based on the difference between the current and previous position of the controller. Change **Control Type** from **Any** to **Delta**.

After defining the action type, we can bind it to one or more control devices:

1. Expand the **Look** action in the central column and select the default entry, **<No Binding>**
2. In the **Binding Properties** in the right column, click **Path**, then **Mouse**, and finally **Delta**.
3. Click the **Save Asset** button and close the window.

Our **Input Action** asset is ready, and we can set it in the **FirstPerson** component.

Assigning the actions

Game objects must know which *Input Action* is being used in a level, so we must set the *Actions* property in our *FirstPerson* character:

1. Select **FirstPerson** in the **Hierarchy** or the **Scene** viewport.
2. Expand **Player Input** in the **Inspector** if it is collapsed. The first field, **Actions**, is set to **InputSystem_Actions**. Click the small circle at the right of the property to open the selection dialog.
3. Select **FP_Actions** in the list.

Player Input will stop displaying the warning about using project-wide actions.

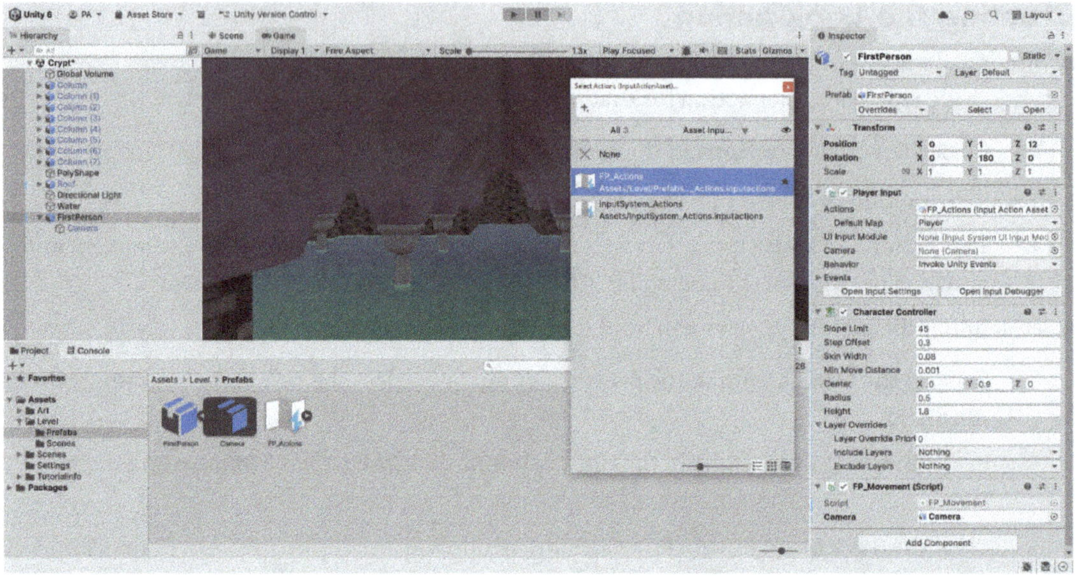

Figure 9.5: Setting Player Input's action and behavior

With our actions in place, we can move to the second requirement and create a component for in-game movement.

Controlling the character

Players can move their characters using input devices like the keyboard, mouse, or gamepad, but unless in the context of an explicit game dynamic, they cannot pass through walls or move a non-flying character upwards. The character movement is mediated by a game component that considers object collisions before applying the desired motion.

By using a Character Controller, we can ensure that our player will not be able to break into objects:

1. Select **FirstPerson** in the **Hierarchy** or the **Scene** viewport.
2. In the **Inspector**, click **Add Component** and type `control`.
3. Select **Character Controller**: we can see that our character is surrounded by a wireframe `Capsule` in the viewport.
4. The capsule is used for detecting collisions. The default height of 2 is perhaps a little bit too much, but still good for our `1.70` tall point of view. In the **Inspector**, we set the **Character Controller** | **Center** | **Y** property to `1.0`, half height, to raise the capsule above the ground.

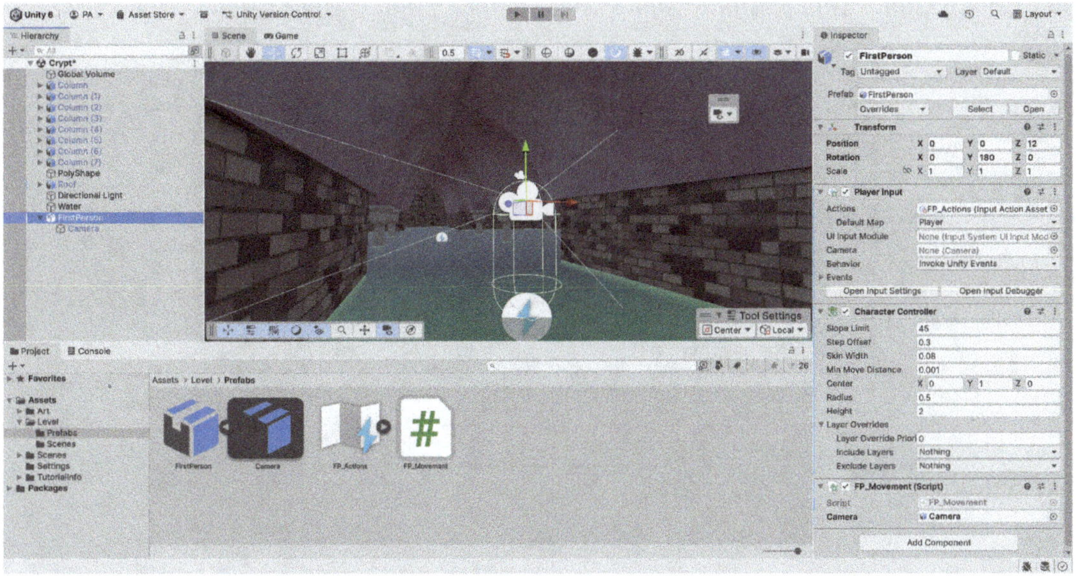

Figure 9.6: A capsule approximates the character's collisions

With a controller in place, *FirstPerson* can be moved in the level without passing through the walls and other objects. To connect the *Player Input* to the *Character Controller*, we need to code the movement logic using the *C#* language.

Writing the control script

While Blender add-ons are written in *Python*, as we learned in *Chapter 4*, gameplay and movement are implemented in Unity using **C#** (read "See Sharp"), a different scripting language. We can create a movement script to move our *Character Controller*.

Creating a script

Scripts are assets and can be created using *right-click* | **Create** | **Scripting** in the Project browser. There are different kinds of script in Unity, the one for controlling game objects is **MonoBehaviour**:

1. In the **Project Browser**, *right-click* the `Assets` | `Level` | `Prefabs` folder and click **Create** | MonoBehaviour Script.
2. Name the new asset **FP_Movement**
3. Drag **FP_Movement** from the Project browser and release it over **FirstPerson** in the **Hierarchy**.

A new component, **FP_Movement (Script)**, is added to **FirstPerson**.

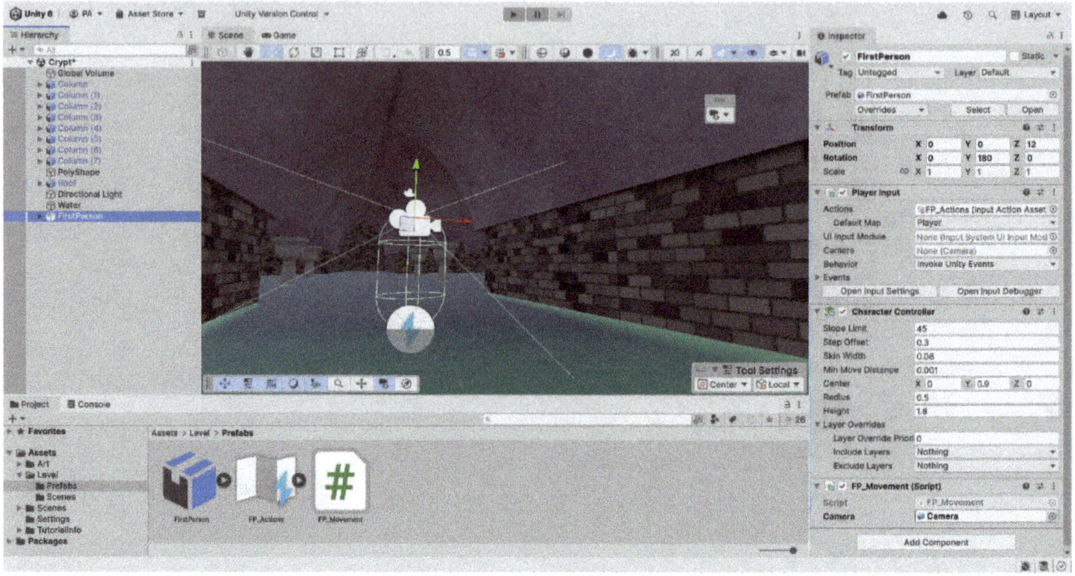

Figure 9.7: The MonoBehaviour script component

Selecting **FP_Movement** in the **Project** browser displays this code in the inspector:

```
using UnityEngine;
public class FP_Movement : MonoBehaviour
{
    // Start is called once before the first execution...
    void Start()
    {
    }
    // Update is called once per frame
    void Update()
    {
    }
}
```

Unlike *Python*, *C#* is a **nominal** language, which means that we need to specify the type of data we are using.

`MonoBehaviour` is a class, a category of programmed objects, and can access and set the properties of game objects; `FP_Movement` is the name for our new class, which inherits all the abilities of `MonoBehaviour` through the syntax:

```
public class FP_Movement: MonoBehaviour
```

In programming, we say that `FP_Movement` is the *derived* or *child* class, while `MonoBehaviour` is the *base* or *parent* class. While the base class is part of Unity and we cannot change it, we can add functionalities to our class by editing the script.

> Note
>
> **What's in a classname**?
>
> When a script is created through the Project browser, Unity generates a class and names it after the new asset. If a different asset name is entered, the name of the class will differ as well; that's not a problem: a class, by any other name, would compile just as well.

Editing our code

Double-clicking **FP_Movement** in Unity opens the application associated with `.cs` files. Alternatively, *right-click*ing | **Show in Explorer** shows `FP_Movement.cs` in the operating system's *File Manager*, from which we can open it in any text editor; a programmer text editor like the ones mentioned in the section *Technical Requirements* is advised.

The first line, `using UnityEngine`, loads Unity's classes and functions in the script: the instruction `using` is similar to *Python*'s `import`, as it gives access to specific facilities available to the language; we need to use the `InputSystem` module as well:

1. In the text editor, move the cursor to the second line and, below the line `using UnityEngine`, type the instruction `using UnityEngine.InputSystem;` and press *Enter*. Don't forget the semicolon, which marks the end of an instruction.
2. To move the controller and rotate the camera, our class must store the following data:
    - A reference to the *character controller*
    - Two-dimensional vectors for the *move* and *look* action inputs
    - A three-dimensional vector for movement
    - A reference to the *camera* object

That information must be declared at the beginning of the class, which becomes:

```
public class FP_Movement : MonoBehaviour
{
    private CharacterController controller;
    private Vector2 moveInput, lookInput;
    private Vector3 move;
    public GameObject camera;

    // Start is called once before the first execution...
```

Data belonging to the class are called fields or members; `camera` is a `public` member because it can be set in the component properties, while `private` members are only accessed inside the class.

Implementing movement

Now it's time to implement the movement logic. Declaring `controller` as a class member creates an empty variable, which must be set when the game starts; `void Start()` is a function, code enclosed within curly brackets that can be executed on command, and Unity invokes that function when the game starts. We change the `Start()` function so that it gets the character controller at the beginning of the game, so it becomes:

```
    void Start()
    {
        controller = GetComponent<CharacterController>();
    }
```

The `Update()` function is invoked at every frame rendered by the engine, and in our case it should apply the movement to the character, so it becomes:

```
    void Update()
    {
        controller.Move(move * Time.deltaTime);
        controller.transform.Rotate(
                              Vector3.up,
                              lookInput.x * Time.deltaTime
                              );
        camera.transform.Rotate(
                              Vector3.right,
                              -lookInput.y * Time.deltaTime
```

```
            );
    }
```

The first instruction, `controller.Move`, applies the move vector to the character controller. It is multiplied by `deltaTime` to account for the interval between the execution of one frame and the next, which is not constant and depends on the available computing power.

The second instruction, `controller.transform.Rotate`, applies the mouse horizontal movement to the character's orientation along its vertical axis (`up`). That's how our character changes direction.

The last instruction, `camera.transform.Rotate`, applies the mouse negative vertical movement to the camera's horizontal axis. The minus sign is due to the relative inversion of vertical vision: to look up, the camera must rotate negatively along its horizontal axis (`right`).

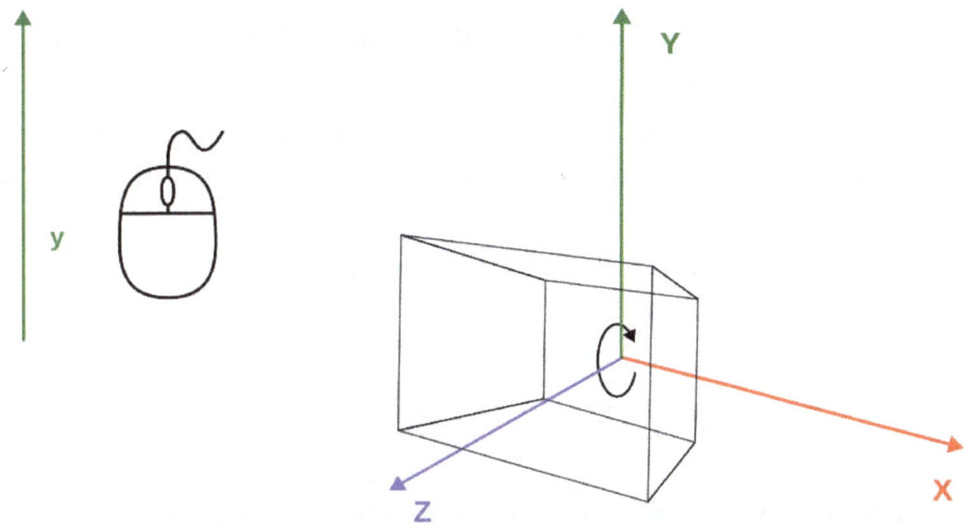

Figure 9.8: X rotation and vertical camera pitch

> Note
>
> **Please don't tilt the controller!**
>
> We apply the yaw rotation to the Character Controller to affect the direction of the character, but that's all the rotation we want to inflict on that component: rotating the character capsule along any axis other than Y is risky, as that might interfere with the physics simulation. To avoid compound rotation on the Character Controller, we apply the tilt separately on the Camera.

Spaces and new lines do not affect the code in *C#*, and here are used to fit the book page. The `Update` function applies the `move` and `lookInput` vectors, but to connect those values to the game controls, we need to implement the `OnMove` and `OnLook` functions.

We can declare `OnMove` after the closing bracket of `Update` and before the last closing bracket, which instead marks the end of the class:

```
    public void OnMove(InputValue value)
    {
        moveInput = value.Get<Vector2>();
        move = transform.right * moveInput.x;
        move += transform.forward * moveInput.y;
        move *= 2.0f;
    }
```

The first instruction reads the input coming from the keyboard, which is then stored in `move`'s `right` and `forward` directions.

The last instruction, `move *= 2.0f;`, doubles the movement speed. The letter `f` stands for **float**, that is, decimal (floating point) numbers. This value should rather be a variable named `speed`, but programming is not our focus.

Next, we handle the input of the look action by implementing the function `OnLook`:

```
    public void OnLook(InputValue value)
    {
        lookInput = value.Get<Vector2>() * 10.0f;
    }
```

`OnLook` is much more straightforward, as it just transfers the action input to the `lookInput` variable. We multiply the input by `10.0`, which, again, should be a variable named `sensitivity` in a more structured setting.

The movement script written so far is about 40 lines long. Here's how it looks now:

`FP_ Movement.cs`

```
using UnityEngine;
using UnityEngine.InputSystem;

public class FP_Movement : MonoBehaviour
{
```

```
    private CharacterController controller;
    private Vector2 moveInput, lookInput;
    private Vector3 move;
    public GameObject camera;
    // Start is called once before the first execution...
    void Start()
    {
        controller = GetComponent<CharacterController>();
    }
    // Update is called once per frame
    void Update()
    {
        controller.Move(move * Time.deltaTime);
        controller.transform.Rotate(
                                Vector3.up,
                                lookInput.x * Time.deltaTime
                                );
        camera.transform.Rotate(
                                Vector3.right,
                                -lookInput.y * Time.deltaTime
                                );
    }
    public void OnMove(InputValue value)
    {
        moveInput = value.Get<Vector2>();
        move = transform.right * moveInput.x;
        move += transform.forward * moveInput.y;
        move *= 2.0f;
    }
    public void OnLook(InputValue value)
    {
        lookInput = value.Get<Vector2>() * 10.0f;
    }
}
```

We can save the file in our text editor and switch back to the game engine: Unity will compile the script and update the *Script* component with the name of our class, *FP_Movement*.

Since `camera` is a public variable, the Inspector displays it as a property of FP_Movement; we must set the property in the scene, or we won't be able to look up and down in the game.

1. Select **FirstPerson** in the **Hierarchy** or **Scene** view.
2. In the Inspector, click the circular button to the right of **FP_Movement | Camera**.
3. Select **Camera** from the list.

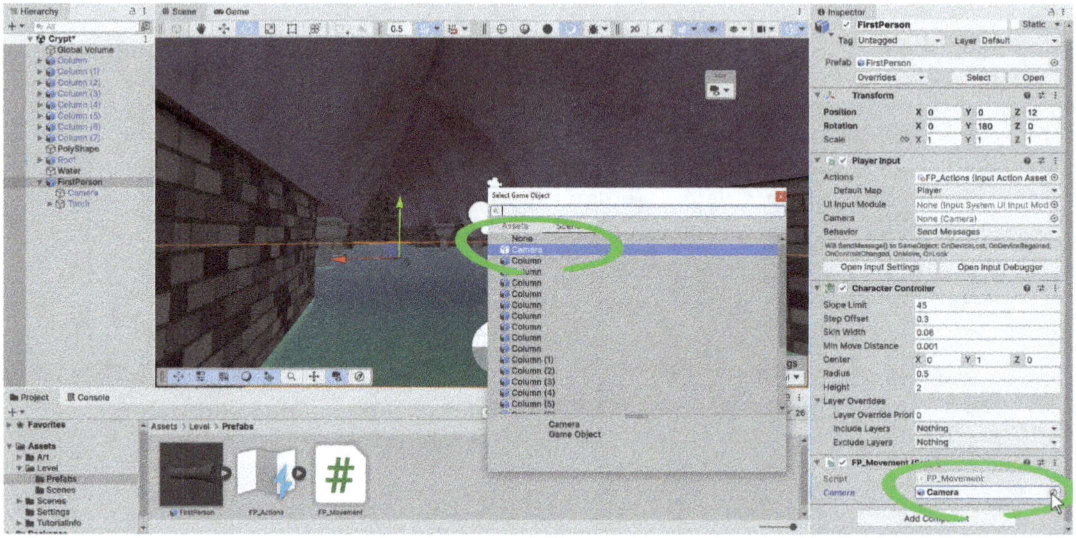

Figure 9.9: Setting the script Camera in Unity

Before we start playing, we may want to remove the collisions from the water plane created in *Chapter 7*, or our character will walk on water, and that could be inappropriate:

1. Select the **Water** plane in the **Hierarchy** or **Scene** view.
2. In the **Inspector**, find the **Mesh Collider** component, *right-click* its header or click the options menu (three dots in the column), and select **Remove Component**.

By clicking the *Play* button in the top bar, we will move in our level using the keyboard and mouse.

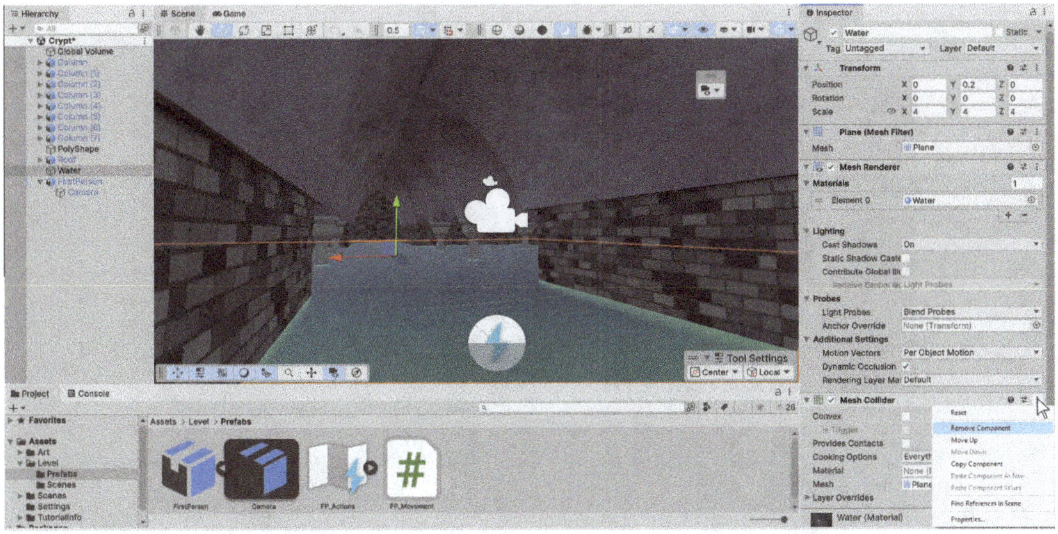

Figure 9.10: Removing collision from the water plane

Note

A matter of focus

By default, the game preview grabs and retains the focus of the mouse pointer, causing jerks in the view when the pointer leaves or enters the game area. That can be worked around by clamping the input in the movement script or switching the preview mode in the Game top bar to **Play Maximized** or **Play Unfocused**; the latter requires clicking the game view to play.

With our character able to move, we can change the lighting and improve our character's immersion.

Lighting and animation

Unity levels are created with a skybox environment that simulates daylight. That helps with lit locations, but it doesn't work well with our underground setting, so we lower that influence:

1. From the top bar menu in Unity, click **Window** | **Rendering** | **Lighting** to open the **Lighting** dialog.
2. In the **Lighting** window, click the Environment button at the top.
3. Reduce the **Intensity Multiplier** slider to `0.4`

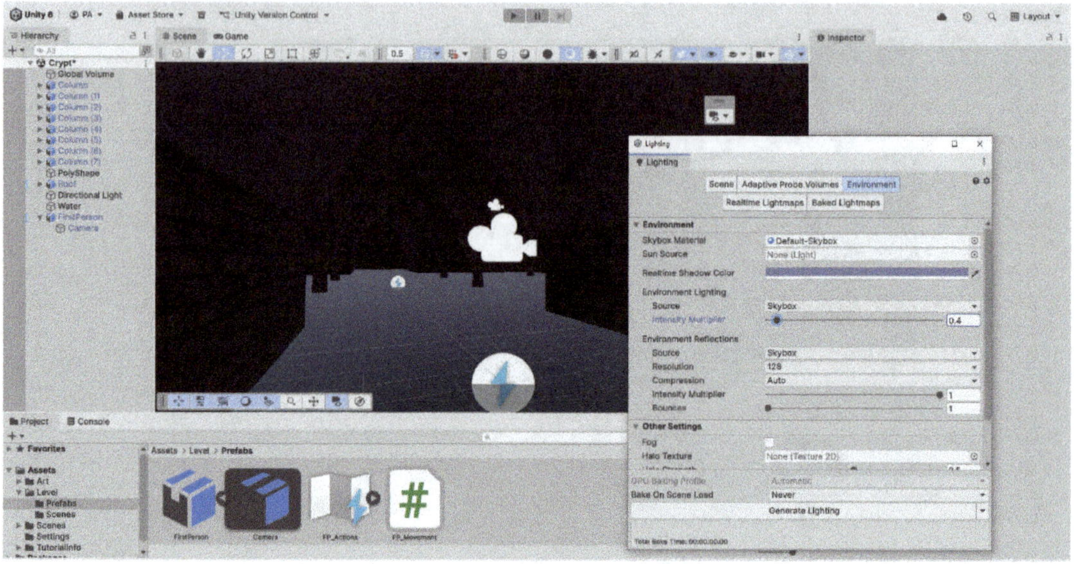

Figure 9.11: Dimming the environment lighting

We can also remove the default light of the level, which simulates sunlight:

1. Select **Directional Light** in the **Hierarchy** view.
2. Press the **Delete** button or use *right-click* | **Delete**

Now that the room has become quite dark, we will better equip our protagonist with a flashlight.

Creating the torch

We haven't modeled a character, since we explore the level from a subjective point of view, but first-person games usually display some handheld object, typically a weapon, as a visual cue for the character's presence.

In our case, we can display an electric torch at the bottom of the view, which will work both as a way of lighting the environment and a hint for the character's presence:

1. Open `FirstPerson.blend` in Blender, either by double-clicking `Assets` | `Level` | `Prefabs` | **FirstPerson** in Unity's **Project**, or from Blender's recent files.
2. The model for our flashlight will be very simple. Press *Shift + A* or click the viewport **Add** menu, and select **Mesh** | **Cylinder**.

3. Expand the operator properties in the bottom left corner and set them as follows:
    a. **Vertices** to `16`.
    b. **Radius** to `0.025`.
    c. **Depth** to `0.15`.
    d. **Cap Fill Type** to **Triangle Fan**.
    e. **Location Z** to `0.1`.

Our flashlight's main body is a 15-centimeter-long, 5-centimeter-wide cylinder.

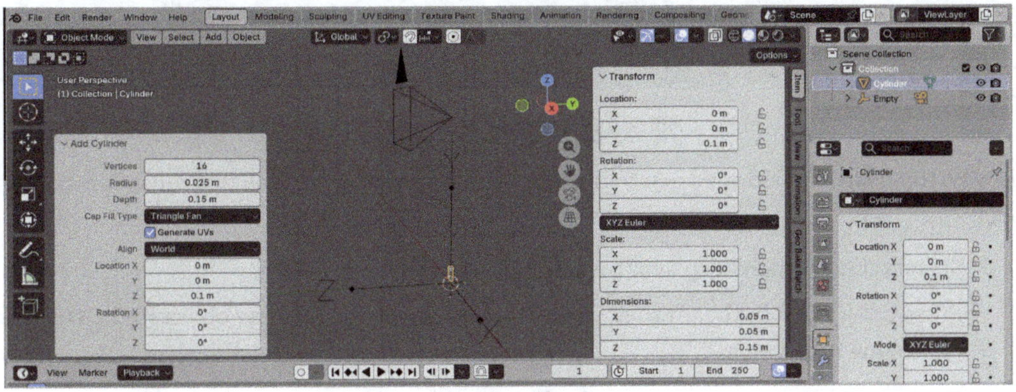

Figure 9.12: Creating the torch handle

We will model the head of the torch using a truncated cone:

1. Press *Shift + A* or click the viewport **Add** menu and select **Mesh** | **Cone**
2. In the operator properties, set:
    a. **Vertices** to `16`
    b. **Radius 1** to `0.04`
    c. **Radius 2** to `0.028`.
    d. **Depth** to `0.05`.
    e. **Base Fill Type** on **Triangle Fan**.

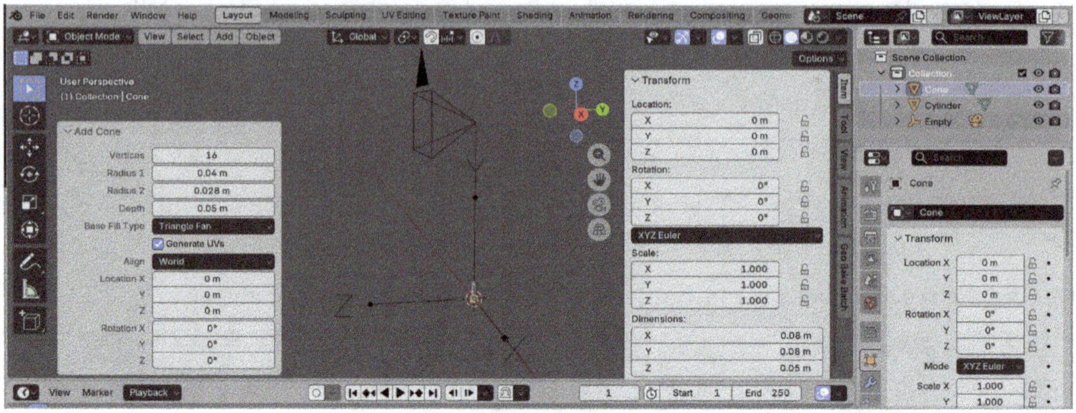

Figure 9.13: Creating the torch head

This way, the head is positioned just below the cylinder; we can join the two meshes into one model:

1. Select *cylinder*, then keep *Shift* pressed and select *cone*.
2. Press *Ctrl + J* to join the meshes; press *F2* or double-click the new object in the **Outliner** to rename it to `Torch`.
3. From the **Object** menu, execute **Shade Auto Smooth**

Once we are happy with the model of the torch, we can create a light to make it work in the level. A spotlight is the best option, as it projects a light cone:

1. Press *Shift + A* or click the viewport **Add** menu and select **Light** | **Spot**
2. Keep *Shift* pressed and select the `Torch`, press *Ctrl + P*, and select the first option, **Object**, in the **Parent** menu.

Once it belongs to the model, the spotlight will follow the torch as we place it in the three-dimensional space:

1. Select **Torch** and, in the **Object** properties, set **Relations** | **Parent to Empty**
2. In the **3D Viewport**, press *N* to display the **Transform** properties if they are hidden.
3. An average person would wield a torchlight at approximately 40 centimeters on the right, at about 1.2 meters above the ground, so set **Location X** to `-0.4`, **Location Y** to `1`, and **Location Z** to `1.2`.
4. Set **Rotation X** to `170`, which is slightly upward.

We can press the *numeric pad* `0` or select **View** | **Cameras** | **Active Camera** from the menu to watch the camera's perspective: on a *16:9* screen, the torch is on the lower border of the view.

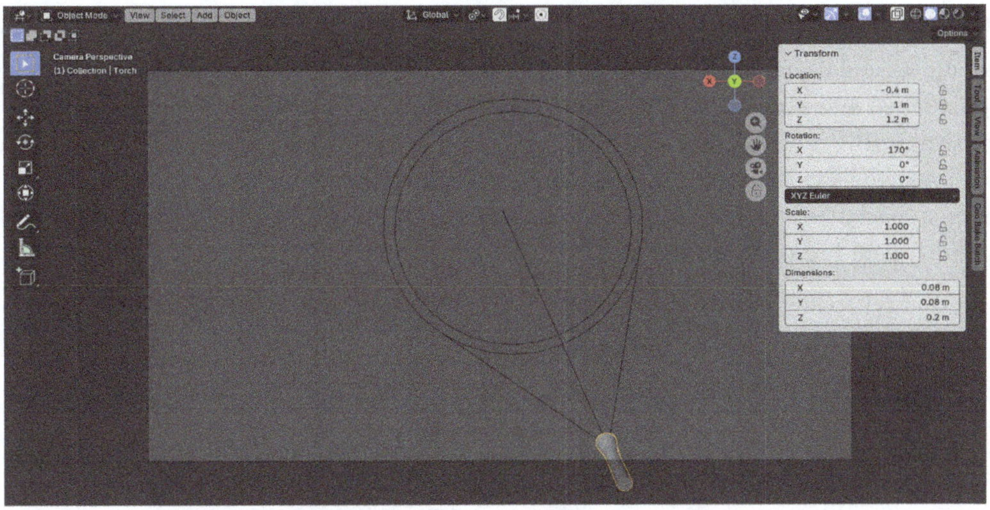

Figure 9.14: Placing the torch in Blender

If we save the Blender scene, switch back to Unity, and play the game, we can see our torch lighting the way; unfortunately, looking down reveals that the torch is floating in the 3D space!

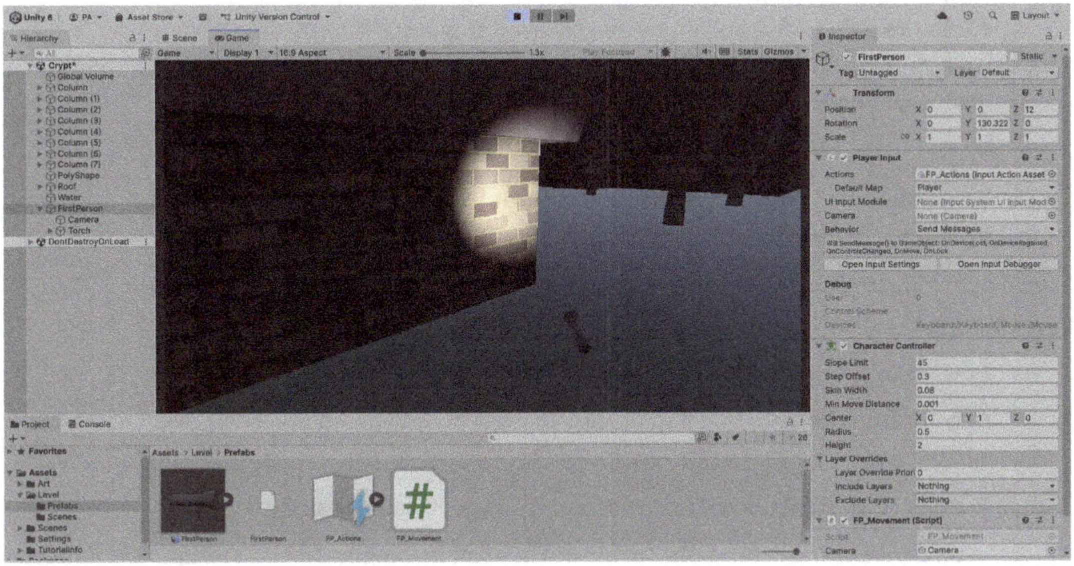

Figure 9.15: Floating torch in the game

Blender cameras are rotated by 180 degrees in Unity, so it is better not to parent the torch or anything else to Camera, as the imported position would be wrong. To fix the issue, we can parent both *Camera* and *Torch* to the limbs of an articulated character.

Creating the armature

Three-dimensional characters are animated by assigning their models to a skeletal structure, which is called **Armature** in Blender. In analogy with actual locomotion systems, each element of the armature is called a **bone**, and each bone can move an object or part of it. The procedure of binding models to an articulated structure is called **rigging**. Full character setup is a laborious, specialized task and cannot be treated in this book, but we can create a very simple armature for our **FirstPerson**.

1. Go back to Blender and, in `FirstPerson.blend`, press *Shift + A* or click the viewport **Add** menu and select **Armature**.
2. Press *Alt + G* to reset the position in case `Armature` was not created at the origin, then, in the **Object** properties, set **Relations | Parent to Empty**.

`Armature` will be rotated so that its default bone is aligned to the floor. By aligning the armature to the Unity space, we ensure the compatibility of poses and animations with the engine. We can add just a few bones to `Armature`; there is no need to create a full human set-up.

Creating the bones

The asset **FirstPerson** contains only two interacting elements: *Camera* and *Torch*. We will create two bones for those objects, and we are also keeping the initial bone as a **root**, that is, the uppermost element of our armature:

1. With *Armature* still selected, press *Tab* to switch to **Edit** m**ode**.
2. The default bone is selected. Press *F2* or **Edit | Rename Active Item** from the top menu, type `Root`, and press *Enter*.

Even if our character doesn't have an actual body, we create a bone where the chest would be, and use it for rotating the visual:

1. Press *Shift + A* to create a new bone.
2. Click the new bone to select it, press *G* to move it, *Z* to lock the vertical axis, then type `1.4` to move it upward and press *Enter*.
3. Press `F2` or **Edit | Rename Active Item**, type `Chest`, and press *Enter*.

As for the torch, we will create a bone to mimic the arm; its hinge point will be approximately where the shoulder would be:

1. Select the `Root` bone, which is parallel to the ground, and press *Shift + D* to duplicate it, `Z` to lock the vertical axis, then type `1` and press *Enter* to place it `1` meter above the ground.

2. Press G to move it again, X to lock the horizontal axis, type `-0.4` to move it sideways, and press *Enter*.
3. Press *N* to display the **Transform** properties if they are hidden, then set **Head** | **Y** to `1.5` to move the bone's head upward.
4. Press F2 or **Edit** | **Rename Active Item**, type `Arm`, and press *Enter*.

Our bone setup will look a bit mechanical, but that's more than enough for our purpose.

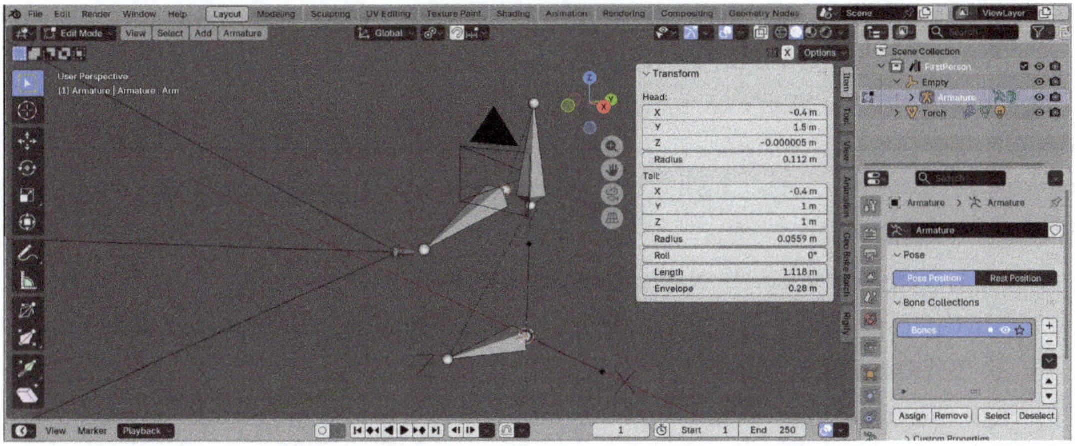

Figure 9.16: Articulated character with a handheld torch

Those bones determine the hinge points of our animations, but to finish the rig, we must define their hierarchy as well.

Creating the hierarchy

What makes skeletal animation useful is that motion is propagated through the limbs, that is, the hip transfers its motion to the leg, which carries the foot, and so on. Our armature doesn't have such a long chain, so we only need to parent the arm to the chest and the chest to the root:

1. With the `Arm` bone still selected, keep *Shift* pressed and select the `Chest` bone, press *Ctrl + P*, and in the **Make Parent** menu, click **Keep Offset**.
2. Select the `Chest` bone, keep *Shift* pressed and select the *Root* bone on the ground, press *Ctrl + P*, and click **Keep Offset**.
3. Press *Tab* to exit **Edit Mode** and switch back to **Object Mode**.

Now we can parent our objects to the bones of the armature; to do that, we will select an object and then switch to **Pose Mode**, which enables bone transformations:

1. Select the **Torch**, keep *Shift* pressed and select the `Armature`, press *Ctrl + Tab* to enter **Pose Mode**.

2. Select the `Arm` bone, press *Ctrl + P*, and from the **Set Parent To** menu, select **Bone**.
3. Enable the **Keep Transform** checkbox in the operator properties to avoid displacing the torch.

To select the camera, we can avoid going back to **Object Mode** using the **Outliner**:

1. Select **Camera** in the **Outliner**; that will also unselect the `Arm`. Keep *Shift* pressed and select the `Chest` bone.
2. Press *Ctrl + P* and, from the **Set Parent To** menu, select **Bone**. **Keep Transform** should already be enabled in the operator's properties.
3. Press *Ctrl + S* or **File** | **Save** to write the changes to the file.

When we switch back to the game engine, Unity will update the **FirstPerson** asset. Because of our changes, *Camera* is not set anymore in the script properties; we will use the `Chest` bone to tilt the visual:

1. Select **FirstPerson** in the **Navigation** or **Scene** View.
2. In the Inspector, click the circular button to the right of **FP_Movement** | **Camera**.
3. Select **Chest** from the list.

Rotating a common parent bone ensures that the position of *Torch* stays constant relative to *Camera*. An articulated character can be used for much more than that, as we can animate the swing of the arm during the walk.

Registering the FirstPerson asset

Unity puts a big restriction on `.blend` file-based workflows: each Blender asset can contain only one animation clip. That wouldn't impact this specific project at all, as we only need one animation for our character, but it is bad news for the character animation pipeline in general, because it is common practice to animate a bundle of animations in one asset.

For that reason, many developers using Blender switch to a `.fbx` workflow when it comes to characters, but that means giving up the ability of `.blend` files to work as assets and generators at the same time.

A workaround to that limitation is creating one asset for each animation to comply with Unity's .blend files policy, but using asset linking and library overrides to animate the same character in separate scenes.

To do that, we must convert our character into a Blender asset:

1. *Double-click* the default **Collection** in the **Outliner** and rename it **FirstPerson**.
2. *Right-click* the **FirstPerson** collection and select **Mark as Asset**.

As we know from *Chapter 4*, new assets are listed in the *Unassigned* category, and they need to be assigned properly using the **Asset Browser**:

1. Click the *Editor Type* drop-down button in the top right corner of the **Viewport**'s header, and select the **Asset Browser** in the list.
2. In the **Asset Browser**, click the **All Libraries** drop-down box and select **Current File**.

The current file contains only one asset, **FirstPerson**; we can create the category **BlendToUni** like we did with the other assets marked for this project:

1. Click the **+** button beside the **All** catalogue.
2. Name the new catalogue `BlendToUni`.
3. Click the **Unassigned** catalogue.
4. Move **FirstPerson** to the **BlendToUni** catalogue using drag and drop.

Once our asset is catalogued in its own file, we need to add its folder to Blender asset libraries:

1. In the top bar menu, click **Edit** > **Preferences**.
2. Select **File Paths** in the left navigation bar.
3. In the **Asset Libraries** panel, click the **+** button to add a folder to the list.
4. In the file dialog, select the folder **BlendToUni_URP** | **Assets** | **Level** | **Prefabs** and click **Add Asset Library**.
5. Set **Import Method** to **Link** and enable the **Relative Path** checkbox to ensure that this asset is read from its original file.

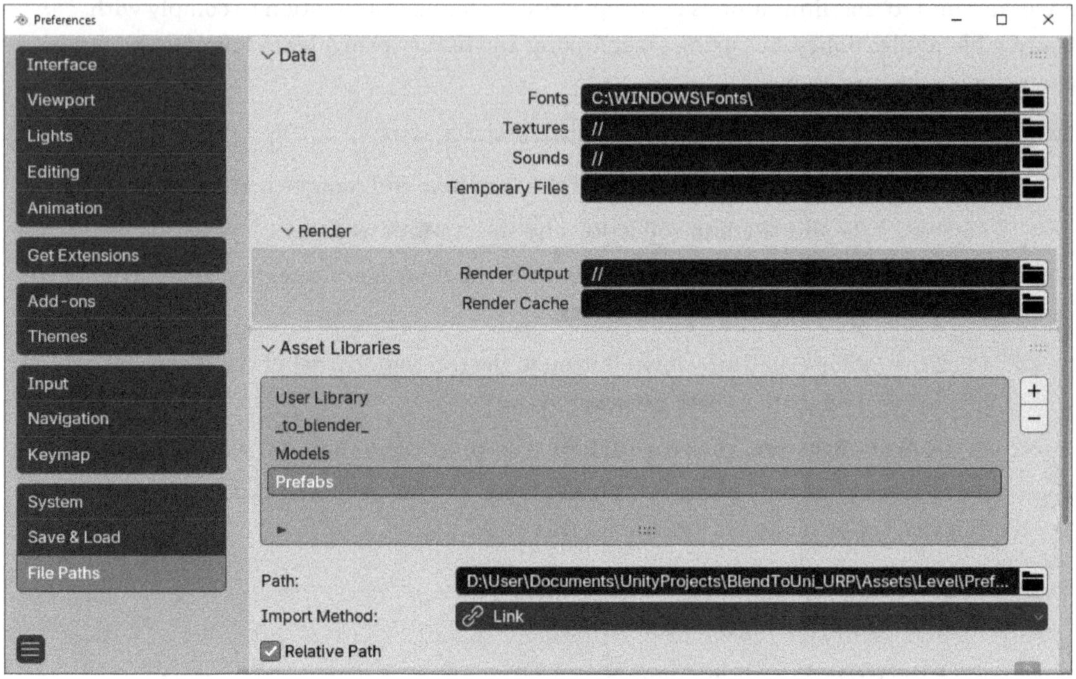

Figure 9.17: Adding prefabs to the Asset Libraries

> **Note**
>
> **The last one sets it all**
>
> Blender saves the preferences on exit, so if the preferences are changed and there are multiple instances of Blender running, it's a good idea to close them all and close the one with the correct preferences last.

Animating our character

Once available in the library, our character can be included in new scenes easily:

1. Open Blender or start a new scene with **File** | **New** | **General**
2. Press A to select all the objects, then press *X* and click **Delete** to remove them.
3. Switch to the **Assets** workspace created in *Chapter 4*, or split the screen to display the **Asset Browser**.
4. Select the **BlendToUni** catalogue.

We can see **FirstPerson** in the assets list, with a frontal view of the torch as the thumbnail:

1. Drag **FirstPerson** into the **Viewport** to add it to the current scene.
2. *Right-click* in the **Viewport** and select **Lock at Origin**, the operator created in *Chapter 4*, or press *Alt + G* to clear its position.

Unless we have changed the import settings of the **Asset Browser**, **FirstPerson** is read from its `.blend` file and displayed in the current scene.

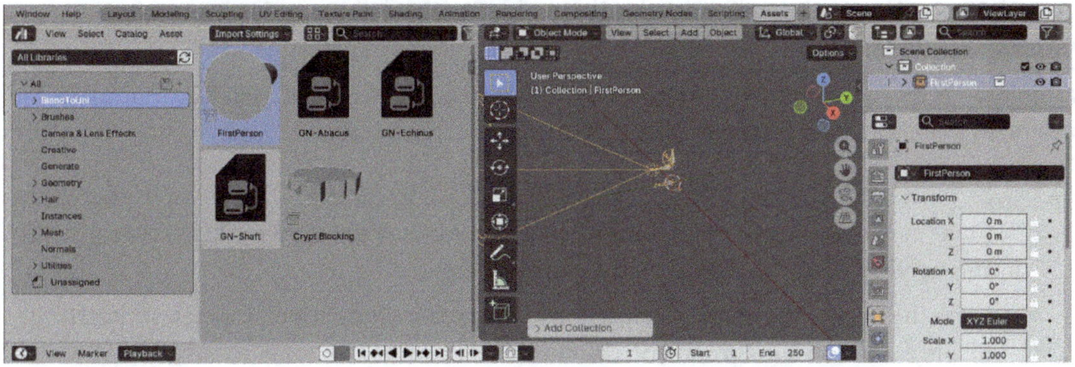

Figure 9.18: Linking FirstPerson in a new scene

Since it is a referenced collection, **FirstPerson** cannot be animated yet. We need to create a library override to access the armature:

1. *Right-click* **FirstPerson** in the **Outliner**.
2. In the menu, click **Library Override | Make | Selected & Content** to make the collection editable.

Once the override is created, the content of **FirstPerson** is displayed in the **Outliner** and can be accessed in the scene.

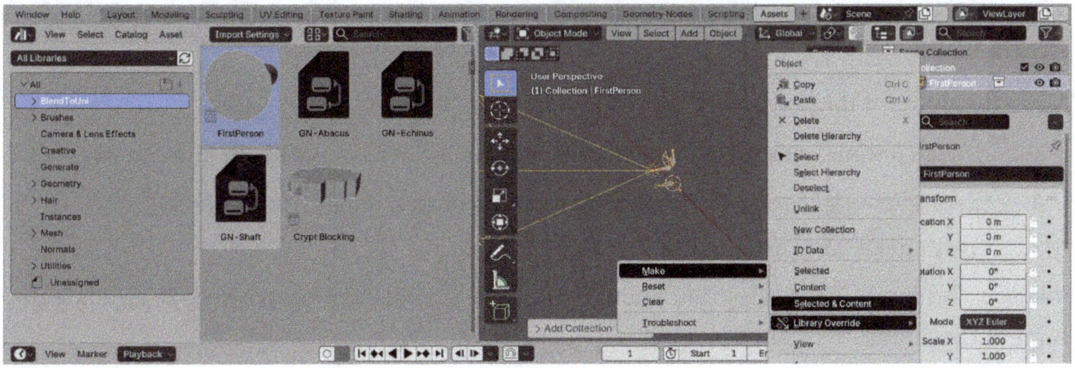

Figure 9.19: Creating Library Override

We can finally work on our animation. First, we need to switch to **Pose Mode**:

1. Click on any bone to select the `Armature`.
2. Press *Ctrl + Tab* to switch to **Pose Mode**.

There is an **Animation** workspace in Blender, but we can work on our simple animation in the **Layout** or **Assets** workspace as well, as all we need is the **Timeline**. The Timeline is displayed below the **Viewport** in the **Layout** workspace. It contains media player buttons to watch the animation in real time and numeric fields that indicate, from left to right respectively, the *current*, *start*, and *end* frame of the playback.

Animation is created by inserting **keyframes**, that is, poses specified at a specific frame. We can insert keyframes to animate the swinging of the arm during a walk:

1. Select the `Arm` bone; it will be outlined in light blue.
2. Make sure that the current frame in the timeline below the **Viewport** is set to **1**; press the **Rewind** button on the left if that's not the case.
3. Press the *I* key to insert a keyframe: showing the transformation properties with N displays a yellow background on the animated channels.

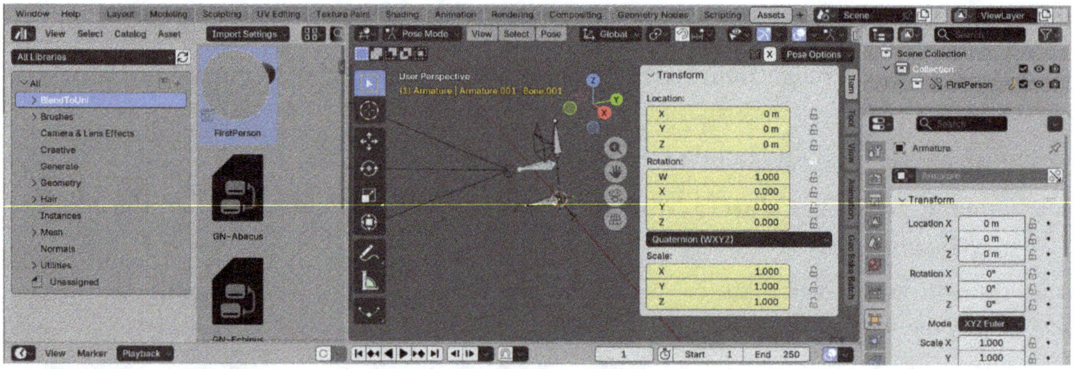

Figure 9.20: Animated channels of arm

We do the same for the last frame; our animation lasts 30 frames:

1. In the *Timeline*, set **End** to `30` so that the playback doesn't exceed our animation.
2. Press *Shift + right arrow* or the **Forward Media** button to jump to frame **30**.
3. Press *I* to key the current pose at frame `30`.

Frames `1` and *30* are identical, so our animation can be played in loops. We need to animate the frame in the middle to create a motion:

1. Set the current frame to `15` in the current frame field to the left of **Start**.

2. With the `Arm` bone still selected, press *R*, then *X*, type `5`, and press *Enter*. That will lower the limb slightly.
3. Press *I* to keyframe the current pose.

If we press the **Play** button or *Spacebar*, we will see the torch swing down and then up, cyclically.

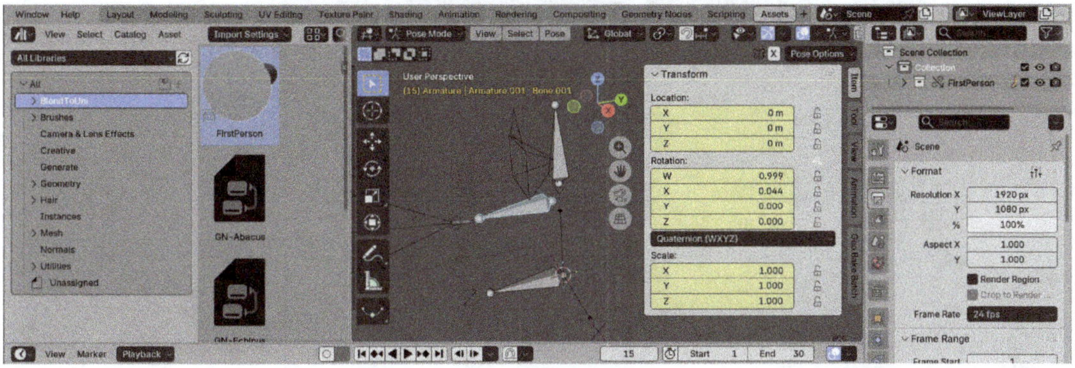

Figure 9.21: Animating frame 15 to create motion

We are almost ready to save our animation, but we need to take care of the clip naming and frame rate:

1. Scene and layer names are displayed at the top right corner of the window. Click the current scene name and change it from **Scene** to `Walk`; this is the name used by Unity for the animation clip.
2. Click the **Output** tab in the properties (the second tab) and change the **Frame Rate** to **30 fps**.
3. Press *Ctrl + S* or **File** | **Save**, name the file `FirstPersonWalk`, and save it to the game folder `Assets` | `Level` | `Prefabs`.

Unity will import this asset and the clip it contains.

> **Note**
>
> **Linked but still imported**
>
> Although the character is read from another file in Blender, it will be fully imported by Unity as the library reference becomes a full copy during export. It's not an issue with our lightweight asset, but it can become a problem with more complex characters. In that case, it is recommended to reference low-poly animation proxies rather than the final version of the character.

Playing the animation in Unity

When we go back to Unity, **FirstPersonWalk** will be imported and displayed in the **Prefabs** folder alongside **FirstPerson** and the input utilities.

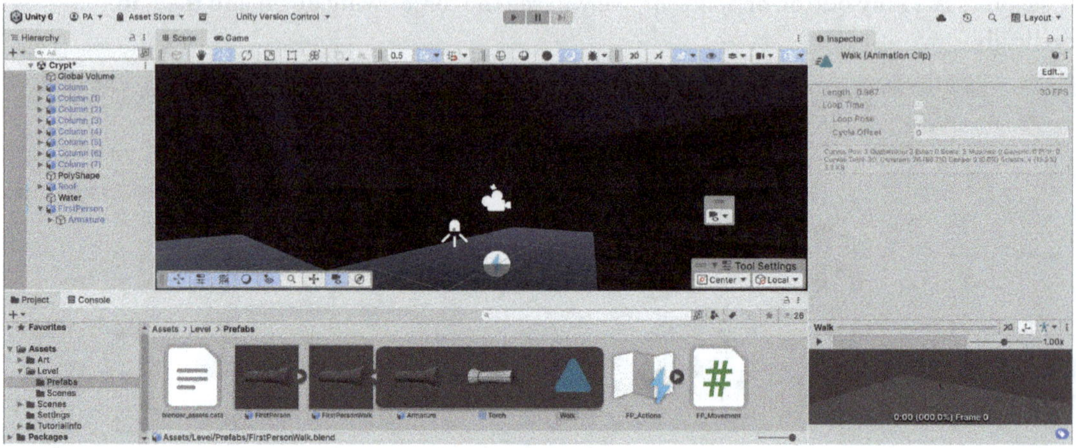

Figure 9.22: The animation asset in Unity

We can play the clip in the **Inspector** and check that it reflects our Blender animation. Unlike the **Inspector**'s player, the game engine doesn't assume the animation plays in loops, so we need to enable that manually:

1. In Unity's **Project** browser, in the folder **Assets** | **Level** | **Prefabs**, select **FirstPersonWalk**.
2. In the Inspector, select the **Animation** view, and scroll down to the clip properties.
3. Enable the **Loop Time** checkbox, scroll down in the Inspector properties, and click the **Apply** button.
4. In the **Project** browser, click **FirstPersonWalk**'s expansion triangle to select the clip, which has a triangular thumbnail, not the asset. Drag the **Walk** clip onto the **FirstPerson** game object in the **Navigation** view.

In the level, a new component, **Animator**, has been added to **FirstPerson**. It refers to a new asset, **FirstPerson.controller**, which was created alongside FirstPerson and can be used to create animation trees for advanced characters.

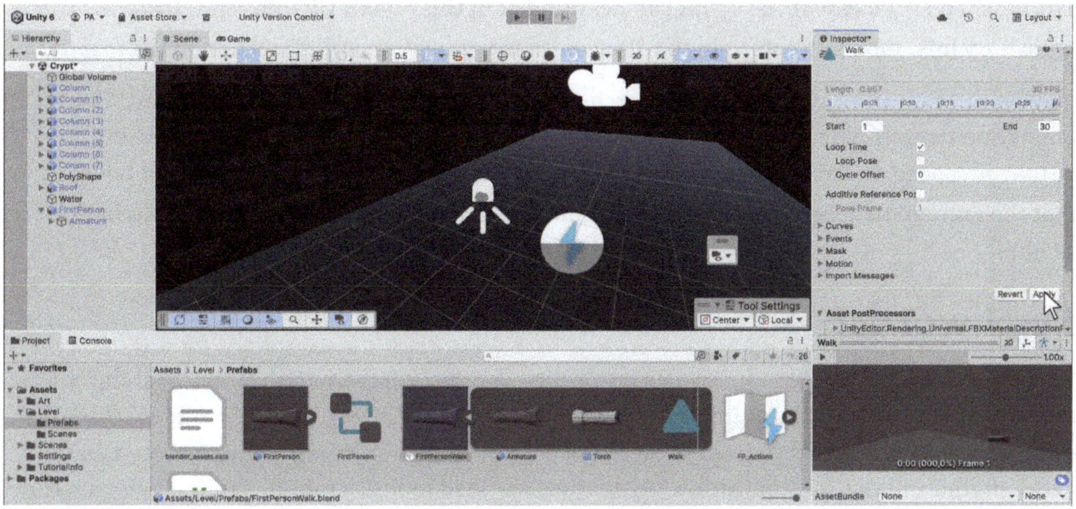

Figure 9.23: Enabling Loop Time on FirstPersonWalk

If we play the game now, we will see the torch swinging all the time during the gameplay. We don't want that though, as the arm should only animate during the walk. We can arrange that in the `FP_Movement` script:

1. Double-click the **FP_Movement** asset in the **Project** browser, or open `FP_Movement.cs` in a text editor.
2. Under the line `private CharacterController controller;`, insert this new line to get the **Animator** component:

    ```
    private Animator animator;
    ```

3. We need to stop the animator when the game starts, so in the **Start()** function, under the line `controller = GetComponent<CharacterController>();`, insert the lines:

    ```
    animator = GetComponent<Animator>();
    animator.speed = 0.0f;
    ```

4. Finally, in the `OnMove` function, after the line `move *= 2.0f;` insert the line:

    ```
    animator.speed = moveInput.y;
    ```

5. Save the script and switch back to Unity.

The finished `FP_Movement.cs` script can be found at in this book's GitHub repo. To access the repository link, follow the steps in the *"Download the example code files"* section in the *Preface*.

Playing the game now, we will see the torch swinging as the character walks forward. The animation doesn't play if the character walks backwards: we could have fixed that using `animator.speed = Mathf.Abs(moveInput.y);` as the last line written in the steps above, so that the animation speed is always positive, but *C#* scripting is not the primary focus of this example.

Final words!

We have integrated our Blender scenes into Unity, connecting them to the input system, the movement control, and the animation system. Despite using a very simple character, the example presented in this chapter shows how we can share non-mesh elements between the game engine and the 3D application. To do that, we need to find a middle ground between the standards of the two software, whether it is the physical units of cameras or the partitioning of animation clips.

This chapter marks the end of our journey in game development, but that's a bare scratch on the surface of such a vast topic. As the book ends, in the hope of sharing useful bits of knowledge, it entrusts the inspired creation to the next page, where the personal adventure of the reader carries on.

Go ahead then, make beautiful games, and carry the torch!

Get this book's PDF copy, code bundle, and more

Scan the QR code (or go to `packtpub.com/unlock`). Search for this book by name, confirm the edition, and then follow the steps on the page.

UNLOCK NOW

Note: Have your invoice handy. Purchases made directly from the Packt website don't require an invoice.

10

Unlock Access to the Code Bundle and the PDF Version

Your copy of this book includes the following exclusive benefits:

Follow this guide to unlock them. The process takes only a few minutes and only needs to be completed once.

Unlock this book's free benefits in three easy steps

Step 1

Have your purchase invoice ready for *step 3*. If you have a physical copy, scan it using your phone and save it as a PDF, JPG, or PNG.

For more help on finding your invoice, visit `https://www.packtpub.com/unlock-benefits/help`.

Note

Note: If you bought this book directly from the Packt website, no invoice is required. After *step 2*, you can access your exclusive content right away.

Step 2

Scan the QR code or go to `packtpub.com/unlock`.

On the page that opens (similar to *Figure 10.1* on desktop), search for this book by name and select the correct edition.

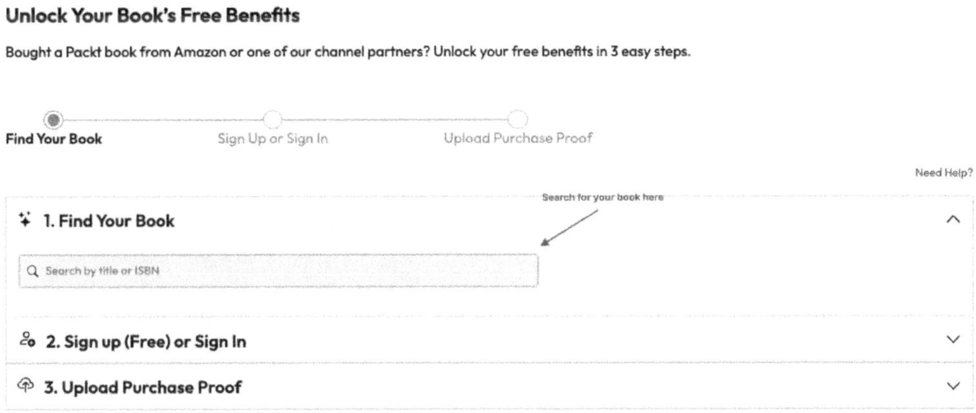

Figure 10.1: Packt unlock landing page on desktop

Step 3

After selecting the book, sign in to your Packt account or create one for free. Then, upload your invoice (PDF, PNG, or JPG, up to 10 MB). Follow the on-screen instructions to finish the process.

Need help?

If you get stuck and need help, visit `https://www.packtpub.com/unlock-benefits/help` for a detailed FAQ on how to find your invoice and more. This QR code will take you to the help page.

> Note
>
> **Note**: If you are still facing issues, reach out to `customercare@packt.com`.

Other Books You May Enjoy

If you enjoyed this book, you may be interested in these other books by Packt:

Learning C# by Developing Games with Unity 6

Harrison Ferrone

ISBN: 9781805808718

- Master programming fundamentals by breaking them into simple, digestible parts
- Understand OOP concepts through clear explanations of C# code samples
- Follow simple steps and examples to create and implement C# scripts in Unity 6
- Divide your code into pluggable building blocks using interfaces, abstract classes, and class extensions
- Grasp game design document basics and then move on to blocking out your level geometry, adding lighting, and a simple object animation
- Create basic game mechanics, such as player controllers and shooting projectiles, using C#

Procedural 3D Modeling Using Geometry Nodes in Blender

Siemen Lens

ISBN: 9781836203018

- Discover the different node inputs and outputs that Geometry Nodes have to offer
- Get to grips with the flow of the Geometry Nodes system
- Work with Geometry Nodes use cases through fun projects that advance with each chapter
- Link Geometry and Material node editors using Named Attributes
- Explore the flow of the Simulation Zone in Blender 4.5 LTS
- Create both simple and complex physics simulations mathematically
- Understand mathematical terms such as velocity, forces, collisions, and vectors
- Work with variables in your Geometry Nodes-based workflow

Packt is searching for authors like you

If you're interested in becoming an author for Packt, please visit `authors.packt.com` and apply today. We have worked with thousands of developers and tech professionals, just like you, to help them share their insight with the global tech community. You can make a general application, apply for a specific hot topic that we are recruiting an author for, or submit your own idea.

Share your thoughts

Now that you've finished *3D Game Development with Blender 5 and Unity 6*, we'd love to hear your thoughts! Scan the QR code below to go straight to the Amazon review page for this book and share your feedback or leave a review on the site that you purchased it from.

https://packt.link/r/1836643217

Your review is important to us and the tech community and will help us make sure we're delivering excellent quality content.

Index

www.ingramcontent.com/pod-product-compliance
Lightning Source LLC
LaVergne TN
LVHW060027210926
848481LV00013B/3810
* 9 7 8 1 8 3 6 6 4 3 2 1 0 *